First Limelight Edition September 1999

Library of Congress Cataloging-in-Publication Data

Hirsch, Foster.
    Detours and lost highways: a map of neo-noir/Foster Hirsch
        p.  cm.
    Includes bibliographical references, filmography and index.
    ISBN 0-87910-288-8
    1. Film noir—United States—History  and criticism.  I. Title
PN 1995.9.F54H57     1999
791.43'655—dc21                                                          99-37006
                                                                              CIP

Printed in Canada

# DETOURS AND LOST HIGHWAYS

## A MAP OF NEO-NOIR

# FOSTER HIRSCH

LIMELIGHT EDITIONS
NEW YORK

# Acknowledgments

Ian Cook, filmography; Henry Fera, Photofest; Kathryn Koldehoff, copy editor; Howard Mandelbaum and Ron Mandelbaum, Photofest; Ruth Nathan, agent; Richard Sawyer, layout; Mel Zerman, publisher.

**Joanne Zyontz, photo editing and book design.**

Courtesy of Photofest: illustrations 1, 2, 3, 4, 6, 8, 9, 11, 12, 13, 14, 15, 16, 17, 18, 19, 20, 21, 22, 24, 26, 27, 28, 29, 30, 32, 33, 34, 35, 36, 37, 38, 40, 42, 43, 44, 45, 47, 49, 50, 51, 53, 54, 55, 57, 58, 60, 63, 64, 66, 68, 70, 71, 73, 74, 76, 77, 78, 81, 82, 84, 91, 92, 95, 98, 100, 102, 106, 110, 117, 119.

Courtesy of Maitland McDonagh: illustrations 7, 39, 46, 56, 83, 85, 86, 89, 96, 104, 105, 107, 108, 109, 113, 114, 118.

Courtesy of Alain Silver: illustrations 31, 61, 88, 97.

# CONTENTS

# HOW MUCH COULD FLESH STAND... HOW FAR WAS LOVE WILLING TO GO!

...how many hours before one man's strange vengeance destroyed them both — and flamed into an international crisis?

She felt his touch once, and never forgot it!

He felt his touch and was turned into a living dead man!

UNIVERSAL-INTERNATIONAL PRESENTS

## CHARLTON HESTON · JANET LEIGH · ORSON WELLES

in

# "TOUCH OF EVIL"

Co-starring JOSEPH CALLEIA · AKIM TAMIROFF

with "Guest Stars" MARLENE DIETRICH · ZSA ZSA GABOR

A 1958 advertising poster for *Touch of Evil* promotes sex and violence and reveals no trace of the film's high place in the history of its genre or of its director's career

# Chapter 1

# Mapping the Route

Set in cities gleaming with menace and telling dark stories of characters trapped by greed and forbidden desires, American film noir flourished from the early 1940s to the late 1950s. Visually and thematically rich, the cycle produced a remarkable number of works that have retained their potency for more than half a century. *Touch of Evil*, Orson Welles's 1958 crime thriller, is often cited as the end of the line, noir's rococo tombstone. At a panel entitled "The New Noir" given during the third Avignon/New York Film Festival in April 1997, noir practitioner and theorist Paul Schrader claimed that noir was "a movement, and therefore restricted in time and place, like neorealism or the New Wave" and that the concept of neo-noir was therefore a mirage. Concurring in the "impossibility" of noir post-1958, a fellow panelist, cinematographer Michael Chapman, defined noir as "the answer to a historical situation which doesn't exist anymore. The techniques used in noir are still available and used all the time—but the soul isn't there."

If noir "expired" in 1958, if indeed Welles' exuberant *Touch of Evil* has come to be widely seen as the film after which noir could no longer be made, or at least could no longer be made in the same way, then by what name do we call all the films released since *Touch of Evil* that bear a striking resemblance to film noir? If post-1950s crime movies that recast elements of noir's stylistic signature are not in fact noir, or are noir without its "soul," then what is the "something else" that has been added or subtracted? What are the ingredients that have estranged noir from itself?

Labeling noir has always been problematic. When the crime thrillers we now call noir were being produced, contemporary filmmakers, critics, and spectators casually identified them as suspense pictures, crime stories, psychological thrillers, or melodramas. "Noir" is a retroactive label, applied first by vigilant French cineastes who discovered an unexpectedly dark tone in a group of American crime films released in France at the end of World War II. (The first book on noir, *Panorama du film noir américain* by Raymond Borde and Etienne Chaumeton, was published in France in 1955.) Once named, however, noir as a label did not gain a foothold on native ground until the late 1960s and early 1970s, when American films began to be studied seriously and seminal articles like Raymond Durgnat's "Paint It Black: The Family Tree of the Film Noir" (1970) and Paul Schrader's own pioneering essay, "Notes on Film Noir," were published.

Even after film noir was named, however, it still proved to be a slippery commodity. Indeed, to this day, there is heated debate about whether or not noir ought to be considered a genre, a style, or a movement. Those who argue against noir as a genre maintain that it is defined by elements of style, tone, and mood that are easily transported across generic boundaries; this view of noir as an ensemble of freely circulating motifs confines it to the category of the decorative. But films retroactively given the noir label are identified not only by "elements of style" but also by such generic markers as repeated patterns in narrative structure, characterization, and theme. If, however, noir is considered a movement rather than a genre, its link to a particular era is enforced. As a movement, noir thrived at a certain time and place: Hollywood in the 1940s and 1950s. "You can't pull a style out from its roots," Paul Schrader argued, "and the roots of film noir are World War II, and German Expressionism, existentialism and Freud as they were filtered into pop culture." As the central crisis around which film noir pivoted, World War II is, to be sure, the movement's subtext, and the crime dramas of the time can be seen as metaphoric representations of the war's traumatic impact on issues of gender, patriarchy, and sexuality. "As a filmmaker you look for rips and tears in the social fabric that can be addressed metaphorically," as Paul Schrader suggestively remarked, and World War II certainly supplied a seismic "rip" that "underwrites" 1940s crime films. Postwar crime stories record the war's lingering aftereffects while, inevitably, new crises—the atom bomb, the

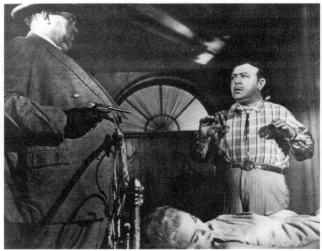

Is *Touch of Evil* (1958) the bravura finale to the classic noir era? Diagonals, shadows, and fog enclose the film's hero, Mike Vargas (Charlton Heston, top); menacing figures ("Pancho" [Valentin De Vargas, left] and his nameless associate [played by Michael Sargent]) surround Susan Vargas (Janet Leigh); a low-angle ceiling shot of crooked cop Hank Quinlan (Orson Welles, left) confronting a local gangster, Grandi (Akim Tamiroff), over a drugged Susan Vargas, maintains the film's high-noir atmosphere.

Cold War, the communist witch-hunts—provided further metaphors that proved grist for the noir mills.

In the decades since the official end of noir, "rips and tears" in the social fabric have continued to be ripe for noir use. However they are labeled, the noir-like crime pictures that have continued to be produced since 1958 testify to the endurance of the noir style and point of view. The films made "after noir," in fact, may well constitute the strongest case for noir as a genre. For over six decades at this writing, stories, settings, and characters with a distinctive dark tone have continued to be made regardless of how they have been named; and audiences, then as now, have recognized noir when they've seen it whether or not they have had a label for it.

It is my belief, in short, that neo-noir *does* exist and that noir is entitled to full generic status. Over the past forty years, since noir's often-claimed expiration, it has flourished under various labels. Noir-like films appeared irregularly in the 1960s and 1970s while in the 1980s and 1990s their number has steadily grown. In the 1960s, "noir" was rarely invoked as a descriptive term for suspense movies with suspicious echoes of a style from the past; and through the 1970s, as well, noirish films, for the most part, remained in a taxonomic limbo. The "real" film noir, which had retreated into a historical mist, began by the early 1980s to be called "classic noir." But what to call the pictures that came after 1958—the crime movies that proved that noir in some form or another wouldn't and perhaps couldn't go away—remained an issue. Since the early 1980s, the films have been called "post-noir noir," "postclassic noir," "nouveau noir," and "neo-noir"; before that and, in casual discourse since, they have been referred to as "suspense films," "thrillers," "crime movies," "psychological thrillers," and "erotic thrillers." "Neo-noir," the most common designation since "classic noir" became an accepted rubric, is graphic but perhaps misleading: "neo," after all, implies a new spin on a traditional style, a promise of a postmodern tease or twist, an advance over the classic formulas. "Neo" acknowledges a difference between now as opposed to then; but for how long can noir continue to be in a "neo" phase? How long does a new period last in any style or genre? When the long and lengthening "neo" phase is exhausted, as it may well already be, and noir, if it can, spirals into another regenerative mode, do we then enter a "post-neo" era? Since neo-noir has already survived at least twenty years longer than the short-lived original, now-classic cycle, the only way out of the naming impasse is the one the media seem to have adopted since the mid-1990s. "The fall will see a huge diversity of films, ranging from the mega-budget sci-fi *Starship Troopers* to the film noir *L.A. Confidential*," reported *Variety* on August 4, 1997. Other magazines and newspapers have followed *Variety*'s lead, and at this writing film noir (sometimes preceded by a qualifying "contemporary") remains the term of choice, thereby demoting neo-noir to a provisional interim designation.

If in 1997 *L.A. Confidential* could be called a film noir without any disclaimer, then surely noir has at last escaped the historical vise (which includes my own study, *The Dark Side of the Screen* [1981]) within which it has been confined since the term first entered film criticism. Nonetheless, post-1958 noir may well continue to be attacked as an impossibility, as an entity so widely dispersed that it can no longer claim an essence of its own, as a dilution of a historically grounded style, or as a figment of the imaginations of journalists and scholars who have wished it into being.

On the rare occasions in the 1960s and 1970s when "noir" was invoked, it was inevitably as a nostalgic term, a reference to a bygone film style. But in the 1990s, noir's retro edge has paradoxically given it postmodern chic. "Noir" is not only the name of a cycle of historical crime movies, it is also a come-on in promoting new crime movies ("a tribute to film noir," the ads for the 1995 B film *Dirty Money* proclaimed), the brand name for a literary genre, the name of an album by Carly Simon and of a perfume; and noir-inspired imagery has invaded fashion and advertising. A kind of shorthand for sex in the big city, a place where greed and desire intersect in fatal attractions, noir has become a potent marketing tool. Co-opted by a range of pop cultural discourses, noir has been dispersed across the social fabric. "Style Noir," an article by William L. Hamilton in the *New York Times* of September 14, 1997, claims that "life's dark side" is "back with a vengeance" in film and fashion. "If modern life appears to imitate noir's art," Hamilton writes, "the low life of noir has established itself as a respectable genre of twentieth-century American art." Hamilton quotes Geoffrey O'Brien, executive editor of the Library of America and the author of *Hardboiled America: Lurid Paperbacks and the Masters of Noir* (1997): "It's become clear that the noir tradition, whether in novels or movies, really is the dominant style of the American twentieth century. It pulls together all the

big themes of the power of money and corruption and sexual obsession—and a kind of craziness. It has seeped so much into the culture
that it's like a vocabulary for people to use."

Noir "lives" but inevitably not in the same form as in its classic
phase. Like any genre with a long run, it has had to continue to rein-
vent itself, to bend and sway, to add and subtract, in order to keep up
with changing times. "How are the conventions of this stylized genre
recast in an age of gender wars and no smoking?" was the topic of
"The New Noir" panel at the Avignon/New York Film Festival. How
has noir survived in the post-noir, post-studio, postmodern period? At
a time when a promiscuous mixing-and-matching collage style has become common filmmaking practice, with boundaries between genres
becoming increasingly fluid, no genre from the studio era has remained
intact. Like the Western, for decades now an endangered species because its sustaining myths (Manifest Destiny, the rugged pioneer spirit,
the dominance of white patriarchs, and the marginalization of women)
no longer evoke loyalty from an audience base broad enough to guarantee profits, noir would seem an unlikely survivor in the age of griev-
ance and political correctness. Noir's three dominant character types—
the femme fatale bedecked in her glittering and deadly sexual allure;
her victim, the unwary, vulnerable bourgeois male; and the cynical
though gallant private investigator observing his own code of honor as
he walks down the mean streets of classic noir's cities of perpetual
night—would seem at first glance to be retrievable only as nostalgic
figures, icons of a pop-culture corpse. Had this been true, however,
noir would have been expressible only as parody or in a form the Marxist
critic Fredric Jameson calls "the imaginary museum," in which objects,
characters, and narrative patterns from the past are placed on loving,
self-conscious display. Jameson cites *Chinatown* (1974), a simulation of
a past narrative and visual style, a fiction about a fictional world, in a
sense a false copy of an original false copy that reflects the filmmakers'
nostalgia for private-eye stories of long ago, as a model of the type.

Indeed, in the long postclassic noir era, quotation and imitation
have been unavoidable. Contemporary filmmakers approach noir with
admiration for its rich history and generic traditions, and a spirit of
homage is built into their work. And as with any genre at a late point
in its evolution, postclassic noir is heavily infiltrated with parody and
pastiche. Parody, in which generic conventions are submitted to vary-

ing doses of irony and burlesque, can be used both to interrogate and to demolish. Pastiche is neutral citation and presupposes a ready familiarity with the genre's topography on the part of both filmmakers and audiences. If scattershot parody leads to a genre's burial, pastiche without attitude or point of view can flatten the terrain, getting you nowhere. In the collage style of the 1980s and 1990s, parody and pastiche frequently coexist within the same film, sometimes perilously, at other times productively. But if noir could accommodate only parody and pastiche it would not have lasted. Jameson's imaginary museum has not been the only form available to neo-noir; renegotiating the rules of desire codified in classic noir, the genre has updated itself, speaking from and to contemporary concerns.

"Noir isn't crime so much as it's existential dilemma," author Luc Sante claims in Hamilton's *New York Times* article on the pervasiveness of *le style noir*. "It's about isolation and wide-ranging but unspecific fear—a kind of fear of being." It is indeed in this sense that noir has continued to thrive: noir names a knot of feelings and intuitions—dread, uncertainty, paranoia—that won't go away. And postmodern life has cooperated by continuing to fuel numerous anxieties easily subsumed under noir. If World War II, the Cold War, and the atom bomb "underwrote" classic noir, the increasing cynicism evoked by Watergate and Vietnam, as well as the mounting tensions in gender politics and race relations, have produced a cultural soil particularly rich in noirish implications. Absorbent and surprisingly mobile, noir has continued to be a reflection of the Zeitgeist—but only up to a point and only obliquely, metaphorically. Noir is not, after all, a documentary style.

As Paul Schrader observes, noir thrives in response to "rips and tears in the social fabric." The fact that noir developed in the 1940s and then revived at full force in the 1990s can be at least partially explained by the realignments in gender relations in both eras. During World War II, when many men were away from their homes and workplaces, women enjoyed unaccustomed prominence; postwar readjustments repositioned women within the domestic sphere. One of classic noir's key ideological projects was to criticize female dominance and to "assist" in returning women and men to their traditional antebellum roles. Like many aspects of Hollywood filmmaking, noir's misogyny functioned as a kind of containment: beware, this is what happens when iron-willed women seize power over men. Archetypal noir narratives in which a luckless head of a family (Edward G. Robinson in *Scarlet Street* [1945] and *The Woman in the Window* [1945] and Dick Powell in *Pitfall* [1948]) succumbs to the siren call of a spider woman (Joan Bennett in *Scarlet Street* and *The Woman in the Window*, Lizabeth Scott in *Pitfall*) dramatize traumatic departures from the status quo. In *The Woman in the Window* the hero's descent into the noir labyrinth is phrased as a bad dream—and it's certain that, after he wakes up, the protagonist who strayed will not make the same mistake in "real life." With relief, this stodgy professor will remain enfolded within the security of what the film has suggested is a safe because sexless marriage. At the end of *Pitfall*, the temporarily errant husband returns to his forgiving but wised-up wife who may well keep as tight a rein on him as he is likely to keep on himself. When a fallen bourgeois, like the insurance salesman in *Double Indemnity* ([1944] played by Fred MacMurray) can't be rescued because he has descended too deeply into a noir inferno, he is killed—another kind of warning notice issued by conservative classic noir.

His masculinity under attack, the vulnerable male of high forties noir had it easy compared to his 1990s counterpart. In recent decades, feminists, racial, ethnic, and sexual minorities have taken aim at the one group perceived to have had it all, the white heterosexual male, the bourgeois capitalist patriarch who has been the traditional protagonist of Hollywood fictions. A number of post-noir suspense films register the many new ways in which this character can be dislodged, while self-defensive male backlash stories record the revenge of the patriarchs against the forces determined to unseat them from their historical place of privilege. Preserving male dominance against escalating threats has continued to be postclassic noir's primary concern. Despite shifts in the real world in the way men and women relate, and despite the effect of feminist arguments on raising the awareness of both genders, noir has for the most part resisted changing its sexist tune.

Stubbornly resistant to the "lessons" of feminism, neo-noir like classic noir presents strong women as Venus flytraps determined to snare unwary men. And neo-noir continues to honor the simplistic opposition in 1940s thrillers between the dragon ladies who take deadly aim and the passive, desexualized wives and girlfriends who stand by, waiting in the wings for their men to act. If sex outside marriage (which is the only place it ever seemed to occur in classic noir) was lined with disaster, the case against sex has increased alarmingly. Indirectly, many neo-noir films of the 1980s and 1990s highlight the risk of sex in the age of AIDS, the new "war" that replaces World War II as the genre's principal subtext. In the 1940s the case against sex could be seen as a general warning to control your libido; in the era of AIDS, neo-noir films about sex gone wrong issue a more urgent declaration. In the past twenty years, the traditional link in noir narratives between sex and catastrophe is no longer merely symbolic or moralistic, although no noir film has addressed AIDS directly or enlisted it as a narrative cause. Nonetheless, the sexual plague in the real world remains part of the background "noise" in noir stories of the consequences of sexual license.

Sex in classic noir, as in all films of the time, was grounded in heterosexual desire, the effect that straight women and straight men had on each other. As in *Double Indemnity*, which ends with an unmarried insurance salesman gone bad dying in the arms of his zealous bachelor boss, homoeroticism left no more than a few traces in the negative space surrounding heterosexuality. Homosexuality, the desire "that could not be named," also could not be seen. But even after homosexuality has become an available subject, its presence in crime movies has remained both rare and contested. While it was always permissible to suggest that heterosexual obsession could lead to crime, the same equation between gay desire and a plunge into noir remains an uneasy coupling. Having emerged from historical invisibility, gays and lesbians are still underrepresented in American movies and therefore any appearance carries a hefty ideological stake. While the straying husband in *Pitfall*, for instance, does not speak for all straight bourgeois heterosexuals with a wandering eye, a gay character driven by desire to commit a crime is more likely to be evaluated, by both gay and straight audiences, as a stand-in for the "gay sensibility." Since most sex in noir is tinged with pathology, the genre is likely to remain dangerous ground for homosexual representations.

Like homosexuality, race in classic noir, as again in most studio-era films, was largely defined by its absence. But in a number of thrillers of the 1980s and 1990s, a significant subgenre has emerged in which being black in white America is depicted as an existential condition steeped in noir. Made in large part by black filmmakers speaking primarily to black audiences, these "noir" noirs forcibly shift traditional themes of paranoia and entrapment from a nostalgic framework—

Jameson's imaginary museum—to a context of immediate social urgency and thereby provide a strong argument for the genre's capacity for regeneration. Simmering cities within cities, densely populated black ghettos in nouveau noir breed crime and psychosis. Stifling in summer, arctic in winter, the ghettos of black noir films have a more heightened glaze of realism than the studio-made cities of the 1940s, but they too are stylized representations, cities, ultimately, of the cinematic imagination.

In contemporary black noir, as in noir's treatment of homosexuals and in its continuing misogynistic undercurrent, there is much to offend the captains of political correctness. Neo-noir's lack of strict moral accountability has deepened in another way as well. In classic noir, as in all American films governed by the prescriptions of the Production Code, crime and punishment were inevitably joined. No matter how slyly audiences may have been coerced into rooting for a criminal, or secretly wishing an audacious criminal act would go undetected, moral order had to be restored. At the end of the day, evil women were dead; men who had strayed were severely chastened, imprisoned, or also dead; any character who had violated the social contract was either eliminated or, where possible, reabsorbed into the status quo, which endured.

Once the Production Code was terminated in the mid-1960s, however, moral laissez-faire quickly became the new mode: the bank robbers in *The Getaway* (1972) were the first movie criminals who lived to enjoy the fruits of their labor. Questioning or jettisoning former codes is a necessary factor in generic recycling, and the freedom to allow criminals to remain unpunished certainly expands noir's narrative and thematic possibilities. It may well be more realistic than the crime-and-punishment couplet of the studio era; and further, the uncaught criminal may even accurately reflect the cynicism, subversion, and haphazardness that lurk at the heart of noir. But the random morality of the post-Code era comes at a high cost. Released from "bondage," filmmakers in the neo-noir period have too often produced crime stories that flaunt a cavalier amorality, and in watching antisocial exhibits in which crime most definitely *does* pay, spectators can be steeped in a potentially depraved point of view.

Photographed in black and white and projected on a specific screen size (the old academy ratio of 1:33), classic noir was a rigorously stylized genre. Skeptics who dismiss neo-noir as an impossibility, a purely imagined category, argue that the noir vision required the format for which it was originally conceived and that the use of color and the wider screen sizes that have become mandatory in the post-studio era have ensured the genre's disappearance. Classic noir was rooted in the visual conventions of Hollywood's classical style, with its seamless "invisible" editing—matching over-the-shoulder shots, shots and countershots neatly joined to afford the illusion of spatial and temporal continuity—and a "well-behaved" camera that was content to remain in place for deep-focus long takes. With the passage of time, the decorum of the classical style has come to seem increasingly formal and even at times rather stiff jointed; but it was an apt style for recording the typical ruptures of a noir narrative. The beauty of classic noir was grounded in elegant simplicity: an artfully placed shadow on a staircase, a rain-slicked street, a flashing neon sign could rumble with premonition. Shimmering chiaroscuro lighting and an occasional canted or distorted angle might be sufficient to suggest the imminence of a nightmarish turn in the plot. As noir narratives became increasingly entangled and the characters' lives unraveled, camerawork and editing continued to observe a measured, logical, centered style. Classic noir typically created a mise-en-scène of minatory *absence*, an ominously still, waiting world. "Less is more" was an axiom the filmmakers, as well as the contemporary audience, had faith in.

It has become an accurate enough critical observation that post-MTV audiences don't have the patience to watch and to listen to films made in the classical style. Weaned on channel surfing and on visual and aural density and fragmentation, the typical generation-*x* spectator may well find the classical style of classic noir both unfamiliar and austere. Like other genres providing visual pleasure in a society enamored of spectacle, noir has had to revise and augment its stylistic menu. To survive, noir has had to make use of (but also to regulate) the staccato editing rhythms, the tracking, craning, restlessly mobile camerawork, the multilayered sound tracks and lush colors that have become part of the post-studio filmmaking syllabus. Now as then, not overload but containment and simplicity are noir's allies, and while it has had to add a crust of superficial dazzle, at heart the genre rejects technological display.

Nonetheless, as they have accommodated changes wrought by the era of "gender wars and no smoking," the most resourceful neo-noir films have also updated without contaminating the genre's potent visual imprint. Postclassic noir has evolved a distinctive color code, as stylized in its way as the high-key black and white of old, and has produced graphic images of enclosure in a wide-screen format. Noir was always intensely self-conscious, even before it had a name; and working within a keen sense of noir tradition, filmmakers in the neo era continue making thrillers that are visually self-aware. Sometimes the films stumble into sheer mannerism or self-parody, while other works reject outright the classic period's visual idiom in order to explore radically different styles that remain true to noir's temperament. Whether imitative or Oedipal, the strongest neo-noirs have created visual textures that honor the genre's legacy.

If, on the one hand, *Touch of Evil*, the film noir that knows too much about film noir, did not terminate the genre in 1958, noir did not, on the other hand, spring full grown in 1941 with *The Maltese Falcon*, as is commonly claimed. (It may be that *Citizen Kane* rather than *The Maltese Falcon* is the 1941 film with the greatest influence on noir's evolving visual style.) Even so, 1941 and 1958 are convenient bookends for a coherent collection of crime movies with echoing titles, visual signifiers, narrative patterns, and character types that can now be labeled "classic noir." But this group of films, among which, of course, there are marked differences in quality and design, should be considered a phase of a larger cycle that began well before 1941 and survives to the present.

The chiaroscuro, canted angles, ceiling shots, and deep focus of *The Maltese Falcon* and *Citizen Kane*, which create a neurotic, unstable mise-en-scène and became key visual elements throughout classic noir, were not new at the time. Silent-screen melodramas, from *Broken Blossoms* (1919) to *Sunrise* (1927), and horror films of the 1930s like *Frankenstein* (1932) and *Dracula* (1931), contain noir-like lighting and imagery. Fritz Lang's *You Only Live Once*, about an outlaw couple on the run, is deeply noir in both subject matter and visual design, and only its "early" 1937 date bars it from inclusion in the classic noir canon. In addition to its long genealogy on native ground, noir has roots in two European film traditions: in German expressionism, regularly cited as noir's principal ancestor, and in the poetic realism movement in prewar France, about which too little has been said. Films like Marcel Carné's *Jour se lève* (1939) and Jean Renoir's *Chienne* (1931) and *Bête humaine* ([1938] remade by Fritz Lang as, respectively, *Scarlet Street* and *Human Desire* [1954]) are potent noir dramas *avant la lettre*, psychological thrillers with compelling anticipations of the mood, the characterizations, and the visual idiom of classic noir. Both during the prewar era and at the end of the classic phase, when prominent critics-turned-directors were the first to rewrite the genre, the French were major figures in noir's history. They played a larger role than simply naming a group of American thrillers. Classic noir's prehistory, longer, more complex, and more widely dispersed than is usually acknowledged, thus matches its equally vast (and equally contested) posthistory.

If, at least for the sake of discussion, we can agree that noir has a decent claim to genre status, then the next problem is which films qualify: How much noir does a picture need in order to merit the neo-noir tag? As Paul Schrader noted at "The New Noir" panel, "It gets easy to use the term to describe a lot of films," and indeed fragments of noir are scattered across a wide spectrum of contemporary movies. But even in the era of postmodern hybrids, noir remains a quantifiably distinct commodity. My approach is to focus on films that continue the themes and the look formulated in classic noir; branch off into fertile or misguided new terrain; or, most typically, combine traditional and nouveau patterns with varying success. Although "neo" implies a new way of making noir, not all the films in the long neo period, of course, take a combative stance toward the original cycle. Applying the strict definition of neo, Jean-Luc Godard's *À bout de souffle* (*Breathless* [1959]) would qualify, *L.A Confidential* (1997) would not: *Breathless* alters noir, *L.A. Confidential* is pastiche, a résumé of familiar elements skillfully assembled to evoke a style from the past.

In canvassing for noir among the crime movies of the last four decades, I have been on the lookout for themes, visual insignia, and a worldview familiar from the classic period (that, inevitably, have been revised to varying degrees). Unlike the classic gangster film, noir in its most compelling form is about middle-class citizens unexpectedly invaded by or lured into crime. Noir is not about Little Caesar fighting his way to the top of the underworld but about Walter Neff (in *Double Indemnity*) taking perverse delight in outwitting the insurance company for which he has been a faithful employee. Pricked by desire and/or inflamed by greed, the luckless noir protagonist commits murder or robbery. Over and over, as it watches its characters stumble into crime, noir sneakily posits the appeal (but also the consequences) of breaking the repressive codes that hold the social fabric in place. A key noir notion is that criminal instincts are innate in even the most sober-seeming citizens and that once they are given in to they become all-consuming, as well as contagious: the cop or private investigator working to solve a crime is often tempted and sometimes succumbs. Characters in noir stories cross boundaries—as victims of bad timing, chance encounters, or their own forbidden wishes; in a fateful split second, typical noir protagonists plunge into the other side of the law.

While there have been many local changes, noir's basic narrative molds have remained notably stable. The private-investigation quest; crimes of passion and profit; stories involving masquerade, amnesia, split identity, and double and triple crosses continue to be the genre's abiding concerns. In the classic era, fragments of noir began to migrate to other genres. With lighting and compositions that exude noir-like neurosis, *Pursued* (1947) is a Western about an unstable hero traumatized by a partial memory that he must recall fully in order to expel. *Reign of Terror* (1949), set in post-Revolution France, is a period noir, one of several made in the 1940s, in which every shot emanates entrapment. "The Girl Hunt" ballet in *The Band Wagon* is a private-eye story danced in stylized Broadway settings ablaze in gaudy Metrocolor, demonstrating (in 1953) noir's openness to co-optation and parody. Noir shadows and atmosphere overtake the small town in the science-fiction-horror landmark, *Invasion of the Body Snatchers* (1956). In the neo era, noir elements have continued to be on the move, in Westerns, science fiction and horror stories, comedies, feminist melodramas, action movies, musicals, and cartoons.

In the high noir of the 1940s and 1950s, whether the film was made in the studio or shot on location, the city provided a stylized setting. Echoing the décor of pulp fiction, the city in classic noir exuded isolation, danger, and bewitchment. Both carnival and purgatory, it was a place in which to hide out, to conceal or transform identity. Its tenements, nightclubs, hotels, side streets, and warehouses promised anonymity, a world bristling with fleeting pleasures, dirty business, and threat. A few classic noir movies had rural settings, and sometimes city characters escaped to beach houses or to mountain retreats or to Mexico, the genre's great foul place. Neo-noir, however, is as likely to take place in vast open spaces as in the pestilential city of tradition. Noir Furies now arise from anywhere, in the bright noon of an infinite desert, as well as from within the canyons of big-city side streets; and open, as well as closed, environments can suddenly become places without exit.

In the following pages, I offer a brief overview of neo-noir's trajectory over the past four decades. I cite key films and trends that I will then return to for closer examination in subsequent chapters. In the third edition of their estimable *Film Noir: An Encyclopedic Reference to the American Style*, published in 1992, the editors, Alain Silver and Elizabeth Ward, place *Harper*, a 1966 film, at the top of their neo-noir chronology. *Harper* proves that a smartly played private-eye story, adapted to the demands of color and wide screen, is as apt for 1966 as for 1946, but the film did not revive noir because noir never died. Between *Touch of Evil* in 1958 and *Harper* in 1966, a few thrillers with unmistakable noir markings appeared. There weren't many, and simply in terms of quantity the entire period from 1958 to 1981 can be regarded as something of an off-season for noir; but a generic tradition endured nonetheless. Along with *Harper*, Silver and Ward list only two other private-eye dramas, *The Detective* (1968) and *Lady in Cement* (1968), for neo-noir's first decade. But I would argue that, in the early post-studio era, noir lingered in the margins, a continuing shadowy presence in the negative space surrounding genres of the moment; and from 1959 to 1966, there were some choice thrillers that began the work of reinventing noir for the "post-noir" era.

Robert Wise's masterful *Odds Against Tomorrow*, produced in 1959, is as aware as *Touch of Evil* of its late place in the history of noir. It uses classic motifs with bracing confidence. Telling a standard noir story about a heist gone wrong, the film features neurotic camera angles, a cool jazz score, and cramped, hideous sets whose walls seem to be closing in on characters sucked into crime because they see no other way out of their existential traps. But, far from wrapping noir in a valedictory aura, the film adds to the genre's possibilities by introducing a potent new subject: racial animosity between two of the thieves.

As if his brand of suspense is sui generis, above the sway and pull of genre, Alfred Hitchcock is usually placed outside noir. But at heart, no director is more deeply noir; and in the period right after the classic cycle ended, he created two symptomatic psychological thrillers located securely on noir grounds (although they usually aren't placed

AT-87

Is *Odds Against Tomorrow* (1959), as intensely aware of noir's visual signature as *Touch of Evil*, the "last" classic noir, or the first neo-noir? In a mise-en-scène saturated with doom, a racist bank robber (Robert Ryan, left) shoots at police after a failed heist, as his boss (Ed Begley) lies mortally wounded.

there). A film noir *en couleur*, *Vertigo* (1958) is an elegant treatment of themes—a romantic obsession that curdles into crime; masquerade; misperception; and the slipperiness and fluidity of identity—crucial to noir in all its phases. Suffering from vertigo, the film's unraveling detective is clearly marked as a noir protagonist whose masculinity is under siege. And the fact that genial, all-American James Stewart plays the character underlines the noir motif that even the sturdiest of us harbors a secret sharer, a criminal other waiting to be released. While the protagonist is conceived securely within a noir tradition, the film rewrites the femme fatale as a victim rather than a manipulator of male desire. Like its protagonists, *Psycho* (1960) has a split personality, part horror show (Norman Bates's story), part classic noir (a drama about a decent, law-abiding secretary who decides to steal forty thousand dollars from her boss). Both of these seminal Hitchcock thrillers anticipated neo-noir motifs, *Vertigo* pointing toward suspense films in lush color that conflate death and desire, *Psycho* a preview of the generic hybrids that have become increasingly common in the 1980s and 1990s.

If Hitchcock disregarded the "end of noir," so did Samuel Fuller, a maverick filmmaker whose early 1960s thrillers—*Underworld U.S.A.* (1961), *The Naked Kiss* (1964) and *Shock Corridor* (1963)—employ noir insignia in a baroque, tabloid style. In Fuller's hands, familiar noir characters (an avenger, a femme fatale, a journalist who assumes a new and dangerous identity) acquire bizarre overtones.

The early 1960s, far from being a limbo for noir, was a particularly rich period. Besides Fuller's eccentric variations and *Blast of Silence* (1961), a no-budget early tribute to classic noir made by a genre aficionado, Allen Baron, there were well-made, noir business-as-usual thrillers, such as the original *Cape Fear* (1962) and *Experiment in Terror* (1962), both on the standard noir theme of innocence invaded. *The Manchurian Candidate* (1962), which grafts noir elements onto a Cold War political thriller, is an early indication of the way the genre has been progressively updated to reflect changing social anxieties.

Thematically as well as visually, post-noir thrillers like *Cape Fear*, *The Manchurian Candidate*, and the already-nostalgic *Blast of Silence* recall the 1950s. *Point Blank* (1967), in color and wide screen and with a nervous new pace, might well qualify as the first truly new post-noir noir. Influenced by French experiments with the crime film in the late 1950s and early 1960s, it is domesticated New Wave noir that introduces

European art-film syntax—fragmentation, stylized color, dream imagery—into a bare-bones genre story of a gunman's quest for revenge. Loyal to Hollywood narrative codes at the same time that it slyly disrupted them, the film established a new kind of dialogue with genre audiences.

Noir appeared more frequently in the 1970s and in a variety of narrative formats. During this period, the private investigator was the most popular character in crime films. Sometimes, as in *Chandler* (1971) and *The Drowning Pool* (1975), in which Paul Newman reprises Harper, the character is played in an entirely straightforward way. A few films add either nostalgic or revisionist touches to the private eye. In *Farewell, My Lovely* (1975), a remake of *Murder, My Sweet* (1944), Robert Mitchum, an authentic classic noir icon, plays Philip Marlowe with an ironic gleam. In Robert Altman's defiantly revisionist *The Long Goodbye* (1973), Elliott Gould plays Philip Marlowe as a slack-jawed buffoon who mumbles to himself and to his cat..

From *Shaft* (1971), who operates on the margins of the crime world, to *Serpico* (1973), who is resolved to oppose widespread corruption on the police force, to *Dirty Harry* (1971), who bends the law to defend and uphold it, policemen in the 1970s became recurrent noir protagonists. Next of kin to some of the era's neurotic police officers, the vigilante emerged as a new noir archetype. The bourgeois citizen driven to crazed vengeance in the notorious *Death Wish* (1974), for example, embodied contemporary fears about big cities. As ever responsive to shifts in the Zeitgeist, noir in the 1970s reflected, in a few telling films, the impact of Watergate (*The Parallax View* [1974]), of the Vietnam War (*Who'll Stop the Rain?* [1978]), and of feminism (*Klute* [1971]).

As in the 1940s, noir thrillers circulated in the 1960s and 1970s without, for the most part, being attached to a definite classification. It wasn't until *Body Heat* was released in 1981 that neo-noir was generally recognized as a distinct formal category. Unlike *Point Blank* or *Klute*, however, *Body Heat* represented a return to narrative patterns of the past. Recalling the story and characters of *Double Indemnity*, *Body Heat* is a skillful pastiche that proved that an old-fashioned noir story about a reckless, sex-minded male who gets entangled with a predatory woman could entertain a new generation. Disguising its retro core in contemporary drag, it efficiently lays out motifs that subsequent thrillers have continued to draw on.

*Body Heat*, a remake in a general sense, was followed by a number of literal remakes. These include *Against All Odds* (1984), based on *Out of the Past* (1947); *The Morning After* (1986), an update of *The Blue Gardenia* (1953); *No Way Out* (1987), a reworking of *The Big Clock* (1948); *The Postman Always Rings Twice* (1981, 1946); *D.O.A.* (1988, 1950); *Desperate Hours* (1990, 1955); *Narrow Margin* (1990, 1952); *Night and the City* (1992, 1950); *A Kiss Before Dying* (1991, 1956); *The Underneath* (1995), based on *Criss Cross* (1949); and *Kiss of Death* (1995, 1947). To date there have been three remakes of films from the post-classic period: in 1991 Martin Scorsese resurrected the 1962 thriller, *Cape Fear*; *The Getaway* (1972) was revisited in 1994; *Payback* (1999) is a reworking of *Point Blank*. The oddest remake so far has been *Breathless* (1983), an American adaptation of Jean-Luc Godard's 1959 *À bout de souffle*, a New Wave tribute to (and demolition of) a Hollywood thriller. Varying both in quality—from *Against All Odds*, strictly d.o.a., to *The Underneath*, nearly sublime—and in fidelity to their sources, the remakes testify to noir's contemporary utility; clearly, a number of filmmakers have felt that the classic noir canon was well worth exploring.

While many crime thrillers of the noir revival of the 1980s and 1990s were not direct remakes, they contained strong echoes from the past. The new faces given to the protagonists of *Johnny Handsome* (1989), *Shattered* (1991), and *Face/Off* (1997), for instance, recall the premise of *Dark Passage* (1947), in which, after plastic surgery, the hero-in-hiding looks just like the film's star, Humphrey Bogart. The wicked sisters of *Final Analysis* (1992), who bedevil a hapless therapist, evoke the doppelgänger motif in *The Dark Mirror* (1946) and *A Stolen Life* (1946), in which there are two sisters, one sweet, the other malefic.

Adaptations of hardboiled novels signal contemporary filmmakers' awareness of noir's usable literary and cinematic traditions. Works by Raymond Chandler, Cornell Woolrich, and James M. Cain, at the high end of the corpus, and by Mickey Spillane at the low end, have been revisited, while Dashiell Hammett appeared as the protagonist in Wim Wenders's film *Hammett* (1983). The works of a number of later hardboiled crime writers, skillful successors to the original "boys in the back room," have also been adapted to film: Charles Williams's *Hell Hath No Fury*, filmed as *The Hot Spot* (1990); Charles Willeford's *Miami Blues* (1990); Elmore Leonard's *52 Pick-Up* (1986) and *Rum Punch*, filmed as *Jackie Brown* (1997); Richard Neely's *Plastic Nightmare*, filmed as *Shat-*

*tered.* Jim Thompson, along with Cornell Woolrich, the most deeply and deliriously noir of all American crime writers who from the early 1940s up to 1964 wrote a series of sizzling hardboiled stories with an often-startling modernist edge, was not discovered by movies until *The Getaway* in 1972. (Thompson's only contribution to classic noir was his screenplay for *The Killing* [1956], Stanley Kubrick's noir masterwork.) The few Thompson adaptations so far, including *After Dark, My Sweet* (1990), *The Killer Inside Me* (1976), *The Grifters* (1990), *The Kill-Off* (1989), and *This World, Then the Fireworks* (1997), in addition to the two versions of *The Getaway*, are a start, but only that: the Thompson canon may be the single richest, untapped source for crime movies.

In the 1940s, noir's deadpan style was embodied by actors who, in effect, became genre specialists: Alan Ladd, Veronica Lake, Robert Mitchum, Humphrey Bogart, Joan Bennett, Edward G. Robinson, Lauren Bacall, and Barbara Stanwyck, among others, perfected a masked, somnambulistic mode ideally pitched to noir's stories of mischance. Neo-noir's long history hasn't produced actors who have become specifically identified with the genre. There have been potent performances in individual films, but no actor has emerged with the iconographic impact of a Stanwyck or a Bogart. But as in the classic era, noir has continued to be a director's showcase. Alongside the mid-level noir thrillers directed in an anonymous style are the works of idiosyncratic filmmakers attracted by the genre's possibilities. Noir still provides a low-budget showcase for novice filmmakers. It has also seduced a number of foreign directors, including Kenneth Branagh, Roman Polanski, Wim Wenders, and Barbet Schroeder, and sparked the interest of established directors, such as Francis Ford Coppola, Ridley Scott, Martin Scorsese, Jonathan Demme, Dennis Hopper, Arthur Penn, Bob Rafelson, Walter Hill, and Michael Cimino, looking for a change of pace. Neo-noir has provided a frame for David Lynch's fever dreams and for Quentin Tarantino's postmodern riffs on crime-movie stencils.

*Betrayed, Frantic, Primal Fear, Fear, Deceived, Body Heat, Fatal Attraction, Falling Down, Shattered, Kiss of Death, Kill Me Again, Masquerade, Deep Cover*—these representative titles from the noir revival of the 1980s and 1990s resonate with themes derived from classic noir. In a single word or phrase, the evocative, echoing titles beckon the viewer into a world of hardboiled pulp fiction.

Caught by the camera: sex and conspiracy radiate from Anna (Yvonne DeCarlo) and Steve (Burt Lancaster), meeting clandestinely at the opening of *Criss Cross* (1949).

Chapter 2

# The Second Time Around

Remakes are always high risk. Unavoidably, they are read against the grain of the original works, and because they confront the widespread cultural belief that the first of any form is the purest version, they are stamped with what amounts to, in effect, a primal curse. A remake is a postlapsarian offering over which the original presides as a nagging, structuring absence. In all genres, remakes have amassed a generally inferior track record; in noir, comparisons are especially cruel because filmmakers and audiences alike fervently admire the original films. Re-creating a work that continues to exert a powerful allure is a process in which the filmmakers are locked in an intimate confrontation with an object of desire. But the aura of homage that surrounds remakes is more likely to result in travesty than in triumph.

All of the classic noir films that have inspired remakes, including *Out of the Past* (1947), *The Killers* (1946), *The Big Clock* (1948), *Murder, My Sweet* (1944), *Criss Cross (1949)*, *Kiss of Death* (1947), *Detour* (1945), *Night and the City* (1950), *The Narrow Margin* (1952), *The Desperate Hours* (1955), *The Blue Gardenia* (1953), and *The Postman Always Rings Twice* (1946), are fully realized works rooted in their own time period. In a strict sense, remakes are valid only when they add to or substantially revise an original. If the primary aim is simply to duplicate or recapture, the remake can be no more than a waxworks simulation. (Some postmodern theorists contend that in any medium only copies are possible.) Since any neo-noir film, however, cannot be made in the same way as in the past—

in its original form, noir was tied to a set of production and technological conditions no longer available—the genre would seem to have
some built-in defenses against slipping into mere imitation.

Classic noir's visual signature—the play of light and velvet shadow
filmed in lustrous black and white; long takes; deep focus; a mostly
sedentary camera—thrived on artful simplicity; and indeed, of what
use are advanced sound systems, frenetic editing and camerawork,
photorealist color, wide screen, and special effects to noir stories of entrapment? Remaking classic noir has embroiled contemporary filmmakers in a series of moral, as well as visual, crises: How can black-
and-white movies conceived originally in a prefeminist, sexually conservative era be post-modernized? And if the visual and moral decorum that imbued classic noir is disturbed or rerouted, are the remains
neo- or anti-noir? Not being able to tell their "old" stories in the same
visual mold as in the classic era, neo-noir filmmakers have had to find
contemporary equivalents. It is precisely in the tensions between contemporary excess and the decorum of the classical style that noir remakes stake their claims to originality.

As I compare them to their sources, adopting the dual reading
strategy remakes impose, the films notify us about the ways that times
have changed, about how "then" has had to be restaged for "now," or,
as the history of noir continues, for a series of "nows." More noteworthy as symptoms than as achieved works, no remake so far either equals
or surpasses the original film. Nonetheless, a few are intelligent revisions while others disgrace the memory of the works that inspired
them. Regardless of quality, the remakes I look at are instructive. As
they return us to classic noir, they also provide guideposts for evaluating neo-noir movies with original screenplays.

The margin for error in all remakes is sizable; in noir, the hazards
are especially steep. I'd like to begin, however, on an upbeat note by
looking at two reasonably successful adaptations. *The Underneath* re-
tells the story of *Criss Cross* with only moderate changes, while *No Way
Out* considerably revises *The Big Clock*.

*Criss Cross* opens, unforgettably, as an invasive camera swoops down
on lovers meeting clandestinely in a dark parking lot. He is clearly
infatuated. Her state of mind is harder to gauge. She speaks of love,
but her eyes are masked. "It will be just you and me, like it always should
have been," she promises. Her words alert us to the fact that, in the

past, something went wrong. The camera's thrusting movement and the ominous lighting—the lovers are caught in a spotlight—suggest that history will be repeated.

It is the night before a robbery, and the reunited lovers, Steve (Burt Lancaster) and Anna (Yvonne DeCarlo), have met to plan how they are to double-cross their partner, Slim Dundee (Dan Duryea), who happens to be Anna's new husband. In a truck on his way to the heist, Steve's voiceover narration, pitted with bitterness and foreboding, takes us into the past, when he and Anna were married. When the marriage foundered, Steve left and tried, unsuccessfully, to forget Anna. But pulled toward the woman he can't get over, he has returned. "It was in the cards. There I was looking for her," he says, intoning the noir antihero's double-stranded anthem: he knows he should have known better, and he also knows he couldn't help himself. "What was the use? I knew somehow or other I would wind up seeing her that night. It was in the cards and there was no way of stopping it. Every place you go you see her face."

Speaking after he has fallen for Anna a second time, Steve's voiceover is thick with a sense of his impending doom. Inevitably, the heist fails. Dundee kills Steve and Anna. But deep in the heart of noir there are no winners: offscreen police sirens warn that Slim, too, has been ensnared by a crisscross. The fated characters are classic noir archetypes. Steve is a born victim derailed by his romantic obsession. Anna is a noir realist and therefore deadlier than the passive male who risks everything for a love grown sickly. (As Steve's mother says about Anna, "In some ways she knows more than Einstein.") "You have to watch out for yourself," Anna admonishes Steve at the end, after she has double-crossed him a second time. "You just don't know what kind of world this is."

Burt Lancaster plays Steve as a character fatally contaminated by desire. As in *The Killers,* using a soft voice and at times bending over from the weight of his character's wounds, he plays shrewdly against his powerful physique. And Yvonne DeCarlo is an insinuating spider woman, at the same time both beckoning and icy, the expert sadist to Lancaster's masochist. Directed by a noir specialist, German émigré Robert Siodmak, *Criss Cross* exudes high tension. Space and chiaroscuro lighting reflect the characters' states of mind. In the heist-planning scene, the mise-en-scène bristles with festering tensions. In the center of the empty, shabby room where the conspirators plot the robbery are poles that divide space in a visual anticipation of the way the thieves will become divided against themselves. At one point Steve and Anna, plotting a double cross, are in the foreground while their partners, in deep focus, remain apart from them in another room. But most of the time, Anna, who will want the money all for herself, remains physically separated from the others. A moodily lighted, deep- focus shot of the Angel's Flight trolley (in downtown Los Angeles) climbing its way up the steep grade of Bunker Hill foreshadows the uphill struggle the characters will face. During the robbery, a startlingly high angle shot of a truck entering the factory that is to be robbed provides another portent of the catastrophe that awaits the criminals.

*Criss Cross* contains a celebrated noir set piece. Suffering from smoke inhalation after the botched robbery, Steve is hospitalized. Outside his room is a long, eerily empty corridor, a space crawling with shadows and ill intentions. In a mirror, Steve catches the reflection of a man sitting quietly, far too quietly, in the corridor. Observing the corridor from Steve's restricted point of view, we are forced to share his sense of enclosure and his mounting dread. Anxious about the stranger—has he been sent by Slim, or is he someone with no connection to his destiny?—Steve asks to see the man, who identifies himself as "Nelson," a husband nervously awaiting news of his injured wife. "Nelson" appears to be who he claims to be; but once again, Steve, a willing victim, is fooled by a masquerade because "Nelson" is Dundee's emissary, a figure of doom.

Steven Soderbergh's adaptation is faithful to *Criss Cross* in letter and spirit. In *The Underneath*, as in the original, the protagonist is a prodigal son who returns home after an enforced absence; resumes an affair with his former wife, now married to a crook; begins a job at an armored-car company; proposes a bank heist; and is double-crossed by both the gangster and the girl. As in *Criss Cross*, as indeed throughout noir, the past retains a firm grip on the present. On the day of the robbery, the hero's thoughts slide obsessively from the present to the past, to the time before his fall, but here there is no voiceover: scenes set in the past are identified by the presence of the hero's beard. Working in color and wide screen, Soderbergh manages to evoke the visual textures of classic noir. With underwater greens and blues dominating, the film's color often achieves an expressionist intensity. The armored car in which the hero is framed is bathed in a sickly greenish blue, a color that seems to emanate from the character's troubled thoughts. In a shot drenched in icy blue lighting, the reunited lovers meet under a bridge, a rendezvous point as ominous as the parking lot in the opening of *Criss Cross*. On the Panavision screen, Soderbergh encloses his trapped characters in a series of frames within the frame. The hero is repeatedly caught behind the barred window of the armored car in which he drives to his noir destiny, and windows with venetian blinds or heavy bars figure prominently throughout. As the film constructs a world in which there is no escape from a probing gaze, the camera seems to spy on the

Venetian blinds frame the uneasy lovers (Alison Elliott and Peter Gallagher), steeped in chiaroscuro, in *The Underneath* (1995), a respectful remake of *Criss Cross*.

characters as they spy on each other. Soderbergh's hospital sequence, a neo-noir highlight, matches Siodmak's in sustaining a sinister atmosphere.

*Criss Cross*, a location noir, was shot in the decaying Bunker Hill section of old Los Angeles, an area of faded Victorian-style buildings long since demolished. Like most neo-noirs, *The Underneath* is partially set in a realistically rendered environment seemingly free of any touch of evil. The remake relocates the story from the city to an unnamed small town, a place of sun and pleasant suburban houses that affords the kind of intermittent respite from noir that was not part of the visual code of the insistently noir original.

While it follows the narrative outline of the original, the remake revises the leading characters. *The Underneath*, set in a cool, post-passionate world, rewrites a story about a mad love into a tale about another kind of loser. The besotted lover of *Criss Cross* is now a compul-

sive gambler and con artist who had to leave town because of his un-
paid debts. Schemes for making a financial killing rather than a two-
timing woman are what's on his mind. The second time around, the
protagonist is in fact a diffident, distracted lover. After being in bed
with him, his new girlfriend (an unnecessary added character) surmises
that he has someone else, and his ex-wife, from whom he is usually
separated within the frame, has to keep reminding him that she is still
around. Burt Lancaster's Steve is dazed by a fatal attraction; Peter
Gallagher plays the character as simply dazed. Although we enter his
mind in the subjective flashbacks, the character remains a remote figure.

In *Criss Cross*, Steve is shadowed by a straight-arrow cop, Pete, who
was his childhood friend and who seems to harbor an unacknowledged
homoerotic attraction to him. (At the time, of course, the character's
feelings had to be repressed, but Pete's squelched passion provides a
provocative corollary to the open way in which Steve expresses his feelings for Anna. Here, as often in classic noir, a repressed sexual subtext
enhances the film's neurotic aura.) Bristling with misogynistic bile, Pete
repeatedly tries to rescue Steve from Anna. In an alley where steam
shoots out of a window, a mise-en- scène that radiates unexpressed
sexual tension, Pete warns Steve against her: "I know it when I see a
bad one." After the failed robbery, Pete says "They used you, they took
you," his dialogue typically coiled with sexual innuendo. In the remake,
Pete is replaced by the protagonist's brother, also a policeman, who is
the film's resident romantic obsessive. A voyeur who watches his returned brother undress ("nice butt," he observes), he desires his brother's
ex-wife and competes with him for their mother's love.

Like the protagonist, who has become more opaque than in the
original, the femme fatale has also been reconceived. If the male is no
longer ensnared by lust, the woman (played by a lackluster Alison Elliott)
is no longer alluring. Seemingly rejecting the femme fatale as an outmoded type, the film replaces her with a more realistic character. In
*Criss Cross*, Anna seems to have been born bad; here the character becomes hard only after she has been seduced and abandoned. In the
flashback scenes, she is a wholesome young woman sincerely devoted
to her husband. It is only in the present, when she is married to a noir
psycho, that she has grown resentful of men; and it is only at the end,
when she becomes greedy about money, that she appears in the kind

of lighting that marks her as a full-fledged femme fatale. The film's attempts to humanize the woman, however, fail to motivate the ending (in which the character runs off with all the money after she has shot both her present and ex-husbands) while at the same time violating the protocols of pulp fiction.

The film's acute awareness of classic noir style gives it a curiously essayistic cast. Rather than the thing itself, *The Underneath* at times seems a primer on how to make noir in color and wide screen. In refrigerating a hot original, Soderbergh turns the spectator into an observer of a beautifully manicured noir ritual.

In its general outline, *No Way Out* adheres to the narrative arc of *The Big Clock*. An employee who unwittingly becomes involved with his boss's mistress is an unseen witness when, in a jealous rage, the boss kills the woman he accuses of betrayal. A patriarch with an empire to protect, the boss concocts a cover story about a phantom murderer, then hires his employee, a man who knows too much, to conduct what is in effect an investigation for himself. Unlike the protagonist of *Criss Cross*, in *The Big Clock* the hunter hunting himself, the man who was in the wrong place at the wrong time, survives.

At the opening of *The Big Clock*, as the camera pans a city at night, we wait for a voice to emerge from out of the dark and, true to the conventions of classic noir, it does. "Only thirty-six hours ago I had a normal life," the voice announces in a tone filled with regret for a paradise lost. Now, thirty-six hours later, the hero, George Stroud (played by Ray Milland) cowers in a dark corner of the company where he had been a valued employee. A long flashback explains how he arrived where he is. A corporate family man stepping out for a little time on the town (always dangerous for men in gray flannel suits in the straitlaced 1940s), he meets a blonde at a bar, a chance meeting that nearly destroys his life. He accompanies the lady, who turns out to be his boss's mistress, to an antique store where she buys a painting, and he then takes her home. It is only in his wishes, not in his actions, that he betrays his elegant and very proper wife, but nonetheless he begins to act as if he is guilty of a crime. Fearing scandal and exposure as he begins to conduct his false investigation, he is forced to hide out in a double sense— from his boss and from the wife he has "betrayed." It's no wonder that this oppressed bourgeois gentleman, a servant of two masters, the corporation and middle-class marriage, has longed for a reprieve. He's a man in the middle, caught between his boss, who always interrupts his vacations, and his castrating wife, who demands his absolute devotion to middle-class propriety.

The film vibrates with another layer of tension as well, one that had to remain submerged in narrative crevices and gaps. As Earl Janoth, the head of a media empire, a possessive heterosexual inflamed by jealousy when he catches his mistress in what he imagines is coitus interruptus, Charles Laughton is not convincing, and surely was not meant to be. Laughton plays the character as a prissy homosexual enraged by a sexual woman who flaunts her sexuality in front of him. On the job Janoth has an effeminate loyal retainer, Steve Hagen (played by George Macready), with whom he speaks in a coded dialect marked by mutual sniping. For this gay couple, the mistress is an intrusion. Tellingly, Stroud saves himself only when he succeeds in turning Hagen against Janoth, making the employee aware that the boss, a monster of egoism, is willing to sacrifice everyone, including Hagen, to save himself. Janoth falls to his death down an elevator shaft, a sexually encoded image: Is Janoth being devoured by a giant dark womb, the visual opposite of the phallic big clock that stands guard over his empire?

*No Way Out* relocates the story to a pre-glasnost Washington in which the serpentine, seemingly infinite corridors of the Pentagon replace the publishing company of the original as a place festering with possibilities for entrapment. The boss is David Brice (Gene Hackman), the secretary of defense, who has a mistress he kills in a jealous rage and a fanatically devoted assistant, Scott (Will Patton). Tom Farrell (Kevin Costner), the man caught in a noir tight spot, is an unmarried officer who has been hired by the CIA. Like his prototype in *The Big Clock*, Tom has a fateful chance encounter that hurls him straight into a noir nightmare. At a Washington party, he meets Susan (Sean Young), the film's equivalent of the original blonde at the bar; but quite unlike the restrained and innocent encounter in the earlier film, the two characters here have uninhibited sex before they even exchange names. Susan is the mistress of the secretary of defense. Her two men meet at night as they pass each other outside her Georgetown apartment. Tom is hired to begin a search for the stranger Brice glimpsed. At the same time Brice's assistant concocts an alibi that Susan was killed because she was having an affair with Yuri, a Russian mole who can pass as an American planted in the Department of Defense by the KGB.

The homoerotic vibrations between Steve Hagen (George Macready, third from left, top) and his boss, Earl Janoth (Charles Laughton, right) in *The Big Clock* (1948) are covert, yet far more charged than the acknowledged homosexual relationship between the corresponding characters (played by Gene Hackman, left, and Will Patton) in the 1986 remake, *No Way Out*.

In a clever twist added to the original story, the seemingly crackpot cover story turns out to be true: Tom is in fact Yuri, a Russian who sounds American. (With all-American Kevin Costner playing him, can the character possibly pass as a Russian?) In the puzzling opening shot, the character looks at himself in a mirror and asks, "When is he going to come out from behind there?" At the end, after the long flashback that carries the character from six months ago up to the present moment, the film returns to the mirror shot and answers the hero's question. The man Tom has been waiting for, a Russian, identifies Tom as Yuri and thereby accounts for the hero's mounting anxiety during the false search he has been forced to conduct. This time the hunter has far more than a disapproving wife to answer to; theoretically the fate of nations rests on his exposure. Unlike the protagonist at the end of the original, who returns to his social place shaken but chastened, Tom walks away from his job as the camera swoops up to a high- angle aerial shot.

The remake on all fronts shreds the conservative sexual morality that anchored the original. The hero is not a guilt-ridden bourgeois but is revealed at the end to be an homme fatale who was sent to the opening party precisely to attract Susan. Playing on generic convention, the film had encouraged viewers to read Susan as the sexual aggressor, but in fact Tom is the sexual con artist. Susan isn't a femme fatale, she is simply a modern woman who's hot to trot. Like everything else in the film, the steamy romance is revealed as a masquerade. In the original, the repressed gay subtext throws out provocative glints; made explicit in *No Way Out*, it is far less potent. Ironically, the acknowledged homosexual relationship between the secretary of defense and his paramour even seems like a charade, a cover-up or alibi for something else. Unlike Charles Laughton and George Macready, whose onscreen relationship bristles with homoerotic overtones, Gene Hackman and Will Patton are a wan couple.

Cleverly, in the film's opening sections, there isn't a trace of noir mise-en-scène. The romance between Tom and Susan, which at the time we are encouraged to take at face value, is photographed in a bland style. A weekend tryst, shot in warm colors, looks like a travelogue. After the pivotal scene in which Brice and Tom spot each other, a new visual register gradually takes over. Without ever edging into mannerism, space becomes infested with noir insignia. The long, tunnel-like corridors of the Pentagon become an intimidating abyss, a place of infinite repetition within which the pursued hero is forcibly confronted with the possibility that there may indeed be no way out.

Unlike Soderbergh's studied re-creation, Roger Donaldson's film is more viewer-friendly. *No Way Out* wears its knowledge of noir with a light touch. Reclaiming noir as a Reagan-era star vehicle, the film achieves a rare degree of independence while still satisfying genre requirements. Soderbergh's dedication to classic noir turned his lovingly made film into a specialist item, a treat for genre aficionados; *No Way Out* has been one of neo-noir's biggest box-office hits to date

If it doesn't have the "look," it isn't really noir is a belief shared by filmmakers and viewers. If the "look" is self-conscious, however, as it tends to be in *The Underneath*, characters and narrative can seem endistanced, housed within a noir-museum framework. The more natural design of *No Way Out* has a contemporary patina. In attempting to re-create a story first told many decades ago, a remake inevitably faces the threat of visual crisis, regardless of whether the material is set in the past or updated to the present.

*Thieves Like Us*, Robert Altman's 1974 remake of Nicholas Ray's 1948 *They Live by Night*, exemplifies the problems that beset the period remake. Acquiring an independent life, the meticulous period reconstruction of a rural Depression America competes with rather than enhances the film's story of a fugitive couple on the run. The film's simulation of the 1930s is insistently picturesque, a visual spectacle in which period artifacts are placed on display in an imaginary museum. Radio programs provide an almost uninterrupted and often ironic aural counterpoint. "Stone's liniment presents *Gangbusters*," a radio voice announces portentously as the thieves enter a bank. A later robbery is accompanied by the voice of President Roosevelt delivering his Inaugural Address. When the vagabond couple Bowie (Keith Carradine) and Keechie (Shelley Duvall) make love for the first time, *The Tragedy of Romeo and Juliet* is on the radio, an announcer sonorously intoning, "Thus did Romeo and Juliet consummate their first interview by falling madly in love." During a scene of sudden, brutal violence, Jessica Dragonette, a popular singer of the time, warbles sweetly. Rudy Vallee, "*The Shadow*," "The Queen of the Norge Kitchen," and "Keep America Safe for Democracy" are among the many other period sounds issuing from omnipresent radios. But the one time the radio provides real news rather than buzz, when the protagonist learns that his partner has been killed, static almost obscures the announcement.

The radio often airs pulp stories to which the characters knowingly respond. Indeed, like the film itself, the characters seem all too aware of their status as cultural artifacts. Hearing about their exploits on the radio and seeing pictures of themselves in "Real Detective," they are self-conscious criminals in an almost postmodern sense. At one point, they rehearse robbing a bank, using children as stand-ins for unsuspecting customers. The practice session, media reports, and the fussy period details, create an aura in which criminality is performed rather than lived.

Like the sound effects, the film's color is self-consciously nostalgic. Photo-album yellows and browns predominate; and the soft, faded, "memorial" tone is another mannerist tic that undermines noir tensions. The panning camera, showing off the film's curatorial relationship to the past, also helps to distance us. Altman's addiction to zoom shots is harmful in another way: since zooms are part of the visual vocabulary of the period in which the film was made rather than the one in which it is set, they call attention to the project's artificiality.

Altman quotes the recurrent high-angle moving shot from the original film of a car racing on country roads. Within the context of the visual restraint of the 1948 picture, the shot becomes a potent image of noir destiny as the characters speed toward an unavoidable doom. With the promiscuous use of high-angle shots in *Thieves Like Us*, however, as well as the nervous, zigzagging camera, the shot no longer has the same iconic force. Its impact squandered, it appears now as a mere flourish added to the film's excessive entrapment imagery. In Altman's imaginary-museum noir, the genre's signature visual motifs have become more ritualistic than thematic.

*Thieves Like Us* is cool where *They Live by Night* is notably warm-blooded, a romantic fable about two young lovers adrift in a world they did not create. Ray's landmark film is a genre rarity, a sentimental noir. Actors with soft personas play the leading roles; moist eyed and fresh faced, Farley Granger and Cathy O'Donnell are surely among the least hardboiled of all noir protagonists. (Although they are typically overshadowed by décor, Altman's actors, Keith Carradine and Shelley Duvall, who seem authentically homespun, are also well cast.) The original con-

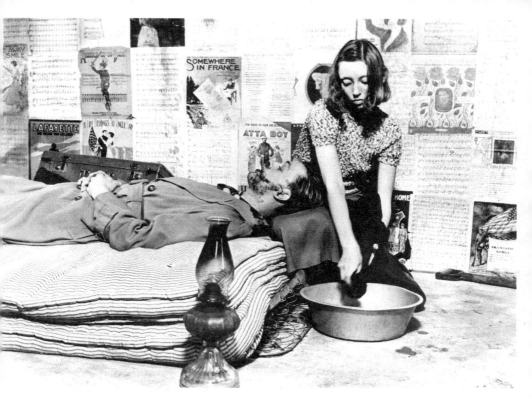

An imaginary museum: Keechie (Shelley Duvall) tends to Bowie (Keith Carradine) in front of prominently displayed 1930s sheet music, part of the insistent period décor that coats *Thieves Like Us* (1973) with a thick nostalgic haze.

cludes, indelibly, with a long, luminous closeup on Keechie (Cathy O'Donnell) reacting to the death of Bowie, gunned down by police. Her expression is both etched with tragedy and alight with the knowledge that Bowie's memory will live on in the child she is carrying. *Thieves Like Us* ends with a long shot of Keechie blending into a crowd in a train station as a voice on the radio urgently requests listeners to "keep America safe for democracy." In the famous last shot of Ray's film, all that matters is our intimate, privileged relationship to the character; in the remake, mise-en-scène and "history" overwhelm the character.

Crime is connected to a social cause, the Depression, in the richly atmospheric novel by Edward Anderson called *Thieves Like Us* on which both films are based. The thieves steal only from those who can afford it; and one of Bowie's older, embittered partners calls lawyers, bankers, and politicians "thieves like us." Neither the original film nor the remake attempts to provide a social context for robbing banks. *They Live by Night*, which is also a period film, is a precursor to Ray's *Rebel with-*

As the original Bowie and Keechie in *They Live by Night* (1949), Farley Granger and Cathy O'Donnell are the sweetest fugitives in classic noir. Fate closes in on them as a waitress (Lynn Whitney) looks on.

*out a Cause,* in which youthful characters embark on a collision course with a world they cannot negotiate. Altman's approach reduces the Zeitgeist to the sounds, images, objects, and décor of a reverently re-created past.

As a visual style, the imaginary museum is risky but not inevitably fatal. Dick Richards's *Farewell, My Lovely,* a remake of *Murder, My Sweet* that uses the original title of Raymond Chandler's novel, starring private eye Philip Marlowe, is a case in point. Unlike *Thieves Like Us, Farewell, My Lovely* re-creates the past with a light touch. A 1970s version of a 1940s movie set in the 1930s, the film doesn't pretend to be the real thing; it's a simulation of a pulp-fiction mise-en-scène made for an era before pulp fiction had acquired the cultural cachet it began to enjoy in the 1990s. The film's sly tone is encapsulated in the noir-revival casting of Robert Mitchum as Philip Marlowe. His face scarred with experience and dissipation, his body bloated in late-middle-aged fatigue, Mitchum looks like an icon in ruins. But his presence onscreen remains as commanding as in his classic noir prime. Mitchum's Marlowe is distinctly world-weary. He's as authentically deadpan as private eyes in the 1940s, but he's also more ironic. The film's nostalgic aura is also carried through in the casting of Charlotte Rampling as the woman with a past she is eager to hide. In voice and bearing, Rampling recalls Lauren Bacall. She's as coarse and as hard-bitten as Bacall, and the scenes between her Helen and Mitchum's bemused Marlowe, in which they are immediately on to each other, generate the sexual spark that emanated from Bacall and Bogart in the 1940s. (Another of the film's in-house touches is the appearance of noir novelist Jim Thompson as the femme fatale's husband.)

Like the performers, the film's design encases classic noir in knowing quotes. "It was one of those transient motels, something between a fleabag and a dive," Marlowe announces, speaking more like a fan of the genre than a participant. The film's Crescent Hotel, with a red neon sign, is indeed classically dingy. A crowded dance hall with a blinking red light; a bar with its name spelled out in flashing neon; Marlowe's office crawling with shadows cast by venetian blinds—the film takes place in locations that look like stage sets. The film's use of color and lighting is also frankly theatrical. Shades of red and amber predominate. In one scene, the femme fatale is dressed in vivid red as she descends a staircase; in another, red backlighting frames her. The burnished lighting and the recurrent use of spotlights, along with the rippling jazz score, enclose the action in a palpitant time-that-was aura. But unlike *Thieves Like Us*, the atmosphere is where it belongs, as embellishment rather than as the film's primary focus.

In *Farewell, My Lovely*, classic noir is recollected as if in a dream. Remakes like *The Killers* ([1964] Don Siegel), *Against All Odds*, and *Night and the City* approach their sources from a more prickly and Oedipal perspective. Determined not to quote the visual motifs and set pieces of the venerated original films, the new works place their stories in blandly rendered contemporary settings. "Fear of noir," however, seems to have drained the remakes of any style at all.

Robert Siodmak's 1946 *The Killers*, inspired by Ernest Hemingway's short story, is noir royalty, an untouchable, and Don Siegel and his collaborators were understandably anxious to avoid imitation. The original opens with a peerless noir set piece, as two gunmen enter a low-ceilinged diner and in a classically hardboiled style bait the patrons.

The remake, announcing at once its refusal to replay the original, opens with the killers hunting their prey in a home for the blind. In the 1946 film, the killers find their victim cowering in the semidarkness of a shabby rented room; in 1964 they find him in a green classroom that contains no visual kick whatsoever. And in place of the voluptuous masochism of Burt Lancaster as the victim awaiting his death, John Cassavetes plays the scene with inapt casualness, as if he too has been infected by the film's refusal to quote its source.

The almost startlingly inexpressive opening is a preview of the way Siegel tells a noir story in a style virtually cleansed of noir motifs. Only one setting, briefly glimpsed, a crummy hotel room with a purple neon sign blinking on and off outside the window, recalls the look of classic noir; otherwise the film takes place in environments that are stubbornly mute. Intermittently, noir motifs are used halfheartedly: there are a few ceiling shots, a few mirror shots, a canted angle at the beginning, a recurrent high-angle moving shot of a car on the way to a heist. Always problematic in noir, much of the film takes place outdoors. For no apparent reason, except to open up the story with action it doesn't need, the protagonist is now a race-car driver. In the original, a factory heist is filmed in a virtuoso single take; here, the heist occurs outside, in mountain scenery no doubt easily accessible to the Univer-

Two versions of Raymond Chandler's always-under-fire private eye, Philip Marlowe: Dick Powell, blindfolded, in *Murder, My Sweet* (1944); Robert Mitchum, postprime and framed within the frame, in the 1975 remake, *Farewell, My Lovely*.

sal production crew. (The shoddy production reveals the film's made-for-television origins; rejected as too violent, it was then given a theatrical release.) In plein-air settings, the tension of the robbery sequence is dissipated.

Except for Lee Marvin, who plays one of the killers with a menacing deadpan, the acting is as noir deficient as the mise-en-scène. In his final screen role, Ronald Reagan as a greedy criminal patriarch (delivering such lines as "I approve of larceny, but homicide is against my principles") exerts a certain grisly fascination, but his interpretation is limp. And as the femme fatale, Angie Dickinson is inappropriately saccharine. Her blank smile, like the film's straightforward realism, denatures a story about romantic obsession.

"And then I saw her coming out of the sun and I knew why Whit [his gangster employer] didn't care about the forty grand," Robert Mitchum as Jeff Bailey says in a celebrated voiceover in *Out of the Past*. Her entrance into the dark cantina where Jeff waits for her orchestrated by the shimmering chiaroscuro of Nicholas Musuraca's cinema-

tography, Kathy (as embodied by Jane Greer) is practically every aficionado's favorite femme fatale, scheming, unregenerate, ineffably desirable. One glance and Jeff is stung. In *Against All Odds*, the shamefully misbegotten remake, the hero (Jeff Bridges) first sees the gangster's fugitive moll (Rachel Ward) picking fruit at high noon in the town square. Wearing beige shorts, her face and figure bathed in bright sun, she looks like an ordinary woman in an ordinary moment.

In *Out of the Past*, when Kathy takes Jeff to her house for their first sexual encounter, rain pelts the roof and windows, a strong wind shakes the trees and blows the front door open as Kathy moves seductively in the shadows. "She walked in and out of the moonlight, smiling," Jeff says in a voiceover that coats the scene with pulp poetry. Observing the decorum of the classical style, the film palpably renders sexual desire through a skein of visual and aural suggestion. In *Against All Odds*, the camera lingers voyeuristically on the entwined, glistening bodies of the new lovers in an extended scene that has none of the erotic charge that jumped from the screen in the original.

*Out of the Past* opens with a long take inside a moving car, the camera placed behind the driver's shoulder. As the car moves through

Classic noir intensity — Swede (Burt Lancaster, left) crouches in a prison cell crawling with something more than night, in *The Killers* (1946) — versus postclassic blandness — the now-dully named Charlie (John Cassavetes) looks blankly up at dead-faced Sheila (Angie Dickinson, in ludicrous 1960s movie star drag), in the 1964 remake.

a small town, the shot signals foreboding, a sense that the vehicle (and the story its forward movement promises) cannot be stopped. *Against All Odds* also begins with a car negotiating its way through a non-urban setting, but this time, with the camera photographing the moving car in neutral long shot, the scene is descriptive rather than tense, casual rather than fateful. In the original, the shot inside the car is an annunciation; in the remake, the car is only a car.

In both films, the protagonist, a detective, goes to Mexico to locate a missing woman. The "Mexico" in *Out of the Past*, as in other classic-era noir films, is a place cut to the measure of an erotic fever, a landscape of hard sun and undulating shadows, of swaying trees and sensual rain. Near the beginning of the film, Jeff is introduced near a sylvan lake, a place that is the opposite of "Mexico," as well as of his soiled urban past to which the unstoppable car comes to reclaim him. The settings in the remake, rather than constructing similarly vibrant contrasts, all look alike. With its fervid sunsets, sun-dappled open-air marketplaces, picturesque Mayan ruins, and a green ocean, the film presents Mexico for the tourist trade rather than for a story of a fatal attraction. From Los Angeles, a city awash with noir possibilities, the film extracts sunny beach settings and sweeping mountaintop vistas.

In *Out of the Past*, chiaroscuro both expresses and frames the characters' duality. Mitchum and Greer, playing masked characters who try to escape from a past they cannot elude, have sculpted faces that seem made to receive the complex play of light and shadow of the film's high-noir cinematography. Victim of an erotic obsession, Jeff Bailey begins to lead a double life as he first pursues and then tries to hide from a hopeless love. Ultimately, Jeff (who has taken on a new identity in the small town he retreats to) achieves a kind of nobility, sacrificing himself , as well as Kathy, so that his new girlfriend is freed to marry the earnest local boy who has always loved her. Aching with love and remorse, Jeff is a powerfully conceived split character, and Mitchum plays him with a suggestion of the existential anguish Burt Lancaster brought to his noir victims of the late 1940s. As with Lancaster, the character's inner wounds play powerfully against Mitchum's hulking physique and lantern jaw.

In *Out of the Past* (1947), a classic-era femme fatale (above), Kathie Moffett (Jane Greer), clearly casts her spell over an investigator (Robert Mitchum). Kathie's contemporary counterpart, Jessie Wyler (Rachel Ward), in the shameful 1986 remake, *Against All Odds*, has been declawed: she is a troubled woman who is sincerely crazy about an ex-football star (Jeff Bridges).

Complexity, penance, self-judgment, and redemption are beyond the scope of the character as he has been reworked for *Against All Odds*. Renamed Terry, the character has been become a horny ex-football player, a has-been who fumbled a pass in front of fifty-five thousand people and is now out of a job and desperate for money. He's a guy with a build (the woman he has been sent to Mexico to find falls for him when she sees him topless) and not much else. Refusing the challenge of re-creating the formidable femme fatale of the original, the remake rewrites Kathy as Jessie, a spoiled heiress under the control of her dominating mother and stepfather and her gangster boyfriend. (The noir-revival casting of Jane Greer as the mother and Richard Widmark as the stepfather is the film's single victory.) Having the character ricochet from one man to another is a curious way to rewrite one of the genre's most independent femmes fatales, a phallic woman indeed, who shoots both of the men who desire her. In the final image of *Against All Odds*, Jessie stands imprisoned between her parents as, from a distance, Terry looks at her with hopeless longing. Defusing the story's femme fatale, the remake turns her into a character whose words and actions coincide: Jessie always means what she says, a fatal formula for noir. She's sincere; she truly loves Terry, who returns her feelings; and

the original story of lovers who expire after pursuing a complicated game of double and triple crosses is diminished to a tale of young lovers separated by greedy capitalists.

In *Out of the Past*, the intermittent voiceover, as throughout classic noir, sets the story in a framework of recollection and lends distance and a kind of enchantment while underlining the deterministic world in which the characters are caught. "I never saw her in the daytime, she seemed to live by night," Jeff muses. "I don't know what we were waiting for . . . maybe we thought the world would end," he says, observing the past with characteristic rue. Adapting from his novel, *Build My Gallows High*, Daniel Mainwaring (under the name Geoffrey Homes) wrote some of the ripest hardboiled poetry in the noir canon and eliminating it is the final insult the remake pays to its source. There is no voiceover and certainly no poetry of any kind in *Against All Odds*. At a moment when he is cornered, Terry says, "I figure, fuck 'em, and fuck you too, lady."

In retelling stories conceived decades earlier, remakes face a double-edged challenge. Maintaining the original time and place risks the kind of embalming nostalgia of *Thieves Like Us*, whereas the moral, sexual, and narrative conventions of an earlier mode may resist or even crumble under the pressure of contemporary relocation. A 1992 remake of Jules Dassin's definitive 1950 thriller *Night and the City*, updated and moved from London to New York, has destroyed the material, while Barbet Schroeder's unpretentious remake of *Kiss of Death* has had a reasonably safe contemporary landing.

To put a fresh spin on aging material, or merely as evidence of the adapters' staking out a new approach, a number of remakes have changed the professions of their protagonists. The insurance agent in *D.O.A.* has been transformed into a novelist who teaches creative writing in a college; the self-sacrificing victim in *The Killers* has become a race-car driver; the detective in *Out of the Past* is a washed-up football player in *Against All Odds*. Far from offering insight, these changes are arbitrary and diminishing. Ironically, the antihero's profession in *Night and the City* ought to have been altered and wasn't. In the original, Harry Fabian, memorably described as a con artist without an art, is a desperate grifter fired up by the notion of becoming a wrestling promoter. His retro ambition is clearly intended to reveal that the character is out of touch. In the remake, Harry, now a crooked, low-rent lawyer, wants to become a fight promoter. Boxing replaces wrestling, but the fight-game milieu seems seriously out of sync with the film's contemporary setting. The film's insistent use of noir signifiers—odd angles, looming shadows, overhead shots—its use of the boxing ring as existential metaphor, as well as Richard Price's gutter dialogue, seem like desperation measures to compensate for material the filmmakers don't trust and sense is not working. Harry's story needs the almost surreal rendering of nighttime London, shot in silky black and white, of the original; in contemporary New York, and in color, the character loses his edge. (The story also needs Richard Widmark's fevered nobility; as the latter-day Harry Fabian, Robert De Niro, providing a pallid imitation of Robert De Niro, is merely vulgar.)

The notable quality about the remake of *Kiss of Death* is that it does not seem like a remake. The film transports a pulp story from the 1940s to the 1990s without visible traces of the material's genealogy. Wisely, it omits the most famous scene in the original, in which Richard Widmark cackles maniacally as he pushes an old woman in a wheelchair down a dramatically steep flight of stairs. In both performance and imagery, the moment is canonic, an indelible classic noir set piece the new film honors by avoiding. In the role that made him a star, Widmark turns his character, Tommy Udo, a marginal thug, into a vivid noir villain who is both glamorously and satanically crazy. Dressed like a 1930s gangster, with a black shirt and a bright tie, and speaking with an almost vaudevillian version of a hoodlum accent, Widmark in his debut plays the role with a deep bow to James Cagney. His over-the-top performance is shrewdly balanced by the stolid, repressed style of Victor Mature as his antagonist, an ex-con trying to go straight by singing about Tommy. As a noir victim who suffers for his past and in whom hope and fatalism contend, Mature performs with the clenched, masked quality of the walking wounded.

Without imitating their predecessors, Nicolas Cage and David Caruso in the remake strike the same balance of performance energies. Deprived of Widmark's picture-stealing moment, Nicolas Cage is nonetheless ignited by the role. Pumped up and looking mean, he transforms the character into a strutting, raging, contemporary psychotic. As the ex-con trying to reform his life, David Caruso acts with a restraint that recalls Victor Mature's high 1940s somnambu-

Ex-cons trying to go straight but tripped by mischance and inducted into noir against their wills: Victor Mature (above) as Nick Bianco in *Kiss of Death* (1947); David Caruso as Jimmy Kilmartin in the 1995 remake. The characters' resistance is reflected in mise-en-scène.

listic mode. With his plug-ugly, lived-in face and his untended body, Caruso is utterly convincing as a noir loser with a decent streak, a victim of bad luck and bad timing who makes the mistake of answering a late-night knock on the front door of his row house in Queens. Like Mature, Caruso plays the role with locked-in tension, the suggestion of a coiled inner life that comes to a boil when a figure from his criminal past returns to claim him. Caruso's naturalistic acting underlines the durability of the noir-loser archetype, a role that may be easier for contemporary audiences to accept than, say, the femme fatale.

Like the characters, the settings are updated while remaining true to the expressionist palette of the original. A dour side-street house in Queens, a warehouse district on the edge of the city, and an auto wreckage shop provide appropriately forlorn backgrounds, which, in an unforced way, reflect the characters' parched lives. The film's main location, new to the story, is the Baby Cakes Night Club where Cage's crackpot kingpin holds court and where, in dark blue and red lighting that is neo-noir's equivalent to black and white, dead-eyed strippers bump and grind as fat geeks gaze up at them lasciviously.

Visual restraint was the dominant mode of classic noir, as of the classical style generally. Most of the remakes contest that legacy by operating within a regime of visual overkill. As if uncertain about classic noir's ability to hold the attention of contemporary audiences, a number of remakes try to compensate for a style that, in the MTV era, might be perceived as forbiddingly sedate by borrowing visual syntax from 1980s horror and action movies.

The blood-and-thunder climax of Martin Scorsese's go-for-broke remake of *Cape Fear* is typical. Throughout the film, Max, an ex-con who haunts the lawyer who helped to convict him, has been placed and photographed like a slithery, omnipresent monster in a contemporary teenage horror tale. He's shot against fire and illuminated by exploding firecrackers; thunder and lightning frame him as he straddles a fence on the lawyer's property. "Is the character human or supernatural?" is an enigma the film seems eager to pose. The generic interbreeding, unthinkable in classic noir, is abetted by Robert De Niro's excessive performance. The motif of the noir nemesis-as-horrific-monster reaches a crescendo in the overdrawn climax in which, in a showdown on a river, the character seems entirely unconstrained by natural laws. When the lawyer's daughter sets the character on fire, he bursts into flame and jumps into the water, where he is quickly restored and ready for further attacks. The character several times seems to expire only to be resurrected against a background of torrential rain and lightning and the crashing chords of Bernard Herrmann's original score, suitably menacing in 1962, overworked into feverish dissonance here. As the heavens crack, Max in a Pentecostal fervor harangues his prey about sin and redemption. The overloaded climax, simulating apocalypse, crushes with religious symbolism a modest and potentially engrossing noir story about a family invaded. In the only remake in his career so far, Scorsese engages in unnecessarily fierce combat with the original film, and loses.

Michael Cimino's fevered climax to his remake of *The Desperate Hours* also reveals a symptomatic trace of neo-noir desperation. In the 1955 original, the showdown is a conversation between the patriarch whose house has been invaded and the escaping con who has led the invasion. Filmed simply, it is a scene in which the director, William Wyler, trusts the dialogue and his two masterful actors, Fredric March and Humphrey Bogart. The only action occurs when the escaping con walks out of the house into a spotlight set up by the FBI and is shot. Cimino "enlarges" the scene into an action-movie coda, pumped up with encircling helicopters and a battery of spotlights. Ignoring the dignity with which Bogart enacted the character's demise, the latter-day con, played by Mickey Rourke, wails hysterically as he dashes from the house to meet his fate.

The final salvo is typical of Cimino's misguided attempts throughout the film to open up a story that depends on claustrophobic confinement. The original film begins, calmly, as the escaped convicts drive down a well-tended suburban street: all of a sudden, there they are, in a place they have no business being. In contrast, Cimino opens with shots of the getaway car tearing along wonderfully scenic landscapes, a desert and snow-covered mountains, that introduce a visual expansiveness altogether beside the point in a drama of enclosure. Itching to get out of the house where the hoods hold a suburban family as their captives, the film includes a number of car chases in a story that originally had none. The most jittery of the three convicts makes a run for it, and as he is pursued by a squadron of cops, his car breaks down in a magnificent desert setting. As police cars surround him, the music swells heroically—a noir story seems dottily to have been momentarily intersected by a scene from a John Ford Western. Overbearing FBI agents set up a monumental command post dominated by huge blowups of

The original *Desperate Hours* ([l955], top) remains, for the most part, confined to an upper-middle-class house invaded by gangsters; the l990 remake (with Mickey Rourke, crouched and ready to shoot) undermines noir claustrophobia with action-movie set pieces that take place outside the house.

the three convicts. As the female FBI special agent barks orders, the camera circles her, "identifying" her as the protagonist in a story in which she is, in fact, irrelevant.

Remakes of *The Narrow Margin* and *D.O.A.* also reveal a characteristic visual crisis. In trying to update their sources, both films embellish lean noir narratives with a kind of visual spectacle the genre cannot comfortably sustain. Both films quote from classic noir's repertoire of images while at the same time pursuing a variety of strategies for maintaining their distance from a filmmaking format that represents Hollywood history rather than Hollywood practice. But in the process of grafting up-to-the-minute stylistic tics onto noir, the films disfigure their sources.

An opening title of the 1990 remake, which announces that the film is "based on the RKO Picture *The Narrow Margin*," might well have added the word "inaccurately." The 1952 original, a modest B noir directed by Richard Fleischer, is basically confined to two classic noir locations, a ratty tenement and a train. "What kinda dame would marry a hood?" asks one of the detectives who must escort a mobster's widow from Chicago to Los Angeles, where she has agreed to testify before a grand jury. The widow lives at the top of a flight of rickety stairs in a tenement that emanates studio-created menace. Like the mise-en-scène, the widow is also made to order: Marie Windsor in a tight blouse epitomizes the detectives' (as well as the spectators') preconceptions about the "kinda dame would marry a hood." She smokes; she spits out her words; she gives as good as she gets. "You're a COD package to be delivered to the grand jury in L.A.," one of the detectives tells her, showing her the kind of hardboiled disrespect he thinks she deserves. The job of getting the widow on the train is made more difficult: the mob is wise to them.

The original is a trim thriller that uses stylized noir accents sparingly. Early on, for instance, there is a perfectly tuned set piece on the stairs outside the widow's apartment. The heavyset detective who leads the way down the stairs is placed in extreme closeup at the bottom right corner of the frame, as in deep focus his partner and the widow remain at the top of the stairs. The scene resonates with unease and foreboding, and indeed the detective who leads the way is the next moment shot by a mob hit man. Later there are occasional distorting closeups, tunnel-like corridor shots on the train, and some reflections

Detectives (Don Beddoe, left, and Charles McGraw) check out a mobster's widow (Marie Windsor), who turns out to be a police officer in femme fatale masquerade, in *The Narrow Margin* (1952).

in windows that provide a thematically pertinent leitmotif of seeing double; but the film's visual syntax is notably subdued, as straightforward as its narrative development. And once the film gets onto the train, it remains there. In a neat twist (an early anticipation of the way neo-noir will rewrite classic motifs), the widow turns out to be in masquerade. Her performance as a mobster's woman—on the train she wears a black slip, listens to jazz, smokes, and slouches in postures of sexual indolence and availability—has indeed been too good, too complete, to be true. The "widow" in fact is a decoy, a policewoman made up to distract the pursuing mobsters from the real widow, who is also on the train, and who turns out to be a pleasant-looking suburban matron traveling with her young son and his nanny.

Appearances are deceiving in this late classic noir. And like the characters, the audience is primed to accept performance as reality. "Why was I stuck with a decoy?" Detective Brown (Charles McGraw), his masculine ego wounded, asks the real widow. "They [the district attorney's office] were testing you," she tells him. "My record's clean," he protests; and by this reversal, the hero becomes a noir victim, the unexpected fall guy. (The film's B-movie status is marked by a curious omission, one that has given the film a permanent wound: nobody re-acts to the policewoman's death; we don't even know if Brown finds out that she was shot by the mobsters.)

Like the 1990 *Desperate Hours*, the 1990 *Narrow Margin* breaks the strict parameters of time, space, and narrative focus within which the original remains confined. And, fatally, it eliminates the original's mo-tif of "performing" noir. There are no longer two widows; there is in fact no widow at all. (Although there is a false blonde here too, em-ployed by the mob and placed on the train to ensnare the detective, she is only a plot device.) The witness has been recast as a middle-class woman who simply happens to be at the wrong place at the wrong time, the victim of what is probably the most catastrophic blind date in movie history. As she's powdering her nose in her date's hotel suite, she wit-nesses his murder through a partially opened door. Without the per-formance motif, the story is flattened, robbed of edge or ambiguity, and the material becomes a simpleminded chase film in which the key witness is always who she says she is. She's a woman in jeopardy, and since the only question the film poses—will she escape her mobster pursuers?—has a foregone conclusion, the focus becomes the ingenu-ity of the chase sequences. Directed by Peter Hyams, a modestly scaled claustrophobic story has been crisscrossed with plein-air action se-quences. Impatient to break away from the train interiors that were the principal setting of the original, *Narrow Margin* oscillates between noir constriction and full-scale action-movie pyrotechnics, complete with hovering helicopters, explosions, and he-man showdowns in the great outdoors.

Hyams knows his noir, as indeed he is also a master of action-movie formulas; but as the film amply demonstrates over and again, the two forms are incompatible. There's a superbly staged noir scene on the train, when the heroine (Anne Archer) confesses what she saw in the hotel. Flashing lights, the relentless noise of the train on the tracks, the shadow of the venetian blinds on the woman's face, the physi-cal separation between the woman and the detective (Gene Hackman), intermittent fades to black when the train passes through tunnels, evoke tension in skillfully composed wide-screen images. But, as if uncertain that undiluted noir can hold the attention of audiences weaned on breakneck editing and visual overload, the filmmakers invent irrelevant high-octane action sequences. For the masquerade fillip of the origi-

A deputy district attorney (Gene Hackman) and a murder witness (Anne Archer) cling to the roof of a speeding train that cuts through the Canadian wilderness in *Narrow Margin* (1990), another remake that turns a tight classic-era noir into a Panavision action spectacle.

nal, the remake substitutes an action-movie climax with the detective taking on two mob hit men on top of the train. Intercut with acrobatic high-angle moving shots, the fight is thrillingly staged but carries no thematic charge; all that is revealed is that Hackman's detective is a better fighter than the hit men.

The film's relentlessly upscale settings clearly reject the original's Poverty Row sensibility and mise-en-scène. The witness is discovered in the burnished elegance of the lobby at the Los Angeles Four Seasons Hotel. And when she hides out from the mob, she retreats to an expensively appointed cabin in the lush Canadian wilderness. The shabby tenement of the original, a set designer's fantasy, may well be a less realistic setting than the Four Seasons Hotel, which of course actually exists, but it is far more congenial to the spirit of noir.

In an unnecessary postscript, the heroine testifies in court; surely, as in the original, it would have been enough to know she had survived the train journey. Flooded with amber, diffused light and indoor fog (insignia that became visual clichés in thrillers of the 1980s and early 1990s and have already begun to look dated and silly), the scene typifies the film's refusal to obey the narrow margins of the original.

On the steps of the Bradbury Building in downtown Los Angeles, a recurring noir backdrop for more than fifty years, the doomed protagonist (Edmond O'Brien, right) of *D.O.A.* (1950) takes aim at a pursuer (Neville Brand).

If *Narrow Margin* tries nervously and intermittently to escape its noir roots, *D.O.A.* tracks an opposite course as, shot for shot, it attempts to offer more noir imagery than its understated original. The film's visual crisis—its intention to compete with its source—is announced in a black-and-white prologue in which the poisoned protagonist stumbles into a police station to report his story. The intensely self-conscious prologue seems like an art-film fantasia of classic noir motifs strained through an MTV filter. Shadows, stripes, diagonals, and Dutch angles are assembled in a frenetic collage that conveys the protagonist's disassociation and at the same time the filmmakers' acknowledgment of the narrative tradition they are working in. Even after the movie melts into color in the flashback, which, as in the original, is the body of the film, it continues a hyperactive visual mode. Rapid-fire editing, blurred images, multilayered sounds register the poisoned hero's progressive disorientation. Camera movement and lighting are "flexed" for noir: foreground objects loom portentously in closeups, and rapid shifts in angle and perspective signal a world in disarray. In a mise-en-scène of insistent enclosure, stairs, doors, and walls frame the hero. Obviously feeling the need to certify its contemporary sensibility, the film has a hipper, sexier protagonist than the original (Dennis Quaid for Edmond O'Brien), and from time to time metal rock blasts onto the sound track. Occasional bizarre settings—an abandoned factory where the hero is pursued and attacked; a tar pit from which combatants emerge looking like creatures from the black lagoon; a raucous bar and a street scene that recall the lurid images of Arthur Weegee's photographs—counteract the blandness of the central college-campus settings and add a spurious neo-noir glaze. The filmmakers seem acutely aware of speaking a historical film language, a borrowed syntax they have tried to update for the 1980s. They haven't trusted their source or their audience; and pursuing visual excess, they have robbed the original story of its existential impact in order to put on a shimmering, superficial display, a sight-and-sound neo-noir spectacle.

The stars (Meg Ryan and Dennis Quaid) of the second *D. O. A.* (1988) are contemporary looking, but the film adheres studiously to such classic noir iconography as high-contrast lighting and banisters that seem to close in on the characters.

If a number of remakes betray the filmmakers' feeling that classic noir's visual signature is dated and no longer usable without extensive postmodern renovations, they also reveal a lack of confidence in the genre's traditional treatment of women. One of the now-standard ways of modernizing stories conceived in and for the classic period is by rewriting female characters. Some of the remakes contain traces of a postfeminist consciousness; and while the shifts may appease the captains of political correctness, they have in every case proven bad for noir. The genre's two customary representations of women, the femme fatale and the patient wife, resist ideological tampering or adjustment; indeed, the impact of many classic noir stories depends on women remaining in exactly the place their original authors assigned them.

Interestingly, three of the most symptomatic examples of a "contaminating" postfeminist influence are in remakes featuring Jessica Lange; the demands of noir storytelling and those of a latter-day performer like Lange turn out to be mutually incompatible. In the remakes of *The Postman Always Rings Twice*, *Night and the City*, and *Cape Fear*, Lange plays roles enacted in the originals by Lana Turner, Gene Tierney, and Polly Bergen, respectively. Lange—a more skillful performer than any of her predecessors, who remain subservient to the demands of plot and of patriarchy—is clearly not content to be so self-effacing. To accommodate her greater range and depth, the roles have been partially reconceived, with unhappy results each time. The original material was not written under a feminist watch and can profit little from a humanizing feminist perspective.

As Cora in the first American version of *The Postman Always Rings Twice*, Lana Turner functioned simply as a noir icon, an object of desire who incites the lust of the itinerant male who stops by the diner she runs with her aged husband. One look and Frank's a goner. Turner was an exemplary Hollywood-made mannequin who walked like a beauty contestant and spoke in a studio-trained voice that had been scrubbed free of any signs of individual identity. As a performer, she simply put herself on display; she's an obedient young woman who emotes in a purely manufactured style. Her performance as Cora has no depth or resonance, and wasn't meant to. Following the mold created by James Cain, her character is simply a cheap, sexy blonde who sets a "real man" on fire. And in an inevitable noir progression, Cora's sexual potency is linked to an act of crime.

Dressed in white hot pants, a skimpy blouse and a white turban—an absurd wardrobe for the proprietress of a backwoods greasy spoon—Turner enters the film as a pure commodity. She stands rigidly in place, framed in a doorway, as the camera travels up her body from bottom to top, openly inviting the character (as well as the spectator) to survey the goods. For Jessica Lange, a modern actress who will not perform the same kind of "demeaning" spectacle, verismo replaces objectification. Her Cora is seen first in the kitchen, sweating among pots and pans. Frank (Jack Nicholson) has a partial glimpse of her through the kitchen door as she bends over. But when he leaves, she gives him a sultry look that clearly announces that this updated Cora claims sexual parity with men to whom she's attracted. Although the story is set in the Depression, Lange signals that Cora is sexually liberated in a distinctly modern way.

But Lange's refusal to duplicate Turner's approach to the character—as a model on display for the male gaze—is contradicted by another contemporary imposition on the material. Unlike their counterparts in 1946, the characters in 1981 are shown in graphic sexual combat. The impassioned lovers copulate on Cora's baking table in a sustained, semi-explicit scene. The steamy passages, reprised throughout the film like song-and-dance numbers in a musical, are purely decorative; the sex scenes are lit with hot yellow "passion" lighting and are explicit in ways that could not have been attempted in 1946. Depicting the characters' rutting embraces, however, violates the decorum that underwrote both the earlier film as well as Cain's novel, in which sexual freedom was not so easily plucked. Indeed, Cora can get rid of her husband only by killing him: simply leaving or divorcing him would have violated the social codes the character was steeped in. Lange's hip, wised-up Cora would never be held by the restrictions of gender and class that govern the character as Cain wrote her and that are part of the essential, if unspoken, fabric of the original narrative context. The characters as Lange and Nicholson play them aren't driven by guilt and fear (prerequisites for noir doom) but are free and easy moderns who exchange one look and hop into bed. Prolonged sex scenes are narrative and visual distractions, not only unnecessary but, in fact, a betrayal of the pinched, essentially straitlaced bourgeois ideology from which most noir stories were written. In 1946, more interestingly, the

Two approaches to Cora, a hashhouse waitress driven by lust and greed in James M. Cain's *Postman Always Rings Twice*: in 1946, Lana Turner (above) played her as a manicured movie star, a studio-created mannequin; Jessica Lange in the 1981 version deglamorized the character. Both performers failed.

cultural taboo against graphic sexual representation forced sex underground, where it simmered provocatively.

Cain wrote flat, iconic characters entangled by their lust and greed and pushed by the plot to their awaiting noir destinies. In her mistaken attempt to deepen Cora, Lange defuses the story. She is too thoughtful, and too soft, to make us believe that Cora would think of killing her husband. Lana Turner's Cora is opaque, and the performer's stylized inexpressiveness fills in the character only as much as she needs to be, whereas Lange's emoting is fatal. She cries when she tells Frank that her elderly husband, Nick, wants to have a baby. After the car accident she and Frank have staged, she runs out into the street in hysterics. When, in jail, she discovers that Frank has signed a confession against her, she breaks into convulsive tears once again. Weepily, after the lovers have been estranged, she says, "If we have each other then we have everything," and seems to mean it.

"You don't know what it's like to be trapped," she tells Frank, but Lange's Cora is too liberated and too resourceful to be trapped by the circumstances Cain has placed her in. Eliminating the entire act three of the original, in which Frank is ironically convicted of a crime he did not commit (killing Cora) after he has escaped unpunished from a crime he did commit (killing Nick), the film ends abruptly with Cora's death in a car accident. Lying near her body, Frank howls in grief. In transforming *The Postman Always Rings Twice* into a story about a couple who really love each other, the 1981 film betrays Cain's noir vision, while Lange's sensitive, tremulous performance only reinforces the immutable noir logic that a femme fatale cannot be humanized: see Barbara Stanwyck in *Double Indemnity*.

In the original *Night and the City*, Gene Tierney, a star at the time, plays a character whose sole narrative function is to worry about, and to support, her troubled man. Irwin Winkler's dead-in-the-water, postfeminist remake casts Jessica Lange as a troubled career woman. In the 1950 film, a fateful web relentlessly encloses the desperate con artist Harry Fabian, while in the remake Harry shares equal time with Lange's character, and as a result the material is diluted into a story of two losers with collapsing dreams. (The film's compromised take on noir is also registered in the fact that its protagonists are given last-act reprieves.) Marked by an inconsistent proletarian accent and studiedly disheveled hair, Lange's performance is as synthetic as the character that has been manufactured for her.

Abetted by her revisionist director, Martin Scorsese, Jessica Lange in the remake of *Cape Fear* attempts to transform the dutiful wife in the original film into a contemporary neurotic. In 1962 the wife was a flat character, another woman on the sidelines who watches anxiously as her house is invaded. A woman of her time (played by modest, unobtrusive Polly Bergen), she is a straitlaced suburban matron content to function within a domestic sphere. The character embodies an ideal of immaculate family values, an ideal that is probably no longer playable; and with a vengeance, the remake sends the original father, mother, and daughter, encased in their innocence, through a postmodern blender. This time, the devoted wife is twitchy, restless, sexually unsatisfied. She has suffered in the past from some unspecified emotional breakdown, and as the film opens she seems to be hovering on the verge of another. Early in the story, before the noir invasion, she interrupts a fumbling lovemaking session with her husband to go to the bedroom window, looking through the venetian blinds as if searching for something that her husband cannot provide and that, instinctively, she senses lies outside the house. What she discovers is Max Cady, the man who will attempt to destroy her already-broken family, surrounded by exploding firecrackers, perched brazenly on the wall that surrounds,

In the original *Night and the City* (1950), Helen (Gene Tierney, top) is a self-effacing helpmate to a troubled Harry Fabian (Richard Widmark). A contemporary Helen (Jessica Lange in the 1992 remake) demands the attention of her partner (Robert De Niro).

but evidently does not protect, her domestic fortress. The opening sets up the wife as a principal character, a woman in psychological turmoil, but again Lange's character is in fact peripheral to the central story, a conflict between the family patriarch and a figure who comes from out of the past to terrorize him and his family. Under the circumstances, as the narrative unavoidably reduces the character to a woman in distress, who shrieks hysterically as Max Cady tries to destroy her family, Lange's performing tics seem like attempts to cover a void.

The character of the wife resists remodeling (the story demands her subservience to the patriarchal code); and while Scorsese's other changes are more fully motivated, they are by no means always successful. Understandably, Scorsese chafed at the neat distribution of good and evil in the original film, as well as its idealized vision of the all-American family. In his neo-noir reworking, each member of the family is impure and therefore susceptible to the forces of noir that the invader embodies. Played by Gregory Peck, the head of the family in the 1962 thriller never loses his balance. His character is an entirely innocent bystander whose eyewitness account of how Max Cady (Robert Mitchum) roughed up a woman sent Cady to prison for an eight-year stretch. Now released, Cady is determined to seek revenge against the prosperous suburban man in the gray flannel suit who testified against him. Without legal recourse to protect himself and his family against the maddened avenger—"men like him are animals and you have to fight them like an animal," a police officer warns the besieged patriarch, instructing him in the law of the jungle—Peck's character has to begin to think and to act like a guilty man, in effect like a criminal, in order to defend his domestic kingdom. "I can't believe we're talking about how to kill a man," his equally straight-arrow wife comments. Under invasion, all the family nonetheless maintain their integrity; shadows may descend on their plantation-style house but not on their souls.

The original *Cape Fear*, late classic noir rather than a harbinger of neo-noir, was directed by J. Lee Thompson, an efficient craftsman with no interest in detonating the story's Holy Family imagery. He finesses the sexual and moral ambiguities embedded in the confrontation between social insider and outsider. After expelling the disruptive Max Cady through vigilante justice—shooting his adversary only once and clearly in self-defense—the patriarch returns to his family, his world

Under attack from an enraged ex-convict, the Bowden family (played by Gregory Peck, Polly Bergen, and Lori Martin, top) in the original *Cape Fear* [1962]) form a united front. The besieged family (played by Juliette Lewis, Jessica Lange, and Nick Nolte) in the 1991 remake are notably divided.

and self-image newly sanitized.

In his 1991 remake, Martin Scorsese attacks the original with the zeal of a die-hard deconstructionist, bringing to a boil all its subtextual implications. The antagonists this time have a closer emotional connection. The head of the family is a lawyer, that most morally problematic of postmodern professions, and Max was his client. Because he felt Max was truly a rapist, he withheld evidence that might have cleared him; and now, after seven years in prison, the enraged ex-con returns to haunt the lawyer and his dysfunctional family. As the lawyer, gravel-voiced Nick Nolte exudes world-weariness and a poisoned aura of bad faith, qualities absent from Gregory Peck's stalwart persona. In addition to being legally culpable, the character is an adulterer who has an incestuous attraction to his nymphet daughter. In the original, the antagonists confront each other across clear-cut differences in class, power, and morality; in the remake, Cady is the lawyer's demonic alter ego who acts out his adversary's forbidden desires. The invader shrewdly exploits this divided family's vulnerabilities, seducing the daughter who is certainly ripe for spoiling, and teasing the restless wife.

In the climactic showdown on Cape Fear River, the lawyer and the ex-con are both covered in the muck stirred up by a torrential downpour. Sloshing about, the American father picks up a stone—the weapon of Neanderthal man—as he attempts to kill his opponent. His attack is not simply self-defense, as in the original film; here the denuded patriarch thrashing in the mud has descended into the primordial slime, and visually, as well as morally, he is indistinguishable from the criminal who has haunted him. At the end, stripped of the vestments of his middle-class armor, he is exposed as the underground man. And this time expelling the invader does not signal a secure restoration. In an unusual framing device, the no-longer-innocent daughter (and with Juliette Lewis in the role, one wonders if the daughter was ever innocent) addresses the camera, claiming that her family never discusses the intruder or the effect he has had on them. It is clear nonetheless that the narrator knows too much about her family's wounds ever to be able to live in the kind of ordered, bourgeois world the earlier film reclaims. (Scorsese's sly casting contains a further critique of the first version: Robert Mitchum, the original Max, plays a police officer who urges the lawyer to pursue vigilante justice against the intruder; and Gregory Peck is a crooked lawyer.)

Engaged in a contest with Thompson's film, Scorsese loses his balance. His swaggering I-can-do-it-bigger-and-better approach, which plunges his revision into moral and visual crisis, is embodied in Robert De Niro's performance. Where Robert Mitchum, whose classically masked face and insinuating gait and voice convey the promise of sex and violence, is a realistic noir villain, De Niro is hyperbolic, performing rather than incarnating a demonic character. Like the inflated film that surrounds it, De Niro's winking postmodern performance is noir in quotation marks.

Placed with reference to prior texts, remakes can never claim independent status. To the genre aficionado, they are more truly sequels honeycombed with allusion and imitation rather than original works. To date no remake of a classic noir film has been a fully achieved piece in its own right; and judged on their own merits, the remake canon does not make a convincing case for the continued validity of noir tropes in the post-noir era. Classic noir has been a risky source for literal remakes; but as a repertoire of images and narrative models, it has served as fertile ground from which many noteworthy neo-noir originals have sprouted.

Before noir: In *Le Jour se lève* (*Daybreak* [1939]), Jean Gabin plays a factory worker who commits murder for love and bears the kinds of psychological scars that will identify many doomed antiheroes in the dark thrillers of the war era that French critics will call noir.

# Chapter 3

# The French Connection

*Film Noir: An Encyclopedic Reference to the American Style* is the name of the essential reference book coedited by Alain Silver and Elizabeth Ward. But as its very name implies, film noir is not strictly or purely an *American* style. American filmmakers have proven to be the shrewdest and most active custodians of that ensemble of images, narrative patterns, and characters we label "noir," but noir's ancestry is only partly rooted on native ground. It is by now traditional to cite two primary sources for American film noir, both of which predate the "official" opening of the Hollywood noir style by several decades: German expressionism, on the one hand, and a homegrown school of hardboiled crime writing on the other. There is, however, a third proto-noir strain – the French poetic realism of the 1930s—that needs to be looked at, a film movement in which many of the elements of noir were already in place. Four representative films from the period, two each by Marcel Carné and Jean Renoir, are richly noir *avant la lettre*. Indeed, when French cineastes applied the noir label to a group of American crime pictures released in France after the war, they were naming a style, a cinematic flavor, already apparent in French filmmaking practice. It is the central theme of this book that noir continued after it was supposed to be dead, and it is likewise my contention that noir existed long before it was named and codified, not only in America but especially in France.

In *The Long Night* (1947), the American remake of *Le Jour se lève*, Henry Fonda's desperate steelworker is trapped in another grim tenement after committing a crime of passion.

Partly because of the enthusiasm of French critics and filmmakers, American film noir has overshadowed all other national brands, including the French. But from the beginning, French noir has been an embedded part of the American genre, and in this chapter I consider the interplay, usually disregarded, between the two movements. Since the 1950s, French filmmakers have kept vigilant watch over American noir. Often citing B-grade American suspense and psychological thrillers and the masters of American pulp fiction as influences, French directors have made dramas that, varyingly, interrogate, deconstruct, imitate (usually inaccurately), and pay homage to the kind of crime movie on which French critics bestowed the noir name. And if French filmmakers have drawn inspiration from American noir, the tributes have flowed in the other direction as well. Over the long international cinematic dialogue that has bound the two countries, American crime films have sometimes imitated French crime pictures made in the first place as a kind of twisted Gallic obeisance to American B thrillers.

Concurrent with the genre's classic phase, French filmmakers produced a string of more or less conventional crime dramas that paralleled the ones "made in the U.S.A." And before the original cycle had run its course, New Wave directors with a fetishistic attachment to previously uncelebrated American studio films produced quirky revisionist crime movies that are the first, and to date the most truly "neo," neo-noirs. For the New Wave cineastes, American crime pictures served only as a casual reference, a point of departure from which to build meditations on—and detours away from—their sources. Deeply, indelibly Gallic, French neo-noir is in effect a collage of fantasies on American themes as interpreted by outsiders who know and love America only through the imaginary prism of the movies.

A critical commonplace, that noir's quickly congealing narrative and compositional tropes exacted a stylistic sameness, is easily disproved by the French, who from the first implanted on noir stories a diversity of individual and at times idiosyncratic authorial signatures. For the canonic directors of the poetic realism movement of the 1930s, like Carné and Renoir, through classicists of the 1940s and 1950s, like René Clément, Louis Malle, and Henri-Georges Clouzot, to the New Wave mavericks of the 1960s, like Jean-Luc Godard, François Truffaut, and Claude Chabrol, noir has provided a rich soil.

Banisters and shadows enclose the emasculated antihero (Michel Simon, top), discovering the infidelity of his mistress, in Jean Renoir's *La Chienne* (1931). In *Scarlet Street* (1945), Fritz Lang's American remake, Christopher Cross (Edward G. Robinson) cowers under a staircase as his mistress's nattily dressed lover (Dan Duryea) arrives.

Carné's *Daybreak* (*Le Jour se lève* [1939]), remade in 1947 in America by Anatole Litvak as *The Long Night*) and *Port of Shadows* (*Le Quai des brumes* [1938]) and Renoir's *Chienne* (1931) and *Bête humaine* (1938) evoke a mood that, in retrospect, is high noir. Indeed, Renoir's two films were adapted during noir's classic American phase, *La Chienne* transformed into *Scarlet Street* (1945), *La Bête humaine* remade as *Human Desire* (1954). Both were directed by German émigré Fritz Lang, who was working for American producers but retained vestiges of his expressionist origins. A mixture of prewar French and German styles adapted to the demands of commercial American filmmaking, *Scarlet Street* and *Human Desire* represent noir's multinational genealogy.

Like American noir during its classic phase, the films of poetic realism vibrate with contemporary anxieties. The films, stories about crime in the lower depths, create enclosed worlds charged with symbolic omens. At least in retrospect, it is tempting to see in the films a reflection of France on the edge of the abyss: *Daybreak* was released a few months before the German occupation.

A gunshot fires offscreen; a body tumbles down a tenement staircase covered with shadows and defeat—the opening moments of *Daybreak* are steeped in what were to become conventional noir signifiers. Barricaded in a grim room and looking into a mirror, Jean Gabin, playing François, the character who pulled the trigger, intones a refrain of the sort that was to instigate many classic noir stories: "What could they understand? You suddenly do it, and that's that. And only yesterday . . ." A crowd gathers outside; police shout into his room as François paces, long shadows spreading in horizontal bands along the walls. The camera moves in on the desperate character, whose intense off-screen gaze serves as a summons to the past. As in many classic noir sagas to follow, it is romantic obsession that has pushed the character into crime. François, a factory worker, has fallen in love with an innocent young woman, a flower seller, but happiness is held before him only to be snatched away when, in the film's opening action, he kills his rival. "I'm a murderer," François pronounces with self-contempt before he shoots himself. After his suicide, his room is flooded with light, and then the screen fades slowly to black.

*Daybreak* is more stately and lyrical (flowers choked by factory smoke is a leitmotif) than American noir was to be. And the central criminal action carries the kind of philosophical twist—François's rival has chosen Francois to be his executioner, to expiate his guilt for having seduced the young woman—that is foreign to the genre's Hollywood strain. But the film is filled with anticipations of classic noir. Like many future noir protagonists, François commits a crime only under extreme pressure; his becoming a murderer is as shocking to him as to his neighbors. "Only a few hours ago he was a normal man, now he's hunted and alone," announces a choral figure in the crowd. The film's flashback structure, as in many noir dramas to come, charges the scenes set in the past with a fatalistic aura; we know the catastrophe that awaits the characters.

*Port of Shadows* is set in a similar end-of-the-world realm, a marginal, hermetic space resonating with Gallic melancholy. A soldier (Jean Gabin again) thumbs a ride on a fog-bound road at night. At the end of his journey, he enters a waterfront bar (of a type that could exist only in France). The proprietor's urgent request not to bring in the fog ("What a fog! Filthy fog!") is soaked in existential dread, and one of the regulars is a painter who says he paints the things behind things. ("If I see a swimmer, I paint a drowned man.") "Do you like life?" the painter asks the newcomer. "It's been pretty beastly to me so far," the soldier answers, taking us deep into the heart of noir. The soldier has a troubled past he keeps alluding to in cryptic fragments (it turns out he is a deserter who has killed someone) as he repeatedly intones, almost ritualistically, "They're after me." The character's noir fate is to enjoy one night of rapturous lovemaking with a young woman who enters the bar, kill her abusive godfather, and in turn be killed by a local gangster.

To construct an allegory of France teetering on the precipice of disaster, the film uses what we can retrospectively identify as noir conventions in visual and narrative pattern. Where doom in most American noirs is local and personal, here it takes on grander dimensions. The world-weary deserter seems to embody the wounded spirit of prewar France, as the gangster who kills him represents emergent fascism. Unlike in American noir, in both *Daybreak* and *Port of Shadows*, crime occurs in the margins, in the negative space surrounding the characters' discussions of romance and the meaning of life. In these philosophical noir dramas, crime is an alibi, a "cover" for larger existential issues by which the films are more engaged. As in classic and neo American noir, death shadows desire, but the equation in both these seminal late-1930s films is embedded within the trauma of a nation confronting apocalypse.

*Scarlet Street* in 1945 restates themes already fully elaborated in Renoir's 1931 *La Chienne*, a story of a fatal chance encounter. But unlike Carné's films or Lang's remake, stamped with noir insignia in practically every frame, Renoir's approach is more realistic. Produced before noir had been either named or industrially codified, and therefore not confined by the rules of a genre or style that did not yet exist, the 1931 film tells a dark story with objective long shots and long takes. Renoir introduces sequences played for boulevard comedy and provides a puppet-show framework. The light touches and humanist grace notes, always a part of Renoir's lexicon, are erased in Lang's more morose, Germanic remake, as in classic noir generally.

If in its visual treatment *La Chienne* is only intermittently noir, *La Bête humaine* in 1938 is noir full-fledged. Based on a novel by Émile Zola, the film pollinates noir with another of its often-overlooked French sources, a naturalist credo that enfolds characters within a deterministic grip. Jean Gabin plays yet another doomed man, a train engineer whose fate is sealed by a tainted inheritance. "I'm paying for all my ancestors who drank," he attests. A prototypical noir antihero grazed with a touch of the psycho, the engineer is subject to fits and suffers moods of depthless despair, "waves of sadness that I can't speak of." The film is a narrative hybrid that mixes a naturalist worldview with pulp fiction for, in addition to suffering for the sins of his forefathers, Gabin's character is also a victim of a nasty noir mischance. In the wrong place at the wrong time, he sees a murder being committed by the stationmaster and his seductive wife, Severine, who then stokes the engineer's lust. The two meet in the train yard at night, and in scenes of fully articulated expressionist chiaroscuro, Severine tries to convince her new lover to kill the husband to whom she feels enchained. But it is Severine he is destined to kill, in a room crisscrossed with shadows. After, he stalks to work on the train tracks. In a montage that rhymes with the film's opening shots, a charging train becomes a portent of an unstoppable fate: his despair mounting in unison with the accelerating train, the engineer jumps to his death. As in classic noir, the film constructs a world in which sex and violence are fused inextricably, and mise-en-scène reflects the characters' passions.

In *La Bête humaine*, as in many French noir films, philosophy precedes plotting. The characters are acutely conscious of their existential traps, with Severine as bound to her compulsive seductiveness as her male prey is to his family curse. Playing a character haunted by an inner life over which he is unable to exert control, Jean Gabin projects depth of a kind that would be unwelcome to most American audiences of noir. His soulfulness, in a sense, halts and "troubles" the pulp story.

Made near the end of the classic noir era, Fritz Lang's humid, gritty, but ultimately compromised *Human Desire* suggests ways in which American and French interpretations of noir differ. Renoir's film unflinchingly propels the characters to a predestined doom; Lang's reserves a noir finale only for the femme fatale. Raped at sixteen by the man she and her husband will kill, Vicki (Gloria Grahame) is the Zolaesque victim of a corrupted sexual inheritance that will ultimately consume her. To attract the returning soldier (Glenn Ford) whom she tries to ensnare in her attempts to kill her husband, she shows him her bruises. As enacted by Grahame, classic noir's preeminent masochist, this femme fatale is marked as a prisoner of both her sexual appeal and her sexual compulsions.

In the American telling of the Zola story, the protagonist escapes the straitjacket the author created for him; this time he is released from a corrupted inheritance and has no history of mental illness. Home

Exacting revenge against the femme fatale in parallel moments in Jean Renoir's *Bête humaine* (1938) and Fritz Lang's American remake, *Human Desire* (1954): Severine (Simone Simon, above) is attacked by her husband (Fernand Ledoux); Vicki (Gloria Grahame) gets equally rough treatment from her husband (Broderick Crawford).

from the Korean War, he takes a room in the brightly lighted house of an all-American family and has simple desires: a job (which he soon gets, as an engineer in the train yards), female companionship, fishing, a night at the movies. Nonetheless, this cleaned-up character is not immune to noir; furtively, he meets Vicki for nighttime encounters, his face and body moving in and out of shadows, and he tries to kill Vicki's husband, as she commands him to. He's sexually starved, and as in the original film, trains charging forcefully across bridges and through tunnels and brushing against each other as they ignite sparks symbolically express the character's incited desire. But unlike the French original, noir is not his unavoidable destiny; rather, he's a basically clean-spirited fellow who took a walk on the wild side and survived. "It's all wrong, Vicki," he declares, in a speech of liberation that Gabin's character, or Zola's original, would be incapable of. "The whole thing's been wrong from the beginning and I feel dirty. I can't tell anymore if you're lying or telling the truth, and it doesn't matter. I'm leaving." At the end, as the vet, snugly enfolded within a middle-class household, looks longingly at a ticket for a dance on Saturday night while he accepts a light from his future father-in-law, Vicki meets her death in a shadowed, isolated corridor.

Renoir's film follows through on the intuition of Zola and of noir that there is no way out, that entrapment, whether internal or external, is a condition of life, the fate, indeed, of *la bête humaine*. *Human Desire*, like most mainstream American films, ends up affirming the sexual, cultural, and economic status quo, which Vicki threatens. In eliminating the character, the film bypasses the truly subversive pessimism of Renoir's treatment. In the American noir version, the forces of good, which have been anemically embodied, triumph – not altogether convincingly—over the dark power of noir, graphically visualized and performed.

The prewar legacy in France of crime movies without a specific designation continued sporadically into the 1940s and 1950s in two divergent directions. There were conventionally made stories about bourgeois crime, on the one hand, and transgressive and often playful interrogations pursued by New Wave directors, on the other. The young directors, who got started just as the original cycle of American noir was coming to an end, often took as their target straightforward thrillers made by their elders on home ground. To audacious young filmmakers like Jean-Luc Godard and François Truffaut, the work of "academic" directors like Henri-Georges Clouzot and René Clément, with its primary commitment to narrative coherence, seemed dangerously antiquated.

Between the prewar poetic thrillers of Marcel Carné and Jean Renoir and Godard's essays in neo-noir beginning in the late 1950s, Clouzot amassed the most substantial crime-film track record. A dirty name to the cineastes clustered around André Bazin at *Les Cahiers du cinéma* in the postwar period, Clouzot, in fairness, was a solid craftsman and a powerful storyteller. From the point of view of filmmakers who want their noir "neo," however, his two most renowned works, *Les Diaboliques* (1955) and *Le Salaire de la peur* (*The Wages of Fear* [1953]), are decidedly old-fashioned. But they are tasty thrillers served with twists of Gallic irony and *tristesse*. (Both films have been remade into lackluster American suspense dramas: William Friedkin "translated" the latter film into *Sorcerer* [1977], while the former was reupholstered into *Diabolique*, a startlingly inappropriate 1996 star vehicle for Sharon Stone.)

Clouzot's tough, lean version of *Les Diaboliques* is set in a rundown boarding school for boys where the lettuce is always rotten. The wife and the mistress of the penny-pinching headmaster conspire to kill him. As frequently happens in classic noir, however, we've been tricked into reading the wrong plot. The mistress and the headmaster, it turns out, are expert masqueraders who have staged his "death" only to arrange his "return" and so to induce a heart attack in the wife, who has a weak heart, is religious and therefore guilt stricken about what she thinks she has done, and has the money the conspirators want. The story, in other words, is a variation on *Double Indemnity*, in which two greedy partners strive to kill a sexual outsider, in this case a high-strung woman rather than an impotent older man. (The film contains one of the most celebrated set pieces in the noir canon, in which the presumably dead husband rises from a bathtub, a horror-movie image of the return of the repressed that, as planned, induces a fatal attack in the gullible wife.)

In place of the straight-arrow conviction of Clouzot's original, the American remake, directed by Jeremiah Chechik, substitutes a detonating postmodern irony. Exuding Continental sensuality, Simone Signoret plays the mistress in the original, unforgettably. Often wearing dark glasses and smoking compulsively, Signoret sizzles with menace as she spits out hard-bitten dialogue. She's the real thing, a tough femme fatale in a traditional tale of a noir setup. Sharon Stone tackles the role by showily and sometimes, in truth, wittily remaining Sharon Stone, glamorous movie queen. Like the film itself, she is unwilling to treat the material seriously. She wears deep red lipstick and, for a teacher, a ridiculously sophisticated wardrobe. Making no effort to relate to the boys in her charge, she keeps her focus securely offscreen, on her fans. The wry quips that decorate her dialogue ("he has enough pills to relax China," she comments about her lover) are tailored to honor and protect her image as a with-it contemporary star.

The attachment in the original film between the female conspirators is only latently sexual; in 1996 Stone brings the repressed lesbian subtext to a full boil. As she strokes and cradles the gullible wife (Isabelle Adjani), Stone's voice softens for the only time in the film, while opposite her male lover (Chazz Palminteri) she maintains a brittle detachment. As a star (or at least as the kind of star she is performing here), Stone must be recuperated in the finale, and so, in effect, she takes back her entire performance. Her character has a last-minute change of heart and returns to stop the show in which the wife will be shocked

Nicole Horner (Simone Signoret, top), a teacher in a school for boys, dominates gullible Christina (Véra Clouzot) in *Les Diaboliques* (1954). Playing Nicole Horner in *Diabolique* (1996), the American remake, Sharon Stone appears in campy movie-star regalia, while Isabelle Adjani as her unwitting pawn looks appropriately vulnerable.

to death by the return of her husband. That she is too late—in self-defense the wife has already bludgeoned her brutish husband to death—is not supposed to undercut the star's nobility. As she apologizes to her former partner in crime, Stone for the first time appears without makeup, as, in tears in the rain, she is "washed clean."

Because the concerns that motivate the crime may no longer be playable, *Diabolique* in the 1990s curdles into camp. For the husband in the original, a fussy, repressed petit bourgeois who won't divorce his rich wife because he is afraid of scandal, it's easier to concoct a plan to kill her. The issue of propriety would hardly constrain the conspirators in 1996 but, unaccountably, the one factor that could still incite their scheme, the fact that the wife has money, has been eliminated and with it the plot's one claim to coherence. In 1996, the only reason the lovers can't simply leave is if the mistress really prefers the mousy wife to the piggish husband. Their elaborate scenario for entrapping the wife now has no rationale except for the sheer (postmodern) pleasure of the game. The conspiracy becomes a charade conducted for its own sake, a play of surfaces in which the intended victim, like the audience, is supposed to be seduced by Sharon Stone's star quality.

Narrative-driven, traditional noirs like Clouzot's *Diaboliques* were a staple of French filmmaking in the 1940s and 1950s (and continue to be made today). Most have had only domestic distribution. Conservative, well-made thrillers, like *Du rififi chez les hommes* (1955), about a caper gone wrong (directed by blacklisted expatriate Jules Dassin, who in the classic era made a number of exemplary American noir films); René Clément's elegant *Plein soleil* (*Purple Noon* [1960]), a change-of-identity suspense film shot on the Riviera in sun-drenched color; and Louis Malle's *Ascenseur pour l'échafaud* (*Elevator to the Gallows* [1957]), about a bourgeois killer foiled by a round-robin of noir misfortunes, provoked the animus of New Wave directors. For Godard and his contemporaries, pioneers eager to liberate the genre from the well-made tradition, classic noir became the ground on which to construct narrative and visual experiments.

When Michel (Jean-Paul Belmondo), the antihero of *À bout de souffle* (*Breathless* [1959]), pauses to gaze intently at a poster of Humphrey Bogart in *The Harder They Fall*, the action comes to a full stop. As he whispers "Bogie," in a tone approaching reverence, he imitates a characteristic gesture of the actor, moving his thumb meditatively over his lips. This emblematic encounter, between an icon from the then-recent past and an icon to be, is Godard's tribute to the American hardboiled tradition that he and his scenarist, François Truffaut, delight in demolishing. Their film has a pulp-movie premise about a hood on the run. At the beginning, Michel shoots and kills a policeman; at the end, he is betrayed by Patricia (Jean Seberg), his American girlfriend, who reveals his whereabouts to the authorities. In an American thriller, the cop killing, the action that turns Michel into a fugitive, would be crucial; in this neo-noir film, it is shot in such a cryptic, fragmented style that first-time viewers might well find the sequence incoherent. Patricia's betrayal, which in an American noir would command extended attention, is also treated in an offhanded way, as a spontaneous action. Intermittently, the film attends to narrative business—newspaper headlines announce the spreading manhunt for Michel; the police question Patricia; the lovers change hideouts; Michel meets with underworld figures—but basically the crime-movie scenario is simply a frame within which the filmmakers improvise jazzlike riffs.

In Godard's *Breathless* the traditional links between figure and ground shift as the plot is pushed into a negative space surrounding the characters. The longest scene, set in Patricia's bedroom, is a virtuoso narrative digression, one of the film's many detours, in which the lovers banter, discoursing on life and love. Hardboiled characters who aren't truly hardboiled, Michel and Patricia, who exude a bohemian glamour of twenty-somethings at a particular place and time, represent distinctly French takes on American film archetypes. Michel, who seems born for crime, is closer to a 1930s gangster than the typical protagonist of a 1940s noir. But unlike the Hollywood gangster, who is often "explained" by a social context, Michel, who exists in the present, moment by moment, is a self-created character with a past that is never accounted for. Patricia is an equally original interpretation of a Hollywood formula. A hybrid of two noir archetypes, the femme fatale and the anxious middle-class matron attracted to a sexy outlaw, Patricia (like Jean Seberg herself) is an American in Paris uncertain of who she is and what she wants. Where Michel is the real thing, a genuine existentialist, she is a dilettante, a mere dabbler in Left Bank counterculture. Betraying a male, she performs the fatal woman's traditional duty, but she is a peculiar and complex embodiment of the type. Unlike the evil sisters of classic noir, Patricia is a bitch in spite of herself.

*Breathless* plays with the narrative and character conventions of noir, but visually the film owes nothing to the American style its young filmmakers admired. This is noir filmed not in the controlled conditions of a studio but in the open, in the streets of Paris 1959. Godard's cinematographer, Raoul Coutard, replaces the artful chiaroscuro compositions of high classic noir with natural lighting devoid of contrasts. Many of the shots have a bleached, rough-hewn, documentary candor. Instead of the doom-ridden mise-en-scène of classic noir, *Breathless* takes place in open, neutral places; the City of Light becomes the playground of two characters dedicated to improvising their lives. The film's famous jump cuts and its unsteady, circling, handheld camera disrupt the illusion of temporal and spatial continuity on which the classical style is founded, and it is the erratic, jerky rhythm, rather than mise-en-scène, that reflects Michel's breathless life. As Godard's "risks" mimic his character's, the film's form and Michel's ideology dovetail. Director and character cavalierly defy the rules of the game.

Godard and Truffaut seem to have chosen noir because they felt it could host a variety of semiotic and autobiographical discourses. Their film is an informal, homemade essay on American noir, an anti-thriller that celebrates their youthful infatuation with the medium. At home and on the thriving art-house circuit in America at the time, their seminal neo-noir movie was a commercial and critical success. Audiences embraced the film's renegade characters and irreverent way with a noir story.

Godard continued to use noir filaments throughout the 1960s, but in determined flight from repeating the popular acceptance of *Breathless*, he pursued an increasingly forbidding style. *Vivre sa vie* (1962), *Alphaville: Une étrange aventure de Lemmy Caution* (1965), *Bande à part* (*Band of Outsiders*[1964]), *Pierrot le fou* (1965), and *Weekend* (1967), among other works, are further essays on neo-noir terrain. In their general narrative outlines, the films evoke classic noir models. *Weekend* is about a greedy bourgeois couple who plan the murder of the wife's rich relatives. *Pierrot le fou* concerns a disaffected middle-class man who, seduced by a bewitching woman, leaves his ordered life for a life of crime. *Bande à part* tells a familiar story of a robbery gone wrong. In *Vivre sa vie*, a prostitute is killed in cross fire between underworld figures. But with the possible exception of *Alphaville*, Godard's version of *Orpheus in the Underworld* in which noir is crossed with science fiction, the films refuse

In Jean-Luc Godard's *Breathless* (*À bout de souffle* [1959], above), we are given privileged access to the intimate relationship between Michel (Jean-Paul Belmondo) and Patricia (Jean Seberg). The 1983 American remake places us as voyeurs ogling partially nude actors (Richard Gere and Valérie Kaprisky).

to observe the customary codes of movie narrative. In picture after picture, the director sets up a noir frame only to ignore it or to dismantle it. For Godard, restless, perpetual avant-gardist, noir served as a jumping off place to the non-cinema of his unwatchable political diatribes of the 1970s.

Early in *Breathless*, as he's driving a car along a country road, Belmondo briefly looks into the lens of the camera, thereby breaking the prohibition in classical cinema against direct address. Allowing his actor to talk to the spectator, Godard is, in effect, thumbing his nose at the filmmaking illusion that the action onscreen is both "real" and unmediated. The authorial interruptions in the remainder of *Breathless* are limited, but in *Bande à part*, based on a pulp novel by Dolores Hitchens that the director clearly regards as disposable, Godard con-

sistently assaults filmmaking conventions. He introduces a (flimsy) story about a heist only to lose track of it; the film's focus becomes the director's discourse about the film. Godard is not interested in telling a story, certainly not this one at any rate; rather, he wants both to expose and to tease the mechanics of pulp fiction, as well as the expectations of the spectator.

Throughout, voiceover narration recalls and mocks one of the recurrent tropes of classic noir. Where traditional voiceover is portentous, saturated with knowledge of how the story ends, Godard's use of the technique here is a playful reminder that this tale of a failed robbery is not for real. "My story begins here," the narrator announces, in a mode of inappropriate grandeur that he is to follow throughout. He introduces the three characters, then for "latecomers" he summarizes the film thus far: "an English class, a romantic girl, a pile of money, a house by the river." "We now open a parenthesis on Arthur and Odile's feelings," he offers, but thinking better of it, adds that, since "it's pretty clear how they feel, we'll let the images speak for themselves."

Odile tells her two classmates, Arthur and Franz, about money in the villa where she lives with her aunt and a mysterious Mr. Stolz; and on the spot, with a capriciousness embraced by all of Godard's faux criminals, the three decide they will rob the house. "Out of respect for second-rate thrillers," Arthur urges his colleagues to wait till night to do the job. Odile asks how they will kill the intervening time. The robbers-in-waiting decide to go to the Louvre, where they race down the long halls. Odile, who has never been to the Louvre before, comments on how much she likes the whitewashed walls. Until the robbery, the conspirators continue to improvise their time, as the film becomes a series of parentheses that resemble the ones the narrator regularly dispenses. Sitting in a café, a place where Godard's self-styled noir players spend much of their time, they have a moment of silence because nobody has anything to say. When they get up to dance, the narrator informs us about what the characters are feeling. Odile wonders if her friends see her breasts move under her sweater; Arthur asks himself if the world is a dream or a dream the world (imagine Bogart, in midnoir narrative, detained by such a consideration), while Franz looks at his feet, thinking of Odile's kisses. Passing a neon sign over a shop that says "Nouvelle Vague," they go down to the metro (or, as the narrator announces augustly, they "descended to the center of the earth") where Odile, looking directly into the camera, sings a song about how people are as alike as grains of sand.

Once the film finally gets to it, the robbery is treated farcically. As if to punish spectators who have made the mistake of reading for the plot, the climactic gunfire is filmed from an unyielding long shot. Events that would be handled in complex patterns of close and medium shots in an American heist thriller are here relegated to a distant, static panorama. Arthur is shot, Odile and Franz run off. In the getaway car, Franz intones an ode to the fact that there is no unity among people, that each of us exists in a separate sphere, an ironic prologue to the happy denouement in which the two decide to go off together to South America. "Do they have lions in Brazil?" Odile inquires (earlier, she has stopped to pet a lion). The narrator interrupts once again, and for the last time, to report that his story ends here, "like a dime novel," at a moment of happiness, and promises that the next installment will find the fleeing lovers in the tropics filmed in scope and color.

Wrapping his characters and story in a coating of reflexive irony, Godard pulps pulp fiction. As in *Breathless*, the film's location shooting and flat natural lighting replace noir with documentary-like realism while, at the same time, Godard exposes the arbitrary, constructed nature of a story about a fouled-up heist. Intersected and blocked by techniques of Brechtian alienation, elements of musical comedy, and digressions on the medium itself, *Bande à part* is for those who not only do not like their noir straight, but really do not like noir at all.

In *Weekend* a prosperous Parisian couple travel to the country in order to kill the woman's rich father. A successful lawyer in *Pierrot le fou* runs off with the babysitter to indulge in a crime spree on the Riviera. Their transgressions lead to grisly fates. The scheming wife in *Weekend*, who has joined with a band of cannibal revolutionaries, eats her husband; the lapsed lawyer in *Pierrot* shoots his new lover and then blows himself up. In both films, genre elements are entangled in worlds that become increasingly surreal and phantasmagoric as Godard batters noir with reflexive declamations and cross-references. "Are you in a film or reality?" asks a character in *Weekend*. "This is not a movie," announces the babysitter in *Pierrot le fou*. A hitchhiker the weekending couple pick up claims to be the son of God as he predicts an era of flamboyance in cinema. At a party at the beginning of *Pierrot*, Samuel Fuller (a classic noir director revered by the New Wave) defines movies as the rendering of immediate experience. As in *Bande à part,* musical interludes play against and defuse noir tension. In *Weekend,* Jean-Pierre Léaud sings a song in a phone booth; Anna Karina in *Pierrot,* taking time off from crime, performs two musical numbers. Surreal incongruities contest the escalating horror shows that both stories become: emerging from a car crash, a woman in *Weekend* cries hysterically about her missing Hermès handbag. More than in *Breathless,* Godard interrupts each film with reminders that what we are watching is indeed a story, a fictional construct. Brechtian titles, which announce the day and hour in flashing red, appear intermittently in *Weekend.* In *Pierrot* the fugitives from time to time narrate their evolving story (such as it is) antiphonally, sometimes calling episodes chapters—there are two chapter eights. Pierrot writes in his diary as the camera lingers on words and parts of words, fetishizing both the process and the end of writing.

Continuing the project begun in *Breathless,* Godard assaults and contradicts noir's traditional visual syntax. His restless camera is sometimes as audacious as his characters. As the wife in a lengthy opening monologue in *Weekend* recounts a ménage à trois, the camera slowly and repetitively zooms in and out, creating a relationship between character and spectator that is at once both clinical and disconcertingly intimate. The most virtuoso camerawork in the film is a seven-minute tracking shot of a massive traffic jam. The moving camera coolly pans the scene until it comes to rest on the cause of the tie-up, a catastrophic accident. At an outdoor concert (the elegant Mozart is in glaring contrast to the world-hurtling-toward-apocalypse the film depicts), the camera undertakes a prolonged circular movement. Passages like these underline a combative directorial presence, one that contests the transparent, "invisible" camera of the classical style. In Godard's noirs *en couleur,* horrific acts erupt in lush settings. Sun-drenched panoramic landscapes become a new site for noir and anticipate a motif in American neo-noir in which crime moves out of the city into hot, wide-open spaces.

Godard's interrogations leave the terrain of classic noir in shreds. Stylistically radical and emotionally disengaged, the director's approach is too theoretical, too "French," actually, to be of much practical use to American filmmakers. To date, the single American attempt to translate Godardian neo-noir into native text is Jim McBride's 1983 version of *Breathless,* Godard's most accessible crime story. Predictably, McBride's

Americanized version of a New Wave take on 1940s American crime movies, starring Richard Gere and Valérie Kaprisky, was widely derided. Nonetheless, McBride's vulgarization with arty touches is a revealing document in the long and ongoing dialogue between French and American strains of noir.

Jesse, Gere's outlaw, is a slick hipster enamored of rock 'n' roll and comic books who dresses in hallucinogenic colors. He wears a bright red ruffled shirt and later appears topless with checkered green and white pants. The character's lowlife dealings—he goes to a sinister-looking bar bathed in red lighting to meet a guy who owes him money—are as vaguely defined as in the original. But where Belmondo's thug seems to embody a contemporary French state of mind, Gere's is a callow Southern California free spirit, a silver surfer with one foot in the underworld. Monica, a French girl in America, an architecture student who wants to make "buildings that last," is an equally vapid adaptation of the original character. Where Jean Seberg's Patricia is a superbly enigmatic femme fatale, a young woman who uses and abuses her allure without fully understanding it, Kaprisky's Monica is a cipher stripped of the moody hesitations that endowed Patricia with a Parisian ethos circa 1960.

McBride's attempts to translate Godard's New Wave neo-noir onto American turf are heavy-handed. Avoiding Godard's use of direct address, he has his character talk to himself instead, a stilted technique that retains a distinctly "foreign" tinge: how many criminals in American noir conduct audible monologues? Where Michel's way of life is reflected in Godard's staccato editing and freewheeling camera choreography, McBride's antihero listens to his favorite song, Jerry Lee Lewis warbling "You leave me . . . breathless." "That's me, breathless," he tells his girlfriend. "You scare me, you're like one of those rides at Disneyland, you make me dizzy," she says, blatantly providing instructions about how we are to read the character.

Godard's cryptic cop-killing sequence and the sustained bedroom scene between the lovers prove untranslatable. Out on the open highway, driving at dangerous top speed through the desert, Gere's hipster talks out loud as a cop follows him. In a sudden, spasmodic gesture, he shoots the cop, then in the next shot he's in Monica's apartment beseeching her to go with him to Mexico. The erratic, fractured rhythm seems inorganic, a self-conscious quotation from the original. From the moment Gere strips in the bedroom scene and joins Monica in the shower, we are placed as ogling voyeurs. For the improvisatory, intimate quality of the original McBride substitutes a brand of American vulgarity. "Do you know William Faulkner?" Monica asks. "Is that somebody you fucked?" Jesse inquires.

McBride's ending is a fumbling clash between traditional and neonoir approaches. Unable to motivate Monica's betrayal and clearly uncomfortable with it, McBride tries to recuperate her as a woman who did what she did for love. As her man is caught in crossfire she screams out her passion for him, a moment that betrays Jean Seberg's self-contained silence in the original. McBride replaces Godard's clipped ending, in which the fatally wounded Michel staggers to his death in characteristic zigzagging movements, with an extended action-movie chase sequence, with blues and reds dominating the conventional neo-noir city-at-night lighting. As he is caught between the police and the woman who has betrayed him, Gere performs a rock 'n' roll number, McBride's miscalculated New Wave grace note.

As a model for filmmakers of noir made in the U.S.A., Godard is clearly dangerous. As both style and substance, noir provided Godard with the ammunition to implode, and his increasingly idiosyncratic generic variations carried him away from both noir and commercial narrative filmmaking—a cinema of attractions designed to seduce and to comfort bourgeois audiences—toward a severe political cinema of diatribe and declamation.

François Truffaut's collisions with American noir proved far more orthodox than Godard's. Only in his screenplay for *À bout de souffle* (*Breathless*) and his direction of *Tirez sur le pianiste* (*Shoot the Piano Player* [1960]) did he exhibit a Godardian combativeness vis-à-vis his American sources. Where Godard approached classic noir models in a complex Gallic spirit of veneration tinged with disavowal, Truffaut had immense and uncomplicated affection for the American hardboiled style. Whether working from an original screenplay or an adaptation of an American pulp novel, Godard treated noir stencils with a brazen disregard. Where Godard seems incapable of homage (unless to himself), Truffaut produced noir stories in a spirit of tribute to the American studio style he had come to love during his apprenticeship as a critic for *Cahiers du cinéma*. As Godard grew increasingly truculent, Truffaut seemed only to soften with age, settling into the role of a basically conventional, sweet-tempered purveyor of audience-pleasing works in a variety of genres.

Godard dabbled in noir for his entire career in bourgeois cinema; Truffaut, following his screenplay for *Breathless*, made only four noir dramas, each time working from a novel by a major hardboiled writer: *Shoot the Piano Player*, based on David Goodis's *Down There*; *La Mariée était en noir* (*The Bride Wore Black* [1967]), drawn from a novel by Cornell Woolrich; *La Sirène du Mississippi* (*The Mississippi Mermaid* [1969]), adapted from a novel by Woolrich writing as William Irish; and *Vivement dimanche!* (*Confidentially Yours* [1983]), Truffaut's final film, from Charles Williams's *Long Saturday Night*. According to the director himself, *Confidentially Yours* was made in homage to Hitchcock and American hardboiled fiction. Strictly speaking, aside from his contribution to *Breathless*, *Shoot the Piano Player* is the director's only full-scale *neo*-noir. His three other noirs are faithful adaptations in which New Wave exuberance has been severely curtailed.

*Shoot the Piano Player* radiates a young filmmaker's delight with cinematic play, and the film is garnished with pauses that recall Belmondo examining the poster of Bogart in *Breathless*. In one scene, for example, the camera becomes momentarily distracted by a passerby, a pretty woman carrying a violin case; forgetting the plot, the camera remains on her for several extra beats just because (or so it seems) she happens to be there. Later, the film halts to present an entire musical number performed by a band member at the low-down bar where much of the action is set. These grace notes, along with jump cuts and jiggling pan shots in which the camera seems to follow an action it hasn't anticipated and over which it has no control, achieve, as in *Breathless*, a fresh, improvised quality. Like other early New Wave noir films, it celebrates cinema. As in *Breathless*, however, the core story is strangely yet productively at odds with the filmmaker's enthusiasm. And from the friction between the new style and the fatalistic noir content, a genre is reborn.

The piano player (Charles Aznavour) is an antihero with a noir secret, a deep wound buried in his past. Feeling responsible for his wife's suicide, Edouard Saroyan walked out on a glittering career as a concert pianist to transform himself into Charlie Kohler, who bangs on a piano in an obscure bar. Playing piano while maintaining a deadpan expression as he stares into off-screen space like Bogart in a classic noir, he has given up. Then he is drawn against his will into a criminal milieu, helping two brothers on the run from gangsters they have double-crossed in a heist. And after he has accidentally killed a man and been responsible for the death of a woman who had been loyal to him, he ends up where he began, staring stolidly offscreen as he continues to beat notes out of his piano.

As in Godardian noir, the crime story is continually broken into, lost track of. Noir, as in *Breathless*, is existential more than narrative. The story of the heist gone wrong is confined to the margins. As in *Bande à part*, a climactic shootout is filmed exclusively in a series of disengaged long shots, the filmic equivalent of a shrug. Gunplay is edited with flagrant violation of eyeline match, as Charlie's brothers and their pursuers are photographed aiming their guns in the same direction. In long shot, the woman who has accompanied Charlie is shot and keels over, presumably killed; the brothers seem to abscond with the money as the gangsters chase after them. Our commitment to the crime plot is presumed to be no more intense than that of the filmmakers.

Crisscrossing the crime-movie sediment with patches of comedy and romantic drama and with intimations of tragedy, Truffaut thumbs his nose at classic noir conventions to a degree he was never to repeat. The gangsters are portrayed as comic bumblers who talk about their clothes as they kidnap Charlie's younger brother. (Their compulsive comic patter anticipates by almost thirty-five years the hit men's conversation about food in the opening scenes of *Pulp Fiction*.) Contradictions between tone and action are doubled by gaps between action and setting: the shootout occurs in a beautiful snow-covered field, so that nearly four decades before *Fargo* (1996), a "white" noir, Truffaut introduces whiteness as a noir mise-en-scène.

Many of the film's surprising, distinctly neo-noir elements are, in fact, based on strategies found in Goodis's novel, *Down There*: this is one instance where hard-core French neo-noir derives from seeds planted beforehand on American ground. A modernist disguised as a pulp writer, Goodis experiments with point of view, as Truffaut does; sets the brothers' hideout in an unusual, snowbound, rural landscape; treats the gangsters as primarily comic figures; and is most interested in his defeated character and in the interactions *among* the denizens of a world "down there," rather than in his pulp story. Where Godard bought slight or marginal noir novels and then proceeded to disembowel them, Truffaut purchased a hardboiled masterpiece he then adapted faithfully.

Frustrating audiences' desire to read for the plot, New Wave noir in its purest and most flavorsome phase teases existential meanings from classic noir motifs. Godard and early Truffaut work crime-movie terrain for its extra-noir residue; in their hands, noir yields material for philosophical inquiry and for reflections on the language and history of cinema. Other directors working at the same fertile period in French film, such as Robert Bresson and (at times) Claude Chabrol, explore another dimension of classic noir more or less untilled in its classic American phase—its spiritual dimension.

Produced during the New Wave era, Bresson's 1959 *Pickpocket* is not connected to any contemporary movement. Both before the New Wave and after, Bresson labored on his own, cultivating a distinctively austere signature through which he tried to pierce—to transcend—the materiality of his medium. An opening title announces that "the style of this film is not that of a thriller," and indeed it is not. Like *Breathless*, Bresson's film is more an essay about a life devoted to crime than a crime film. But where Godard's style is vaudevillian, Bresson's is unrelieved neorealism that seeks through its documentary starkness an otherworldly aura. Bresson's antihero, like Godard's named Michel, is a loner who lives in a rooming house with bare walls that exudes existential despair and an unadorned staircase straight out of classic noir. Flaccidly, the character claims that inadequate parents led him into a life of crime. Unlike characters in American noir, Michel chooses crime not out of passion or greed but as an intellectual experiment. His goal is to explore an abstract question, Can a clever man sometimes break the law? Studying with a master pickpocket, he trains for his profession with monastic discipline. Alert, distant, steeped in his thoughts about crime, he is at first a tentative thief, but he soon becomes habituated to his chosen profession, exhilarated by the control his work affords. "My boldness had no limits now," he announces in the intermittent spoken and written commentary that punctuates his story. His life is immersed in crime; he rehearses his crimes rigorously and then records in a diary his thoughts about what he has done. Arrested at the races, one of his habitual haunts, he is jailed. His mistress, Jane, comes to visit him and, seeing her face bathed in light through the bars of his cell, he realizes that he loves her and that this is his reason for living. "Jane, in order to reach you what a strange way I had to take."

Like Michel, the film itself, which records the character's repetitive m.o. with an uninflected documentary exactitude, is a student of crime. Yet, like the character as well, the film wants crime to lead to something else. Michel's petty thievery is both sign and substance of his twisted desire to connect to others, as it is also in Bresson's audacious and perhaps even blasphemous scheme a route to redemption. It is Bresson's singular intent to investigate a pulp-fiction subject for religious awakening; like his character, the director enters a noir world only to renounce it. After having debased himself in a life of petty crime, Michael achieves, from his place of physical confinement, spiritual insight; and the film's trajectory parallels the character's: its matte acting and Bresson's stark, ascetic, meticulous accumulation of detail ultimately achieve at least an illusion of transcendence.

A decade later, Claude Chabrol in his masterpiece, *Le Boucher*, transformed another improbable noir subject, the story of a serial killer, into a philosophical meditation. Like everyone else, Chabrol works in a lusher style than Bresson, and he does not keep so great a distance between his film and the visual and narrative conventions of classic noir. But *Le Boucher* nonetheless is a major addition to a rarefied canon, French neo-noir discourse on crime and philosophy. Among New Wave directors, Chabrol has remained the most devoted to noir and has been the most prolific. Producing a string of suspense films that might have been made in the same way even if there had been no noir movement in America, Chabrol has pursued a more conventional course than either Godard or Truffaut. His work, which ranges from distinguished to routine, does not engage American noir in the same fertile ways that Godard and early Truffaut do, but at his strongest he creates stories of middle-class crime that fully justify his critical sobriquet as the French Hitchcock.

A bucolic village is built near caves bearing material that dates to the Cro-Magnon era—the setting of *Le Boucher* rustles with symbolic import. The film opens with lyrical pan shots of an outdoor spring wedding and closes with images of the town and surrounding countryside enshrouded in fog. Noir invades the green world of the opening as the title character (played by Jean Yanne, whose brooding quality recalls Jean Gabin), gripped by a compulsion that overtakes him "like a nightmare," kills a series of young women. His uncontrollable urge to kill women he desires is ignited when, at the opening wedding, he meets the reserved new schoolteacher (Stéphane Audran). Wounded by a love affair eleven years ago, the teacher is content to lead a serene life devoted to her students, until her encounter with the butcher stirs up feelings she has repressed. The butcher says people go mad without love; the teacher says people go mad with it.

When she discovers near the body of one of his victims a cigarette lighter she had given him for his birthday, she realizes her butcher is a killer. Instinctively, she decides to shield him. As she puts on a mask of innocence and so becomes complicit with her murderer-lover, the mise-en-scène reflects her plunge into noir schizophrenia. Bluffing to the police, she is framed in a low-angle ceiling shot; later, alone in her apartment, she is shot from a high angle, her shadow indicating her self-division. At the climax, as she hides in her apartment, locking herself in and closing the windows, the space, previously splashed with sun, is now dark with something more than night. The camera zooms in on her, as shadows seem almost literally to bisect her. When the butcher appears out of the darkness flicking his knife, she closes her eyes as if preparing to sacrifice herself to his mania. But it is himself he has come to murder, not the woman he knows he cannot be with in a normal way.

From a conventional story of a psycho killer who causes panic in a regulated community, Chabrol has constructed a cool, elegant meditation on a universal inner criminal, repressed yet lying in wait. Pitting civilization (the orderly village) against the underlying atavistic darkness from which it emerged (the prehistoric caves with their images of hunters stalking prey), the film extracts philosophy rather than sensationalism from the story of a serial killer. Chabrol's somber, reflective style sustains the kind of vast symbolic armature that an American film noir on the same subject would almost certainly shun.

In its upper reaches, as with Godard and Chabrol at his most cerebral, French neo-noir refuses the code of violence that governs the classic American crime movie. For Godard, movie-made violence is patently not for real, and in his anti-thrillers, shootouts and showdowns are confined to the margins, filmed cryptically and with a defiant casualness, as if to challenge audience expectation. Godard seems to take an impish delight in either underplaying violence or eliminating it altogether. In *Le Boucher*, in observance of a cinematic decorum no longer generally acknowledged by 1969, violence takes place offscreen. And representing the killer's violent acts only by the traces they leave is one of the film's strategies for converting crime into a subject for metaphysical speculation.

Compared to Godard, who filters fragments of noir into semiotic satires of contemporary French life, and Bresson, who sifts noir for its spiritual yield, Jean-Pierre Melville takes his noir straight. Melville's attachment to high 1940s American noir is purer than any other French director's. (Indeed, the director who venerates an American film style adopted an American name, that of novelist Herman Melville.) Unlike New Wave directors who interrogate and, to varying degrees, puncture noir archetypes, Melville fashions his noir dramas as tributes. His underworld antiheroes are distinctly Hemingwayesque as they exhibit grace under fire and maintain a code of honor with comrades and ultimately toward themselves. As they confront their noir destinies, Melville's protagonists in speech and gesture act out a masculine ethic steeped in an ethos derived from a hardboiled American idiom. His stoic underground men have an austere dignity; and as they keep a tight rein on whatever emotions may be lurking beneath their frozen expressions, they seem to be playing a kind of macho camp. For Melville and his characters, however, being manly is no laughing matter.

The director's adulation of the American hardboiled manner is expressed in his lean, tight style, which often seems to be as masked as his characters. He is at the same time a documentarian of a French underworld that models itself on a 1940s film prototype and its elegist, who celebrates hard, icy, well-behaved criminals. Like his disciplined characters, Melville seems to have his mind only on the task at hand; the philosophy of crime and the moral issues raised by his adoration of criminals do not concern him. *Bob le Flambeur* (1955) and *Le Samouraï* (1967) are two representative Melvillean homages to an American style that are nonetheless unlike any film any American director made during noir's classic phase.

In *Bob le flambeur*, in a leisurely opening sequence, which evokes the deadpan realism of such location noirs of the late 1940s as *The Naked City*, Bob the gambler makes his nightly rounds. Walking the streets of Pigalle and Montmartre till the bleak dawn, he visits bars, nightclubs, and a casino whose neon and deco décor recall settings in American crime films of the 1940s and have been photographed by Henri

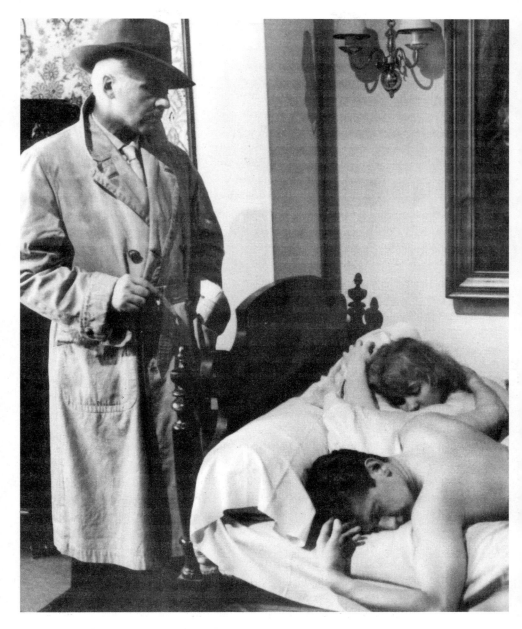

In regulation trenchcoat and fedora, Bob (Roger Duchesne) confronts his sexual alienation as he watches his protégé, Paolo (Daniel Cauchy), with a friend (Isabel Corey), in *Bob le flambeur* (1955), Jean-Pierre Melville's tribute to a 1940s American genre.

Decaë in ravishing black and white. The film's interiors exude a fragrance of low life conducted in high style. Clearly the director is as enamored as his character of this seductive after-hours underworld. The protagonist's occasional voiceover performs the typical noir functions of precisely locating time and place while also hinting at the destiny lurking in the wings.

Establishing the rhythm of his nightly ritual, the film's own measured rhythm echoes that of the title character. Only gradually does a story emerge. Bob, who has been straight for twenty years, after having been sent up for a failed robbery, is planning a heist of the Deauville Casino. As he hires and then trains his crew, he works with scientific concentration. But there's a leak on the team, and the robbery is foiled before it even happens. As he is being taken away, Bob boasts to his policeman-friend that he will beat the charge of criminal intent and bring a countercharge of harassment: brisk curtain banter in which Melville's antihero maintains, indeed flaunts, his customary sangfroid.

Bob's self-containment is the film's focus and point. The character's style (underscored by the cool jazz score, another element of American noir Melville idolizes) is held up for our approval. Like the private eyes—the Sam Spades and Philip Marlowes—of American pulp fiction, Bob knows how to do the right thing, behaving with honor in low circumstances. Most of the time the detectives uphold the law while Bob violates it, yet like the Americans he conducts himself righteously, both expecting and receiving deference from colleague and foe. Part of his "purity" rests on his courtly treatment of women. He disapproves of pimping, and he never abuses women, in fact seems to have no interest in women at all. His hardboiled style seems to be a cover for his not-so-submerged homoerotic impulses. Early in the film, he picks up a girl, not for himself but as a present for Paolo, his young stud protégé. Bob is most himself as a man among men; his one "love" scene is when he cradles Polo in his arms, after Polo has been shot.

Style is substance in this crime movie about a crime that does not take place, as it also is in *Le Samouraï*, where again Melville lionizes a frozen-faced loner engaged in the methodical daily routines of an undercover life. Like the hit man played by Alan Ladd in *This Gun for Hire* (1942), Melville's underground man (Alain Delon) hides out in a gray room that oozes criminality. In a virtuoso opening shot, the cam-

Only in the movies: Alain Delon plays a soulful hit man, a hired killer who follows a rigorous code of honor, in *Le Samouraï* (1967), a powerful work with a pernicious legacy.

era at daring length remains stationary as in long shot it observes a room ingrained with alienation. The only hint of movement is a puff of smoke rising from a shadowy figure reclining on a bed. Outside the single bare window it's raining, and passing traffic sounds faintly. Within the room, a chirping caged bird provides the only sound. "There's nothing lonelier than a samurai, except for a tiger in the jungle," is the film's epigraph, Melville's sly joke, a quotation from an imaginary volume called *The Book of Bushido*.

Like Bob, the samurai says little and moves at a deliberate pace. And as in the earlier film, the character's precision and his icy control are inscribed within the film's style. The camera follows Melville's "warrior" as he prepares for a hit, observing him as he steals a car, pays a visit to a girlfriend, stops by a card game in order to arrange an alibi, then descends to a jazz cavern where he proceeds imperturbably to stalk his quarry. "Who are you?" the victim asks. "What does it matter?" "What do you want?" "To kill you." Following the job, the hunter, betrayed by his employees and pursued by an inspector whose persistence matches his own, becomes the quarry. The character, knowing he is doomed, stages his death. He stalks into the jazz club to shoot the pianist who has helped to set him up, but his gun is empty; gunned down, as he knows he will be, he dies as he lived, a hit man of honor.

*Le Samouraï* is cinema of cool in excelsis. Dressed ritualistically in trench coat and fedora, his face half-hidden in shadow, Alain Delon is transcendently icy. Only his alert, wary eyes, which betray signs of an inner life, disrupt the immobile perfection of his face. With its monochromatic colors, its repetitive tunnel imagery, and its narrative enigmas—we learn nothing about the gang who hires the hit man nor about the hit man himself, who remains a nameless figure without a past—*Le Samouraï* is a brilliantly designed noir about noir. Derived entirely from other movies, the essentially banal narrative is enhanced by Melville's fragrant style, which, however, is too self-regarding and too pleased with its own "wickedness" to pass as the real thing. This is a noir masquerade, a bravura impersonation. And both as a simulation and in its coolly defiant amorality, the film anticipates moves to be made by American neo-noir.

Using classic noir as the stage on which to construct homage or demolition, Godard, Truffaut, Chabrol, Bresson, and Melville, each in his own way and to varying degrees, have reinvented American noir. But, of course, assertive and idiosyncratic neo-noir films have not been France's only contribution to the genre, and a steady stream of straightforward, impersonal thrillers were made before, during, and after the heyday of French experimentation in noir. Narrative-driven "pop" noir, tailored to prevailing trends, has continued to be a staple in France up to the present. Let Luc Besson's commercial hit *La Femme Nikita* (1990) stand as an example. In line with action-movie formulas of the 1980s, the film uses a noir story as an alibi for fetishizing violence. Nikita, a brutal street junkie, is transformed in three years into a lethal weapon, a woman with a gun who is sent on top-secret government missions. Programmed to become a killing machine—the film conflates femininity with apocalyptic violence—Nikita yet longs for a normal life. Like the protagonists of classic noir, however, Nikita is unable to escape the claims of her past. She is forced, like the antihero in *Out of the Past*, to confess her past to an innocent loved one, the man she knows she must leave to pursue her unavoidable noir fate, serving the government that created her.

What fascinates Besson about this twisted, squalid material, a male fantasy about a monstrous woman who retains an atavistic need for men, and what marked both the film and the director for American co-optation, was the erotic spectacle of a woman with a gun. Nikita, indeed, is gun crazy, and the film turns her expertise into a state-of-the-art display of violence. It's no wonder that *Point of No Return*, the 1993 American remake, is the most faithful translation of any French noir: unlike *Les Diaboliques* or *Breathless* or *La Bête humaine*, the original required no significant alterations. Besson's ode to violence seemed ready-made for the American action-film market. And unlike Godard or the other New Wave directors with a new take on noir, Besson was quickly imported to Hollywood, where he made *Léon* (*The Professional* [1994]), a bicultural hybrid that is as talented, and as fetid, as *La Femme Nikita*. Working in America with his favorite actor, Jean Reno, who plays a hit man who becomes enamored of a teenage neighbor, Besson pursues the same mix of sex and violence. As in the earlier film, violence is soaked in sexual sublimation: unable to have sex with his "daughter," the hit man shoots his big guns. The final, prolonged gunfire, spectacularly staged and edited, does indeed achieve an illusion of orgasmic release.

Unlike the New Wave directors who rethought noir and whose films were phrased as tribute and commentary, Besson is a commercial filmmaker who grafts a European art-house sensibility onto the conventions of the American action-film blockbuster. Despite its obnoxious subject matter and point of view—the film never disavows its protagonist's pathological violence or his pedophilia—*The Professional*, unsettlingly, is a formidable performance. Besson films violent action at a stately pace, accompanied by elegant classical music. Like Jean Gabin, Jean Reno creates a character shadowed by an aura of tragic destiny and so adds unwarranted depth to Besson's lurid pulp fiction. And conforming to the codes of postmodern display, visually and aurally the film asks to be read, to be consumed, as sheer spectacle. Besson's dazzling surface, however, does not conceal his queasy allegiance to a false theme that has infested the genre in the 1990s, the underlying belief that a contract killer is able to retain a pure inner self. The pernicious holiness-of-the-hit-man contemporary motif has plunged a branch of neo-noir into a cesspool.

At least since the 1970s, noir has become an international style. Filmmakers in Germany, Japan, Hong Kong, England, Belgium, Denmark, and Australia have made noir-based thrillers that use elements of classic American noir as a starting point. As with Besson, foreign directors with a noir track record have sometimes been summoned to Hollywood to make American suspense movies. But the kind of cross-cultural fertilization that enriched the original cycle, when German and Austrian émigrés in retreat from Nazis directed a new kind of crime film, has not happened. Having already absorbed the traces of a foreign signature, postclassic noir has so far resisted outsiders. To date no foreign director in the neo period has had the definitive impact of a Fritz Lang or a Billy Wilder on evolving noir, nor is it likely that any ever will. As in France, the most distinctive international directors of noir have not wanted to work for an American studio, and have not been invited to. And the noir "imports," like Besson, have worked in America with decidedly mixed results. I briefly consider the way in which three foreign directors have intersected with American neo-noir.

One of the artists whose work in the 1970s and 1980s galvanized the long-dormant German film industry, Wim Wenders, like his colleague Rainer Werner Fassbinder, admired American noir and paid tribute to it with films that could not be mistaken for homegrown products. Wenders's *Amerikanische Freund* (*The American Friend* [1977]), based on two Tom Ripley novels by Patricia Highsmith, is a landmark neo-noir, one of the first works that in fact suggested noir's accessibility to post-studio-era filmmakers. The film's protagonist, Zimmermann, is a picture framer, an unusual but apt noir profession, enclosed repeatedly in frames within the frame and therefore visually marked as the marked man he is. In an eerie chance meeting, he crosses the path of Ripley, a mysterious character who sells forgeries and has obscure links to the mob. Zimmermann's noir destiny is set when at an art auction he haughtily refuses to shake Ripley's hand. Because of the insult, Ripley gives Zimmermann's name to his mob associates, who are looking for a hit man. When Zimmerimann later asks Ripley why he gave him to the Mafia, Ripley says it was because of the snub. "Only that?" Zimmermann asks. "Isn't that enough?" Ripley answers, voicing a quintessentially noir perception about the way of the world in which for a minor misstep or perhaps for no reason at all, the noir Furies descend. When Zimmermann is diagnosed with a fatal blood disease he does not hesitate to become a killer for hire.

Like French New Wave noir, Wenders's film stresses atmosphere, *Stimmung*, over narrative coherence. Details about the gang warfare are deliberately sketchy; what interests Wenders about noir are the doom-ridden undertones that can be teased out of the story. Far more than

Zimmermann (Bruno Ganz) is trapped in the city in *The American Friend* (*Der Amerikanische Freund* [1977]), Wim Wenders's neo-noir tribute to classic American noir.

do any of the Gallic directors of noir, Wenders returns noir to its brooding, Teutonic roots. Bruno Ganz plays Zimmermann, deeply repressed and alienated, as a character who suffers from a terminal case of European melancholy. Throughout, Zimmermann is confined in spaces that seem to choke him as he moves sluggishly through a world drained of color—*The American Friend* is a film noir in black and gray and dark, heavy browns. The narrative enigmas, the despair that seems ingrained in every image, the slow pacing mark the film as a European essay on noir rather than a facsimile of the original style. And, beginning with the title, Wenders carries the noir motifs of masquerade and double-dealing to an almost dreamlike degree. The American "friend," a cowboy in Hamburg, is a fake philosopher who deals in forgeries, lives in a mansion that resembles the White House, and betrays Zimmermann by giving him to the mob. A seducer in an oversized cowboy hat, he's an homme fatale whom Zimmermann's wife instinctively recognizes as her rival, the "other" man in her increasingly mysterious husband's other life. (In the film's politically incorrect moral syllogism, homosexuality and criminality, as in Highsmith's *Strangers on a Train* and *Purple Noon*, are deeply connected.)

Despite the Germanic angst, Wenders's "complicity" with American noir is evident in his casting. As Ripley, Dennis Hopper gives a sly performance that, in retrospect, looks like a dress rehearsal for his emergence in the 1980s as a neo-noir crackpot; his enigmatic cowboy anticipates the dark sexual powers he unleashes in films like *Blue Velvet* (1986). Two American masters of classic noir, Nicholas Ray and Samuel Fuller, appear in cameos. Ray, blind in one eye and wearing an eye patch, is a forger; and Fuller plays a cigar-smoking New York pornographer.

Enamored of Wenders's Germanic take on noir, Francis Ford Coppola hired him to direct an American-made noir. Wenders, unlike most other foreign directors working for an American employer, was free to make the film he wanted to; the result, *Hammett* (1983), was a legendary misfire that is nonetheless a genuine contribution to the neo-noir canon. The film's hero, Sam Hammett (a conflation of Sam Spade, the aboriginal private eye, and his creator, Dashiell Hammett), is a writer of pulp fiction. When the camera "crawls" into his typewriter in the opening shot, the film immediately announces its distance from classic noir. "It isn't like one of your stories," an Asian femme fatale tells

Frederic Forrest (right) as Dashiell Hammett trailed by a thug (David Patrick Kelly) in the surreal settings of Wim Wenders's *Hammett* (1983), an outsider's approach to American hardboiled terrain.

Hammett at the end of the film. "It never is," he says, before he begins writing the story we have just seen. Master of the penny dreadful, Sam Hammett becomes a character in the kind of story he writes, led into a narrative maze by a detective named Jimmy Ryan, who believes he is the real-life inspiration for the Continental Op, the real Dashiell Hammett's first successful series character. "The agency and I taught you everything you know, and you sell it on the street in a cheap magazine," Ryan tells Hammett. "Who are you now, Hammett the writer or Hammett the detective?" his downstairs neighbor asks. "You left out Hammett the fool," the hero responds, the way a wry Spade might in the real thing, a Bogart noir. Wenders's "not-real" noir thus engages throughout in Pirandellian spirals of illusion and reality that mark it as art-house noir, a usually fatal commodity.

Strewn with double crosses, *Hammett* takes place in a highly stylized Chinatown, configured as a maze of narrow, minatory alleyways and criblike rooms. "Nothing in Chinatown goes unobserved," a local promises. "What brings you down to the depths?" a policeman who would like to rope off the area asks Hammett. This world of shadow and silhouette, dizzying diagonals, and boxes within boxes is a racist construction, recalling 1940s high noir, when Asians were the enemy. Within limits the inner story of Hammett's journey into Chinatown is played straight, but the sumptuous, surreal, hothouse mise-en-scène, a show all on its own, is the film's real focus. *Hammett* is American pulp fiction observed and commented on by an artistically ambitious outsider.

Despite his "un-American" perspective, Wenders in both *The American Friend* and *Hammett* is working within noir tradition, and indeed, along with Godard, he is one of the primary international revisionists. To claim Hong Kong action-movie-meister John Woo's connection to noir may at first glance seem an act of critical sleight of hand; nonetheless, I would argue that Woo can be securely placed within the genre's precincts. Shades of noir underline Woo's Hong Kong festivals of bloodletting; with good reason, Woo dedicates his seminal thriller *Die xue shuang xiong (The Killer* [1989]) to both Jean-Pierre Melville and Martin Scorsese, both of whom he has cited as major influences on his work. In *The Killer*, the title character clearly knows his noir and is able to express the central noir irony of the story, that the law officer who pursues him is his alter ego. And he's also wise to the fact that the choice he has made, to become a hit man, ensures that for him there will be no way out. In a world where figures of authority on both sides of the law are almost equally corrupt, the killer and the police chief bond together against gangsters.

The moral ambivalence suggested in the "cross-dressing" between cop and killer, however, and the film's glaze of existential angst are ultimately only alibis for Woo's trademark scenes of expertly choreographed violence. The film opens and closes in a church, filled with doves, that looks like a set built only to be demolished; in the same way, Woo has borrowed a noir premise only to detonate it with action-movie overload. His signature film subverts noir into a bravura sight-and-sound spectacle.

The worldwide acclaim Woo received for his Hong Kong specials earned him an invitation from Hollywood: American money courted a foreign director who had outperformed homegrown action-movie masters. In Hollywood, as in his native Hong Kong, Woo starts from and then proceeds to obliterate a noir-based libretto. *Face/Off* (1997), for example, hinges on a double masquerade, multiplying the literal change of face that was the fulcrum of a classic noir like *Dark Passage* and contemporary noirs like *Johnny Handsome* (1989) and *Shattered* (1991). An

Action noir: terrorist Castor Troy (Nicolas Cage, left) baits FBI agent Sean Archer (John Travolta) in John Woo's *Face/Off* (1997), in which the director's trademark action set pieces are embedded uneasily within a noir change-of-identity narrative.

FBI straight-arrow (John Travolta), determined to prevent a terrorist (Nicolas Cage) from setting off a bomb, undergoes a medical procedure in which he acquires the face and body of his adversary. In an equally extreme and equally magical countermove, the terrorist is surgically reconstructed to look like his pursuer. Imprisoned in the terrorist's body, the FBI agent finds himself in a classic noir tight spot. As he "performs" the FBI man, the terrorist gives him an incestuous itch for "his" daughter, thereby providing an ironic twist on the classic noir theme of a solid bourgeois whose id has leapt out of control. Wife and daughter suspect something's wrong with the normally repressed agent.

As in *The Killer*, the audience is not expected to believe the film in the old-fashioned way but rather to enjoy it as sheer spectacle. A scene of orgasmic violence in a church filled with pigeons recalls the "blasphemous" church scenes in *The Killer*. A prison-escape sequence is a high-octane set piece. And an extraneous final showdown on speedboats is the action-movie equivalent of a rousing production package that in the musical theater is called the "eleven o'clock number." Audacious sentiment following torrential violence is the Woo formula, and the film ends with the family reunited as the agent, accompanied by a little boy, a new "son," returns to the nest in his own body. Performance is embedded in the narrative, as the two actors "do" each other in vaudevillian turns; the actors' "show" underscores the film's performance as a sideshow hybrid, with noir collapsed and folded into horror, action, black comedy, and family melodrama.

Unlike earlier émigré directors like Fritz Lang and Billy Wilder, who had to conform to studio house style, in the post-studio era latter-day filmmakers like Wim Wenders and John Woo, who had international reputations before being abducted by Hollywood, have been allowed greater creative freedom. In Wenders's case, artistic license produced a famous noir failure, while Woo's crossbreeds have been box-office bonanzas. The fate of an obscure director is perhaps more symptomatic of Hollywood's appropriation tactics. In 1988, a Danish director, George Sluizer, had a hit with a noir thriller called *Spoorloos* (*The Vanishing*), in which, virtually in plain sight, a woman is abducted from a highway convenience store. The film ends darkly as the woman and her husband share the same fate of being buried alive. Hired by an American studio to remake his film with an American cast and setting, Sluizer was asked to discard his original ending. This time, the hero who searches for his missing wife is allowed to survive; his feisty new girlfriend pulls him from his untimely grave and also defeats his abductor. Sluizer was thus forced to "take back" the unyielding noir vision of his original story, now improbably transformed into *The Vanishing* (1993), a tale of feminist empowerment. Even so, the material has not been wholly Americanized. Sluizer retains a philosophical motive for his kidnapper: having in the past performed a valiant deed, saving a drowning child, he now feels compelled to commit a gratuitously evil act, kidnapping and killing a female victim chosen purely by chance.

Classic noir, itself a melding of disparate influences from German expressionism, prewar French poetic realism, American crime movies, and hardboiled pulp fiction, has provided the ground on which non-American directors in the post-studio era have continued to model a certain kind of crime film. Directors as varied as Godard, Wenders, Fassbinder, Truffaut, Chabrol, Melville, Bresson, and Woo have engaged in a frequently contentious dialogue with archetypes solidified in the original noir cycle. As in all debates, the directors making their anti- or neo-noir films have been bound to the terms set by the "other," the conventions of classic noir. Even Godard, the director most determined to refuse the codes of the classic form of the genre, was nonetheless crucially dependent on them as a means of defining the shape of his partial noirs. In opposing directions, Godard and Woo have exploded noir motifs into shards that bear scant resemblance to their original placement and intention. While Godard's experiments with noir are hermetic, Woo's cannibalization of pieces of noir for his postmodern spectacles may well represent a global trend.

A despairing, alienated Cornell Woolrich antihero, Harlan (Dennis Lipscomb), confronts his destiny in *Union City* (1980), a rare adaptation in the neo era of a work by Woolrich, the pulp master of stories of lower-class bad luck.

# Chapter 4

# "The Boys in the Back Room"

Edmund Wilson called them "the boys in the back room," the crime writers in the twenties and thirties grinding out stories and novelettes for pulp magazines, so called because of the cheap-quality paper on which they were printed. For characters on either side of the law who walked the mean streets of big cities, these genre specialists developed a terse, staccato, hardboiled literary style that, flavored with a distinctive brand of tabloid poetry, became the model for the dialogue in the best of the classic noir thrillers. As Geoffrey O'Brien writes in his authoritative study, *Hardboiled America: Lurid Paperbacks and the Masters of Noir*, pulp fictions "were a microcosm of American fantasies about the real world. They took the ordinary streets, the dives, the tenements, the cheap hotels, and invested them with mystery—with poetry even—turning them into the stuff of mythology."

In the 1940s, adaptations of novels by hardboiled maestros like Dashiell Hammett (*The Maltese Falcon*), Raymond Chandler (*The Big Sleep*), and James Cain (*Double Indemnity*) provided quintessential examples of a new kind of crime movie retroactively called noir. Genre aficionados know that the truest noir author was not one of the "big three," however, but Cornell Woolrich, who also wrote as George Hopley and William Irish. *Rear Window*, *Phantom Lady*, *The Window*, *Night Has a Thousand Eyes*, *Fear in the Night*, and *Black Angel* are among the Woolrich tales of mischance, deprivation, and paranoia that became part of the classic noir pantheon. *Dark Passage*, *Nightfall*, *The Burglar*, and *Shoot the*

*Piano Player* are among the films derived from the work of David Goodis, celebrated in France as the black prince of American pulp fiction. Like Woolrich, Goodis created hermetic urban settings rumbling with the discontent of castoffs and misfits whose lives seem drawn ineluctably toward crime. Goodis, as Geoffrey O'Brien writes, "was a poet of the loser, transforming swift cut-rate melodramas into traumatic visions of failed lives. The desperation of his characters appears to have been that of their creator."

Filmmakers in the studio era raided the work of other, less well known hardboiled writers, recognizing their merit decades before the pulp canon gained a literary seal of approval. John Farrow's *Big Clock* is adapted from a daringly constructed novel by Kenneth Fearing in which point of view shifts from chapter to chapter. Nicholas Ray's celebrated romantic noir, *They Live by Night*, is derived from one of the treasures of the hardboiled tradition, Edward Anderson's *Thieves Like Us*. "Mesquite trees persisted even into this foothills country, but the plains were far behind now," the novel opens, immediately establishing a rich sense of place and time sustained throughout. "There were Spanish oaks and cedars and in the late afternoon this way the sage grass had a lavender flush. Away ahead, in the distance, a long range of sharp hills embroidered the horizon." Working in a homespun tradition, Anderson uses vernacular similes and metaphors: "Outside, the sun stung Bowie's face like a shaving lotion and his knee-bones felt like dry sponges." And also adhering to a hardboiled literary code, Anderson keeps us close to Keechie and Bowie, his two fugitives on the run in rural America during the Depression, recreating the world from their limited perspectives. "If she stays much longer, Bowie thought, I'm going to duck in that bar and get a beer. It takes a woman a lot longer to do things than a man." From the first extreme closeup on the lovers, isolated against a black background in their own romantic world, to the final transcendent shot of Keechie reacting to Bowie's sudden death, Ray's film maintains the novel's intimacy. And it captures Anderson's aura of rural fable, an outlaw's folktale in which the protagonists are "trapped in a world they didn't make."

Their stature enhanced by powerful film versions, the best crime novels of the 1930s and 1940s are now recognized as constituting a significant literary movement, deeply American in tone, setting, and language. In 1997, edited by Robert Polito, the Library of America published *Crime Novels*, a collection including *Thieves Like Us* and *The Big Clock*; James Cain's *Postman Always Rings Twice*; Horace McCoy's *They Shoot Horses, Don't They?*; William Lindsay Gresham's *Nightmare Alley*; and Cornell Woolrich's *I Married a Dead Man*. The book's subtitle, *American Noir of the 1930s & 40s*, retroactively applies the now-commercial noir label to works written before noir had been identified.

Filmmakers in the post-noir era have continued to draw on some of the canonic hardboiled writers. Except as the title character in Wenders's idiosyncratic postmodern thriller, Hammett remains untouched, and Cain is represented only by the misjudged remake of *The Postman Always Rings Twice*. But both writers continue to exert a potent influence on noir thrillers. Hammett's version of the private eye may be a rare figure in contemporary crime movies (the neurotic cop seems to have replaced the private investigator as a noir staple), but his depiction of an urban setting sweltering in corruption, and his politically incorrect equation of Asians with criminality and deception remain central to nouveau noir. The network of vipers that runs the city in films like *Chinatown* and *L.A. Confidential* recalls Hammett's San Francisco, a setting steeped in Asian duplicity. At the time of its release in 1981, *Body Heat* was loosely described as a remake of *Double Indemnity*, as indeed in a loose sense it is. But then every noir with a scheming wife, a complicated money scam, and a gullible protagonist who thinks with his phallus owes a debt to Cain's novel. The writer's vision of a ravenous, depleting female sexuality—the woman as bad sister, the embodiment of male castration anxiety—has achieved totemic status in noir. It's the image second-, third-, and fourth-generation filmmakers continue to draw on, whether, like John Dahl or the Coen brothers, they are self-conscious imitators fully aware of their debt to a literary tradition or filmmakers simply copying other movies. Either way, and despite the protests of some feminists and the self-appointed guardians of political correctness, Cain's elemental notion of male vulnerability confronting a dangerous female sexuality has become part of the American grain.

To date Raymond Chandler's private eye Philip Marlowe has made four appearances in the neo era: in remakes of *The Big Sleep* and *Murder, My Sweet* (now called by the novel's original title, *Farewell, My Lovely*); in an adaptation of Chandler's late novel *The Little Sister*, called simply *Marlowe*; and in Robert Altman's revisionist *The Long Goodbye*. Woolrich adaptations range from an independent work, *Union City*, to Truffaut's

*The Bride Wore Black* and *The Mississippi Mermaid,* and to *While You Were Sleeping* and *Mrs. Winterbourne,* two comic recyclings of the distinctly non-comic *I Married a Dead Man.* French filmmakers have adapted a series of David Goodis novels, from Truffaut's beloved *Shoot the Piano Player,* based on *Down There,* the Goodis novel in which the writer's characteristic themes are sounded with the purest note, to the notorious *La lune dans le caniveau* (*Moon in the Gutter*).

Now as then, Mickey Spillane occupies the bottom of the hardboiled barrel, and his private eye Mike Hammer, the poor man's Philip Marlowe, to date has appeared in the neo period only once, in a 1982 remake of Spillane's signature novel, *I, the Jury.* (Although Spillane's *Kiss Me Deadly* served as the basis of one of the most respected and stylish of classic noir films, the director, Robert Aldrich, and his screenwriter, A. I. Bezzerides, borrowed little more than Spillane's title, his leading character, and a general milieu. The film transformed the novel's routine hunt for drugs, in 1955 an unrepresentable subject, into a search for the Great Whatsit, which turns out to be a radioactive Pandora's box brimming with symbolism for the newly atomic age. The film's status as an apocalyptic noir has little connection to Spillane's novel.) While it updates Spillane's story from the 1950s to the 1980s, *I, the Jury* is faithful to its source. It keeps in place Spillane's trademark paranoid anticommunism and his espousal of vigilante justice. As in the original, his Mike Hammer (played with swaggering sex appeal by Armand Assante) is a loose cannon, a killing machine with a macho strut. As the CIA agent who hires him to kill "commies" observes, Hammer has "a refreshing Biblical attitude, a dozen eyes for an eye." The private dick as Rambo, Hammer here is a hardened Vietnam vet who enacts Spillane's down and dirty code of ethics.

To date the neo-noir track record of adaptations of the original hardboiled stylists has been spotty. More consistently successful have been the film versions of second- and third-generation writers working in a literary mode now generally called noir. All but forgotten at the time of his death in 1977, Jim Thompson is now widely regarded as the most imposing successor to the territory worked by writers like Cain and Woolrich. Not only has Thompson's satanic muse been resurrected in a series of films, including two versions of *The Getaway* (1972 and 1994), *The Grifters* (1990), and *After Dark, My Sweet* (1990), his novels are mainstays in the Vintage Crime Black Lizard series, and he has been the subject of a major literary biography published in 1995, *Savage Art* by Robert Polito, winner of the National Book Award. Works by Elmore Leonard—including *Jackie Brown* (1997), based on *Rum Punch*, and *52 Pick-Up* (1986)—and by James Ellroy (*L.A. Confidential* [1997]), the most acclaimed of a third generation of hardboiled crime writers, have been successfully adapted. And filmmakers still have an eye for the stray noir novel of literary merit, with Charles Williams's *Hell Hath No Fury*, the source of *The Hot Spot*, a first-rate 1990 noir, and Richard Neely's *Plastic Nightmare*, made into a 1991 thriller, *Shattered*, cases in point.

Two postclassic versions of Raymond Chandler's Philip Marlowe: traditional (James Garner, left, getting knocked out by a mystery woman in black [Gayle Hunnicutt]), in *Marlowe* (1969); and revisionist (Elliott Gould, a doltish, clodhopping Marlowe, in *The Long Goodbye* [1973]).

In the postclassic era, Chandler's Philip Marlowe has had three distinct incarnations: as a straightforward star vehicle for James Garner in *Marlowe* (1969), as a fading-star vehicle for Robert Mitchum in *The Big Sleep* and *Farewell, My Lovely*, and as a comic turn for Elliott Gould in *The Long Goodbye*. As Geoffrey O'Brien notes in *Hardboiled America*, "when someone speaks of the Private Eye, it is generally Philip Marlowe he is talking about. . . . Philip Marlowe . . . is the raison d'être of Chandler's novels. The blondes and gunmen come and go; the dingy offices, the hallways, the dark parking lots and glittering nightclubs remain the same; bodies are discovered; guns poke out from behind curtains; Marlowe gets hit over the head; the plot develops as it must; and it turns out to be the same story we have already heard. None of it would amount to much without the consciousness of Philip Marlowe. It is his presence as a living, thinking being that gives the books their life." Among the neo-noir interpretations of the canonic character, James Garner's unheralded, no-fuss Marlowe is the closest to Chandler's original, described by O'Brien as "unmistakably chivalrous, a quixotic figure who is also disillusioned and increasingly bitter . . . a man who perceives his own goodness as useless, and who is most himself when the heroism wears thin."

"This has been an average day in a detective's life," Marlowe announces in the style of self-mocking wit that lines Garner's performance. "I've been stabbed, my office qualifies for urban renewal, I've been generally snookered, and the cops want to take my license away." A ladies' man, suave and confident, Garner's shrewd private eye is wise to female masquerade. "You're good," he appraises a rich client whose "acting" doesn't convince him. "You're so good you act your way out of a safe deposit box." "You're vamping, Miss Wald, stalling for time," he chastises her at a later point when once again he isn't fooled. Like his creator, Marlowe is suspicious of women, and has good reason to be: every woman in sight is either working an angle or not what she seems. The "little sister," dressed in prim blue and white, turns out to be greedy; the ice queen, who certainly looks guilty, a television actress who wears an assortment of wigs, is actually only trying to protect her sister, whom she incorrectly thinks has committed a murder. It is the actress's best friend, a stripper in a bright blonde wig, who is the killer, a deduction Marlowe makes as he watches her strip act—as she peels down, in a parallel "move" the detective uncovers the mystery. While the women are in disguise, Garner's Marlowe seems not to be performed at all. The actor has a light, deft, contemporary touch, and he delivers Chandler's sardonic asides without evident signs of quotation marks.

Chandler's story is updated from the 1930s to the 1970s, yet throughout there are unforced echoes of classic noir. One of two ice-pick murders occurs in the Alvarado, a dump with grungy brown walls, mirrors that look like relics from a B noir circa 1947, and a retro neon sign. (The other murder is set in a hippie pad with shrieking hallucinogenic colors.) Marlowe's grubby office is located in the historic Bradbury Building, a downtown Los Angeles landmark featured in a number of vintage noir films, and a key scene takes place in Union Station, another popular high-noir location. Marlowe's blackout, after a doctor gives him a drugged cigarette, recalls the noted blackout scene in *Murder, My Sweet*. Produced in 1969, at a time when noir was generally believed to be an unretrievable historical style, Paul Bogart's sensible film proved that a solid private-eye drama can transcend the sway of fashion.

Made only a few years later, Dick Richards's *Farewell, My Lovely* and Robert Altman's *Long Goodbye* are, in different ways, self-conscious simulations. The stylized sets and color in *Farewell, My Lovely* do not interfere with a commitment to tell Chandler's story seriously, but still the film has a noir-revival glaze the simpler *Marlowe* avoids. And the quotation-marks tendency is reinforced by the presence of Robert Mitchum as an aging Philip Marlowe. To be sure, Mitchum is the real thing, but in 1975, well past his movie-star prime, he projects a terminal world-weariness that exceeds the boundaries of Chandler's genre narrative; and in a subtle way, he seems to be outside and above the material. When he announces that he has "a hat, a coat, and a gun," pastiche threatens to tumble into parody. His voiceover narration is tinged with irony, and combined with the old-photo-album color and the undulating jazz score, his commentary enfolds Chandler's story in retro heaven. Mitchum's detective has walked down entirely too many mean streets; "everything I touch turns to shit," he sighs. Beyond his sardonic exit line, "what a world," a too-long-postponed retirement seems to be lying in wait. The film indeed concludes on a valedictory note: Marlowe has a soft spot, not this time for a dame (Mitchum's character seems beyond that kind of desire), but for a kid, a fatherless boy. Despite the postmodern wrappings, Mitchum's presence contains echoes of an authentic 1940s deadpan style. His great ruined face, the formerly chiseled features collapsing in bulges and puffs, and his signature somnolence evoke the original hardboiled mask beneath which there are suggestions of a festering inner life. Jim Thompson, as Mr. Grayle, politically powerful and sexually impotent, and Charlotte Rampling, playing Mrs. Grayle, a dragon lady at once sultry and hardboiled through and through, the woman Marlowe searches for, compound the noir-revival aura.

Unlike *Farewell, My Lovely*, which places Chandler's story in its original time, *The Long Goodbye* takes place in a contemporary Los Angeles from which chiaroscuro and claustrophobia have been scrupulously banished. This is a Marlowe investigation shot in wide screen and bright color. Altman replaces the mirror shots of classic noir with the film's primary visual motif, reflections in sliding glass doors that evoke the slippery characters Marlowe encounters once he is hired to find a missing husband. And Altman creates a new sound to match his new look for noir. In the dense, multilayered sound track, only snatches of Chandler's hardboiled dialogue are decipherable. Like sound and image, the film's approach to narrative is also notably contra-noir; the plot meanders through the film, as wispy as the reflections in glass.

Altman's nouveau touches provide the stage on which his "un-Marlowe" (Elliott Gould) ambles. Disregarding the tight-lipped, macho style of all previous impersonations of Chandler's gumshoe, Gould plays the character as an out-and-out schlemiel. Sounding like Mr. Magoo, he delivers his dialogue in a throwaway manner, as if we aren't really supposed to be listening to him. Unshaven, this Marlowe lives in a mess, and often seems as distracted as his neighbors, a bevy of post-1960s Los Angeles airheads who bake hash brownies, dance half naked on their balcony, practice Yoga, and become increasingly vague. Gould's Jewish Marlowe is a Borscht-belt jokester, a compulsive wisecracker whose irony deliberately avoids the same pitch as Chandler's. Altman surrounds Gould with other comic characters: two gangsters are vaude-villian buffoons; the gatekeeper at the Malibu Colony where Marlowe's client lives performs imitations of movie stars.

Engineering mood swings that are far steeper than in Chandler or in the 1940s Marlowe movies, Altman crosses comedy with eruptions of violence. A joking gangster suddenly slashes his girlfriend's face with a Coke bottle to prove to Marlowe that, all kidding aside, he means deadly business. The ultimate payoff in the film's oscillations between "Jewish" comedy and "Italian" violence is reserved for the showdown between Marlowe and his former best friend, Terry Lennox, in which the truth finally emerges. "I had to kill [my wife]," Terry says, "and I had to get out. Now no one cares. Marty [the gangster] has his money, people think I'm dead, I have my girl [the woman who hired Marlowe to look for her "missing" husband]." Savoring his well-constructed crime scenario, Terry admits that he had to set up Marlowe as a patsy; "that's what friends are for." "No one cares?" an incredulous Marlowe repeats, then takes out a gun and shoots his turncoat friend. "You're a born loser," Terry says, and indeed that is the way Gould has played him. And coming from a character that has seemed so curiously inert, the sudden killing, as intended, is a shocking gesture, capped by further assaults on Chandler's hardboiled mode. After Terry falls dead, Marlowe at last assumes the patented mask of the classic noir private eye, becoming inscrutably frozen faced as he walks away from the crime scene he has himself produced. His "performance" is only momentary, however. When "Hooray for Hollywood" filters onto the sound track, Marlowe violates movie realism (and the actor reclaims his comic persona) by dancing a spontaneous jig with an old lady passerby and then continues strolling merrily down a tree-lined lane and out of the film.

Altman's subversive version of Chandler's courtly private eye is prime early neo-noir. For all its self-indulgence and contradiction— the film both satirizes and seeks acceptance as a cool, contemporary L.A. mystery story—Altman's "new age" noir suggested the genre's elasticity at a time when it was considered passé. Produced before nouveau noir had taken root, *The Long Goodbye* anticipates the full-force genre revival of the 1980s and 1990s.

As Geoffrey O'Brien notes, Cornell Woolrich "is quite simply the premier paranoid among crime writers. His is the realm of the impossible coincidence, perceived as a cosmic joke at the expense of man. . . . The perennial unanswered question of his protagonists is: Why me?" Set typically in working-class urban environments that evoke the peculiarly American isolation captured in the paintings of Edward Hopper, Woolrich's contrived, engrossing stories are richly movie-friendly. His tales of sudden mischance, rumbling with a wide range of timeless anxieties, have continued to supply scenarios for neo-noir thrillers.

In the 1960s, during the "ban" on noir in America, François Truffaut directed two French films based on Woolrich novels. *La Mariée était en noir* (*The Bride Wore Black*) and *La Sirène du Mississippi* (*The Mississippi Mermaid*, adapted from *Waltz into Darkness*) lack the spark of *Shoot the Piano Player*. Bristling with bravado and something to prove, Truffaut's approach to David Goodis's hardboiled classic *Down There* is that of a youthful rebel, while his Woolrich adaptations unroll with stately, middle-aged grace. The two films, in effect, represent a second generation of French neo-noir, the residue left in the wake of the New Wave's initial thrusts at the genre. But even with fewer directorial flourishes, there is no mistaking the fact that Truffaut's perspective is that of an outsider who is offering a foreigner's take on an American master of noir.

Woolrich's premise in *The Bride Wore Black* is basic and relentless. On his wedding day, the groom is killed accidentally, the victim of a prank. Seeking and then eliminating each of the five men involved (strangers who, during a sodden bachelor's party taking place near the wedding, had been playing around with a gun), the bride becomes an avenging angel who dedicates her life to acting out the biblical injunction of an eye for an eye. As each man in turn is caught in the bride's web, Woolrich's prose builds to a boil; in contrast, Truffaut keeps his cool. His deadpan style, which recalls Jean-Pierre Melville's distinctly Gallic sangfroid, is matched by Jeanne Moreau's tight, dry, droll performance as the efficient heroine. Fashionably dressed in either black or white, she catches her victims off guard because she doesn't look the part; like the film itself, she doesn't appear to be noir. Telling a story similar to Woolrich's *Phantom Lady*, filmed in 1944 by Robert Siodmak, Truffaut's film looks nothing like the classic noir thriller. Truffaut, defying tradition, sets an indelibly dark story in a bright, realistic world

The fateful Cornell Woolrich moment: the men on the twisting stairs are to become the victims of the bride whose husband they have just accidentally killed, in François Truffaut's adaptation of *The Bride Wore Black* (*La Mariée était en noir* [1967]).

in which there are only occasional reminiscences of noir: a virtuoso high-angle shot of the bachelor-party celebrants racing down a spiral staircase; a jail scene at the end that oozes entrapment.

In more marked ways, Truffaut's *Mississippi Mermaid* is a French version of Woolrich in which a hot subject, a tale of a fatal attraction, is presented in a detached style. Truffaut's distance is not the mordant Teutonic irony of a Fritz Lang or a Robert Siodmak; rather it "speaks" another kind of remoteness. The director has transformed Woolrich's novel of dangerous desire into a vehicle for two glamorous stars, Catherine Deneuve and Jean-Paul Belmondo, placed against ravishingly color coordinated settings. In the translation, Woolrich's noir vision, the typically mounting hysteria with which he orchestrates his narrative, curdles into a sickly French romanticism.

Alcoholic, hermitic, and homosexual, Woolrich was a misogynist who evinced intense castration anxiety in his writing; Truffaut was a heterosexual who loved women and believed in a romantic ideal, and he has rewritten Woolrich's novel of a contaminated, impossible love into a story about redemption through love. In the novel, a spider woman fatally poisons the antihero, who grows sick from his passion and the knowledge that the woman he loves has betrayed him. When he discovers that she is poisoning him, he is willing to sacrifice himself on the altar of her greed and duplicity, assuring her that she has been worth the sacrifice. The woman breaks down, declaring, or at least recognizing, her love after it is too late. Typically, Woolrich has constructed

Louis (Jean-Paul Belmondo) looks longingly up at Julie/Marion (Catherine Deneuve) in François Truffaut's *Mississippi Mermaid* (*La Sirène du Mississippi* [l969]), a romantic, and therefore distorted, adaptation of Cornell Woolrich's decidedly noir novel, *Waltz into Darkness*.

a no-exit scenario for his characters and watches as they descend irretrievably into the noir pit he has laid out for them. Truffaut wants to believe in the femme fatale's conversion; and, in a sense, he has directed the entire film from the perspective of the last shot, in which the fated, united lovers walk through a pristine, snow-covered landscape. Truffaut's ultimate commitment is to the "truth" of their love, whereas Woolrich's original story creates a world in which a genuine romantic bond will be and must be forever frustrated. Woolrich's narrative contrivances are designed to ensure romantic failure; Truffaut interprets the story as a romantic idyll and so downplays a fact that finally cannot be disregarded, that in *Waltz into Darkness*, as in all his fables, Woolrich has made a world that mocks and forbids love.

As in *The Bride Wore Black*, Truffaut's mise-en-scène in *The Mississippi Mermaid* is built against the noir grain. For the most part, a story of a spider woman sapping her prey is filmed in open vistas and bright colors. Not set in the American South but on a lush Caribbean island, the film opens in an elegant plantation where there are no noticeable noir undertones. Only as the characters succumb to the descent Woolrich has prepared for them does a noir signature begin to intrude. The doomed lovers leave the plantation and inhabit increasingly shabby hotel rooms and hideaway apartments. But rather than moving from a day to a night world, the expected noir trajectory, the damaged couple end their odyssey in the snow, where, ironically, their romance, only a charade in the sensuous tropical heat at the beginning, finally ignites.

*Union City* (1980), written and directed by Mark Reichert and based on a short story originally published in *Detective Fiction* in 1937, returns Woolrich to native ground. Most of the picture is set in the kind of bleak side-street tenement where Woolrich characters are trapped in dead-end lives. There are only a few exterior shots, of ominously blank city streets that resemble Edward Hopper's *Sunday Morning*. Harlan, Woolrich's impotent antihero, leads a cramped domestic life tied to a straying wife whose biggest treat is to go to Friday matinees with the super. On the job, he's an accountant who works at a small desk pushed against a window covered by venetian blinds.

As always in Woolrich, bad luck, obsession, and violent crime shadow the protagonist. Enraged that someone is taking his milk, Harlan sets a trap for the presumed perpetrator, a neighborhood vagrant, and then kills him, dragging his body through the hallways to place him on a Murphy bed in an empty apartment. Guilt ridden by his crime, Harlan no longer takes milk in his coffee—and becomes sexually alienated from his distracted wife. Milkless, he has visions of the dead man returning. In his distinctive vein, Woolrich has written a mocking black-comic fable about a sexually immobilized male haunted by images of the return of the repressed. Woolrich's loser wants to confess, to be exposed; when newlyweds rent out the empty apartment down the hall, he brings them a hammer to help them open the jammed bed. When he hears the new tenant gasp, he assumes that what he has wished for has finally happened, his crime has been discovered, and he jumps out the window. But typically for Woolrich, the last laugh is at his character's expense: there is no telltale corpse; it was only a trace of blood that prompted the tenant's response, and the vagrant Harlan thought he had killed is seen among the crowd that gathers to observe Harlan's corpse.

Updated from the Depression to 1953, the film still confines Woolrich's story to a "distant" past. Loving attention to the bad taste of low-class 1950s décor and the stylized red and blue lighting re-create a bygone era of pulp fiction in movies and paperbacks. Affection mixes with condescension, yet despite the andante pacing and matte acting, this obscure movie comes as close as any in the neo period to evoking a B noir from the 1940s. *Union City* reveres Woolrich, unlike two mainstream 1990s rewrites that convert *I Married a Dead Man* (filmed for the first time in 1950 as a melodrama called *No Man of Her Own* starring Barbara Stanwyck) into romantic comedies.

Woolrich's novel opens at the end of the story as the first-person narrator announces irreversible doom. "The summer nights are so pleasant in Caulfield. . . . But not for us. . . . We've lost. That's all I know. We've lost, we've lost." At the end of the novel, sustaining the opening lament, the narrator intones, "I don't know what the game was. I'm not sure how it should be played. No one ever tells you. I only know we must have played it wrong, somewhere along the way. I don't even know what the stakes are. I only know they're not for us. We've lost. That's all I know. We've lost. And now the game is through." Both *While You Were Sleeping* and *Mrs. Winterbourne* remove the original story's thistles while retaining Woolrich's general outline. Throughout both adaptations, noir remains a possibility that is perpetually defused. In Woolrich's noir premise, a pregnant woman with no money, in flight

from her abusive husband, has a chance meeting on a train with another pregnant woman traveling with her new husband to meet his
rich family for the first time. When the train crashes, the wife is killed,
her husband is thrown into a coma, and the fugitive heroine, who survives, is mistaken by the husband's family for the wife they have never
met. At first reluctant, the woman decides to play the role fate has
pushed her into.

*While You Were Sleeping* (1995) reframes Woolrich's story as a
charming star vehicle for Sandra Bullock. The heroine is now a single
working woman who saves the life of a man who falls into a coma. In
the novel, the character is motivated by greed and her masquerade
leads to murder, the inescapable destination in most Woolrich narratives; in the film, it's romance rather than money that prompts the
heroine to assume another identity when the man's wealthy family
mistake her for his fiancée. Closer to Woolrich's story, but a less successful film, *Mrs. Winterbourne* (1996) phrases the same basic plot as a
comedy of class conflict. A distinctly proletarian character (played by
Ricki Lake), pregnant, is mistaken for a patrician woman, also pregnant, who is killed when the train on which they meet crashes. Adopted
by a wealthy family, this noir Eliza Doolittle is schooled in how to
imitate the manners of her betters. When her lowlife husband appears, he is murdered, as in the novel; but the film plays the crime
for comedy rather than suspense. Each member of the heroine's new
family, eager to protect her, claims to have killed the husband. Murder is treated blithely, as a nuisance to be dispensed with, so that the
new Mrs. Winterbourne can enjoy the happy ending her adopted family wants for her.

As the pulp poet of the darkness and loneliness at the core of
urban American life in the 1930s and 1940s, the laureate of all-night
cafeterias, tenements with peeling walls, and empty nighttime streets
and subways, Cornell Woolrich is unsurpassed. Although grim irony
pervades his work, to the author the world etched in his fiction was no
laughing matter. It may indeed be that in the postmodern era Woolrich's
brand of noir, which lacks the graphic violence and sex, the cynicism
and the deft verbal comedy of most contemporary crime writing, is too
sincere to attract filmmakers. If Woolrich has come to seem like a back
number, the work of an equally brilliant, second-generation crime writer,
Jim Thompson, has at last found its way to the screen.

As Robert Polito writes in *Savage Art*, his superb literary biography of Thompson, the novelist's "most characteristic performances mark him as the blackest beast of what is coming to be known as *série noire*." While Thompson published twenty-six novels between 1942 and 1973, it is his astonishing string of paperback originals in the early and mid-1950s that display at a virtuoso level his "dismaying gift," as Polito notes, for "spotlight[ing] edgy, disturbed, insidiously engrossing criminals who often unravel into psychopathic killers." Surely the most experimental and artistically daring of all crime writers, Thompson "recreate[s] his monsters from the inside out . . . root[ing] deep within their snaky psyches . . . to embody through imaginative art their terrifying yet beguiling voices on the page." Thompson at his strongest is a bona fide literary modernist, a master of first-person narration, evoking the tortured, disintegrating minds of his protagonists through the creation of a fluid subjectivity that recalls Joycean stream-of-consciousness. In *The Killer Inside Me* (1952), *A Hell of a Woman* (1954), and *After Dark, My Sweet* (1955), Thompson takes his readers deep inside the minds of criminally warped characters. Part of the frisson of his conceits is that each of his psychopaths appears to be one of us, but beneath a seemingly normal façade a murderous violence continually simmers, waiting to erupt.

Lou Ford, the antihero of *The Killer Inside Me*, Thompson's masterpiece and a work whose merit transcends its genre, is a sheriff in a small Texas town, an affable good ol' boy whose homilies mask an inner rage. "'Well, I tell you,' I drawled. 'I tell you the way I look at it, a man doesn't get any more out of life than what he puts into it,'" Lou engages a customer in the restaurant where he is having his customary pie and coffee. "'Every cloud has its silver lining, at least that's the way I figure it. I mean, if we didn't have the rain we wouldn't have the rainbows, now would we?'" Beneath the patter, Thompson shows us his character's awareness of his performance, the way in which his genial clichés are a form of attack. "Striking at people that way [his way with words] is almost as good as the other, the real way," Lou chillingly informs the reader. Likable Lou has lived all his life in the same town, trying to hold his sickness at bay. As the novel opens, Lou's repressed demons are about to return in a hideously distorted form. He embarks on a spree of killings, becoming gradually and irreversibly unhinged. And as he reports his crimes, the line between objective reality and

Lou's warped perspective blurs until, by the end, the reader is uncertain about how much of what the narrator reports is true and how much his deranged fabrications.

Lou narrates most of his story in a cool, clipped, colloquial voice that echoes the traditionally terse style of the hardboiled hero. Even as suspicions against him mount, Lou's language is reportorial, delivered with a willed matter-of-factness. "It was almost three o'clock in the morning when I got through talking—answering questions, mostly—to Sheriff Maples and the county attorney, Howard Hendricks; and I guess you know I wasn't feeling so good. I was kind of sick to my stomach, and I felt, well, pretty damned sore angry." But filtering into the commonsense veneer are recurrent leaps into pathology when, without warning, the narrator enfolds us in his mania. "I'd done everything I could to get rid of a couple of undesirable citizens in a neat no-kickbacks way. And here one of 'em was still alive; and purple hell was popping about the other one." By the end, as his grip on reality weakens, his syntax reflexively unravels as well. " 'Two hearts that beat as one,' I said. 'Two — ha, ha, ha—two—two—ha, ha, ha, ha, ha, ha, ha—J-jesus Chri—ha, ha, ha, ha, ha, ha, ha, ha—two Jesus . . .'" "And I sprang at her, I made for her just like they'd thought I would. Almost. And it was like I'd signaled, the way the smoke suddenly poured up through the floor. And the room exploded with shots and yells, and I seemed to explode with it, yelling and laughing and . . . and . . ."

Sutured to a mind in the grip of madness that cannot be contained or controlled, the reader is left with no way out. We begin, are indeed forced, to see the world as he does, exulting in his elaborate subterfuges to avoid detection, his brazen (though at first carefully constructed) alibis, and hoping he won't be discovered. Lou's insinuating style has "called" us within his circle of transgression; and for the length of the novel, we are allied with him against the world outside his fevered consciousness. At the end, as he goes up in smoke, the narrator explicitly inscribes us within his mania. "Our kind. Us people. . . . All of us that started the game with a crooked cue, that wanted so much and got so little, that meant so good and did so bad. All us folk. . . . All of us. All of us." Just as he does every character he interacts with, Lou also contaminates us. "Read Jim Thompson and take a tour of hell," a blurb announces on many of the Black Lizard reprints of Thompson's work.

In *A Hell of a Woman*, Thompson's schizophrenic narrator is another killer hiding behind a mild demeanor who achieves remarkable criminal success before he arranges his self-destruction. The sexually frustrated narrator plans to rob and kill a rich old woman and then to run off with the woman's enticing niece. This routine scenario is periodically interrupted by the narrator's diaries as well as by a novel in progress he is writing under the pen name of Derf Senoj, his real name, Fred Jones, spelled backwards. Once the killer within him is released, the novel, like the character himself, breaks in two. As we enter the mind of a killer no longer able to separate reality from fever dream, the novel begins to decompose. Italics are used to indicate the "fictional" version of the character's increasingly incoherent report of a life spinning out of control; as his delirium intensifies, italics and regular type crisscross with increasing frequency, until in the finale the two stories intersect on alternating lines: "she was the / I was really wide awake. But still I was sleepy; and if / most beautiful woman in the world and all I wanted was to do / that doesn't make sense I can't help it. I went and / something nice for her, show her how much I appreciated and / stretched out on the bed, and she came in and sat beside / loved her. And I didn't have but the one thing, the only thing, / me. She had a big pair of shears in her hand, and she sat." In one of the two alternate endings, a woman cuts off the narrator's penis ("all he ever had to offer a woman") and in the other he commits suicide.

*After Dark, My Sweet* is another Thompson tale told by an unreliable narrator, a brain-damaged former professional fighter named Collie. Uncertain of his own reactions and vacillating in his responses to people and events, the narrator is aware that his point of view is limited and possibly untrustworthy. As Collie analyzes himself and others, Thompson never steps away from his character. Scenes are dramatized through the grain of Collie's struggles for comprehension. "Fay had to care, didn't she? Or did she?" Collie asks himself, as the reader is made to follow his doubts. "She hadn't been faking, but maybe that didn't mean that she really cared. She'd been batting around on her own a long time. Drinking so much she didn't know what she was doing, or not giving a damn if she did know. . . . A woman like that. . . . But Fay wasn't a woman like *that*. Like it seemed she might be." Even more than in the earlier novels, the underlying story in *After Dark, My Sweet* is standard pulp: through a chance meeting in a roadside bar, the hero

A Jim Thompson loser, a brain-damaged ex-boxer (Jason Patric), enclosed in a frame within the frame with a troubled widow (Rachel Ward), in *After Dark, My Sweet* (1990).

becomes involved in a kidnapping. But out of the threadbare plot, Thompson has woven a crime novel that resonates with philosophical and poetic overtones. Throughout, Collie steps back from recounting what happened to reflect on what happened, and why. In a distinctive vernacular voice ("I waked up when I heard the back door slam"), a blend of Hemingway crossed with Camus that achieves the heights of pulp lyricism, Collie ruminates about his existential status as a drifter with no luck—as someone who's always on the move, always betrayed, and because of his illness, always marked. Thompson's novel is a sturdy noir story at the same time that it offers, through the voice of its bruised protagonist, a meditation on noir themes.

Thompson's descents into noir subjectivity present a steep challenge for film adaptation. His narrators' voices produce, and coexist with, the image; in film, audiences accept as convention that voiceover and image are not a precise match. Voiceover narration, in essence, only reinforces the essential objectivity of cinematic representation. The first-person voice that springs from the screen can never create and saturate the image as it can in a novel, nor can it duplicate the reader's sense of being confined within a consciousness in the process of cracking.

The initial attempt to render a Thompson psychopath's consciousness on film was in the 1976 adaptation of *The Killer Inside Me*. Inevitably, the film relies on voiceover narration only sporadically; otherwise, Sheriff Lou Ford, as in the novel, would be simply telling us his story. But seemingly frustrated by having to remain outside the character, the camera periodically moves in on the actor's face, as if trying physically to penetrate an unhinging mind. The more insistently the camera moves in toward the character, however, the more it confronts the impassable external status of the filmed image. Many of the noir touches through which the character's schizophrenia is signified—mirror shots, strategically placed shadows that bisect the character's face, sounds and images the sheriff recalls from his past, presented in distorted, repetitive fragments – are, in fact, appropriate filmic parallels to Thompson's literary devices. And as Lou Ford, the sheriff who is everybody's friend, Stacy Keach sustains an expert masquerade, his character's genial veneer disturbed by increasingly frequent emanations from within. But ultimately the film cannot recreate the novel's two crucial and colliding voices, Lou Ford's unbroken inner monologue and, hovering above and beyond it, the darkly ironic, shaping voice of the novelist himself, a potent presence no film, even a far more skillful one than this pioneering effort to decode Thompson, could possibly seize.

While the film's attempts to translate Thompsonian subjectivity are partial and fragmentary, the adapters of *This World, Then the Fireworks*, a 1955 Thompson short story, go for broke in trying to find film equivalents for first-person narration. Another Thompson sociopath (fixated by a childhood trauma of witnessing his father being killed after having had sex with a neighbor's wife), the narrator has an incestuous attachment to his sister, harbors murderous feelings for his mother, and kills an obese private eye who has been trailing his sister. In trying to depict the subjectivity of a deranged character for whom sex and death are deeply intermingled, the 1997 film employs nonstop visual and aural overload. Rat-a-tat editing, rapid shifts of focus and distance, and a hyperactive, rotating camera create narrative incoherence. The frenzied efforts to capture the protagonist's progressive mania achieve the opposite result; what the film displays is a knowledge of noir and of MTV techniques rather than the inner workings of a troubled consciousness. As the psycho-narrator Marty Lakewood, an intolerably mannered Billy Zane matches the surrounding bluster. Mumbling in an elaborately throwaway style, he mimics a hardboiled tone while signaling that he is not the real thing, only an ironic, wised-up, postmodern copy.

In contrast, James Foley's *After Dark, My Sweet*, shot in hot desert colors and played in eerily empty rooms and landscapes, makes little effort to resuscitate the voice of the novel's narrator or to ingrain the character's subjectivity within the image. Voiceover is used sparingly and only to suggest the vein of existential alienation that marks Collie's narration in the novel. "For years I kept going when going didn't seem to make any sense, and now I had to keep going to the end, to make the end come," Jason Patric as Collie announces, intoning a classic litany of a noir antihero. Collie's inner monologue, pivoting around his distrust, his misperceptions and hesitations, is more accessible to filming than Lou Ford's psychosis. The character remains connected to others—his desire to stay in touch is, in fact, his primary motive—in a way that the hermitic sheriff cannot. Foley keeps us close to his confused protagonist, placing us in the position of interpreting the other characters at the same time that Collie does. We ask the same questions he does about the woman who picks him up in a bar and seduces him into a kidnapping scheme: Can he trust her? Is she using him? Does she really care for him? "Look, Fay, if only I knew what you wanted, if you just talked straight to me," he pleads with her, and because of the wonderfully veiled and ambiguous way in which Rachel Ward plays the character, we are made to share Collie's anxieties. At times Ward plays her as a traditional femme fatale, a woman who has adopted Collie because she is attracted to him and knows she can capitalize on his attraction to her. At other times, her façade of sexual confidence cracks and she seems a troubled, sincere character trapped in desperate circumstances.

To date the most popular and most mainstream Thompson adaptations—the two versions of *The Getaway* and *The Grifters*—have been derived from novels with conventional narration. "Carter 'Doc' McCoy had left a morning call for six o'clock, and he was reaching for the telephone the moment the night clerk rang," begins the novel *The Get-*

*away*, in a cool, impersonal, third-person style that presents no particular obstacle or challenge to the screenwriter. Nonetheless, Thompson typically throws the filmmakers a curve; his novel is a taut, straightforward story of a bank heist and its aftermath until it reaches a coda that is unlike any other in the hardboiled field. After outwitting their partners and getting away with the loot, the master thief and his wife seek refuge in a hideaway for criminals, a "kingdom" governed by a strict and ruthless code of universal dishonor. As Thompson describes it with an ironic gleam, "The tiny area where El Rey is uncrowned king appears on no maps and, for very practical reasons, it has no official existence. This has led to the rumor that the place actually does not exist, that it is only an illusory haven conjured up in the minds of the wicked. And since no one with a good reputation for truth and veracity has ever returned from it . . . Well, you see? But it is there, all right. Lying in a small coastal group of mountains, it suffers from sudden and drastic changes in climate."

Trapping his fugitives in a noir nightmare world, in which betrayal and murder flourish in epidemic proportions, a world in which even the most intense paranoia is entirely justified, Thompson transports his tale of bank robbers on the run into a borderline area that strains against genre parameters. Significantly, neither the original 1972 film nor the 1994 remake attempted Thompson's bitter finale, in which his thieves can never be freed of their suspicions that one of them will arrange to kill the other. Rather, both films end with a literal getaway as the criminal couple escapes into Mexico with the money they have stolen.

Thompson expressed deep disapproval of the happy ending the 1972 film pasted onto his story; but at the time, the getaway was a climax almost as daring as the novel's. Released after Hollywood terminated the Production Code, which mandated punishment for all criminal acts, *The Getaway* was the first film in which crime pays. Despite the film's intentional misreading of Thompson's novel, it is nonetheless fitting that a story by the defiantly rule-breaking Thompson should have provided the opening wedge in Hollywood's rejection of the moralistic Code.

Even the tamed and truncated 1972 version of *The Getaway*, however, as directed by Sam Peckinpah, whose surly disposition is a good match for Thompson's, is not business as usual. The film establishes an unsavory, hot-weather atmosphere that captures the novelist's distinctive edginess. Peckinpah and his canny screenwriter, Walter Hill, himself to become something of a noir specialist, have gleaned from Thompson's novel its vivid set pieces of fugitives on the run. "Flight is many things," as Thompson writes in one of the novel's many pulp-poetry asides. "Something clean and swift, like a bird skimming across the sky. Or something filthy and crawling; a series of crablike movements through figurative and literal slime, a process of creeping ahead, jumping sideways, running backward. It is sleeping in fields and river bottoms. It is bellying for miles along an irrigation ditch. It is back roads, spur railroad lines, the tailgate of a wildcat truck, a stolen car and a dead couple in lovers' lane. It is food pilfered from freight cars, garments taken from clotheslines; robbery and murder, sweat and blood." The film captures many "phases" of Thompsonian flight. In the most aromatic, a scene that typifies the sensibility of the director as well as the writer, the couple on the run hide out in a garbage truck and are dumped with the garbage onto a flat, stifling Texas landscape, the word TRASH seen prominently behind them. The showdown among rival thieves takes place in a dilapidated hotel located in a Mexican border town as memorably seedy as the one in *Touch of Evil*. Following descriptions provided by Thompson, the hotel is one of the most pungent foul places in neo-noir, its long, empty, dark brown corridors

Two images of Jim Thompson tawdriness: above, a spectacle of sexual sadism as a wife (Sally Struthers) and a lusty intruder (Al Lettieri) humiliate the woman's bound husband (Jack Dodson), in *The Getaway* (1972). On the run, a master criminal and his partner-wife (Alec Baldwin and Kim Basinger) land in a garbage dump, in the 1994 version of *The Getaway*.

evoking the end-of-the-world mise-en-scène at which Thompson is a master.

Wisely, the film retains Thompson's subplot of sexual humiliation. A rival hood, whom the fleeing couple presume dead, rises up like a monster in a horror film to pursue them, kidnapping a meek veterinarian and his horny wife. The burly intruder makes love to the wife as the husband watches; after the doctor, emasculated beyond endurance, hangs himself in the bathroom, the callous criminal crouches on the toilet beside the corpse. The ribald black humor and the tragicomedy of sexual shame are accurate translations of Thompson at his most down and dirty.

The problem is with the leading players, a husband-and-wife team unable to project onscreen sparks. As Thompson's shrewd, hardened con man, Steve McQueen, with an unvaryingly dumb expression, is too flaccid. He's a movie star walking through the role in his characteristically laconic style. Doc's wife, Carol, may be Thompson's ultimate tough cookie, a phallic woman who is an equal part of the gang and who has sex with a politically powerful criminal to spring Doc from jail. The couple have a volatile relationship in which lust and deep mutual distrust are enmeshed. As Thompson's tart, able to give as good as she gets and driven by greed and desire, Ali MacGraw is fatally miscast. With her boarding-school manner and hopelessly bland voice, she is a misfit in the Darwinian world of Thompson's outlaws. Her approach to the role is to seem to want to hide in plain sight.

The 1994 *Getaway*, the first neo-noir remake of a neo-noir, directed by Roger Donaldson and starring a real-life married couple, is a faithful rendition of the original film rather than of Thompson's novel. All the visual and narrative set pieces are reconstructed, and this time the desert backdrop is more graphically rendered: this is noir in hot colors, with the outlaw couple often bathed in bright yellow light. Thompson's pulp story, minus his surreal coda, remains swift and compelling, and the film was worth remaking because the second couple, Alec Baldwin and Kim Basinger, are more potent than McQueen and McGraw. With more muscle than their wan predecessors, the Baldwins re-create the sizzle that both drives and divides Thompson's characters. The remake opens with Carol being instructed in how to use a gun—she's being prepped to become the phallic woman her husband and her career plans require. This time the subplot is even harsher than in Peckinpah's version: the pursuing criminal is played by a vividly sour Michael Madsen, the hot-to-trot wife he seduces is Jennifer Tilly, who with her Kewpie-doll appearance (and voice) seems a pulp-fiction cover come to life. "I think it's time to leave," Madsen snaps, as he urinates beside the fresh corpse of the husband he has humiliated, providing a moment of cryptic Thompsonian cynicism.

The most critically acclaimed of the Thompson adaptations so far, Stephen Frears's *Grifters*, is also the most unflinching. A mother-son love story that ends in an act of murder, the film preserves Thompson in his most morbid mood. In the showdown, Lilly, the mother, a veteran small-time crook, confronts her son, Ray, whom she has told to get off the grift because he hasn't got "the stomach for it." "You don't know what I'd do to live," Lilly warns, her voice edged with icy desperation. "I gave you your life twice, I'm asking you to give me mine once." Lilly seduces Ray, suggesting that maybe she isn't his mother, before hurling a piece of glass into his neck. Her body heaves over her son's, as she seems at once to be killing and humping him. At first shocked by what she has done, then momentarily grieved, she quickly assumes the deadened expression with which

Mother love, Jim Thompson-style: to save herself, a mother (Anjelica Huston) will first try to seduce, and then kill, her son (John Cusack), in *The Grifters* (1990).

she will now confront the outside world. After her crime, she descends in a barred elevator in which the crisscrossing shadows and the ominous lighting from below transform her into a ghoulish apparition, a noir fiend. With the money she stole from her son, she drives off into the night.

An episodic account of the penny-ante con games played by Lilly and Ray and Ray's girlfriend, *The Grifters* is one of Thompson's most loosely plotted narratives. True to the novel, the film, dominated by Anjelica Huston's chilling, monochromatic performance as the beyond-hardboiled mother, is a character study steeped in acid. Recalling the noir deadpan of the 1940s, Huston speaks in slow, insinuating rhythms as her masked face intermittently betrays suggestions of her character's demonic inner life. The film opens with a montage of black-and-white images of Los Angeles in the 1950s before it switches to contemporary settings shot in color. Yet, as in many neo-noir films, the action seems suspended in a temporal limbo. The characters, who speak in a distinctive pulp-fiction lingo, seem still to be living in the era when Thompson created them. And the stylized color and lighting—orange, yellow, and red predominate, intersected by liquid shadows that have a different texture from those in classic noir—help to place the characters in a noir never-never land.

"Well, sir, I should have been sitting pretty, just about as pretty as a man could sit," the narrator of Thompson's *Pop. 1280*, the sheriff of Potts County, confides in the opening sentence. A supreme nihilist, the sheriff is a self-appointed savior, doing what he considers God's work as he goes about eliminating the unworthy. "All I can do is follow the point of the Lord's finger, striking down the pore sinners that no one gives a good god-dang about. Like I say, I've tried to get out of it; I've figured on runnin' away and staying away. But I can't, and I know I'll never be able to. I got to keep on like I'm doin' now." Nick is another Thompson killer who dons a fool's mask, another small-town Texan with a Christ complex. He's a noir philosopher who shares his dark epiphanies with us. "Well, sir, it was a funny thing, a funny-terrible thing, a strange crazy thing. Because what caught my attention wasn't what you'd have thought it would be at all. . . . Not something that was in the room itself. Not somethin' but nothing. The emptiness. The absence of things." Unlike Lou Ford, Nick remains undetected, free to continue his version of the Lord's work.

Bertrand Tavernier's acclaimed *Coup de torchon* (*Clean Slate* [1981]) sets Thompson's character in French West Africa of 1938 and converts the novel's Deep South good ol' boy into a cool, solitary, melancholy Frenchman. These external changes only reinforce the universality of Thompson's themes, and Tavernier's may indeed be the purest filmic distillation to date of Thompsonian irony and nihilism. Without forsaking the writer's swift pulp plotting—the sheriff schemes to eliminate people who have taunted or offended him—Tavernier injects the film with the kind of Gallic meditation on a noir worldview that also happens to fuse with Thompson's philosophical asides. More fully than any American version of Thompson so far, *Coup de torchon* captures Thompson's particular pitch-black comic tone and his poet-*maudit* sensibility.

The African setting works well on a number of levels. The dry, vast, uninhabited landscapes seem, after a while, to reflect the protagonist's parched soul. The piercingly bright African sun that enfolds the dark story counterpoints the mad police captain who pursues dark errands under a benign mask. Like Joseph Conrad's *Heart of Darkness*, the film exploits the African setting for mythic overtones; relocated, Thompson's Texas sheriff becomes like a Conradian colonizer unhinged by his perception of a universal heart of darkness. "Good and evil are meaningless concepts in Africa," he proclaims, as if he is using "Africa" to rationalize his self-appointed role as moral arbiter come to "wipe the world clean." The film opens and closes with the character observing black children; at the end, he points a gun at them, then at himself, shaking his head in befuddlement at himself and the human condition. In the novel, one of Nick's victims is black, and while the character evinces the racial bias of a Southern bigot, blackness is not promoted to an existential theme as in the film. For the crazed character, blacks become image and embodiment of the other, the lesser beings it is his duty to eliminate. First-person narration in the novel "frames" Nick's madness; the film makes no attempt to penetrate the character's subjectivity. We observe him from the outside, yet it is clear that the racism emanates from the character, not from the filmmakers.

As it aligns a pulp-fiction story of unsolved murders in an isolated community with the killer's ruminations on the meaning of his crimes, the film crosses genre boundaries in a way that is distinctly Thompsonian. Like Thompson's, Tavernier's approach is at once corrosively comical and terrifying. When the demented protagonist confesses to a schoolteacher he admires that he has been dead a long time, it is a perception the film has richly demonstrated.

Unlike Thompson, David Goodis was not overlooked during the classic noir period. His 1946 novel, *Dark Passage*, about a man on the run who hides out behind a remade face, became a highly regarded noir movie with Humphrey Bogart; and two B films of the 1950s, *The Burglar* and *Nightfall*, based on Goodis novels, have acquired a cult reputation they fully deserve. But Goodis's particular brand of melancholia continues to be appreciated in France far more than at home. In the nouveau noir period, Goodis so far has been entirely overlooked in America, whereas in France he is the subject of a major literary biography, *Goodis: La Vie en noir et blanc* by Philippe Garnier, that remains untranslated, and his novels have formed the basis of a notable *série noire* that includes such films as *Le Casse* (*The Burglars* [1972]), *La Course du lièvre à travers les champs* (*And Hope to Die* [(1972]), *La Lune dans le caniveau* (*The Moon in the Gutter* [1983]), *Rue Barbare* (1984), *Descent en enfer* (1986), and the little-seen *Street of No Return* (1989), directed by

Samuel Fuller. Of the series, *The Moon in the Gutter*, based on Goodis's 1953 novel and directed by Jean-Jacques Beineix, is both the most widely seen in America, as well as the most notorious. Like Wim Wenders's *Hammett*, it is an unmistakably "foreign" interpretation, a French art-house fantasia on American noir.

*The Moon in the Gutter*, like Goodis's significantly titled *Down There*, is set in one of the novelist's typically closed-off underworlds. As in *Down There* and Goodis's archetypal 1951 novel *Cassidy's Girl*, the story takes place mostly in a waterfront bar populated by outcasts destined to remain where they are. In this separate realm, the weather is a perpetual gray, and the air is coated with both literal and existential grime. Echoes of Zola and Hemingway, Eugene O'Neill and Theodore Dreiser are sounded, yet Goodis's fevered, hardboiled style has a distinct individual cast. The antihero of this lower-depths outpost, named Gerard and played by Gérard Depardieu in a hulking, somnambulistic style, is a dockworker who lives on a dead-end street with a woman for whom sex is a primal weapon. Like many Goodis protagonists, he is haunted by a tragic event from the past; each night he returns to the dark cul-de-sac where his sister was raped and then committed suicide. Gerard tries to escape with a woman from the world beyond the waterfront, only in the end to return to his woman from the gutter.

Beineix eliminates the novel's naturalistic underlining and sets the story in a surreal, painterly mise-en-scène, an artificial world that recalls the theatrical Chinatown Wenders constructed for *Hammett*. All too literally, Beineix translates Goodis's world "down there" into a cinematic world apart, a dream of a noir universe rather than a realistic representation. "Gerard dreams of a white city . . . but was afraid to enter it, feeling he would be out of place there," a voice of God announces portentously in the film's opening. "TRY ANOTHER WORLD" is written in big letters (in English) on an advertisement that hovers over the squalid waterfront streets. The airy white place depicted in the oversized sign is both a lure and a mockery for the characters trapped in their end-of-the-world harbor enclave. The sets, clearly marked as sets, recall the cluttered spaces of Josef von Sternberg's early 1930s vehicles for Marlene Dietrich. Nets, fallen beams, broken stairs, rubble invade the rooms in which Goodis's waterfront rats are caged. Hot orange rectangles of light pierce the blackness that seems to emanate from the characters' poverty; dockworkers are silhouetted poetically against a tinted orange-pink sky. Furnaces belch apocalyptic fires, and rumbling thunder provides an almost unbroken obbligato.

"You came to see the dirt," Gerard tells Loretta, the outsider in a red car played by Nastassja Kinski, costumed and lighted like a movie queen making a guest-star appearance. "You're in rough company," he warns her. "It's magnificent," she twitters as she takes photographs. Fatally, her stance is the same as the filmmaker's—Beineix regards Goodis's down-and-outs as "magnificent" objects to be placed on display. With dream interludes, a swelling romantic score, a camera that swirls around the newly formed and doomed romantic couple, Beineix loads the material with a mushy, faux-mystical glaze that is a misreading of Goodis's basic American hardheadedness. Delirious where Goodis is stoical, the director offers a skewed version of a homegrown master that is a fascinating neo-noir failure.

"Currently repackaged out of a sense of nostalgia and a need to profit from the past, it's not surprising that original pulp culture paperbacks have become consumer objects fetching extraordinary prices," Woody Haut notes in *Pulp Culture: Hardboiled Fiction and the Cold War*. "At the same time," he continues, "pulp culture reprints are avidly consumed, allowing fin de siècle readers both to investigate the past and, in noting the literature's language, place, attitudes and politics, make connections with the present. This, in turn, has helped create a new generation of crime writers—James Ellroy, Walter Mosley, James Crumley, Sara Paretsky, and Elmore Leonard, for example—who have gone beyond parody to examine the new urban reality in which they find themselves." Among the third generation of hardboiled writers Haut cites, writers who have indeed ventured "beyond parody" to carve out contemporary crime-story idioms, Elmore Leonard to date has proven to be the most movie-friendly. Four Leonard novels—*52 Pick-Up*, *Get Shorty*, *Rum Punch*, and *Out of Sight*—have been made into well-received crime films shaded with varying inflections of noir. His sensibility more comic than noir, Leonard bypasses the despair and profound unease that permeate the work of Woolrich, Thompson, and Goodis. For Leonard, crime scenes are occasions for bright repartee rather than springboards into paranoia. Released in 1986 before he became a star of crime fiction, the film *52 Pick-Up*, directed by John Frankenheimer, is a modest B thriller about a prosperous married man who takes justice into his own hands. The protagonist pursues and out-wits three hoods who blackmail him with photographs of his sexual encounters with his mistress, a stripper. While it preserves chunks of the novelist's rapier dialogue, the film stresses noir over the comic ele-ments that are always part of Leonard's signature, whereas the dispos-able movie versions of *Get Shorty* and *Out of Sight* play Leonard's stories primarily for hardboiled comedy rather than for noir suspense.

That Quentin Tarantino, in his first film since *Pulp Fiction*, chose to write and direct *Rum Punch* had all the makings of a literary match brokered in crime-movie heaven. Like the novelist, Tarantino extracts unlikely, bracing wry comedy from scenes of criminal action and inter-cuts banter with sudden violence. Filmmaker and crime writer are en-amored of jazzlike verbal riffs laced with profane humor and enjoy tak-ing pauses from their narratives to pursue collateral issues. Leonard's dialogue always remains at true pitch even as his plots often collapse, but in *Rum Punch* he keeps his story of an intricate scam afloat until the end. Tarantino changes Leonard's title to *Jackie Brown*, the story's heroine, and turns her into a black character (played by Pam Grier). Otherwise, as in the novel, she remains a sexy, likable, somewhat world-weary trickster who outwits both sides of the law as she succeeds in stealing money from a psychopathic gunrunner. Taking cues from Leonard's solid construction, but adding distinctive curlicues of his own, Tarantino plays with time—events are repeated out of sequence from differing vantage points—and periodically retards the action. Jackie and a middle-aged bail bondsman she ensnares meditate on aging, and many times the camera lingers reflectively on characters after a scene appears to be completed. The filmmaker's relish for punctuation—titles announce the place, the time and sometimes the content of a scene; there are slow fades and dissolves—recalls the early, jubilant experi-ments of the French New Wave directors. (Tarantino named his pro-duction company A Band Apart in honor of Godard's eccentric riff on noir, *Bande à part*.) Moving the action from West Palm Beach, Florida, to a more resonant American wasteland, the Los Angeles suburbs of Torrance, Carson, and Compton, awash in soulless shopping malls, anonymous fast-food dumps, and decrepit apartments with hideous décor, Tarantino even improves on his source material. And unlike Leonard, he does not allow Jackie and her bondsman to consummate their mutual attraction: who has time for sex when you're plotting a major scam?

A fresh, delicious crime caper, *Jackie Brown* confirms Tarantino's position as the premier director of pulp in the 1990s. Like Elmore Leonard, Tarantino breaks traditional noir codes to create a brand of quirky, ironic, postmodern neo-noir in which ribald comedy and violence play off against each other in a deft, delicate balance. It's a formula that other contemporary filmmakers have tried and so far failed to match.

James Ellroy, like Elmore Leonard, has amassed a large readership with a group of crime novels published in the 1980s and 1990s, but with the exception of *Cop*, a 1987 film based on his novel *Blood on the Moon* (also called *Killer on the Road*), until the 1997 film of *L.A. Confidential* his work, unaccountably, remained untapped by American filmmakers. Where Leonard is only marginally and fitfully committed to traditional noir, Ellroy is a noir loyalist. "The master of postmodern crime fiction," as blurbs on his novels announce, he has evolved his own brand of hardboiled prose built of short, stabbing sentences, often no more than fragments, strung together at a restless pace. A review in the *Detroit News* accurately described Ellroy's style as "noir with a vengeance, related in a speeding shorthand."

Set in the 1950s, but layered with flashbacks to the 1930s, *L.A. Confidential* is Ellroy's noir epic, the story of three soiled police officers whose careers following a mass murder at the noir-named Night Owl Diner are deeply enmeshed. Exley is entangled in an Oedipal conflict with a powerful father. Bud, overwhelmed by the childhood trauma of watching his father beat his mother to death, is driven to a life of violence. Jack is a self-loathing "celebrity" cop, who works in collusion with the editor of a slimy true-confessions scandal sheet and can't remember why he joined the force. Each of the characters is haunted by an event from the past. Bud obsessively replays his mother's death. Exley is scalded by the memory of a cover-up in World War II that earned him a Medal of Honor he knows he did not deserve. Jack tries to suppress evidence of a murder he committed when he was drunk. The cops' boss and surrogate father, Captain Dudley Smith, turns out to be the most corrupt character in Ellroy's demonic L.A. He challenges mobster Mickey Cohen and, improbably, wins.

Ellroy transforms what could be a routine police procedural about a puzzling and at first incorrectly solved crime into an indictment of a city in which the police, gangsters, politicians, and movie moguls are locked in a vast web of deceit and collusion. In Ellroy's tainted City of Angels, there is plenty of trouble in paradise; and after five hundred pages, the moral rot that runs this noir L.A. remains firmly entrenched. Ellroy turns up cynicism to a screeching volume, and his plotting is intricate. Folding in on itself, the many-stranded narrative keeps burrowing deeper and deeper into the past as the characters, for their own sakes as well as the reader's, periodically offer miniature plot summaries of what they know so far. *L.A. Confidential* is crime writing as postmodern theater. Ellroy's brand of noir is so virtuoso, his writing struts with such macho swagger that his novel seems poised on the edge of parody. Asking the reader to follow the serpentine story lines, which none of his characters, with their partial knowledge of events, seems able to do, Ellroy plays fast and loose with the issue of his sincerity. Is his massive novel a crime story "for real," or is it, after all, an elaborate masquerade, noir *en travestie?*

Confounding novelistic illusion with real life, Ellroy surrounds his trio of lapsed policemen with historical figures such as the gangsters Mickey Cohen and Johnny Stompanato, Lana Turner, and Police Chief William Parker. A character named Ray Dieterling, an entertainment mogul who builds a fantasy amusement park, is clearly a stand-in for Walt Disney. (The scandalous family history Ellroy provides for the character would surely have incurred lawsuits if he had been called Disney rather than Dieterling.) The play between historical reality and its fictional copy is epitomized in a stable of prostitutes who are cut to resemble Hollywood divas of the day. While the real Lana Turner makes a cameo appearance, fake versions of Veronica Lake, Ava Gardner, and Rita Hayworth are among the simulacra the customers of a brothel can select. The masquerade motif is Ellroy's metaphor for L.A. itself, a city of illusions.

The dense, at times virtually impenetrable plotting is reinforced by Ellroy's experimental approach to point of view. Without ever resorting directly to first-person narration, he presents the subjective impressions of a large cast of quasi narrators, wrapping their often-colliding deductions in a muscular, profane tabloid prose alight with crimeworld and police jargon. An Ellroy sampler: "Dudley could bend you, shape you, twist you, turn you, point you—and never make you feel like some dumb lump of clay. But he always let you know one thing:

he knew you better than you knew yourself." "Jack heard rumors: an ex-cop named Buzz Meeks heisted the summit, took off and was gunned down near San Bernardino—Cohen goons and rogue L.A. cops killed him, a Mickey contract: Meeks stole the Mick blind and fucked his woman. The horse was supposed long gone unfound." "The music inside went off key—wrong, not really music. Bud caught screeches—screams from the jail. The noise doubled, tripled. Bud saw a stampede: muster room to cell block. A flash: Stens going crazy, booze, a jamboree—bash the cop bashers. He ran over, hit the door at a sprint. The catwalk packed tight, cell doors open, lines forming."

Occasionally intercepting Ellroy's reports from the front are supposedly objective newspaper accounts of the crime as well as internal police memos on the three officers. Written in a conventional style, these parallel chronicles prove to be as unreliable as the eyewitness accounts.

The screenplay by Brian Helgeland and Curtis Hanson wisely makes no attempt to duplicate the novel's tricky manipulations of point of view, eliminates many characters and subplots, and cleanses the three central policemen. Rather than the sociopaths Ellroy drew, the leading figures are now conventional noir neurotics with most of their burrs and stigmata excised. The character who has been changed the least, Bud, a self-appointed protector of battered wives who resorts to extreme force and allows himself to be used by his boss, Captain Smith, emerges as the film's hero, its least compromised figure. (Russell Crowe, an actor with an appealing presence whose noir tough guy recalls the macho bravado of 1940s icons like Bogart and Dick Powell, plays Bud.) The adaptation also pulls its punches in the way it handles Ellroy's darkest villain, criminal mastermind Captain Dudley Smith. At the end of the novel, he is still in power; the film kills him off. But the screenwriters find a shrewd substitute for the novel's mordant conclusion. Since the chief of police cannot admit the truth, that one of their own engineered the Nite Owl massacre, Smith is enshrined as a hero killed in the line of fire. Participating in the charade, Exley, who killed Smith and who has been the lone idealist among the cops, has finally learned the rules of the corrupt L.A. game that Ellroy has constructed.

Despite its period setting, the film, like the novel, percolates with contemporary overtones. Captain Smith's successful attempt to place the blame for the Nite Owl massacre on a group of young black men exposes the racism that saturates the police force, the media, and the entire white power structure. Racial antagonism, the power of the media to shape and distort public opinion, a distrust of everyone in a position of power—the film vibrates with up-to-the-minute concerns. A *Chinatown* for the millennium, *L.A. Confidential* is an "imaginary museum" with its eye on contemporary headlines. Like most postmodern artifacts, the film uses reflexivity as a sign of its informed point of view. In a key moment, Exley mistakes the "real" Lana Turner for a hooker cut to look like Lana Turner. His inability to distinguish the original from a copy is a crucial sign of his cultural ignorance. Like the novel, the film places the "reader" in a superior position to Exley, as someone able to identify simulations and, at the same time, alert to the fact that facsimiles are a condition of postmodern life.

Even with its hefty excisions of Ellroy's novel, the film is still more densely plotted than any noir since the famously indecipherable *The Big Sleep* in 1946. The film's epic canvas and its massive indictments (all the characters, to one degree or another, are complicit in the image manipulation and the abuse of power by which the modern metropolis is run) are at heart anti-noir. Unlike *L.A. Confidential*, which exposes too many crimes and has too many characters to keep track of, noir in its truest incarnations is leaner, more sharply focused in narrative and theme. Although it received more rapturous reviews than any noir in either the classic or neo periods, *L.A. Confidential*, like its source,

Two of James Ellroy's compromised cops (Russell Crowe, left, and Guy Pearce), cornered in the frame, in *L. A. Confidential* (1997).

and unlike, say, *The Maltese Falcon* or *Double Indemnity*, is a dangerous and probably unproductive genre model.

Into the maze: James Stewart as an obsessed detective, in Alfred Hitchcock's *Vertigo* (1958), an early film noir *en couleur*.

# Chapter 5

# The Quest: Errands into the Maze

Classic noir yielded a few basic, recurrent narrative patterns: the private eye's investigation of a missing person or a murder; the bourgeois male seduced into crime by a femme fatale; a bourgeois home or safe place invaded by criminals; a caper that misfires; a bystander sucked into a crime scene merely for being in the wrong place at the wrong time. Significantly, in the period right after the "end" of noir, prime examples of these staples were produced. Samuel Fuller's legendary *Naked Kiss* (1964) submits the femme fatale to a startling twist. *Cape Fear* (1962) and *Experiment in Terror* (1962)) are strong examples of the bourgeois fortress invaded. *The Manchurian Candidate* (1962) represents a remarkable variation on the noir patsy. And heists gone wrong are presented with compelling changes in *Odds Against Tomorrow* (1959) and (Fuller again) *Shock Corridor* (1963).

The private-eye investigation, the kind conducted by Sam Spade in *The Maltese Falcon* and by Philip Marlowe in *The Big Sleep*, may be the narrative mold that most readily connotes "noir" in the popular mind. In the classic period, despite their reputations and their familiar iconography, the private-eye stories were rarely the most enticing of noir's offerings. As a narrative lode, *The Maltese Falcon* isn't as rich as *Double Indemnity*. Interestingly, however, some nouveau variations built on the private-eye quest are among the choicest and most influential entries in the postclassic canon. Over neo's four-decades-and-counting trajectory, the private-eye investigation begins with some straight-

forward renderings and then undergoes a number of creative muta-
tions. The quest motif has, in fact, proven to be the most elastic of
noir's narrative pedigrees, the one most receptive to postmodern in-
scriptions in tone, plotting, and visual design.

At the end of *The Maltese Falcon*, Sam Spade announces, in Dashiell
Hammett's beautifully cadenced prose, "If your partner is killed . . .
you do something about it." The private eyes created by the original
hardboiled writers walked down the mean streets of the noir city guided
by a knightly code. Following their own personal sense of morality, they
remained ethically distinct from the people they interviewed, as well as
from the ones they were hired to find. As the form has evolved in the
nouveau era, the hunter can no longer be distinguished from his quarry
simply as a matter of course.

Silver and Ward cite *Harper* as the inaugural neo-noir, a designation I contest. Except for the novelty of a private eye's search filmed in
color (burgundy and hot pink predominate) and wide screen, the film
is strictly retro, a by-the-numbers account of a narrative type no longer,

Paul Newman as a traditional private eye, charging to work, in *Harper* (1966), a revival of a
classic-era prototype.

in 1966, in active use in mainstream American filmmaking. Based on a series character created by Ross Macdonald, *Harper* (played by Paul Newman) is an old-fashioned detective, a sexy loner with a busy inner life of the kind embodied most typically by Humphrey Bogart in the 1940s. The contemporary 1960s décor and music and Newman's time-lessly cool style camouflage the material's noir-revival flavor. *Harper* is efficient entertainment, a hit at the time that, if nothing else, proved a no-frills private-eye story was still doable. The film in fact is strongest when it takes a business-as-usual approach, as in the deadpan opening sequence of Harper performing his morning rituals. Except for Mike Hammer (Ralph Meeker) in *Kiss Me Deadly*, private eyes are slobs who camp out in shabby rented rooms. Harper inhabits one of the grimi-est. Awakened by a ringing phone and badly hung over, he accepts an assignment, then proceeds to make himself some very bad coffee, all the while shielding his eyes from the light that seeps through the vene-tian blinds.

He is summoned by a rich, acid-tongued woman (Lauren Bacall, evoking shades of 1940s noir), who reports the disappearance of her hated husband. "Water seeks its own level," she announces, "which means my husband would be at home in a sewer." "You were hired by a bitch to find scum," the district attorney tells his friend Harper, nicely summing up the plot. As he conducts his search for the missing mo-gul, Harper encounters an assortment of kooky, morally contaminated characters pretending to be who they are not. Among them are a jazz singer-junkie, a religious charlatan, and an overweight former starlet. The bitch that hired Harper turns out to be the one character who's on the level, while the sardonic district attorney is the most masked. He's the culprit, who killed for a kiss. Paul Newman plays Harper in a brisk, no-nonsense style that matches Jack Smight's direction. The detective's job has left him jaded. "The bottom is loaded with nice people; only cream and bastards rise," he observes in one of his philosophical asides. Even so, he's a conscientious professional sleuth eager to give good value for his salary and still able to believe in a world where evil can be overcome. "I'm going to crack this thing, I swear to you," he promises. He's so devoted to his job, in fact, that his wife has evicted him and wants a divorce.

In 1975 Paul Newman reprised Harper in *The Drowning Pool*. Sum-moned once again into a world of weirdos with secrets—this time the

Although he plays the title character, a private investigator, Donald Sutherland is not the focus of *Klute* (1971), as these two stills attest. Directing his gaze at a prostitute, Bree (Jane Fonda), Klute helps to center our attention where it belongs.

dramatis personae are viperous Southern gentry—Harper has his first interview in an intimidating mansion presided over by a sexual neurotic (Joanne Woodward, oozing Southern Gothic menace). Plunging into forbidden territory, Harper is knocked out, tied up, and hosed down, the standard occupational hazards for the physically vulnerable private eye, and he has to endure numerous women who hurl themselves at him. Following a genre code, however, the detective resists all emotional entanglements that last longer than a night. At the end, as at the beginning, he's on his own. "Harper, you're not such a tough guy," one of the women who wants him to stay around says to him. But Harper won't be pinned down; and on the way to catch a plane to take him out of the infested Southern waters in which he's been swimming,

he lifts his hand to her in a gallant salute, an Apollo acknowledging a devotee.

This routine thriller, capped by Newman's predictably stolid private eye, would seem to suggest the end of the line for the quest formula. Yet in the 1970s, three private-eye dramas—*Klute* (1971), *Chinatown* (1974), and *Night Moves* (1975)—significantly expanded the genre's possibilities in tone, characterization, and thematic reach. Each is a neo-noir landmark.

A detective descends into the noir city's sexual underground to track the disappearance of a friend: the start-up premise of *Klute* conforms without a ripple to the conventional terms of the private-eye quest narrative. The fact that Klute, the detective, and his missing friend are out-of-towners wide-eyed in Babylon underlines the film's view of the city (New York) as both corrupt and corrupting. True to the rules of the game, the audience knows what Klute knows, sifting clues along with the character, and the mystery isn't solved until the end. Also typical is that the story is littered with red herrings. Along with Klute, we are led to suspect that the absent friend, who has led a double life, is guilty of murdering a prostitute and is obsessed with another hooker, Bree. But the missing man turns out to be a victim rather than a killer. With its loops and detours, the quest plot does nothing to disturb genre convention, and Klute (as played by Donald Sutherland) is a dull hero. Lacking the acrid humor of a Lew Harper, Klute is a matte character who regards the world of sex for sale with puritanical disapproval. A minimalist, Sutherland performs with a fixed, opaque expression that occasionally breaks to reveal the character's simmering sexuality. Despite the fact that the film is named for him, Klute isn't the central figure. Rather, the mystery plot evolves into a character study of Bree, the woman Klute is trying to find. Bree (Jane Fonda) becomes the focus, and her feelings about her role as an object of desire for repressed suburbanites are far more compelling than solving the crime.

Rethinking noir's usual representation of the femme fatale, the film offers a fresh twist: it depicts the way a woman views her own sexual allure. It is as if, for the first time, the character assigned the femme fatale role is allowed to speak for herself and so to break free of the male anxiety through which she had traditionally been perceived. The mask of the fatal woman, the woman whose sexuality is deadly to the men who desire and are entrapped by her, is pierced to reveal her own awareness of how and why she exploits her looks. At times we are permitted to see Bree up close, from her own perspective. During a quickie with a commuter, we see how she performs a sexual masquerade, faking orgasmic cries as, behind her john's back, she glances at her watch. In sessions with her analyst, she confronts her need to turn tricks as she examines her own complicity in presenting herself as a sexual object. And we see her "offstage," alone in her apartment, reading, a rare glimpse in a mainstream movie of a woman in her private space.

Alternating with the shots of Bree unmasked are the countershots in which she becomes the focus of the camera's or a character's voyeuristic gaze. When she goes on modeling auditions, prospective employers evaluate her like a consumable, disposable item. And in a recurrent point-of-view shot, Bree is spied on by an unidentified stalker whose obsessive watching radiates a fetishistic and criminal aura even before he is revealed as a killer. In a daring move, the film equates the voyeur's murderous gaze with the "look" of the camera itself. The stalker has a tape, which he compulsively replays, of Bree speaking on the phone; like her image and her body, Bree's voice has also been appropriated, "stolen" from its owner.

Some feminist critics have claimed *Klute* (despite its misleading patriarchal title) as a key text, one that challenges the historically male preserve of the private-eye story. For all the ways in which it rewrites gender codes—Bree is a sexual woman who is also innocent, a genre rarity—ultimately, however, the film does not resist the pull of masculine dominance. For all her strength and self-awareness, Bree finally needs a man to save her; in the climax, as she confronts the stalker, Klute is the male cavalry come to rescue the damsel in distress. And in the last scene, her apartment stripped, Bree is about to depart the wicked city to start a clean new suburban life with her heroic rescuer, the somnolent detective. When the phone rings with a job offer, she says she's going to be gone for a while.

In the traditional private-eye stories, professional sleuthing solves all mysteries and restores at least an illusion of moral order to a fallen world. No matter how devious the detective's adversaries may be, or how infested the noir world into which he must descend, a Philip Marlowe, a Sam Spade, a Lew Harper, or a John Klute proves equal to the challenge. With a prizewinning screenplay by Robert Towne, Roman Polanski's *Chinatown*, a period noir set in Los Angeles in the 1930s, reverses genre convention with a private eye unable to control the crimes his detective work unveils. Unlike the usual investigator with his trademark fedora and trench coat, Jake Gittes dresses nattily in spanking white suits and spats and, as embodied by a smiling Jack Nicholson, enters the film with the air of a confident movie star. Like practically everything else in *Chinatown*, appearances are deceiving.

Jake is nonetheless true to his profession in many ways. A shrewd observer, he looks at photographs with scientific scrutiny; he is a superior snoop, peering through windows; he's suspicious of appearances, casting a skeptical glance at the veiled woman who initially hires him; he asks probing questions; and he even solves the crime. But for all his professional expertise, he cannot accomplish what private eyes had always been able to do before: he fails to protect a woman who desperately needs him, and he watches helplessly as the criminal remains at large. As savior and restorer of a moral order, he's a complete washout, a genre first. On his errands into the noir maze, it's traditional for the private eye to be beaten up, knocked out, bruised, and assaulted in ritualistic set pieces that carry sadomasochistic overtones. But even here, Jake Gittes's fate is singular: early in the film, his nose is cut; and for the rest of the story, as a continual reminder of his emasculation, he

In *Chinatown* (1974), the unheroic bandaged nose of detective Gittes (Jack Nicholson) foreshadows his inability to provide a happy ending for a client.

wears a decidedly unheroic bandage.

Gittes's nemesis, Noah Cross (played by a reptilian, terminally obnoxious John Huston), is a patriarch of biblical potency, a Faustian overreacher who survives. The secret that Gittes uncovers is that Cross has fathered a daughter by his own daughter. In the showdown, Cross kills his daughter, the veiled woman who hired Gittes, and runs off with the daughter, who is also his granddaughter, as Gittes is reduced to the role of a speechless bystander. Instead of remaining after the wreckage to make some summarizing pronouncements, the dazed and defeated detective is hustled offstage by a cop who urges him to go home. "This is Chinatown," the police officer says; and in the film's politically incorrect symbolism, "Chinatown" represents both infernally bad luck and masquerade. In the past, in Chinatown, when Jake was a cop, he "tried to keep someone from being hurt and . . . ended up making sure she *was* hurt," a preview of his inability to save Noah's daughter. Chinatown, a place where "you can't always tell what's going on," a place that "bothers everyone who works there," is, finally, the place where the crime story unravels entirely against the detective's wishes and intentions. In Chinatown, the investigator's emasculation is completed.

The film also challenges genre boundaries in the kind of crimes the detective's search uncovers. It is standard for the private eye's quest to be played out within a limited sphere, a hunt for a missing object or person. Here, Gittes's investigation into what at first he assumes to be a purely private matter spirals into public issues. In his obsession for power, Noah Cross has conspired with a gang of robber barons to gain control of the Los Angeles water supply. His capitalistic and sexual exploitations run hand in glove, and Noah "owns" Los Angeles almost to the same degree that he possesses his hapless daughters. Cross and his corrupt power brokers, entering a vast conspiracy to deceive the public and enrich themselves, evoked images for viewers in 1974 of the Watergate scandal, as did the film's paranoid, cynical attitude toward all figures of authority. On a more personal level, Jake's failure to rescue Noah's daughters has been interpreted as a metaphor of Polanski's inability to save his pregnant wife, Sharon Tate, from the Manson "family" and his mother from the Nazis. In this autobiographical reading, Noah Cross would be a combination of Charles Manson and Adolf Hitler, who unlike the real-life monsters, endures.

If the crimes in *Chinatown* are identified but ultimately uncontainable, the mystery in *Night Moves* proves to be impenetrable. "I haven't solved anything," the private eye, Harry Moseby, announces. As in *Chinatown*, the investigator's quest forces him to confront his own limitations, and like Gittes, Harry exits the story with a physical wound

Harry (Gene Hackman) in *Night Moves* (1975) is a burnt-out case, and another neo-noir detective outwitted by a crime scene he cannot control or solve.

that marks his emasculation. Shot in the leg, he pounds his foot angrily on the deck of a boat that spins dizzily in circles as the film ends in narrative chaos. As the film's director, Arthur Penn, claims, "*Night Moves* is anti-genre."

Hired by an ex-actress to find her missing daughter, Harry tracks the young woman to Florida and retrieves her from her stepfather. When she is later killed, Harry returns to Florida, where he discovers that on his first investigation he had misread almost all the clues. In act two, the case slips from Harry's control as the body count escalates. *Night*

*Moves* suggests that, in post-Watergate America, solving crimes is problematic. Stumped by his case, Harry is a new kind of detective, far more neurotic than the sleuths of the classic era. Like other postclassic private eyes, Harry expresses disdain for his profession; and indeed, after act one, when he returns the missing girl to her unloving mother, he retires, reentering the case only after the girl's sudden, mysterious death. A loner who plays chess with himself, Harry is a compulsive clue seeker and a voyeur both on the job and off. Tracking quarry becomes for him an inescapable way of life—he conducts a massive search for his long-lost father; and when he finds him, a lonely old man in a rooming house, he observes him without saying a word. When he discovers his wife is having an affair, he repeatedly spies on the couple and seems to experience masochistic pleasure from the spectacle of his wife's betrayal. Unlike Klute or Harper or Gittes, Harry is not merely a disinterested professional but a character who suffers from wounds of his own.

Playing this burned-out case, Gene Hackman projects a kind of weariness that is unusual in an American detective story. For this investigator, detection is a form of self-defense, a way of being that ensures his emotional detachment. His wife tells him he has grown more distant, yet ironically his strained marriage is the only thing he rescues from the rubble. (Harry is also more intellectual than the standard-model sleuth. His comment about the film that his wife and her lover go to see, *My Night at Maud's*, that it is "like watching paint dry," is a bon mot of the sort Philip Marlowe would be unlikely to utter.)

Alert to its genre—"Are you going to hit me, the way Sam Spade would?" asks the boyfriend—the film stops short of being a postmodern send-up. We're expected to take seriously the tangled family romance, aflame with twisted desires, that Harry uncovers, and for the most part the film's visual signature is straightforwardly realist rather than self-consciously noir. Harry's investigation takes place in open, neutral settings that make no attempt to evoke the world of classic noir; for a new kind of noir quest, the film creates a mostly anti-noir visual style.

During the high neo phase of the 1980s and 1990s, the private eye has become a back number. If he appears at all it is likely to be in a period setting, "protected" by a nostalgic framework. In contemporary noir, the kind of investigation usually the province of the private dick is now more likely to be conducted by a cop who becomes tarnished by

Despite the promise of the neon sign, it is the maverick cop (Clint Eastwood) who saves San Francisco from a sniper, in *Dirty Harry* (1971).

the world he must enter to solve or combat a crime. Indeed, for a *policier* to qualify as legitimately noir, the cop must be attracted to or in some way be complicit with the cry of the city at night. If he remains an observer who is innocent of any transgression, the film is a crime movie that has not earned its noir stripes.

*Dirty Harry* (1971), the picture that inaugurated the tainted-cop investigation dramas, is only marginally noir. The title character is a police officer dedicated to terminating a serial killer on the loose in San Francisco. To target his quarry, he must defy his conservative bosses and the political establishment and break the law. Rejecting a system he believes is fairer to criminals than their victims—the psycho sniper has been released because his rights have been violated—Harry, in effect, goes outside legal boundaries to uphold his sense of a higher law. The indignant, crusading policeman embodies both a late 1960s counterculture ideology (he defies authority, here represented as either dead faced or utterly callow) and a right-wing distrust of government, phrased as an incipient vigilantism the film applauds.

Harry Callahan, as enacted by Clint Eastwood, is an unbreakable straight-arrow. Uncontaminated in his search for the psycho, he never goes undercover and remains immune from the after-hours world he must plow through to reach the killer. He spies on his quarry, yet his surveillance, as it might in a genuine neo-noir film, never becomes tinged with an erotic charge, nor does it become obsessive. In later variations on the same narrative pattern, cop and killer become doppelgängers, while here they remain distinct adversaries in a moral allegory of good versus evil. For a quest story that refuses noir ambiguity, Eastwood is exactly the right icon. Neurosis and inner conflict are outside the actor's minimalist range; to express emotion, Eastwood squints, clenches his teeth, or tightens his lantern jaw. At the end, when he tosses his badge after he faces and finally kills the sniper, he remains unfazed. And like its stalwart hero, the film itself believes that evil can be contained; whereas in a typically 1990s crime picture, like *L.A. Confidential*, evil is systemic and no cops operate with Harry's cleanliness. Indeed, from the perspective of later, truly neo cop quests, *Dirty Harry* seems ironically misnamed.

*Serpico* (1973) carries the police-investigation narrative more deeply into noir territory. Like Harry, Serpico is a righteous policeman who must defy the system to uphold the law. Where a mannequin with angular features plays Harry, Serpico is embodied by Al Pacino, an intense Method actor whose wary eyes register the scars of a turbulent inner life. And unlike Harry, Serpico has a noir fate. He's an undercover agent in a double sense: masquerading is a regular part of his job, but once he begins his crusade against widespread police corruption, he begins to hide out from his coworkers as well. The character is visually marked as an outsider. Throughout the film, he is isolated in one-shots; and in group shots, there is usually a significant space between him and his partners. His apartment is a stark, white, open space that becomes progressively cluttered and barred windows transform it into a noir hideout. As Serpico the hunter becomes, or at least begins to feel as if he is himself the hunted, he cowers within imprisoning interiors. In outdoor shots as well, he is hemmed in, dwarfed by a towering bridge in one shot, framed by the city's vertical canyons in others. In a beautifully choreographed scene, his fellow officers surround him as they question him on his loyalty. When they determine that he is not one of them, they break the circle and move away in different directions, abandoning Serpico in a park that has become suddenly and menacingly emptied.

Throughout the film, in classic noir fashion, Serpico is depicted as a marked man. But unlike the truly doomed protagonists of hardcore noir, he is redeemed. At the end, reclining in a hospital bed after he has been shot, and framed against a sterilized white background, he looks washed clean. The elegiac music (typical of director Sidney Lumet's emphatic touch) adds a baptismal aura; Serpico may have to leave the country, but his exposé of police corruption has begun a process of renewal. Quite unlike most police-investigation thrillers of the 1980s and 1990s, *Serpico* believes in the system—it is only rotten individuals that tarnish it—and, in constructing a heroic if neurotic protagonist, the film keeps its distance from noir. Nonetheless, in visual inflection and in Pacino's performance, the film sizzles with intuitions about blurred boundaries between enforcing and breaking the law, which later, more authentically noir *policiers* are to develop.

The crusading cops in *Dirty Harry* and *Serpico* resist the dark worlds their quests uncover. A decade later, the investigating cop has a less certain purchase on his difference from the "other" side. Will Graham (William L. Petersen) in *Manhunter* (1986), a prequel to *The Silence of the Lambs* (1991), is an investigator who tracks serial killers and is a star in

FBI forensics detective Will Graham (William Petersen), obsessed with tracking a killer, plunges into his own dark side, in *Manhunter* (1986).

the field because of his uncanny ability to read psychotics' minds. "The reason you caught me is we're both alike," the infamous Hannibal Lecter tells him. Graham, who nearly "lost it" when he pursued Lecter, is a man on the edge, haunted by demons that are aroused when he pursues killers. Lecter's confession, that he likes to kill because "it makes me feel like God, and once you do what God does often enough you begin to feel like him," stirs up feelings in Graham that he can't fully repress. Directed by Michael Mann in a bombastic style, the film emphasizes spectacle over psychology, treating its tortured protagonist more as a horror-film hero with alarming powers of self-transformation than as a noir victim or as a case study of a man who knows too much. The film's glibness is apparent in the finale, where Graham performs Hollywood heroics in nabbing the killer and then reclaims his place as head of the family. Nonetheless, the theme of the similarity between hunter and hunted is one that a number of later neo-noir quest narratives have drawn on.

In *Heat* (1995), Michael Mann returns to a story of an investigator obsessed with his quarry. A master cop (played in customary overdrive by Al Pacino) pursues a master criminal (played by Robert De Niro, whose intense self-infatuation matches Pacino's). The film sets up the two characters as mirror images. Like the manhunter in the earlier film, Pacino's officer confronts his own dark side as he tries to interpret his criminal adversary. Hunter and quarry have only one face-to-face meeting, in which they confess their mutual admiration—the audience, clearly, is encouraged to read the scene in an extracurricular sense, as two crack actors, famously high-strung about their work, pay fulsome compliments to each other. As in *Manhunter*, however, a promising premise is lightly developed.

The investigators in *Manhunter* and *Heat* struggle to repress the calls from the noir wild that lurk within; but by the 1990s, characters on the hunt typically succumb. The fallen cop has become a neo type, persuasively dramatized in *Internal Affairs* (1990) and *Mulholland Falls* (1996). *Internal Affairs* overturns the standard quest saga by making the police officer himself the subject of surveillance. Unlike Harry, the cop here is truly "dirty," a Machiavelli in blue. Conceived with vaudevillian excess, Dennis Peck (Richard Gere) is a compulsive, conscienceless womanizer with a stake in many scams, an artist of corruption. While the premise plays on the post-Watergate distrust of authority that has become endemic, it also sneakily turns the cop-as-felon figure into a character the audience enjoys. The scale of Peck's treachery and his bravado, embodied in Richard Gere's strutting performance, turn him into an antihero for a jaded era.

Continuing its subversion of genre patterns, the film dethrones the investigator. The usual hero of a quest drama, here the character (played with jaw-clenching intensity by Andy Garcia), in effect, is a spy who uncovers wrongdoing within the police force. Obsessed with his job, Raymond Avila is an unstable, pious hypocrite, and quite unlike his lubricious quarry, sexually dysfunctional. Estranged from his wife, Avila bonds on the job with a humorless, dead-faced lesbian. As this hunter becomes progressively unhinged by the hunt – he's out for blood after Peck seduces his wife – Avila must confront his attraction and similarity to his adversary. Punning on its title, the film becomes an exposé of the hunter's own turbulent internal affairs. The thrill of the chase incites and derails him; and when he ultimately kills his opponent, he cannot, and knows he cannot, claim a victory

Police detectives or hoodlums? The elite team (left to right, Chris Penn, Nick Nolte, Michael Madsen, and Chazz Palminteri) on inspection, in *Mulholland Falls* (1996).

for virtue over vice.

The police investigator guilty of transgressive behavior on the job and in his personal life has become an entrenched neo-noir conceit. In the commercially unsuccessful but symptomatic *Mulholland Falls*, for example, the protagonist (Nick Nolte) is part of a four-man Los Ange-

Walker (Lee Marvin), a persistent hunter, watches one of his quarries (Michael Strong), who thinks he is making a secretive getaway, in *Point Blank* (1967).

les police unit that brazenly takes the law into its own hands. The film opens with the team abducting a gangster from Chicago, new to town, and throwing him to his death from the top of a steep hill. These officers not only behave like criminals, they dress like them too, wearing hats and pinstriped suits that bring to mind the sartorial code of the traditional movie gangster. Two of the squadron are played by actors, Michael Madsen and Chris Penn, known for their roles on the other side of the law; and with his scratchy voice and bruised face, Nick Nolte's Sergeant Hoover could easily pass as a criminal. Unhappily married, Hoover has an affair with a call girl whose death sends him on a quest that uncovers noir in an unusual place.

In the contemporary mode, then, the sleuthing cop is a soiled figure, but because mainstream films rarely erase anointed conventions in toto, he is permitted to solve the crime. Despite his subversion of legal as well as sexual boundaries, Hoover occupies the narrative place of the good guy. And to a certain extent, he is even redeemed (in a male "love" scene in which he cradles his dying partner). The squad breaks up; his wife walks away from him; but as an investigator, he has done his job well. Unlike the outmoded private detective, however, Hoover is on the trail of something much weightier than a precious objet d'art or a misbehaving missing heiress. As Hoover's search leads him to the Atomic Energy Commission working in league with the U.S. Army and the FBI, what is potentially at stake is nothing less than the fate of the earth. Set in the early 1950s, this film, like both *Chinatown* and *L.A. Confidential*, imposes on the past a distrust of authority, a cynicism and take-no-prisoners paranoia born out of the present. A *Chinatown* wannabe, *Mulholland Falls* is a failed second-generation neo-noir picture that, that because of its imitative, absorbent qualities, is a good marker for the state of the investigation story as it has been transfigured since the 1970s. Over the years, the hunter has become steadily more tarnished by his descents into noir, while the crimes he uncovers have grown exponentially vaster.

Inviting variation and "play," the two coefficients of the quest narrative—the investigator and the world he must enter to solve the mystery—are wonderfully elastic. In the course of neo-noir over the past four decades, both elements have undergone significant migrations. I now look at four landmark neo-noir films that rewrote genre formulas in ways that have been widely, though rarely successfully, imitated. Cov-

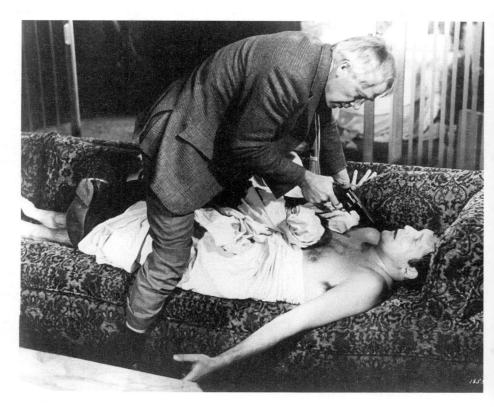

Violence with a hint of homoeroticism in *Point Blank* (1967), as Walker (Lee Marvin) confronts Mal (John Vernon), a former partner who stole his money and his wife.

ering a nineteen-year span, from 1967 to 1986, the movies demonstrate the versatility in theme and visual design that has helped to keep noir in business. Instead of private detectives or cops, a hard-core criminal (in *Point Blank* [1967]), a neurotic surveillance expert (in *The Conversation* [1974]), a slick journalist (in *The Parallax View* [1974]), and a sexually curious postadolescent (in *Blue Velvet* [1986]) perform the work of tracking and interpreting clues. The kinds of foul play these neo-noir investigators uncover are also new to the genre, in varying ways both more intimidating and more amorphous than the crime scenes the original private eyes were likely to confront.

Based on a novel by Donald E. Westlake (writing under the name Richard Stark) with the unpromising generic title *The Hunter*, the antihero of John Boorman's terrific *Point Blank* is something of a pre-terminator, a masked, stolid avenger of deadly efficiency, a hunter indeed. Lee Marvin's opaque deadpan performance as the hunter recalls the stoniness of the private eyes in classic noir yet contains a sinister edge that sets the character apart from a Sam Spade or Lew Harper. Walker (an apt name for a character whose heavy footsteps sound repeatedly throughout his search) is not a private eye; he does not have a merely professional relationship to a crime he has been hired to investigate. He is a master thief, betrayed by his partners, his employers, and his wife; his hunting strategies therefore are driven by a personal motive. Determined to reclaim the ninety-three thousand dollars that was to have been his share of the take on a heist, he also is eager to avenge himself against his wife and his partner, who ran off together after shooting him. Doubly unmanned, Walker at the start is hurled into a pit of male anxiety. Throughout his quest, he recalls the moment at a party when his accomplice Mal (the name could be male or female) knocked him down and then straddling him seductively whispered, "I need you." For Walker the event, which he replays in his mind over and over, epitomizes the attack that has been committed against his manhood and suffuses his quest with a lingering homoeroticism that the 1967 film only glancingly acknowledges. Rising up from his "grave," Walker with ferocious tenacity tracks those who have wronged him.

Each step of his way, Walker is advised by a mysterious figure, Yost (Keenan Wynn), who seems to be a law-enforcement officer using the hunter's expertise to eliminate the kingpins of the vast Organization that employed Walker. Both chorus and avenging angel, Yost uncannily supplies Walker with the information he needs to continue his pursuit. But in this tricky neo-noir movie, there is no representative of the law; "justice" is worked out from down below, among the sharks; and Yost is revealed at the end to be Fairfax, the head of the Organization, who has been using Walker to kill his associates. Just as the investigator in *Point Blank* is different from his antecedents in classic noir, crime too is conducted on a new basis and in new settings. Crime is now corporate, conducted not in side-street back rooms at night but from nine to five in brightly illuminated steel-and-glass skyscrapers. The top criminals Walker hunts for are men in gray flannel suits, power brokers with their place in a vast pyramid, the Organization that is never clearly defined.

Like most noir detectives deeply committed to the chase, Walker is incapable of intimacy. He begins an affair with his wife's sister, Chris

*Point Blank* (l967) creates a mise-en-scène of constriction in color, wide screen, and the outdoors.

(another name of ambiguous gender) who runs a nightclub called The Movie House, but he is only using her. Sleeping with her he has, in a sense, reclaimed his wife. Indeed, as Walker is in bed with Chris, in a subjective montage she turns into her sister, Lynn, as Walker is replaced by his two-timing partner, Mal, the sexual rondelay reflecting the erotic currents washed up by his hunt. In one of Walker's hits, Chris becomes the bait that ensnares Mal; when Walker tries to pay her for her sexual masquerade, in effect treating her like a prostitute, he seems to be enacting revenge against her for the way her sister emasculated him. "Do you know my last name?" Chris asks, as these curiously detached lovers are about to part. "Do you know my first name?" Walker responds, employing the kind of hardboiled repartee that recalls the way characters in classic noir expressed sexual attraction.

Larger than all these local changes is the question the film tauntingly introduces at the beginning. Is Walker's quest all a dream, a wishfulfillment fantasy through which the hunter recaptures his own sense of masculine sufficiency? In the opening sequence, set in Alcatraz, Walker gets up after he has been shot several times and stumbles into the treacherous currents surrounding the prison. In the next shot, resurrected and dressed in a neat blue suit, he is on a tour boat as a guide claims that Alcatraz Island is a place from which escape is impossible. The last scene also casts doubt on the film's realism. It is only in the final moments that Walker discovers Yost's identity and Yost's use of him to rub out his partners. When Yost-Fairfax offers him a job, Walker, who has been lurking in the shadows, seems to drift away, disappearing into the darkness as mysteriously—as magically—as he survived his escape from escape-proof Alcatraz. Seemingly evaporating, he doesn't even come forward to claim the money his boss promised him. Defying logic and probability, the rhymed prologue and coda encase Walker's quest within a dreamlike glaze, an estrangement compounded by the film's final image. After Walker slinks away, the camera pivots from the prison the film has claimed to be Alcatraz and pans to a shot of the real Alcatraz, a visual grace note that informs knowledgeable viewers that they have been fooled.

Not only in the opening and closing sequences but throughout, distortions in time and space and an odd, decorative use of color distance the film from the usual photorealist style of mainstream cinema. Like other films of the so-called New Hollywood of the time, *Point Blank* adapts some of the syntax of European art films of the 1950s and early 1960s. As in the work of Jean-Luc Godard, Alain Resnais, and Federico Fellini, the film treats time and space fluidly and often subjectively. Sound and image sometimes seem to emanate from the hunter's fevered consciousness. In the difficult opening, which clearly announces that the film will not play according to crime-movie convention, scenes of Walker's betrayal and "death" at Alcatraz are chaotically intercut with shots of the earlier party scene in which Mal "seduces" Walker. Out of the time-space jumble, Walker's voiceover emerges to impart a sense of order but then vanishes once the character begins tracking for revenge. Fragments of the prologue are then distributed throughout the action, encoded as Walker's disordered recollection of a double trauma.

The film's overly vivid, limited range of colors, with bright yellows, red, and lime predominating, also underlines the enigmatic status of the action. In a bizarre (though representative) scene in a car lot, colors are strictly limited to blue and white; a customer, with no more than a tangential link to the story, wears a blue dress with white circles. Eerily, wardrobe and décor are rigorously color-coordinated, drenching a quest story in a neo palette of 1960s psychedelia. *Point Blank* was the first neo-noir film in America to use color and the wide screen to conjure an environment of enclosure and displacement. Glass is everywhere, yet all the characters are hiding out, and the vast open spaces of the film's unpopulated, depersonalized mise-en-scène become as ominous as the traditional mise-en-scène of classic noir. On the enlarged, horizontal screen, the characters are often caught in frames within the frame, separated from each other by glass or drapes or windows.

In 1967, near the beginning of the post-noir period, one year after the conservative *Harper*, Boorman's thriller reupholstered a narrative form presumed to be as dead as Walker. A foundational postclassic noir film, neo before the fact, *Point Blank* (paid tribute to by the title of a third-generation, postmodern noir, *Grosse Pointe Blank*) proved decisively that the genre need not be segregated automatically to the retro bin. And the film's narrative "problem," that the quest itself may be a dream, remains one of the most intriguing puzzles in the canon.

Like *Point Blank*, chronologically as well as creatively, Francis Ford Coppola's *The Conversation* is genuine nouveau noir. Harry Caul (Gene Hackman) is a wiretapper, a hot profession in the era of Watergate, who both lives and invites noir. Skulking in shadows as he bugs others, and harboring a paranoid's fear of himself being invaded, on the job and off Harry hides out. He ascends to his loft in a cagelike elevator, and at work in his vast, mostly empty room, which is bathed in a sickly green color, he looks as if he's underwater. On a routine surveillance job (the director of a corporation has hired Harry to wiretap the director's wife and her suspected lover), Harry overhears a troublesome sentence. In the middle of a seemingly bland conversation, as she walks in circles with her supposed lover in a public square, the wife says, "He would kill us if he could." When Harry replays the tape over and over (repetition and going in circles are endemic to the noir world the film sets up), the "us" seems to him to become increasingly emphasized. Despite warnings from a representative of the corporation not to get involved, Harry takes on the role of an investigator driven to decipher the mystery he is convinced is enfolded in the conversation.

Harry is a pious, guilt-ridden Catholic who confesses his sins. He claims he is pursuing the case to atone for the murder that resulted from his noninterference on an earlier job. But his motives are not humanitarian. He is afflicted rather with the hermeneut's compulsion to find out, to see and to hear what is obscured or forbidden. Like other neo-noir investigators, the frenzy of interpretation consumes him. Harry desperately wants to fill in the gaps of the narrative he has wiretapped, to master and even in a sense to ingest a text that remains maddeningly elusive. At the climax, as he hides out in a motel room adjacent to the room in which he thinks the conspirators are committing a mur-

Harry Caul (Gene Hackman), surveillance expert, doing what he does compulsively, observing those who can't return his gaze, in *The Conversation* (1974).

der, he frantically plants listening devices on the bathroom wall in order to penetrate the other space to which he can never gain complete access.

The other scene, the inner story Harry thinks he has discovered, is presented cryptically. We never know more than Harry does. The murder scene is especially problematic. Is it being presented as imagined by the investigator, crouched against the wall in the adjoining room, a product of his escalating delusions, or did the scene "really" happen? We never get an unobstructed view of the crime, and the sound is either blurred or suppressed. However partial our access remains, we know enough by this point to realize that Harry has misread the story. It is the wife, her lover, and a top corporation executive, not the director, who have hired him. The "conversation" he was hired to wiretap was a masquerade, a pretext to lure the director to the motel room where the lovers kill him and afterward announce his death in a car accident as they prepare to inherit his wealth and power.

But in this truly new noir, it isn't the mystery, framed as the "other" text, that is the focus; it is the investigator himself. The mystery plot exists only to mirror and to reinforce Harry's noir vision of the world and of his place in it. His distrust of others is so deep that he plays saxophone with a recorded band. He is so secretive with his girlfriend that she asks him not to stop by anymore. When a coworker asks too many questions, Harry explodes. Investigating the "conversation," he is deceived by the conspirators, and he is himself bugged. "We know you know and we will watch you," the executive in league with the lovers hisses at him over the phone. Fully convinced that the world is as dark as he has always assumed it to be, Harry dismantles his apartment to strip it of any possible bugs. Observant Catholic to the end, the last object he breaks is a plaster Virgin Mary. Alone, he plays his sax in the eerie blue-green light that has permeated the film. The repetitive, rotating camera movement of the last shot, which echoes Harry's encircling surveillance of the conversation at the beginning, underscores his utter isolation. Watched from without by the all-seeing Organization, he is also trapped from within by the coils of his unraveling psyche.

Like *Point Blank*, *The Conversation* locates noir within a seemingly omnipotent corporation operating out of impersonal glass-and-steel high-rises. Each time Harry approaches headquarters, on a long bridge with high enclosures, he seems to be entering the jaws of hell. But if its use of architecture recalls the earlier picture, *The Conversation* is distinctly a noir for the mid-1970s—a Watergate noir. An anxious citizen reacting to conspiracy at the highest levels of power, Harry is a post-Watergate paranoid. And in his compulsive taping of others to uncover evidence of conspiracy, he also has Nixonian overtones. With its palace coups, its manipulation of the media, its cover-ups and counterplots, the unnamed corporation can be read as a metonymy for a remote and shadily operated federal government.

*The Parallax View* (also 1974) is even more expressly a topical noir in which the investigation motif is entwined with two national traumas, the Kennedy assassination and Watergate. When eyewitnesses to the assassination of a senator are killed one by one, Joe Frady, a macho maverick reporter (Warren Beatty) becomes convinced that the culprit was not a lone crackpot, as an official investigation panel claims. He asks his editor to print his obituary and goes undercover to pursue his

Noir triumphs in *The Parallax View* (1974), a Watergate-era thriller, as an undercover journalist (Warren Beatty) is about to confront an emissary of doom.

hunches. When the trail leads him to Parallax, a company that recruits and trains assassins, he applies and, answering the questions as a homicidal maniac would, he's hired. As he assumes a new identity, the star reporter is placed and photographed like a paranoid noir misfit. He cowers in darkened rooms, his face half hidden by shadows, the space around him pierced by diagonally placed beams and staircases. His hunt uncovers a conspiracy that stretches from a sheriff in a small mountain community to the nefarious Parallax Corporation to government commissions. The ultimate source of power, crouching vigilantly offstage, remains unseen.

With Warren Beatty as the intrepid hunter, exposure and ultimate triumph would seem to be preordained. In the thick of Watergate America, however, movie-star heroics and a sexually secure hero do not ensure victory; it is the film's clever trick to cast a winner like Beatty as a noir loser for whom, finally, there is no way out. Outsmarted by dead-faced executives in Brooks Brothers gear, fronting for a corporation with uncontainable power, the hero is executed. It isn't the hunter who, as in the traditional private-eye story, has the honor of the last word, it's a faceless government commission concealing the truth from the public. The film ends as it began, with a government agency squelching rumors of conspiracy. A bland spokesperson, in a voice that admits no challenge, announces that Frady, a solitary psycho, is responsible for the assassination of another senator. As the camera pulls back, the members of the commission, suspended in a surrounding pitch-black darkness, sit in perfect symmetry, an image that attains an almost abstract representation of monolithic, unapproachable government authority.

Alan J. Pakula's film doesn't try for the revisionist style of the three other neo investigation dramas I have bracketed it with, but its view of a hero embattled with a massive conspiracy is a prime example of noir's absorbency, its ability to react to changes in the Zeitgeist. The film is a potent example of how noir devises nightmarish narratives out of contemporary social anxieties. "Underwritten," in a sense, by the national catastrophe of Watergate, *The Parallax View* is a slick left-wing fable denouncing a corrupt government that has seized unlimited power. This story of a failed investigation is set not against the city at night of classic noir but in cavernous, intimidating, fascistic spaces, the visual emblem of the Parallax world. Cowering high in the rafters of the monumental convention hall in which he will meet his doom, Joe Frady is dehumanized by architecture that is as incinerating and mazelike as the conspiracy he has uncovered.

*The Conversation* focuses on the investigator rather than on what he investigates; in *Blue Velvet*, the investigator is merely a conduit for the investigated scene. Yet in both films, the mystery at the heart of the traditional noir quest is almost beside the point. The crime scene in *The Conversation* is of use only insofar as it's a catalyst for the protagonist's breakdown; the crime scenes in *Blue Velvet* are of value purely as spectacle, as titillation for the investigator himself, as well as for the audience. As if it is being mocked as a remnant of a passé nar-

In the closet: an amateur sleuth (Kyle MacLachlan) witnesses a scene of sexual degeneracy in David Lynch's fetish-strewn *Blue Velvet* (1986).

rative code, the quest in *Blue Velvet* is something of a put-on, and like *Pulp Fiction*, another cool postmodern neo-noir movie, David Lynch's fantasia is intoxicating, delicious, and meaningless.

The investigation formula in *Blue Velvet* is a pretext for a carnivalesque tour of the director's fascination with the bizarre. In a quest that uncovers nothing for sure, sight is privileged over sense. The film acknowledges its attraction to shimmering surfaces in the hyperreal opening montage, an evocation of a bucolic small town with a picture-perfect blue sky, brilliant red roses, and vivid greenery. This vibrant, orderly world, a new terrain for noir—Edward Hopper mixed with Grandma Moses—rumbles with menacing undertones. "It's going to be a beautiful day, get out your buzz saws," a radio announcer says, setting up all too clearly the contrast between a pretty surface and what's underneath. In a virtuoso movement, as overstated as every other element in the opening, the camera burrows beneath manicured, luminously green shrubbery to discover a war among insects and thereby exposes the rot that lies beneath the enameled surface.

Jeffrey, the straight-arrow, repressed young protagonist, stumbles by chance into an investigative role when he discovers a severed ear, another piece of rot in the picture-perfect community. His search for the ear's owner sends him on a downward journey into his, and the town's, dark side. As this quester-by-chance, Kyle MacLachlan has an appropriately matte style that ensures that the hunter doesn't interfere or compete with the characters and scenes his search leads him to. The investigator is no more than a device, our way into a strange other world. Unlike, say, Harry Caul in *The Conversation* or Walker in *Point Blank*, who charge into their searches fired by paranoia or revenge, Jeffrey is merely passive—he's curious about the ear just because it was there. And as a detached, unformed observer—aroused by the ear, he becomes a voyeur—he can be molded, played with, and ultimately discounted.

In a general sense, Jeffrey's journey into noir constitutes a rite of passage from dim-witted adolescence to sexual awakening. At the beginning, Jeffrey's father collapses when he's watering the lawn and has to be hospitalized; midway through his forays to the other side, Jeffrey waters the lawn, replacing his father. His wanderings take him to the Deep River Apartments, where he encounters another set of "parents." "Mother" is a torch singer, Dorothy Vallens (Isabella Rossellini), whose husband and child have been kidnapped (the severed ear may be her husband's, but it doesn't matter); "father" is a maniacal drug dealer, Frank Booth (Dennis Hopper, aflame with Method intensity). In the film's most infamous scene, a neo-noir set piece unlike any in the classic canon, through a slatted closet door Jeffrey spies on the torch singer and the drug dealer having violent sex. Later, inaugurated into the other side, Jeffrey enacts his own sadomasochistic charade with "mother" Dorothy, mimicking in a milder version her kinky liaison with the whacked-out drug-dealing "daddy" who has a sinister hold over her. And he's taken by the drug dealer to a house of distinctly David Lynch-like weirdos where a fey Dean Stockwell in semi-drag presides.

Turning the tables on the noir quest, Lynch not only rewrites the investigator but also the crime scene, as well as the genre's traditional gender politics. The collusion between the drug dealer's gang and a crooked cop in a bright yellow jacket would be, in a conventional narrative, the focus and limit of Jeffrey's investigation; but in *Blue Velvet*, the crime story is dismantled into fragments that never seem to cohere. The raven-haired torch singer who oversees Jeffrey's sexual baptism occupies the traditional narrative place of the femme fatale; but this time, the siren is distinctly more victim than catalyst. Beneath her sexual masquerade is a conventional woman longing to be reunited with her missing husband and child. Her opposite number is Sandy Williams (Laura Dern), Jeffrey's dippy blonde girlfriend, the daughter of the chief of police; she becomes his assistant as he walks on the wild side yet remains blithely unaware of it. Seated in a car with Jeffrey in front of a church with stained-glass windows and with organ music swelling on the sound track, Sandy makes a sentimental speech about innocent robins. The sheer, staged excess of the scene sets up the good-girl-in-noir as the target of Lynch's ironic disapproval: the character's virtue is hopelessly inadequate in the world that Jeffrey uncovers.

At the end of Jeffrey's search, everything is restored, yet nothing is quite resolved. The hero's father returns from the hospital. Jeffrey is reunited with his still-unknowing girlfriend, although he has betrayed her; and their two families meet to have lunch on a brilliant sunny day. Dorothy is reunited with her son (although her never-seen husband remains absent). All the criminals have been eradicated. Bracketing the search with a visual rhyme, the same sequence of shots as in the opening montage is repeated, and all's right with the world. Yet the supremely ambiguous chief of police, who may have colluded with the drug dealers and the crooked cop, remains at large. And a robin, one of the "innocents," according to Jeffrey's girlfriend, devours a worm outside the kitchen window as Jeffrey's prudish aunt expresses disdain at the same time that she stuffs a hot dog into her mouth. Like the pretty town, the "happy ending" is extremely unstable: the world underneath is there still, palpitating, threatening, minatory, alluring.

*Blue Velvet* replays the noir quest as an Oedipal narrative in which Jeffrey marries his "mother" (has sex with Dorothy) and is responsible for the death of the "daddy" (the drug dealer he replaces in Dorothy's bed). Homage collides with mockery in Lynch's satiric jabs at the character types, settings, and narrative arc of the traditional investigation format. The film is both elegant and haunting, but finally the variations it spins are merely modish. Its simplistic oppositions between surface and underneath, between sunny appearance and dark core, are too facile to carry a genuine or lasting thematic impact. As cued by his hip-sounding but ultimately meaningless title, a fetish object, as well as a cheesy pop tune of the 1950s, Lynch's primary interest is in making a spectacle out of bizarre behavior. Weirdness and sexual transgression are displayed to tickle, please, and in a superficial sense, disturb our vision. *Blue Velvet* is noir conceived as pictures at an exhibition, an approach that already seems dated; and the director's limited palette and apparent addiction to grotesques have catapulted him into obscurity. Like Jeffrey's quest in the film, Lynch's inquiry into noir has led to a dead end.

A postmodern Circe (Sharon Stone as Catherine in *Basic Instinct* [1992]) serenading one of her victims, detective Nick Curran (Michael Douglas).

# Chapter 6

# The Wounds of Desire

Mistaking the woman whose back is turned to him for his new mistress, the man casually inquires, "Do you want to fuck?" "This is a friendly town," the woman, a stranger, answers, turning to face the man with the proposal. A cool 1980s type, with an up-to-the-minute take on sexual politics, she's amused rather than insulted. "It's hot," the characters in *Body Heat* (1981) announce repeatedly, and indeed in this symptomatic neo-noir film about the enticements and perils of lust, the heat is turned up, in dialogue and sexual display. In classic noir, restricted by the decorum that governed all genres, sex was signified indirectly through codes—the screen fading slowly to black after a lingering kiss, for instance, or half-extinguished cigarettes smoldering on an ashtray—the audience understood as surrogates for intercourse. The mechanics of sex remained unspoken, while bodies in sexual communion were something the audience was primed to imagine rather than witness.

Classic noir rested on repression, the characters' as well as the spectators'. Femmes fatales tempted the genre's cloistered males with what they could not and had never been able to get at home: the promise of a raw and liberating sexuality. Sex lit such fires in the bourgeois protagonists of the classic era —the bachelor insurance salesman in *Double Indemnity* "married" to his job and to his father-surrogate boss; the fuddy-duddy professor in *The Woman in the Window*, vulnerable to noir just after he has said goodbye to his straitlaced wife and their son, off on a holiday—precisely because it represented a forbidden realm, a world elsewhere. Issuing their transgressive siren calls, the genre's brigade of treacherous sexual women embodied a bewitching terra incognita.

In a postclassic film noir like *Body Heat*, the protagonist is sexually liberated right from the start. Good times with available women

Men in trouble: his arms crossed and trapped in a low-angle ceiling shot, a shady lawyer, above (William Hurt, in *Body Heat* [1981]), is clearly under the thumb of Matty Walker (Kathleen Turner), an expansive, cigarette-smoking, postfeminist femme fatale; in *Final Analysis* (1992), a psychatrist (Richard Gere) looks more like a prisoner than his jailed temptress (Kim Basinger), shrouded in protective shadow.

seem to be part of his birthright, the way of his world. The film opens with the character in bed with a bimbo. When he gets up to go to the window to look at a building going up in flames, he reveals a naked backside to his partner and to us, and neither the character nor the camera seems to blink. Somewhere in offscreen space, fire engines howl while the frame is suffused with a sensuous pink glow. "It's hot," Ned Racine (William Hurt) says, adding hyperbole to exaggeration. The randy hero, who already knows about sex with strangers, hasn't even encountered the femme fatale.

Why would he need her? To thrive in an atmosphere that is already liberated, the femme fatale would have to be exceptionally clever and her victim exceptionally horny and dim—exactly the way a neo-noir picture like *Body Heat* rewrites the sexual politics of its classic noir story of sex entwined with crime. And in place of the verbal and visual allusiveness of classic noir, the film traffics in voyeuristic display.

"My temperature runs high, around 100 degrees," Matty Walker (Kathleen Turner) boasts moments after she has insinuated herself into Ned's life. "Maybe you need a tune-up; I have the right tool," Ned counters, not wasting time with courtly maneuvers. Ned spies on Matty through the shutters and mullioned windows of her big house as she undresses. Not accustomed to censoring his impulses, Ned, aroused, a bull in heat, crashes through the heavy front door of the massive Spanish colonial house, lunging hungrily for the prize Matty has been tempting him with. "You shouldn't have come, you're going to be disappointed," she warns him, speaking, as she is often to do, with absolute truthfulness. "You shouldn't wear that body," he says, now, as ever, guided by his gonads.

In unflinching, lascivious closeups, the camera travels up and down the actors' bodies. And although they are mere parentheses to the story, prurient peekaboo shots of vigorously entwined torsos recur throughout. "You never quit, you just keep on coming," Ned compliments Matty. Later, noting her apparent insatiability, he tells a friend, "She'll fuck me to death." Sex in *Body Heat* is graphic, casual, and a topic of frank discussion; and in rewiring the sexual dynamics for a contemporary, post-sexual liberation audience, the film inevitably sacrifices the poetic indirection and the palpitating sexual subtext of the best classic-era thrillers. Yet for all its strident touches, the film did confer a contemporary sheen on a narrative pattern from the Golden Age, and *Body Heat* was a hit that began a full-scale neo-noir resurgence.

Set in Florida, in a town apparently without air-conditioning, bodies steam in the killing tropical heat and the burnt-sienna walls in Matty's house perspire in sympathy with the characters. Despite the lumpen literalness with which it acts out the promise contained in its crass title, the film ultimately inscribes extramarital sex within traditional noir parameters, equating it with both crime and death. "Are you trying to kill me?" Matty's ailing, elderly husband asks her following a sexual workout. And as Ned and Matty make love, their entangled bodies are often crisscrossed with premonitory shadows, a time-honored signifier of entrapment and doom. Stained with the puritan streak that underwrote classic noir, "body heat" is not finally heroic; on the contrary, it makes Ned dumb and gullible, and with his neatly trimmed moustache, an emblem of the wounds of his desire, he's a prisoner of his lust.

Because from the start Ned is already sexy, he is also already, in the perhaps not-so-liberated-after-all early 1980s, when promiscuity in the real world would result in a medical catastrophe, a little corrupt. In fact, he is much riper for the noir pickings than the typically corseted males of the 1940s and has far less distance to fall. Ned is a shady lawyer who has already done what Matty has recruited him to do; without the knowledge of a client, he has rewritten a will to benefit unscrupulous heirs. In the film's moral reckoning, Ned's sex drive is part and parcel of his willingness to break the law, and Matty chooses him as her fall guy precisely because she already knows he is corrupted and corruptible.

The film modernizes its femme fatale along with her victim. Grazed by the spirit of a distinctly Hollywood-style feminism, Matty is a new age spider woman with greater agency and initiative than most classic-era predators. In *Scarlet Street* and *The Woman in the Window*, the sirens played by Joan Bennett need a male accomplice (Dan Duryea in both movies), and even Barbara Stanwyck's ultimate hardboiled dame in *Double Indemnity* is crucially dependent on her male prey to carry out her scheme. Matty needs only her powerful will and her body heat. Infernally clever, she has stage-managed the entire scenario: having already chosen Ned, she contrives their first meeting; and each step of the way, through her complicated plan to kill her husband and run off with his money, she remains in full control. Nothing about her is genuine, not even her name, which is really Mary Ann Simpson. "Matty Walker" is the name of her best friend. Matty has constructed her noir plot to realize the goal stated in her high school yearbook (where Ned discovers her true identity), "to be rich on an exotic island."

All along she had planned to have three corpses, those of the real Matty, her husband, and Ned. That she allows Ned to live suggests a momentary pause in her deadly stratagems but doesn't contradict the fact that she has performed her role as femme fatale to obtain the only things she cares about: money and freedom. A character who succeeds by expertly *performing* femininity, Matty is revealed at the end to have conducted a masterful house of games. A contemporary type, writer-director Lawrence Kasdan, less threatened by the specter of a voracious femininity than his classic-era predecessors had been, fairly openly admires his woman-as-con-artist-extraordinaire. As a result, the film treats its cunning female in more overtly contradictory ways than noir dramas have done in the past. Matty is both threat and warning to the unwary male, but she is at the same time a figure whose sheer cleverness as a performer is meant to elicit an approving smile. And unlike her earlier sisters in evil, Matty lives to savor the rewards of her charade. While Ned is in jail, she lies in the sun on her tropical island. Next to her is a partially glimpsed reclining, muscular male torso, the trophy her money has claimed and another mechanism for generating more body heat. Looking offscreen contemplatively as she puts on dark glasses, she doesn't look deliriously happy, but—existentially if not psychologically—she is free. In 1981, punishment does not necessarily either fit or follow the crime, and *Body Heat* presents the phenomenon, novel at the time, of a femme fatale who may be fatal to her male victims but not to herself.

Playing these updated conspirators, Kathleen Turner and William Hurt (who have had disappointing subsequent careers) are resplendent neo-noir icons. Neither is the eye-popping knockout the text demands, but Turner's smoky tone, strutting walk, and hard edge ripple effectively against Hurt's gluelike voice and air of privacy. While they seem sexual equals in a way not permissible in classic noir, ultimately her sexual swagger overtakes his. (Complicit with the newfangled morality of its own time, the film sounds a further contemporary note in supplying Ned with a virtuous black colleague. A choral figure who upholds the law, the black lawyer helplessly observes Ned's fall into a noir abyss.)

As it shrewdly distances itself from classic noir archetypes, the film is suspended in a curious temporal limbo. Not set in the 1940s, it is mum about exactly when it takes place. The ambiguity is a fitting frame for a story that despite revisions retains a retro pull.

*Body Heat* knows classic noir but renders it as distinctly pastiche rather than parody. Like Matty's plot, the film itself, as it quotes from classic noir iconography with ceiling shots, overhead angles, and images of entrapment, is self-consciously staged. Noir is being "performed" by filmmakers who have studied the genre, but this is not a postmodern rewriting that exposes the scaffolding to demolish it. *Body Heat* takes its noir story seriously, and the spectator is implicated in and made desirous of the characters' body heat, not outside or above it. Embellished with contemporary touches, the film is nonetheless a straightforward genre piece that was exactly the right kind of noir for the time—a mocking, wised-up rendition would not have performed the same historical service of ratifying noir's durability.

Matty represented a nouveau kind of femme fatale, a successful schemer who remains free of the entangling narrative loops she weaves. Thirteen years later, the character of Bridget in *The Last Seduction* embodies what is surely the climactic version of this neo-noir castration threat. Hard in the style of a contemporary evil sister, Kathleen Turner performs her dance of death with a certain grace. As Bridget, Linda Fiorentino is pure frontal assault, a male-baiting demon with a coarse, braying voice. "Come on, you eunuchs," she snaps at the men she supervises on her job. "You're an idiot," she berates her husband. Attacking male pride and privilege, this femme fatale is a die-hard capitalist whose conversation is littered with references to making sales. Conceived and performed at a terminally crude level, Bridget's does indeed feel like the "last" seduction, a final turn of the narrative screw for a noir icon.

Although she is accorded greater latitude than the typical classic

The spotlight, and the protagonist's gaze, are fastened on the meanest, toughest fatal woman in neo-noir, Bridget (Linda Fiorentino), the antiheroine of *The Last Seduction* (1994).

femme fatale, Matty in *Body Heat* must still share screen time with a male, and her story, ultimately, is framed as a sideshow attraction within a story of what happens to a man. It is Ned's fate, his missteps, his desire, his defeat, that provide the narrative fulcrum. In *The Last Seduction*, from first to last the spider woman drives the plot, in the process occupying the narrative space traditionally reserved for males. Where Matty is a "screen" observed and interpreted by a male, there is no barrier between the spectator and Bridget: this is entirely her show; and as she lays each of her traps we remain privileged witnesses.

Fleeing with drug money her husband brings home, Bridget moves to another place where, under cover of a new identity she selects a new male victim. She walks into a bar in upstate New York where she sets her stakes, throwing off a scent that attracts exactly the kind of male she needs to launch a new scheme for making dirty money. Her victim is a hick who boasts that he's "hung like a horse." After she opens his pants to see, they have sex outside in an alley behind the bar and again in his van. The new "man" in town, Bridget treats Mike like a sex object, and he's so easily beguiled—he was briefly married to a man in drag, thinking he had married a woman—that he quickly cedes his "masculine" control to her. Bridget, in effect, is the second "man" Mike has misidentified. "You can't stop reminding me that you're bigger than me," he tells her, nailing her compulsion not only to compete with but to conquer, in a sense to replace, men. When she tries to enlist him in a scam to "sell" murder to wives with straying husbands (she calls it "bending the rules, playing with people's heads"), he calls her "sick." But he's also turned on. "You want to live bigger but there's nothing you'd kill for," she taunts him when he begins to falter. "I don't want to be with you enough to be like you," he says.

Nonetheless, she seduces him one last time, in a plot to kill her husband. In this noir fever dream, it's the gullible (though sexually capable) male who has a sense of limits, and he cannot bring himself to carry out the plan. Like Ned Racine in *Body Heat*, however, the male patsy ends up behind bars while his seducer is free to construct other noir narratives with other male victims. In addition to Mike and her husband, Bridget also outwits two detectives her husband has hired, a porcine private eye and a particularly dim black investigator. While driving, she asks him to show her his penis so she can see if the rumors about black men are true. Falling for her appeal to his male vanity, he unzips his pants as she smashes his car into a pole. With her luck, she escapes unharmed and he's killed.

In extricating herself from the trammels of her own labyrinthine B-noir plotting and in her victories over men, she begins to acquire a demonic aura, and the film itself threatens to become a hybrid in which the noir vamp is melded with the horror-movie vampire. Verbally as well as visually, Bridget is presented as an almost supernatural femme fatale, a noir witch. As if voicing, while at the same time attempting to disavow, audience disbelief, Mike says she isn't "human," and her husband seems to have a sixth sense about where she is, as if her scent can cross barriers of space and time. In climactic scenes, lighting from below casts otherworldly shadows onto her face. In her empty white living room, she is sometimes literally bisected by shadows; and as Mike is pulled into her orbit, he is photographed with progressively ominous lighting that seems to have its source in—to emanate from—his succubus.

Like Matty, Bridget is a character who elicits contradictory responses—resentment, fear, admiration, and lust—from spectator and filmmaker alike. We are primed, all at once, to desire, root for, and despise her; and at the end, as she savors her triumphs, leaving town in a limousine, we are placed as her conspirators, enjoying, indeed sharing, her sly smile. The misogynist undercurrent, standard for classic noir stories about femmes fatales, is here so vigorous that it washes up either as camp or as postmodern cynicism, depending on the viewer's predilections. Installing a psychopathic heroine as the star of a primitive theater-of-the-noir-absurd scenario, *The Last Seduction* emanates the kind of noxious odor unknown in classic noir. The only way out of the film's moral quandary is by rationalizing that it's only in a movie that we could root for a monstrous character like Bridget.

John Dahl, directing Steve Barancik's script, is an overrated but knowledgeable contemporary noir-meister whose approach mixes homage with parody. He deploys classic noir insignia, such as high-angle shots and neon signs blinking in a sea of shadows, with the kind of self-consciousness that wraps the film in a faux-retro frame. *The Last Seduction* is a noir replicant.

*Body Heat* re-created a character type familiar from historic noir. Yet the fatal woman was hardly a noir original. The genealogy of the woman whose sexual allure is a threat to her masculine victims can be traced back to the very origins of storytelling. In film, she appears at least as early as a 1915 work called *A Fool There Was*, in which Theda Bara made her debut playing a character designated only as "the Vampire." In *Evil Sisters: The Threat of Female Sexuality and the Cult of Manhood*, Bram Dijkstra describes the climactic scene in which the Vampire kisses the bourgeois hero, an exemplary husband and capitalist and all-around model citizen:

> Audiences saw the vampire woman triumph with what must still be one of the most graphically sexual kisses ever recorded on screen. . . . Clearly there continues to be a direct connection between the lurid, bestial intensity of that single kiss and our own lingering suspicions about the function of human sexuality in a civilized environment. This was not merely the bite of a fantasy vampire. Instead, it was an evocation of sexual intercourse as the deadly attack of a cannibalistic usurper. It showed vividly that to get involved with a sexual woman was equivalent to death itself. . . . Theda Bara's brazen and prolonged depradation of this civilized man's mouth . . . was a violation of more than a dramatic taboo. In depicting a woman's absolute erotic power over a man, this kiss also became a violation of the principles of manhood itself: here was a woman who was, in essence, raping a man.

Noir's femmes fatales continued the vamp's nefarious campaign against masculine structures of order and power. Their sexuality, which has been registered in displays far more graphic than Theda Bara's "brazen and prolonged" kiss, remains threatening, fearsome, indeed potentially annihilating. Despite changes in sexual politics, despite the work that feminism has accomplished in raising awareness about gender, the woman who exudes a potent sexual force still arouses the anxiety of many (male) filmmakers and spectators. To the extent that the femme fatale is an essential part of noir's texture, the genre remains scarred by a politically incorrect substratum. Regardless of the story's point of view—and in the high neo period the evil sister is just as likely to be admired as condemned for her craftiness in subduing prey—the character type is marked by her monstrous threat to a "civilized environment." Indeed, as the genre's dragon ladies have won greater authority than in the classic period, noir has grown correspondingly misogynistic, as well as increasingly fearful about the consequences of sexual indulgence. Produced in a society more liberated than the one to which the original cycle was addressed, neo-noir remains—and is probably destined to remain—a sexually conservative, perhaps even reactionary, genre. Any noir story in which a woman whose wickedness is tied precisely to her sexual power is condemned to the sexual rear guard; for no matter how brazenly the films may depict the woman's sexuality, at heart they are driven by an elemental fear of sex. And as negative depictions of the consequences of sexual straying, the films are designed to maintain the status quo. Beneath the enjoyment with which the viewer is expected to take in the sheer spectacle of the characters' male bashing, these are cautionary fables marked in essence by the label "(male) viewer beware."

From its origins up to the present, noir reflexively represents sex outside marriage as at once enticing and potentially fatal. In the classic era, noir's (extra-marital) sex-equals-death coupling was grounded in the moral conservatism mandated by Hollywood's Production Code; in the age of AIDS, the equation has received a different kind of sanction, and the fate of characters who act out forbidden desires has acquired a ghastly relevance. In real life, as on the noir screen, sex indeed can be a lethal weapon. To date no noir film has directly addressed the medical crisis; to do so would puncture noir's sheen of erotic fantasy. But just as, regarded from a certain remove, 1940s noir reflected the tensions of a country at war, so erotic thrillers of the 1980s and 1990s are metaphors for the dangers of sex in the time of AIDS. A simmering offstage "noise," like World War II in 1940s noir, AIDS is a significant structuring absence. The punishment that dare not name itself, AIDS is a sediment floating in the negative space surrounding noir's galaxy of sexually misbehaving characters. At a time when unsafe sex has caused a global medical crisis, the vamp that drains her (or his) sexual partners of their life's blood has acquired an unexpected contemporary jolt. Rather than retreating into a merely retro or nostalgic limbo, the fatally oversexed woman (or man) has become a disturbingly updated figure.

*Body Heat* set the mold for a contemporary femme fatale that, in a sense, *The Last Seduction* both completed and exhausted. Matty Walker remains neo's exemplary preying mantis, spinning tortuous narrative mazes for an unguarded male. I look now at four key neo variations on the type, three from the high neo period of the early 1990s and one, Samuel Fuller's *Naked Kiss* (1964), from early in the postclassic era, long before neo was an acknowledged entity. In *Romeo Is Bleeding* (1993) and *Shattered* (1991)—the titles define the fates of the male protagonists wounded by their involvement with beckoning women – and in *Final Analysis* (1992), the audience is sutured to the male victim's perspective. Typically, we don't know much more than he does, and it isn't until the finale that each woman's masquerade is fully uncovered.

*Romeo Is Bleeding* is narrated by its debilitated antihero after the story has already been completed. Jack (Gary Oldman) was a cop on the take who played a dangerous double game, delivering mob witnesses to the FBI then revealing their whereabouts to the mob. He was also a lady-killer. Now he is a hermit who hangs out in an isolated diner in the middle of a desert, endlessly ruminating on his downfall. "This is a story of a guy who fell in love with a hole," he narrates in a mournful tone, referring to his past self in the third person. Like many motifs in the film, his statement is double-edged: the hole is the one he dug in his backyard, where he stashed his dirty money, and it is also the one that belongs to, is part of, Mona (Lena Olin), the hit woman he became obsessed with. As he looks through a photo album of his past life, Mona is represented only by her name, written in white on a black background; she is indeed only a hole, an absence, unrepresentable and uncontainable. Glancing up, he sees a phantom Mona framed in

Male masochism: the femme fatale (Lena Olin as a foreign hit woman with almost super-natural skill) chains up her victim, a cop on the take (Gary Oldman) severely punished for both his desire and his greed, in *Romeo Is Bleeding* (1993).

the doorway of the diner. One moment she's there, the next she has disappeared.

The femme fatale is transformed in this grisly nouveau noir into an idea lodged in the mind of her possessed victim. Eluding the male gaze and patriarchal control, she is a mystery woman who over and again escapes from her pursuers, including the mob, the FBI, and Jack, and who ultimately transcends her human form to become a ghostly vision that bedevils her bleeding Romeo. Even in her merely human form, however, Mona is a femme fatale on the verge of transforming into a vampire. Rolling around on a bed in fetishistic underwear, she licks her lips as she leers at Jack. Driving with Jack at the wheel, she wraps her legs around him in a powerful grip. Repeatedly she appears as a vision in Jack's fever dreams; in one dream, dressed for s & m in leather with her breasts exposed, she ties Jack to a bed, takes off one of her arms as she makes loves to him, and then, winking, points a gun at him. Mona embodies desire promised but delayed—she's a siren whose sexuality is nothing but an image, a performance, which she admits near the end when she confesses to Jack that she could never stand him. Even after he fatally shoots her, however, she continues to be both fetish and enigma to her victim.

Having killed the woman who has tried to kill him, Jack is given his freedom and a new identity. But he has been irreversibly unmanned, and all he does with his time is wait, a traditionally feminine role in films, and brood about the woman who "cut" him. At the end, he walks out of the diner into a vast, bright, empty desert—a new noir place of dread—as the camera moves up and away from him. Like the vampire, her victim too dematerializes, erased by his desire.

Mona is a femme fatale who practically breaks the mold. The duplicitous women in *Shattered* and *Final Analysis* provide more localized variations. They run truer to type, bewitching their victims by orchestrating virtuoso masquerades that stamp them as neo rather than classic-era Circes. Both turn out to be other than their victims, or the spectator, assume them to be.

In *Shattered*, the femme fatale (Greta Scacchi), in an unusual twist, hides out through most of the action in the guise of a dutiful wife trying valiantly to help her husband (Tom Berenger) recover from a nearly fatal car accident. The husband is in a double noir bind, having had to undergo extensive plastic surgery on his face and suffering from amnesia. Both characters are playing roles. The amnesia victim is not the husband but the woman's lover; instead of being a sympathetic wife, the woman is a murderer who has taken desperate measures to hold onto her lover, Jack, after she killed her husband and Jack, horrified, refused to run off with her. To keep Jack, she caused him to have the accident. (Only one of the many implausible narrative turns is that, post-accident, the lover's face has been reconstructed to look like the husband's.) In the end, her own ruse having returned to bedevil her, the scheming wife is killed in a car accident while her victim, the lover she has tried to cling to, is reunited with his own identity (although, ghoulishly, he wears the face of the man he betrayed).

The femme fatale here is an unusual example of her type. Masquerading as a loyal wife, she is not visually encoded as a spider woman, and she commits crimes not out of greed or hatred or envy of men, but only to keep her departing lover. It's genuine passion that kindles the femme fatale within her.

With its surgically reconstructed antihero, *Shattered* recalls the classic noir *Dark Passage*. *Final Analysis*, a tale of two sisters, evokes *The Dark Mirror* (1946), in which Olivia de Havilland plays twins, one virtuous, the other irredeemably twisted. In *Final Analysis*, a conventionally cynical nouveau noir, both sisters are con artists who use sex to bait men. A steamy blonde, Heather (Kim Basinger) seduces a therapist (Richard Gere), who in court has used a diminished-capacity argument to help free criminals. She convinces the doctor that she has a drinking problem—after one drink she goes crazy—and therefore she is not responsible when she shoots and kills her abusive, very wealthy husband. Her plan works: the deluded therapist gets her off; but the kicker here is that the femme fatale is outfoxed by her sister, Diana (Uma Thurman), an inmate who conceals her wickedness under the cover of being ill. Contriving Heather's death, the supposedly incapacitated woman continues the family trade. In the last scene, Diana is out on a date with a handsome, presumably wealthy man, informing him of her drinking problem; then facing the camera and out of sight of her intended victim, she drops her mask to reveal a chilling, transfixed gaze. Here is a femme fatale in full control of her performance, manipulating another unsuspecting male.

Although the fatal women in *Shattered* and *Final Analysis* are cleverer than their targets, they are nonetheless reduced to accessories in

A woman with a past, a reformed ex-prostitute (Constance Towers), is expelled from town by a disapproving committee (from left to right: Betty Bronson, Patsy Kelly, Marie Devereux, and Linda Francis), in Samuel Fuller's idiosyncratic *Naked Kiss* (1964).

male melodramas. Only the traduced men are permitted inner lives and have a chance to be redeemed postcoitally. The women remain flat characters, their wickedness simply a narrative given, although— unlike the studio-era dragons—they have not been consumed by their misdeeds. While the remarkably disengaged sex they offer is bad news for their partners, they themselves seem to have escaped unscathed and ready for more.

The depiction of a femme fatale in *The Naked Kiss* early in the "after-noir" period is a forceful reminder of how vast a span neo encompasses. While classic noir is confined within clear-cut borders, neo is dispersed across an expansive and heterogeneous cultural topography. From the vantage of the 1990s, Samuel Fuller's heroine pursues what seems like an antediluvian occupation for a femme fatale—she's a prostitute who, quite unlike the evil sisters of neo, wants to reform. The film opens, unforgettably, with an oblique low-angle shot of the heroine, Kelly (Constance Towers), hitting the camera, a stand-in for the pimp she is attacking, as her wig falls off. Under the titles and facing the camera, Kelly then applies makeup, putting on her feminine mask. Two years later she appears in Grantville, a quiet small town, looking worn but respectable. Selling champagne ("Angel Foam guarantees satisfaction"), her new occupation, she immediately attracts male attention. "Are you giving free samples?" Griff asks Kelly. (Fuller gives his characters deliciously pulpy names.). They recognize each other at once: Griff sees that Kelly is or was in the sex trade, while Kelly spots Griff as a cop. "Why did you buy my merchandise?" she asks later, after they have had sex (for which Griff pays her twenty dollars). "I was thirsty," he says. (The morning after, when she gives herself a hard look in a mirror, Kelly sees "the buck, the bed, and the bottle" for the rest of her life.) He sends her across the river to Candy's whorehouse in a wide-open town that is the moral antithesis to puritan Grantville, but Kelly instead seeks out a pleasant room at Miss Josephine's and goes to work at a hospital for handicapped children. As Mac, a nurse, says, "She came out of the clouds one night without a single reference."

Griff pursues her, foiling her desire to go straight. She begs him to let her redeem herself, to "purify" and exorcise her past, a quest none of the later femmes fatales would even momentarily consider. "Your face might fool a lot of these people, but not your body: your body's your only passport," Griff claims, trying to brand her as a once and future fatale. At the hospital, Kelly warns Buff, a young nurse with a body that underlines Griff's assertion that anatomy is destiny, away from the life: "You'll be sleeping on the skin of a nightmare for the rest of your life. . . . You'll become a social problem, a medical problem and a despicable failure as a woman."

The son of the town's founder falls for Kelly, giving her a chance to elevate her social and financial status. But when she first kisses Grant, an ambiguous expression crosses her face. Later we find out what Kelly knows intuitively, that Grant is a child molester—"the naked kiss" is prostitute lingo for pervert. When she discovers Grant attacking a child, she kills him, is jailed, and then freed after the child speaks up. The people of Grantville gather to pay tribute to her. Yet in the film's stern moral code, a woman with a past is stuck there; and though she has been vindicated, Kelly must leave town, alone, condemned by what she once was. In Fuller's tabloid early neo-noir melodrama, sex carries an aroma that's corrosive, depleting, and fateful; the film endorses Grant's declaration that he wants to marry Kelly because she is one of his kind, a pervert. Because she has a sexy body and has used it—indeed, for all her good works at the hospital, uses it still—Kelly must be punished. A deeply conservative 1950s morality underwrites Fuller's pulp poetry: to maintain "a civilized environment," the femme fatale cannot be redeemed and must be expelled alone into a moral wilderness.

Confounding the historian's predilection for erecting borders, maverick Fuller made a classic noir after the fact. In black and white, shimmering with chiaroscuro, its call girl branded with an ineradicable mark of Cain, *The Naked Kiss* looks as if it *had* been produced in 1954 rather than 1964. It is a noir back number that bristles with the director's pulpy B-movie temperament. By the time the femme fatale was resurrected as a neo icon in *Body Heat,* she was more likely to be a wife than a woman of the night. In the 1980s and 1990s, in fact, the prostitute is more likely to be the heroine of a queasy romantic comedy, such as *Pretty Woman*, than a noir thriller. In 1987, in the phenomenally successful *Fatal Attraction,* the fatale was given a distinctly new spin as a career woman, a dignified, unmarried publishing executive played by severe-looking Glenn Close. Underneath her confident veneer, her ability on the job to hold her own with high-powered men, Alex Forrest is extremely dangerous.

At a New York publishing party, Alex (note the gender ambiguity) meets a happily married Dan (Michael Douglas). "If looks could kill," Dan's partner observes after Alex shoots him a withering gaze. Accounting later to Dan for the deadliness of her look, Alex explains, "I hate it when guys think they can come on like that." The exchange should have been fair warning to Dan. But when his wife and daughter leave town, always a recipe for sexual catastrophe in noir, Dan allows himself a dalliance with Alex. Curiously, she lives in a loft in the meat-market district of the West Village, and when Dan visits her he has to pass through an inferno of fire and smoke set by groups of homeless men. To reach her loft, he has to take an imprisoning, cagelike elevator. Dan wants and needs no more than casual sex, but Alex becomes contaminated by desire. When Dan tries to back off she becomes unhinged. She threatens and then attempts suicide, and she begins to invade Dan's house. By the time she rises up from a bathtub after Dan thinks he has drowned her, Alex seems to have transmogrified from a femme fatale into a horror-movie monster with supernatural powers. Dan's wife, to protect her home and family, shoots the madwoman.

The film's underlying conceit is that a single working woman without a mate is "of course" a sexual hysteric. Alex is fatal, all right, but as much to herself as to her partner. She is less masked, more desperate and vulnerable, and she cracks up in more spectacular ways than classic-era femmes fatales, who typically work their sexual wiles encased in a hardboiled deadpan glaze. And where traditional dragon ladies enter noir already in sexual heat and fatal, Alex becomes deadly only after she is sexually aroused –presumably, if she had kept her mind on her work she could have continued to repress her inner demons. As the character unravels, she is like a cubist version of the old self-contained siren.

At first Dan, who really does leap before he looks, blithely ignoring the cues Alex and her meat-market loft give off, is the woman's partner rather than her victim; their initial "crime" is mutual. Mistakenly operating on the assumption that what's sauce for the goose is also sauce for the gander, he misreads her cool, sexually forthright aura as meaning that she wants what he does, a fling with no strings. But despite the up-to-date window dressing, Alex (as well as the film) conforms to the old-fashioned sexual code in which men treat sex casually while women demand commitment. If a little sex drives Alex insane, releasing the femme fatale lurking beneath her self-possessed career-

Michael Douglas, the quintessential vulnerable male in neo-noir, wounded by desire: above, in *Disclosure* (1994), with Demi Moore as his persecutor; in *Fatal Attraction* (1987), confronting, with his unaware wife (Anne Archer) at his side, a fatal woman (Glenn Close) who, this time, suffers more than her partner from the consequences of unleashed eroticism.

woman drag, it turns Dan, a middle-class family man, into a near murderer. "If you tell my wife, I'll kill you," he warns her, then later crashes into her apartment and tries to choke her to death. He doesn't, because *Fatal Attraction* is a postfeminist, male-backlash noir in which the errant man is ultimately reinstated within the fortress of marriage and the family, and the sexually out-of-control woman is conveniently eliminated. The film validates patriarchy, like most mainstream Hollywood products, and puts the voracious career woman in her "proper" place—as a corpse. In this cautionary drama, marriage is salvation, while sex outside marriage has lethal consequences.

Written by James Dearden, this erotic thriller with especially nasty misogynist curves is noir as a kind of designer porn. It's slick, shallow, predictable, compelling. And as its extraordinary commercial success attests, this antiromance for the age of AIDS tapped into the nation's sexual unconscious.

*Disclosure* (1994), based on a novel by Michael Crichton, is another warning to and vindication of the bourgeois male, this time Tom, a

prominent lawyer in a high-end corporation (Michael Douglas again). Like *Fatal Attraction*, the film rephrases the femme fatale as a denatured professional, a dressed-to-kill career woman who horns in on sanctified male terrain. Without husband or children, with no attachments whatever to spheres traditionally marked as feminine, she is indeed a phallic new woman. Where Alex is truly voracious, however, the career woman here, Meredith, is a sexual pretender, sent by men at the top of the corporate ladder to do the woman's work of seducing a colleague and then claiming she was raped. Despite the fact that he once had an affair with his new coworker, Tom is unwary enough to accept her invitation to come to her office in the evening to celebrate their reunion. The dopey male is thus placed in the role of the woman who cries foul when, with sex sizzling in the air, her date pounces after she accepts an after-hours invitation to his residence or invites him to hers. After the male has been "molested," and so, in his own mind, feminized, he has a dream in which, in the enclosed space of an office elevator, his boss (Donald Sutherland) kisses him. To help him out of his unmanly impasse, he hires a lawyer, a tough, homely woman called Alvarez, who clearly poses no sexual threat or temptation.

As if designed to kindle feminist wrath, the 1994 film subverts the then-hot subject of sexual harassment on the job by confounding statistics and probability to set up a woman as the instigator. The victim is a male chauvinist who pinches his secretary's bottom, a misdemeanor for which he is metaphorically slapped on the wrist—Tom just needs his awareness level raised a little, the film implies, and he'll be all right. (The fact that his secretary is an Asian he is clearly not attracted to is part of the film's racist erasure of Asian sexuality.) But his predator (Demi Moore), like Alex, cannot be let off so lightly; to ensure the perpetuation of masculine dominance, she must be expelled. More ruthless than Tom (one of the guys at work says she used to be a man), Meredith is set up only to be defanged. Working according to a male script, sent by men to discredit Tom, she is really less than meets the eye, a faux femme fatale. When she is disgraced at the end and escorted from the corporate boardroom by the solemn big boss, the audience has been primed to cheer. And since joyless, hardworking Demi Moore plays the character, the film has made it easy to hiss the villain.

*Disclosure* stakes a spurious claim to feminist enlightenment by refusing the scorched male the promotion he wants. The job goes to a woman, an attractive, reassuring, distinctly middle-aged woman who, unlike tough Demi Moore, is truly "womanly" and not sexually threatening. The unguarded protagonist at least gets to keep his job and his family (although his wife, also a lawyer, will have lingering doubts about him), and his misadventure can be read as a yuppie nightmare that almost came to pass. Like *Fatal Attraction*, *Disclosure* issues a warning to middle-class married men who might be thinking of stepping out. While it is nominally critical of men who stray and of the male habit of sexual objectification and allows a "feminine" woman a near-the-top corporate position, its heart is pledged to validating the way things are, with the genders in traditional alignments of power and subservience.

The crimes in *Disclosure* are strictly white collar—there is no murder—yet the film qualifies as full-fledged noir, not only in its appropriation of the femme fatale ensnaring her victim but also in the way it skillfully updates the genre's compositional patterns. Brightly illuminated corporate offices replace the dark city as the site of noir. In this brave new noir world, characters are always on view through the glass partitions that separate offices, while omnipresent computer screens that tell all but also block and "screen" information provide another kind of invasion. Encased in and by technology, the corporate drones are doubly trapped within their workspace. (Technology may threaten the characters but it also provides the smoking gun that rescues the besieged lawyer, as his non-rape is recorded on Meredith's answering machine.) And the film's shrewd use of the Panavision wide screen enforces an oppressive aura, the sense that in this contemporary business empire, as in the noir city of old, there is no privacy and no exit.

Counting on audience familiarity, filmmakers in the later stages of any genre subvert archetypes. As one of the foundational icons of classic noir, the femme fatale, usually so easy to spot, is an especially ripe target for this kind of replay. The leading female characters in *Still of the Night* (1982), *China Moon* (1994), and *Sea of Love* (1989) look and sound like traditional spider women and occupy the narrative place usually reserved for women up to no good, but in the end they are revealed to be innocent. Assaulted by miscues that depend for their full impact on prior knowledge of noir, the audience has been set up.

She smokes; she has bright blonde hair; she makes mysterious entrances and exits; she emerges out of a dark basement elevator; she exudes sexual tension and neurosis; she breaks a figurine on her therapist's desk. The character played by Meryl Streep in *Still of the Night* is clearly marked as a fatal woman. Even her therapist (Roy Scheider), drawn to her against his will and better judgment, thinks she is guilty of having murdered her lover and begins to lie to protect her. But he hovers on the edge of noir for no reason. Although the character is a genuine neurotic, haunted by a trauma identified only in the last act (guilt over her mother's suicide and father's death), she's no femme fatale. Her lover's previous, rejected mistress, is the killer. The heroine is an evil sister in appearance only, and the film, in a sense, is a neo-noir anti-noir planted with red herrings for both the enamored therapist and the spectator.

"You do strange things under a china moon," Kyle, a cop (Ed Harris) says, in a rowboat with Rachel (Madeleine Stowe), a woman he met in a bar. Rachel, with a rich, unfaithful husband, is unstable, sexually enticing, and repeatedly emerges out of shadows and rain. She certainly looks guilty. Out on the lake, at her invitation, the cop strips off his clothes and plunges into the water, beginning a journey into noir that is to terminate with his death. But the woman who beckons Kyle into the water is not an instigator, only a neurotic. It is Kyle's crooked partner who has scripted a scenario of murder for profit and then framed Kyle for the death of the woman's husband. When the apparent femme fatale confesses to the cop that "it all changed" once he entered, that against the script she really fell in love with him, she is speaking the truth. And as she cradles the fatally wounded officer, she shoots the partner who set them up, thereby erasing any trace of the Gorgon that may still cling to her.

In *Sea of Love*, the audience, like the investigating police officer (Al Pacino), is in the position of questioning whether or not the sexy character played by Ellen Barkin is a serial killer who places singles ads and then knifes her dates. Divorced and with a little boy to support, the woman works in a shoe store. She's hungry for male companionship; she has a wild side; and after hours she becomes a sexual outlaw. The cop, married to his job and estranged from his wife, breaks the rules by going out with her, then wavers neurotically in his opinion of her, thinking now she is the killer he has gone undercover to find, now she isn't. But even when he thinks she is the psycho, he has sex with her because for him sleeping with the enemy is an aphrodisiac. Once again the film plays with genre stencils in order to mislead the audience; the shoe clerk may look guilty, but it is her pathologically jealous ex-husband who kills the men she has dated. (In a

Sexual outlaw: a wary and harried New York detective (Al Pacino), in a noir tight spot, in *Sea of Love* (1989).

homoerotically tinged compulsion fetish, he makes his victims mime how they penetrated his ex-wife. Early on, as he seems to "beckon" to the killer, the intense cop lies facedown on an empty bed in the anally receptive position in which the corpses are discovered.) While killing his ex-wife's dates, the husband compulsively plays a 1950s pop tune, "The Sea of Love," thereby linking "love" to death. The equation between Eros and Thanatos insisted on throughout casts a shadow over the conventional happy ending in which the woman and the undercover police officer get together. She may not be a femme fatale, but—like the volatile and erratic investigator—she seems too damaged to be able to swim in a "sea of love" without drowning. The film has made a convincing case that, in the era of AIDS, sex is more likely to lead to death than to romance.

In classic noir, fatal sexuality was traditionally encoded as female, whereas male sexuality, especially if it was contained within the boundaries of marriage, was rarely depicted as poisonous. It became so only when infected by the feminine other summoning her male prey to games of lust. But in neo-noir, instigation is not as tightly gender segregated, and so the homme fatale has become a recurrent character. In these revisions of fatale-ism, attractive men are set up to inspire and to receive the gaze of the camera and of other characters—that sexually appraising gaze formerly reserved for the sexual woman only. Matt Dillon in *A Kiss Before Dying* ([1991], a remake, actually, of an obscure 1956 film with Robert Wagner making trouble for Joanne Woodward), Jeff Bridges in *Jagged Edge* (1985), Rob Lowe in *Masquerade* (1988), and Tom Berenger in *Betrayed* (1988) play tempters whose sexual allure contains potentially fatal traps for the women they arouse.

In *A Kiss Before Dying*, the antihero's villainous sexuality is revealed at the beginning, when we see him push his rich new wife off the roof of a tall building. For the rest of the story, we remain tied to the character, placed so as to enjoy his scheming as sheer spectacle; and even with a tainted male as its focus, the film observes the genre's traditional misogyny—it offers no sympathy for his victim, played impassively by Sean Young. In the other representative hommes fatales narratives, the seducers are seen from a greater distance. Like the wicked women of classic noir, they are presented as objects to be scrutinized and decoded; and along with other characters, we're prodded into wondering, Is he or isn't he? In usurping the narrative and visual space traditionally occupied by women, the homme fatale is a genuinely transgressive figure who casts into sexual shadow the female costars hostage to his appeal. To "repay" him, and to reassert the heterosexual male gaze with which the camera is usually aligned, the films link beefcake to bad news. Like the femme fatale stories, these films betray a fundamental fear of the unleashed libido that their devious protagonists embody.

In *Jagged Edge*, Glenn Close is unflatteringly cast as Teddy (the male name echoes the performer's), a dressed-for-success lawyer, a fatal profession in neo-noir for women who want to enjoy being women. The film takes pains to feminize the character—she has an estranged husband and two cute kids—but there is no doubt that in the game of love Jack Forrester (Jeff Bridges) is the knockout. When Jack enters, flashing a come-hither smile, his blonde hair gleaming, Teddy, like the audience, is—and is supposed to be—dazzled. Because he is so good-looking, she wants to believe him when he claims he is innocent of having killed his very rich wife. And even after she discovers a first crack in his armor—he has had an affair, but hadn't told her because he wanted her to take the case—she continues to take him at his word. Jack is so certain of his sexual power that, when Teddy confronts him with a smoking gun (a typewriter with a faulty *t* that seems to confirm his guilt), he coolly insists on his innocence.

New woman that she is, Teddy faces her client on her own, waiting in her bedroom for his arrival. When he appears, masked and wielding a knife, she whips out a gun and shoots him. The ending rhymes with the film's baroque opening, in which, on a stormy night in a house overlooking a turbulent ocean, an unidentified stalker enters the bedroom of a sleeping woman, takes out a knife, and bestrides her. His knife penetrations are lethal, phallic thrusts into the body of a woman he detests and fears; it is the film's dominant conceit, devised by screenwriter Joe Eszterhas, meister of porno noir, that the homme fatale is, *au fond*, as virulently antisex as his female counterpart.

Attracting the gaze of the camera and of the female characters, Tim (Rob Lowe) in *Masquerade* is an outsider in a wealthy community. His body drenched in golden, tinted lighting, he often appears shirtless and just as often bare-bottomed; and, like many femmes fatales, he conceals his eyes with dark glasses. The heiress (Meg Tilly) who falls for him has given him a red car, which becomes the equivalent of a scandalous dress worn by a femme fatale. From the first, when we catch him sleeping with his boss's wife, the character is clearly guilty until proven innocent. Rob Lowe plays him in a suitably hidden style, refusing to reveal what lurks beneath Tim's glossy façade. As it turns out, the character, unlike the lady-killer in *Jagged Edge*, undergoes a moral reformation. He develops feelings at the eleventh hour for the dim heiress he plots to kill; and in a misguided attempt to rescue her onboard her deceased father's boat, the *Masquerade*, he gets blown to bits. He may have changed, but in the film's traditionally conservative perspective, the character is still too sexy to live, too pretty for his (and our) own good.

Male revenge: an homme fatale (Rob Lowe) seduces an heiress (Meg Tilly), in *Masquerade* (1988).

In this turnabout thriller, the men have all the looks. Tim conspires with a crooked cop (Doug Savant), who is also sexier than their female prey; and the film, in a typical strategy, flirts with and then disavows the homoerotic spark between them. One scene, in which the brawny cop, in his underpants, threatens to send Tim up for murder if he doesn't cooperate, bristles with a different kind of sexual masquerade than the one that is the film's ostensible subject.

In *Betrayed*, the heroine (played by the charmless Debra Winger) performs a role customarily enacted by males: she's an undercover FBI agent. Katie Phillips, taking the name Cathy Weaver, is sent to the Midwest to investigate Gary Simmons (Tom Berenger), suspected of complicity in the murder of a left-wing Jewish radio announcer. To study her subject, Katie masquerades as a farm gal new to the area. The suspect, a widower with two children and a sweet mother, is devastatingly handsome, and at first the cowed agent convinces herself that he is innocent. Conforming to the noir axiom that appearances are indeed deceiving, the film's poisonous sexual male is not a city slicker but a heartland farmer, a family man who lives in a sylvan, ecologically balanced world that contains inner rot. Written by Joe Eszterhas and directed by Constantin Costa-Gavras, master of the international political thriller, the film introduces a spin on the homme fatale, here envisioned as a political rather than sexual crackpot. Gary Simmons is part of a vigilante movement of neo-Nazis whose power reaches into the highest levels of the government; driven by a mission "higher" than lust or greed, he uses his sex appeal to indoctrinate his female victim into sharing a utopian belief in a racially cleansed world.

In classic noir, homosexuality was strictly confined to subtextual currents the audience wasn't really supposed to, and often didn't, notice. Buried or camouflaged, it added to the fund of sexual neurosis that informed most psychological thrillers. Cases in point: the relationship between a publishing executive and his fanatically loyal assistant in *The Big Clock*; the Oedipal tie in *Double Indemnity* between an insurance agent and his puritanical supervisor, who resents the younger man's interest in women. More charged than the protagonists' heterosexual liaisons, these male bonds are never specifically defined as homoerotic. In the studio era, they couldn't be. And when homosexuality was an integral component of the source material, as in Kenneth Fearing's novel *The Big Clock*, or in the novel by Richard Brooks on which *Crossfire* (1947) was based, it was erased and rephrased. The criminal in *Crossfire*, for instance, has been changed from a homosexual to a racist. But a residue of sexual "difference" remains, washing the narratives with an unspecified turbulence.

While homosexuality is no longer a proscribed subject, it is still heavily segregated, and certainly in neo-noir it remains marginalized. Touching on it at all within the context of a psychological or erotic thriller seems to lead to a moral quicksand. If heterosexuality in noir usually is a dirty deal, then, almost reflexively, homosexuality is even more disruptive and dangerous. On virtually every occasion in which homosexuality appears in noir, it has been branded as the narrative's noir element, the source of aberrant, criminal behavior. Written, directed, and for the most part performed by and addressed to a heterosexual audience, *Cruising* offers a prime example of why noir and ho-

An undercover cop (Al Pacino, center) enters noir in an underground gay club scene in the notorious *Cruising* (1980).

mosexuality are a negative match. A tightly wound straight cop (Al Pacino, who else?) goes undercover to track a serial killer preying on gay men. As the officer plays out his masquerade, cruising parks and after-hours bars where compulsive men engage in sexual prowling, he loses a firm hold on his prior identity. He becomes estranged from his girlfriend and seems (like the film itself) to become fascinated by the sexual carnival in which he is immersed. Enacting the role of a hot, cruising gay man acquires disturbing possibilities for the investigator. His new identity begins to "take," and at one point, he goes off with a male partner. As his character contemplates the world of orgiastic revelry his assignment has opened to him, Pacino looks offscreen with dark, soulful gazes.

Lured into a homosexual netherworld, the cop may have killed his neighbor's lover, with whom he has had a bitter quarrel (the film is deliberately ambiguous on this point). And after the case is finished, he may return to "the scene of the crime," the cavernous bar where he repeatedly witnessed Rabelaisian rites. The film leaves open the possibility, then, that the investigator may be both a homosexual and a murderer, which in the film's warped perspective are almost equivalent.

But like the bourgeois antiheroes in classic noir who are goners once they see and are seen by a femme fatale, he is stamped as a fallen figure. Possibly having "turned" gay, he has succumbed to noir.

In the film's primitive Oedipal framework, the serial killer is drawn to and resents other men as a reaction against a withholding father. For both the nominally straight cop and the psychopath, homosexuality replaces the lure of money and of the femme fatale in classic heterosexual noir. It is the inspiration for noir, the summons to the dark side. And furthermore, it is catching: not only is the policeman drawn into its vortex, so at the end is his uninteresting girlfriend, who dons a leather cap and dark glasses, part of the fetishistic costume the s & m players wear, which she discovers in his apartment. Caressing the objects before she puts them on, she too becomes "gay" while, standing at a marked distance from her and evidently stunned by what he has seen and possibly done, the cop one last time looks off into deep, dark offscreen space.

Released in 1980, a year before the AIDS crisis in the U.S. gay population, the film clearly brands homosexuality as a contaminating practice. Confined to underground sex clubs, the dark streets of the meat-market district lined with menacing hooks and cleavers, parks after dark, and video arcades with blinking lights and cacophonous sounds, homosexuality is depicted in the film as an ensemble of chaotic, depersonalizing rituals. As the camera glides slowly past scenes of group sex that look like couplings from paintings by Hieronymus Bosch, the film "enshrines" outlaw sexuality for the curiosity, disapproval, and perhaps covert desire of outsiders. At the time, the film was considered a scandalous spectacle, and both "middle America" and many gay spectators were up in arms; a document of sorts of a gay subculture that since AIDS no longer exists in quite the same way, *Cruising* is still strong stuff. Understandably, gay activist groups protested and a disclaimer stating that the film represents only "a small fraction" of the gay community was an unsatisfactory response. In the absence of other mainstream representations, the film did seem to be presenting a global picture of how gay men express desire.

As if scorched by the example set by *Cruising*, neo-noir films have kept their distance from homosexuality. When it surfaces, like the kiss of the spider woman, it is almost invariably fatal. In *Frisk* (1995), a little-seen independent film made by and primarily for gays, homosexuality is subjected to an equally unenlightened treatment, depicted as the eruptive overflow of sexual desire gone mad. The film's protagonist is Dennis, a young gay man who, like the killer in *Cruising*, murders men after having sex. Mesmerized since he was thirteen by pornographic images of s & m and of young boys who seem to be dead, Dennis is driven by his fatally perverted desire to turn these forbidden images into reality. He moves to San Francisco to carry out his obsession, devoting his life to trying to slake an insatiable need. As it annexes noir to conventions of the slasher film, *Frisk* attempts to present its excremental vision with postmodern neutrality, but this gay ghetto fantasy exudes self-loathing; and while it did not arouse protests from activists, it certainly deserved to.

As in straight pornography, where gay men are rigorously excluded and lesbianism is a fetishized, acceptable aphrodisiac, so in mainstream neo-noir lesbianism, either explicitly named as in *Basic Instinct* (1992) and *Bound* (1996), or not-so-subtextual, as in *Black Widow* (1987), is more admissible than homosexuality. In Bob Rafelson's erotic thriller *Black Widow*, Theresa Russell plays Catherine, the black widow, who marries and kills off three rich husbands. Debra Winger is (again) a federal agent, Alexandra, who tracks her and becomes progressively obsessed. Her boss accuses her of being a workaholic who shows no interest in men, and indeed Alexandra spurns a dinner date from a male coworker so she can spend time studying and pursuing the black widow. As she becomes entwined in the widow's web, the plain-Jane agent acquires a sexual glow. Knowing what the agent wants, the black widow kisses her erotically. Each woman is aware of the other's true identity, as killer and agent, but each is also hip to the other's real sexual interests as well. In alternating, over-the-shoulder shots, the two husky-voiced actresses seem to mirror each other.

Although it remains undeclared, if only partially repressed, lesbianism throughout the film is relatively untainted. The black widow's bisexuality is not identified as the source of her madness, and the formerly drab agent's desire for the sexy killer animates her. In contrast, *Basic Instinct* almost reflexively equates being gay and being evil. The killer, Catherine, is a novelist (played by Sharon Stone) who writes about the murders she commits. Hiding in plain sight —"everybody I know dies"—Catherine conceals nothing and gets away with it. In the film's most notorious scene, a police interrogation, she wears no underwear.

This manipulative heroine, who turns life into best-selling fiction, has a tendency to kill the men she has sex with; after they climax, she stabs her partners with an ice pick, her weapon of choice. Catherine is a polymorphous femme fatale with a look-alike girlfriend, Roxy, with whom she takes dope and who enjoys watching her having sex with men. Sexually liberated and a confident professional, Catherine is also a psycho. Nick, the detective who pursues her (a typecast Michael Douglas), is drawn by her illicit aroma. Her bisexuality turns him on, as does his on-again, off-again suspicion that Catherine may be the serial killer he's looking for. "Let me ask you something, man to man," Nick, a heterosexual male threatened and enticed by lesbianism, chides Catherine's girlfriend, whom he calls Rocky. "Rocky," a tough one to tangle with, later tries to run him down in her car. Both women are killers of men, which the film more or less phrases as a lesbian compulsion; its not-so-repressed subtext is that, of course, lesbians hate men, indeed they kill them every chance they get.

But *Basic Instinct* isn't a serious treatment of lesbianism; it's an adolescent male's version of lesbianism packaged for the voyeuristic gaze of the moviegoing heterosexual male. In the film's titillating view of sex, lesbian coupling is no different from the heterosexual kind: both are packaged to serve and stroke the vicarious pleasure of the male spectator. Written by kinky-sex neo-noir specialist Joe Eszterhas (with Gary L. Goldman) and played by glamorous Sharon Stone, Catherine is indeed a visual spectacle, a figure of both desire and fear—Catherine is alive at the end, undetected and therefore free to continue her assault on men she ensnares.

In *Bound*, two lesbians outwit the Mafia and get away with the money. Gina Gershon plays a plumber who works in the apartment next door to where a femme fatale with a Kewpie-doll voice (Jennifer Tilly) lives with a Mafia thug. The attraction between the women is presented openly, with a kind of directness unusual in American films: on first meeting in an elevator, they give each other deep looks of sexual appraisal. But like *Basic Instinct*, this is lesbianism as fantasized by straight men; the women may be more cunning than their lowlife male opponents, but in the end are as much objects of curiosity as the Mafia goons. When the plumber goes to a lesbian bar, the place appears distinctly illicit, a breeding ground for noir. Addressed to and counting on a liberal, sexually tolerant spectator, the film frames the heroines' sexuality as an alibi for their crime—if we don't root for them, we're branded as homophobic. Pro crime, really, more than it is pro lesbian, *Bound* is revolting.

In classic noir, sexual dalliance invariably led either to death or to post-trauma recuperation within marriage and family. In neo-noir, sexual outsiders and predators sometimes triumph, free to reenact their scenarios of seduction. But for their victims, sex is no less catastrophic than it ever was in the days of the Production Code; and neo-noir films about sexual straying are just as severe as thrillers in the 1940s and 1950s. Sex in noir, now as then, is almost guaranteed to be a raw deal, and for the normally repressed middle-class citizen, a walk on the wild side is a certain invitation to self-destruction. Noir erotic thrillers are thus both therapy and warning. They offer a vicarious release that, in a sense, endorses the value of sexual fantasy—so long as it remains fantasy. Seeing the consequences of what happens when their alter egos on the screen step out of sexual line, presumably spectators will either reform, if they have strayed, or continue to monitor their sexual behavior.

A middle-class businessman (Johnny Depp) traveling with his daughter (Courtney Chase), the moment before noir mischance descends, in *Nick of Time* (1995).

# Chapter 7

# Melodramas of Mischance

In *Scarlet Street*, a mild-mannered cashier and a creature of habit takes a detour on his way home. The decision changes his life. A chance encounter—he witnesses a man attacking a beautiful woman—catapults this innocent and therefore vulnerable character into a noir maelstrom from which he emerges a murderer and a destitute recluse who wanders the city in a deranged state of mind. In *D.O.A.* the protagonist is a truly innocent bystander who is fatally poisoned because he notarizes a letter. This small-town accountant may have his faults—he seems unable to commit in a relationship, and on a business trip to the big city he is tempted by its usual dissipations—but his noir punishment is surreally in excess of his "crimes." A cruelly disinterested god of mischance oversees his descent into noir. In these quintessential classic noir stories, the antiheroes are simply in the wrong place at the wrong time.

Noir's narratives of mischance, in which bourgeois characters are sucked into a criminal undertow, follow two basic formats. In the first, passersby crash into crime scenes through mere happenstance, and the films therefore posit a world in which misfortune can overtake anyone for no reason at all. In the second, and much larger and more varied narrative group, noir assaults characters who seem either to invite or to deserve it. Both kinds of stories force characters to confront a slippery, unstable universe pitted with traps. Moral reckoning in traditional noir had to be exacting, and characters scorched by noir had to pay for their tumbles. The moral uncertainties of postmodern noir sometimes allow fallen characters to outwit the odds and to live to savor the fruits of their crimes, a circumstance that reflects the sheer, absurd randomness that has always lurked at the heart of noir.

The first kind of representative mischance films I want to examine are the ones built on the pattern of a bourgeois house invaded. I use "house" literally, as well as figuratively, to connote a protected world of moral order. In the original version of *The Desperate Hours*, the family whose house is overtaken by escaped convicts embodies an idealized, all-American high-mindedness. The stern father, the poised, dignified mother, and their two children, one of each gender, all know their place in the national chain of being. In the early 1960s, near the beginning of the post-noir period, and intermittently from the mid-1980s, a number of noir stories have followed the archetypal scenario of *The Desperate Hours* in which innocent characters are challenged but not significantly bruised by their brush with noir invasions. Although the tone inevitably shifts—the staunch uprightness of the invaded family in the 1955 *Desperate Hours* is no longer playable unless it is tempered with irony—the stories rest on a remarkably similar set of distinct oppositions between innocence and guilt, bourgeois propriety and criminal transgression. The invaded-house narratives may be the purest, as well as the most simplistic, of noir molds, illustrating the axiom that virtue is no prophylactic against noir, because in a fickle, indifferent universe, terrible things can happen to perfectly good people.

*Experiment in Terror* (1962) preserves a clear-cut moral distinction between villain and victim that was rare in classic noir and virtually eradicated in the nouveau period. The heroine is, pure and simple, a lady in distress. She's a bank teller stalked by a criminal who wants one hundred thousand dollars from the bank; and to persuade her to help him in his quest, he has kidnapped her sister. The FBI agents called onto the case are straight-arrows who, recalling the decorum of the studio era, dress in jacket and tie at all times and speak in a language pruned of any profanity. The stalker is an embodiment of abstract menace, whose only defining trait is that he is asthmatic. In this entertaining bare-bones noir, there is no transference of guilt, no resemblance whatever between the heroine and the noir situation that overtakes her.

As the woman in a tight spot, Lee Remick is imperturbably wholesome. Entering her garage at the end of a typically normal day—she

There's trouble just offscreen for an innocent bank teller (Lee Remick) in *Experiment in Terror* (1962).

commutes to her city job from her house in a pleasant suburb presumably safe from noir—she is accosted by the desperate villain, encased in shadow. The experiment in terror begins right away, transforming the heroine's bright, familiar world. Once her suburban haven is invaded, everyday places and things acquire a noir-like sheen. A striped coat the besieged heroine wears begins to seem like a prison uniform. Menacing shadows appear on walls and ceilings, augmented by the sinister wheezes that signify the stalker's mostly offscreen presence. Directed by Blake Edwards and strikingly photographed by Philip Lathrop, this elemental, skeletal post-noir noir, stripped of psychological resonance or ambiguity, is in essence an homage to the iconography of the then recently "deceased" classic noir style.

The original *Cape Fear* that same year—a family stalked by a convict—also adheres to an old-fashioned division between straight and crooked characters. *The Manchurian Candidate* (also 1962), in contrast, provides one of the canon's most unusual variations on the fate of an innocent bystander. If *Experiment in Terror* harnesses noir to a horror-film scenario, *The Manchurian Candidate* cuts noir to the demands of a political thriller. Recalling the maladjusted soldiers in classic noir who return home from the war as sitting targets for noir misfortune, the victim here is a shell-shocked Korean War vet brainwashed into becoming a presidential assassin. The vet is thrown into the narrative space of a noir antihero whose masculinity has been fatally attacked, and Laurence Harvey plays the character in a high 1940s deadpan style. Where noir protagonists were traditionally dazed by the events that overtake them, the vet is quite literally a zombie, unmanned not by a ravenous femme fatale but by his mother (a deliciously wicked Angela Lansbury). The wife of the vice president and in league with Communists on a plan to take control of America, this maternal Gorgon harbors an incestuous attachment to her son yet, at the same time, is willing to sacrifice him to achieve her mad dream of political conquest. Deprogrammed at the last minute by a fellow soldier, the tainted victim shoots his mother and stepfather before killing himself.

The notorious film (which in retrospect seems to have anticipated the circumstances of the Kennedy assassination) grafts a fable of Cold War paranoia onto the noir paradigm of a vulnerable male undermined by female treachery. While *Experiment in Terror* may be too bare to qualify as full-scale noir, *The Manchurian Candidate* might be too thematically overloaded. At the crux of both films, however, is the essential noir theme of innocent characters inscribed within noir scenarios. And in both films, a victim and a stalker are figures placed against a specifically noir ground. *The Manchurian Candidate*'s occasional canted angles and low-angle ceiling shots, the shadows that engulf the dragon lady and her innocent prey and mark them as characters caught in a noir web, pay tribute to classic noir. Typical for the house-invaded noir, both *Experiment in Terror* and *The Manchurian Candidate* end with the restoration of the status quo: the bank teller is saved from her stalker; the country is spared the unimaginable traumas of an assassination and a Communist government spearheaded by a woman.

In the early 1960s, a basic victim-of-noir story like *Experiment in Terror* was safe from postmodern irony. The film's A-list director, Blake Edwards, "reads" the B-movie scenario strictly for its tidy plot. Two decades later, Edwards's brisk, straightforward approach to formulaic material seemed no longer possible; cases in point, three films by major directors with a similar invasion premise: *The Morning After* (1986), directed by Sidney Lumet; Ridley Scott's *Someone to Watch Over Me* (1987);

and Roman Polanski's *Frantic* (1988) are about middle-class characters whose lives are overtaken by noir. But unlike Blake Edwards, the insecure directors of these later films pump them up with romantic, psychological, and visual embellishments that only dilute serviceable narratives. Aided by "artificial respiration," these are noir films in only a partial and apologetic sense.

In the opening scene of *The Morning After* (a loose remake of Fritz Lang's 1953 *Blue Gardenia*), a woman who doesn't know where she is and doesn't remember what she did last night wakes up to discover a corpse lying next to her. In *Someone to Watch Over Me*, a rich woman attending a party sees another guest knifed to death. In *Frantic*, an American doctor traveling abroad with his family mistakenly inherits a suitcase containing a device for unleashing nuclear destruction. The three films for different reasons fail to capitalize on the perfectly decent innocent-bystander premises that jump-start the action.

The A-list casting in both *The Morning After* and *Frantic* undermines the pulp fictions. As the woman who wakes up with a corpse, Jane Fonda does entirely too much emoting in a story that requires an anonymous deadpan style. The solid narrative—the woman, a blackout drunk, has been set up by her ex-husband, who is protecting the murderer, his new and very wealthy fiancée—is downplayed to allow Fonda and her equally A-list costar, Jeff Bridges, added space in which to develop their characters. He's a redneck ex-cop and recovering alcoholic, and after a chance meeting the two characters fall in love, a process the film elaborates at unnecessary length. Indeed, the romantic plot contends with and occasionally overtakes the suspense plot. The two stars attempt to deepen characters who need only arouse our suspicion. Is the woman guilty? Has the redneck set her up? Is it wise to trust a guy she met by chance as she was on the run from a murder she doesn't know whether or not she committed? At the end, crying over her man as he lies in a hospital bed, her voice trembling, Fonda, with a loaded Method pause, says, "You . . . you make me happy," ending this fainthearted noir on a non-noir chord of romantic resolution. (That Fonda received an Oscar nomination only underscores how inappropriate to noir her performance is.)

Like the stars, the film's odd color design seems intended to resist the pull of noir. The heroine lives in an apartment with tangerine walls; the hero lives in a shed with a red staircase and yellow walls; a hospital room is a bright lemon-lime; and most of the buildings the characters pass are pink or blue. Trying to convert a noir story into a sentimental romantic comedy, the film subverts both genres.

Innocent characters in classic noir collapse when terrible events impinge unexpectedly. But as the distinguished doctor under fire in *Frantic*, Harrison Ford remains hopelessly heroic. After his wife vanishes, the doctor adheres to a noir formula by starting to behave like a criminal. He crouches in darkened stairwells and lies to authorities, but his masculine prowess is never seriously challenged. The movie star as stalwart action hero, Ford is immune to the insecurities that were the unmaking of the victim protagonists in the studio era. Throughout, Ford holds onto his big-budget action-movie persona; he's a winner, a valiant American abroad who is equal to any reversal the story hurls his way. Better-looking and braver than his Arab adversaries, he resists all the usual noir temptations and pitfalls and, of course, succeeds in reclaiming his missing wife. To protect his star's iconography, Polanski directs in an uncharacteristically flaccid style, with no residue whatever of the lure of darkness that underwrites his masterful American-made essays in noir (*Chinatown*) and horror (*Rosemary's Baby*).

*Someone to Watch Over Me*, like *The Morning After*, denatures a noir witness-to-murder plot with romance. Across class boundaries, the rich witness and Mike, the (married) detective assigned to protect her, fall in love. (Tom Berenger lays on the working-class accent, but as the swanky Upper East Side matron, a badly miscast Mimi Rogers sounds equally proletarian.) Sleeping with his charge, the detective opens himself to noir retribution. "I'm all messed up," he confesses to a colleague. Mike botches the case and nearly loses his family. Crossing a solid if conventional story with a moralistic warning against sex outside marriage, especially if your partner is from a different class, this is noir that pulls its punches. Too slick to play a chance-witness premise in a straight style, Ridley Scott bathes the film in absurdly elegant lighting. And as the camera cranes and tracks gracefully through the vast rooms of the heroine's imperial apartment, baroque music pours onto the sound track as mist illogically swirls through the rarefied air. Noir tension is sacrificed in order to construct a mise-en-scène intended to extract from the spectator the same kind of awe it evokes in the gawking cops assigned to guard the witness. In this "segregated" film, noir is reserved for the working-class world. The detective's ride home to

Queens on a subway, beautifully designed in neo-noir reds and blues, clearly registers Scott's familiarity with the genre he spends most of the film avoiding.

In the film's sexist, class-biased finale, the hero who has "sinned" is recuperated within his patriarchal role, while the victim of noir mischance, who has been guilty of nothing, is punished for being rich, single, and female. The detective with the screeching Queens accent is forgiven, reunited with his wife and son, presumably because he is an ego ideal for much of the target audience, while the rich woman is banished. Sitting alone in the back of a police car, she looks wistful as she is escorted out of the film.

Seemingly ashamed of the decidedly pre-postmodern simplicity of the innocent-bystander trope, films like *The Morning After*, *Frantic*, and *Someone to Watch Over Me* would appear to have been the end of the line; but less than a decade later the innocent witness-to-noir re-emerged. *Nick of Time* (1995) and *Breakdown* (1997) are refreshingly retro invasion narratives that recall the formula of the exemplary no-frills 1953 thriller *Jeopardy*, in which a car accident hurls a bourgeois woman (Barbara Stanwyck at high octane) into a race against the clock. Both of these neo-noir pictures take a minimalist approach, sacrificing psychological reverberation for sustained suspense. Unlike the overweening 1980s misfires, these B noirs are played strictly for the plot.

A businessman dressed in a regulation suit, carrying a briefcase, wearing horn-rimmed glasses, is moving anonymously in the crowd at Union Station, and is about to become a victim of a ghastly noir scenario in *Nick of Time*. Criminals with a plan to assassinate the California governor (Marsha Mason, a Dianne Feinstein look-alike) choose the businessman because he is so clearly an upright citizen and because, as a father traveling with his young daughter, he is particularly vulnerable. Holding the girl as ransom, the conspirators (played by the always-creepy Christopher Walken and the equally minatory, unlovely Roma Maffia) box the businessman into a classic noir tight spot. One minute you're a normal civilian in a busy train station; the next you're marked as the intended assassin of the governor; the cut-to-the-chase narrative catapults the protagonist into a race against time, which becomes the emblem of an implacable noir deity.

Audiences didn't accept Johnny Depp, usually an actor with tricks up his sleeve, in an uncharacteristic straight part, and the film was a

In neo-noir, wide-open spaces are often as threatening as the city streets of classic noir: a traveler from the city (Kurt Russell, above) in *Breakdown* (1997) is coerced into noir as a sheriff (Rex Linn) and a seemingly uninvolved truck driver (J. T. Walsh) look on. To survive, the traveler must, in effect, become an action hero, able to prove his masculinity against a redneck (Walsh).

decided commercial failure. As happens all too frequently in neo-noir, the writers were more adept in setting up their story than in resolving it. Fractured editing and pumped-up volume attempt to conceal the narrative's illogical turns. (The film's nods to political correctness—all the patriarchal white men, including the governor's husband, are maleficent, and only black and Hispanic characters are helpful to the besieged protagonist—are irrelevant.) But despite these flaws *Nick of Time* is a trim, satisfying B thriller that has the courage of its unimportance.

Other yuppies, a pleasant couple driving through the desert on their way from Massachusetts to San Diego, collide with noir mischance in *Breakdown*. Because they are outsiders (the man is dressed conservatively in a blue dress shirt and tan slacks, inappropriate survival gear for the desert), redneck thieves attack them. The visitors in no way beckon or deserve their noir detour; the thieves in no way reflect character traits the bourgeois couple might have repressed: good and evil

inhabit distinct realms. Set in spectacular John Ford country, the film is a neo-noir Western, with the East Coast couple untested pioneers unable to read the landscape and the trailer-trash predators taking the narrative space of "Indians on the warpath." For the unprepared refugees from civilization, naive about the customs of the country, the vast desert, bright with blinding sun, replaces the city at night as noir's new place of treachery.

Like many popular American movies, *Breakdown* justifies the hero's use of violence to fight violence. The truth his experience in noir yields is that, to save himself and his wife, he will kill if he must, and the film applauds the macho prowess he exhibits under duress. Staying the obstacle course, the yuppie displays greater brawn than his aboriginal opponents. In the climactic battle, a joust between physically powerful adversaries that is staged as the kind of fevered, deliriously excessive sight-and-sound spectacle standard in action movies, the hero's physical resilience and his moral worth become indivisible. Bound and thrown into a freezer, the wife meanwhile is a female victim whose genealogy can be traced to *The Perils of Pauline*. In its gender politics, as well as its narrative design and moral voice, *Breakdown* is almost startlingly antediluvian. Primitive noir fodder that adheres to and successfully animates B-movie stencils of the distant past, it is a distinctly retrograde guilty pleasure.

*Breakdown* and *Nick of Time* are almost defiantly non-neo neo-noir films about completely innocent bystanders. More in the neo line are stories in which the characters tossed precipitously into noir aren't altogether guiltless, seem, in ways that remain unspoken, somehow to deserve their noir destinies. In four remarkably similar narratives—*Blood Simple* (1984), *The Hot Spot* (1990), *Red Rock West* (1992), and *U-Turn* (1997)—itinerant males are quickly encased in tangled domestic crimes. Sexy women are their downfall, but it isn't the femmes fatales on which the films focus. Rather, the vulnerable, wounded males, themselves exuding a potent sexual availability, are the stars. And there's something about these guys, adrift on the open road and with no particular game plan, that makes them ripe for noir picking. Once they succumb, these four prototypical neo-noir victims, who consistently misread the characters and situations that engulf them, turn out to be remarkably naive criminals.

The films draw from the same classic source, the paradigm set by *Double Indemnity*. As if in tacit acknowledgment that they are in the business of recirculating well-worn tropes, however, and that therefore it's difficult to play out their stories with a completely straight face, they inject varying levels of comedy into the noir mix. In each movie, sudden violence erupts to still laughter or disbelief; pastiche sometimes shades into parody in the films' labyrinthine plottings. An epidemic of twists, coincidences, double and triple crosses underwrote many classic noir tales, of course, but these updates are gilded with a postmodern disregard for (or at least a casual attitude toward) narrative coherence. Like the addled outsiders who wander into violent scenes of domestic retribution, spectators can easily lose their moorings amid the narrative landmines.

All four cognate thrillers take place in the great American outdoors, in deserts and prairies parched by searing weather. The films transform spare, rocky, limitless vistas and isolated small towns baking in relentless sun into places that seem poised for noir. "Nothin' comes with a guarantee, something' can always go wrong," Ray (John Getz),

Looking baffled and out of place in a stripper bar, Abby (Frances McDormand, left) in *Blood Simple* (1984) is a femme fatale who doesn't know the score.

the protagonist of *Blood Simple,* announces in an opening voiceover. "What I know about is Texas, and down here you're on your own." The rugged settings suspend the films' characters and narratives in a protective temporal limbo that suggests that the films' old-fashioned stories can only occur far from the madding contemporary urban crowd.

Ray's problems in *Blood Simple* begin with his spontaneous decision to spend the night with his employer's wife, Abby (played by Frances McDormand). Abby's suspicious husband Marty, has hired a private detective to trail her, and so once Ray yields to a sexual urge he at the same moment relinquishes his privacy. The new lovers are not the usual noir conspirators: Abby is not a femme fatale, and Ray is a likable oaf rather than a huckster. They're both hicks, simple indeed; and through chance and inertia, they tumble into a noir vortex. As thinly conceived by the Coen brothers, devotees of classic Hollywood, these characters are defined primarily by their differences from the sophisticated schemers of the *Double Indemnity* stripe. Led by his hormones, Ray is remarkably dim; while, with her freckles and plain corn-fed appearance, Frances McDormand makes Abby a counter-fatale, who never seems quite to understand or to connect with the rules of the noir game her infidelity has hurled her into.

When Ray discovers his boss's corpse, he naively assumes Abby killed her husband for him. He instinctively follows a noir mold and begins to act like a criminal. Planning to bury his former boss in an incinerator, he clears up traces of Marty's blood and places the corpse in the back of his car. After Marty turns out not to be dead, Ray, enacting the kind of noir-comedy sketch that is a Coen specialty, takes out a shovel and goes after his prey on the highway before attempting to bury him, still barely alive, in an impromptu grave in an open field. Two of a kind, Abby, like Ray, also misreads the unfolding noir plot, assuming Ray killed Marty for the money she knows her husband kept in a safe in his office; but Ray didn't know there was any money to take, and most likely wouldn't have been interested anyway. The killer is the greedy, crooked private eye, who is also a simpleton; after killing Marty, he leaves his calling card, a watch that will ultimately incriminate him. In the showdown, which the luckless characters bungle as much as they do all the other stations on their criminal Calvary, Abby fatally shoots a man she never sees, assuming he is her husband when it's the private eye, everyone's nemesis, who has already killed Ray.

In this rural *Double Indemnity* the characters are compelled to play roles for which they are poorly cast, and their inexpert performances turn a noir plot into a black comedy of errors. The Coen brothers' typically ironic treatment spills over into visual style as well. Throughout, overdrawn images—a low-angle shot of Marty in his office, with red and black shadows dancing on the ceiling; a high-angle overhead shot, with the camera placed in an impossible position behind a whirring fan as it peers down on a not-quite-dead Marty slumped on a table—are the cinematic equivalent of purple prose. In the process of

The new man in town, Harry Madox (Don Johnson), striped with foreboding shadows, in *The Hot Spot* (1990).

making a film noir, movie-savvy Joel and Ethan Coen are also commenting on and lightly satirizing the form.

If Ray stumbles into noir because of stupidity, the drifter who drives into a steaming Texas town in *The Hot Spot* is punished because of his excess sexuality. Where Ray and Abby are strangely mismatched for noir, Harry Madox, X-rated wanderer, is typecast. An extreme high-angle overhead opening shot of the protagonist in his car whizzing through an "erotic" desert landscape, the contours of which resemble buttocks and breasts, immediately identifies him as a noir victim-to-be. The hot setting is a suitable frame for the story of a car salesman, the new stud in town, who in no time flat is involved with two women. Harry Madox is tender with the nice girl who works with him in the office, while he treats the bad girl, the boss's wife who takes one look at him and goes into sexual overdrive, with contempt. Nonetheless, drawn ineluctably by her scent—she entices him with a peekaboo wardrobe, a lush drawl, and penetrating stares—he takes the bait.

Harry's sex appeal leads him straight into noir. Quickly entangled, he robs the town bank, setting fire to an abandoned building to create a diversion, and he kills a blackmailer. But the Circe of the film's godforsaken hot spot outwits the homme fatale. The good girl has to leave town, but the vamp, who has listed all Harry's crimes in a letter to her lawyer, to be opened in the event of her death, has him just where she wants him. Harry's first response is to try to choke her, then he laughs at his existential plight: he's in one hot spot, and he knows there's no way out. With bitter self-awareness, he observes that he has found his own level and he's living it. Chained to a woman he despises, he drives off with her into a scorching landscape lined with phallic telephone poles, an image of the sexual entrapment that has become his unavoidable fate. Sex is Harry's birthright, but it is also his prison.

As this sexual winner as a noir loser, Don Johnson exudes an erotic confidence curdled by a rippling undercurrent of the character's self-loathing. Playing a stud who's a failure at anything other than sex, Johnson is wonderfully cheesy. He vividly projects Harry's bitterness, his cynical recognition that sex is a weapon men and women use against each other. Like the film itself, directed by Dennis Hopper (whose claim that noir is every director's favorite genre is self-evident here), Johnson's witty, intense performance is a neo-noir highlight.

The protagonist of *Red Rock West* (played by Nicolas Cage) is a wounded vet who has a partial cast on his leg. A sign of impotence and a portent of the bad luck ahead, his encased leg stretching out of his car is our first view of the character. Like other characters marked for trouble in neo-noir, Michael is on his way across the open spaces of America, driving from Texas to Wyoming looking for work. When he enters a roadside bar, he is mistaken for a hit man. Desperate—because of his leg he has been turned down for construction work—he takes the job. In the noir maze he falls into, which he is completely unable to decode, nothing is what it seems to be. For a start, the bartender who hires Michael to kill his wife turns out to be the town sheriff and a former thief. Like the plotters in *Blood Simple*, Michael is not cut out for noir. He always tries to do the right thing: he doesn't steal money from a gas station even though he is flat broke; and falling for Suzanne, he warns her that her husband is trying to have her killed. Michael becomes a pawn in the deadly warfare that ensues among three vipers, the embattled couple, and the real hit man (Dennis Hopper in high neo stride, dressed in obligatory black, in contrast to the blue jeans the protagonist wears). Every time the hapless antihero tries to leave town, he is recalled and inducted into a new turn of the narrative screw.

Dumb and sexy, Michael is an easy mark for noir. But because he commits no criminal acts, unlike the derailed males in *Blood Simple* and *The Hot Spot*, he's allowed to escape from the undertow. At the end, when Suzanne turns on him as they are finally leaving Red Rock West, Michael throws the temptress and her money from the train. Discovering that one packet of the money remains, he tucks it into his shirt, figuring that through his detour into noir he has earned it.

*U-Turn*, directed and cowritten by Oliver Stone as a noir fever dream, plays like a parody of *Red Rock West*, which itself nudges parody. Another wounded, impaired stud (Sean Penn), this time with a bandaged hand (we learn that the mob has cut off two of his fingers), the antihero is another traveler on the open road heading straight into noir. When his car stalls, he takes a wrong turn into an end-of-the-world town called Superior. Within seconds, as if she has been waiting for him, he meets a babe with a brutish husband who, with a bow to *Chinatown*, turns out to be her father. Both the husband-father and his wife-daughter quickly enlist the trespasser into plots to kill the other, and as in *Blood Simple* and *Red Rock West*, there's money stashed in a safe. Other than the fact that mobsters are pursuing him, we're told little about the wanderer. (It's axiomatic in road-movie noir that the drifter protagonist is a man without a past.) He's a shady character to begin with, but sex turns him into a killer. After the small-town siren turns on him, throwing him over a cliff, he rises up and slays her. As at the beginning, his car again blows out, and he ends up where he started from, only this time he is near death, trapped with a broken-down car in the middle of the forbidding American nowhere.

Compensating for the familiarity of character and story, Oliver Stone, a director for whom way too much is clearly never enough, practices visual, thematic, and aural excess, at every moment transforming plenitude into hyperbole. Distrusting the noir-retread premise of the fateful wrong turn (recall Joe Gillis turning by chance into Norma Desmond's driveway in *Sunset Boulevard*), Stone treats it as the excuse for a shrill sight-and-sound show, a shallow noir spectacle. The virtuoso techniques, including insistent spatial, temporal, and narrative fragmentation, complex punctuation, oscillations between color and black and white, and aural slides between pop tunes and Ennio Morricone's stately, menacing score, are replacements for, rather than enhancements of, content. Sex is presented operatically. The femme fatale (a lubricious Jennifer Lopez), shot mostly in fragments, is frequently reduced to a set of devouring eyes and an engorging mouth. Closeups on vultures, snakes, and other desert reptiles italicize Stone's already-excessive depiction of an animalistic female sexuality. A commercial misfire, the film is so out of control that some reviewers read it as a comic fantasia on noir themes, a hip postmodern parody. But no; directorial overkill here does not represent a stance of postmodern cool but rather sheer flop sweat. Stone's hyperventilating take on a noir wrong-turn formula is less a U-turn than a dead end.

Incorporating state-of-the-art technology, *The Net* (1995) and *The Game* (1997), both written by John D. Brancato and Michael Ferris, bring the trope of bystanders pressed into noir—the format handled in unfashionable ways in *Nick of Time* and *Breakdown*—up to postmodern speed. In *The Net*, cyberspace provides contemporary window dressing for a story that's retro at heart, whereas *The Game* is a neo-noir knockout that takes the genre to a dangerous new level. Like the wanderers in the above four movies, the protagonists here also seem to invite their bad luck.

Angela Bennett (Sandra Bullock), the heroine of *The Net*, is a woman who knows too much. An ace computer hack, she finds and fixes problems in cyberspace. By mischance, she possesses a disc that becomes for a gang of computer thugs a veritable noir grail, the equivalent of the Maltese falcon or the mysterious black box in *Kiss Me Deadly*, the thing they must have at all costs. Providing

A computer specialist (Sandra Bullock) confronts the screen, adversary as well as nemesis, in *The Net* (1995).

myriad frames within the frame, computers represent a new emblem of noir entrapment. The heroine's journey through noir is instigated by, and largely conducted on, omnipresent screens. Angela, both master and servant of this technological godhead, is also erased by it. "It's a nightmare, I'm not me anymore," she wails, intoning the classic lament of a noir victim suffering from a loss or confusion of identity, here given a novel high-tech spin. "Give us the disc and we'll give you your life back," her pursuers offer. But this postfeminist heroine chooses instead to go on the lam, combating a noir threat by entering a noir world. On the run, she holes up in a motel that seems made to order for a victim of mischance. The machine is Angela's enemy—with a few strokes her identity is voided—but it is also her salvation, for with some deft counterstrokes she is able to expose the underworld network that is after her. Complicated computer technology serves in a sense as an alibi for the film's illogical hare-turn narrative twists; as in many neo-noir thrillers, *The Net*'s tortuous plotting ultimately undermines its clever premise.

True to the genre's conservatism, Angela's noir detour is constructed as warning and riposte. Isolated with her computer and communicating to the outside world through a network of screens and disembodied voices, Angela is a workaholic who keeps dangerously to herself. "Computers are a perfect hiding place," she admits, but they are also paradoxically a perfect place to be found out because, as she also says, "Our whole lives are on the computer." "They know everything about me," she realizes at the end, confronting the fact that the brave new techno-world is steeped in noir possibilities. After her identity has been restored, however, she returns to her computer screen a little wiser than she was before her misadventure. Unlike bourgeois males who succumb to temptation, either sexual or financial, Angela is innocent at heart. And where their brush with noir instructs them to stay at home, Angela's collision with techno-noir has perhaps encouraged her to step out a little more, to open herself (gingerly) to the world beyond the screen. At the end, as if to demonstrate her enhanced outreach capacity, she has taken in a housemate, her mother, suffering from Alzheimer's disease.

In *The Game*, technology invades another isolated character, a venal investment banker who's divorced and lives alone in a gated mansion. A cold, hard fat cat, the character (played, of course, by Michael Douglas) seems ripe for a fall. After his television begins to talk to him (an unnerving parody of how the media interpellate us, reaching directly into our lives), the banker becomes the target of what he interprets as a vast conspiracy to separate him from his wealth. He is quickly transformed into a noir victim and hounded by relentless, largely unseen pursuers. He is drugged and taken to – and must find his way back from—Mexico, the fatal other place and the site of last resort in numerous classic noir films. His whole fortune gone, his mansion padlocked, his former position of dominance is now but a bitter memory. Like *The Net*, the movie pivots on a noir perception that, in a high-tech world, wealth is a fragile membrane.

It turns out that, in a narrative move that converts the film into a prime postmodern artifact, the maze in which the protagonist's world and identity are demolished has been elaborately staged. "The game" has been a birthday present from a resentful, bad-seed brother. The film's intricate, twisting plot, its periodic violence, its neon-lit Chinatown, its sleazy Mexico, its dark alleyways, its ominously impersonal corporate offices, and its insistent diagonal compositions that create a menacingly unstable mise-en-scène have been staged to intimidate and mislead the protagonist, as well as the spectator. *The Game* creates a virtual-reality world of gleaming surfaces; beneath the images, there is no substance or truth whatever; and, like the banker, we've been deliciously fooled. This is trompe l'oeil noir, glistening with devilish irony.

At the end, after thinking he has shot his brother, the former banker jumps off a roof and crashes through a skylight, landing on a net in a huge banquet hall where his friends and family and all the actors in the charade are gathered to applaud him. After he has finally learned the truth, one of the actors, a woman who has played her femme fatale role with notable skill, asks him to go for coffee. He hesitates, as the screen fades slowly to black. Now that the game is over, can he trust her? Can he ever again separate reality from masquerade? Is there any tangible, verifiable reality in a world that functions like an uncontainable, interactive personal computer?

Brilliantly directed by David Fincher, *The Game* is a dare, a boldly reflexive neo-noir film that submits the genre's innocent-bystander motif to a novel rewrite. It is, however, a perilous model that if pursued could lead only to the death of noir. Treating the form as only a game, as carnivalesque theater of the absurd, a sequence of what in retrospect are vaudevillian turns, the film contains the seeds of the genre's deconstruction.

Unlike the white bread bank teller in *Experiment in Terror*, the alienated characters in *The Net* and *The Game* are not altogether innocent; it is unlikely in postmodern neo-noir for innocence to be reclaimed in other than an ironic context. The techno-wizard self-imprisoned in front of her computer and the investment banker puffed up by his overweening sense of entitlement seem prime candidates for noir visitation. Nonetheless, even as their lives are overtaken by noir reversals, the characters maintain immunity from their inner demons; they're victims who never become criminals and, at the ends of their bizarre journeys, are reinstated within a non-noir world. In contrast, other middle-class characters whose lives are crisscrossed by noir do slip into crime. As opposed to the more or less innocent bystanders who pass in then out of noir, these characters edge into another realm. For them, mischance instigates transgression, for which they pay either with their lives or at the least with their moral integrity. After noir, if they're still standing, they've been irremediably branded.

For these victims, crime releases impulses coiled just beneath their social masks. Whatever their motives for embracing noir, whether to exact revenge against an unjust fate or to realize a forbidden desire, they become complicit in their own moral and psychological unraveling. If they begin as victims, they often end on the other side and thereby both ensure and earn their dark destinies. A barely covert axiom of these melodramas of mischance is that the bourgeois characters,

Bizarre noir: a poster for Samuel Fuller's *Shock Corridor* (1963) promotes the film as a pulpy brew of sex, violence, and insanity; a receding institutional corridor is a noir metaphor, reflecting the disordered minds of inmates (Peter Breck, center).

whom we first take as decorous, harbor an inner criminal waiting to be expressed. To varying degrees, these fallen characters are "always already" guilty, and so their brush with noir is simply the mechanism for unchaining their instinctive, immanent desire to be subversive.

I now look at some representative "not-innocent" victims of noir misfortune who succumb to crime. This popular narrative trope, a genre staple, ranges across the long and still-lengthening neo-noir canon, from the early 1960s, when noir was a dead letter, up to the know-it-all present, when the form has become increasingly the target of self-conscious jibes, noir in quotes. Clearly, working from a cineaste's knowledge of noir motifs and conventions, latter-day movies about bourgeois descents are colored with varying shades of irony, reflexivity, and play.

As in his idiosyncratic take on the femme fatale in *The Naked Kiss* (1964), Samuel Fuller offers a distinctive interpretation of a criminal in the making in *Shock Corridor* (1963), another early, postclassic bizarre noir. Unlike the purely victimized characters in pictures like *The Net* and *Nick of Time*, Fuller's protagonist in *Shock Corridor* actively beckons

F101·9

noir. Fuller's Faust, the character is a journalist who hungers for a Pulitzer Prize ("to be in the company of the newspaper greats"), and reaching for glory he is willing, even eager, to barter his soul. He contrives to have himself committed to an insane asylum where he believes that, masquerading as a patient, he will be able to solve a famous murder case. Staging his own madness, he does indeed catch the criminal as, almost at the same moment, he slips into a state of irreversible catatonic schizophrenia. "An insane mute will win the Pulitzer Prize," as one of Fuller's choral figures comments, underlining the film's pitch black irony.

Neither the journalist's goal nor his means are precisely criminal; yet in both a narrative and visual sense, the character occupies the place of the lapsed bourgeois. Like homosexuality in *Cruising*, insanity functions here as the noir contaminant, and, as in William Friedkin's thriller, it's contagious. As the journalist's girlfriend, another divided character, who strips to earn money "for a normal life," says, "Their sickness is bound to rub off on you. This Jekyll-Hyde business will make a psycho out of you." The journalist in Fuller's punitive scenario, playing crazy, hastens his descent into darkness. As in regulation-model middle-class noir, the character's "criminality" is marked by his increasing detachment: as he pursues his goal, he dehumanizes the inmates, regarding them as fodder for a potentially prizewinning story. His distance from them is the prelude to his ultimate self-estrangement.

As the character unravels, he is visually branded as a trapped criminal. Barred windows, looming shadows, seemingly endless hallways— Fuller and Stanley Cortez, his master cinematographer, construct a space spiked with noir doom, in effect a noir stage that "opens" to receive memory fragments (in color) of the three deranged key witnesses the journalist interviews. The shock corridor to which they are confined is a symbolic noir world that, through a glass darkly, mirrors social ills identified by Fuller as emblematic of a decentered contemporary America. The mad witnesses are a GI, who reverted to communism because he was raised on hate ("I would have defected to any enemy"); a black, who has turned racism inward, claiming he is the founder of the KKK; and a scientist, who went insane working on nuclear fission ("we've become too sophisticated in the act of death").

Fuller, in his characteristically lurid style, has fashioned a slip-into-noir narrative as a metaphor for a contemporary society gone haywire. In a far more pedestrian style, *Death Wish* eleven years later also grafts a story of a newly-minted criminal onto a tabloid declaration of "what's wrong with America." Although aficionados are reluctant to claim it, *Death Wish*, alas, is steeped in noir terrain. Within a classically noir story, Michael Winner's thriller, in its way just as dotty as *Shock Corridor*, exploits contemporary fears of the American city at night.

The wife of a prominent architect (played by Charles Bronson) is killed and his daughter badly beaten when two hoodlums break into his apartment while he is at work. The bereaved architect is a former conscientious objector who hadn't "touched a gun" since his father, a hunter, was killed in a hunting accident. But as he boils with revenge against the invasion that destroyed his family, he begins to take nightly walks armed with a weapon. He comes to his "calling" as a vigilante with signal reluctance. When from the window of his apartment he sees punks breaking into a car, he draws the shades to screen out the scene of random violence. After he bashes a mugger, he runs home shattered by his violent outburst. As he pours himself a drink, his hands tremble. But he quickly grows bolder and, walking in parks at night, seems to be setting himself up as a target for crime. And when a junkie holds him up at gunpoint, he takes out his new gun and shoots: his first hit. Shaken by his act, and not quite believing he was capable of it, he goes home and vomits.

But in this cracked neo-noir picture, it's crime rather than sex or money that seduces the antihero. Wasting muggers begins to turn the architect on. He shoots when he catches thugs beating up a man. Two muggers strut through a subway: he shoots. In a traditional noir, this sociopath with a new affinity for guns and violence would be counted among the damned, a character lost in an ebony underworld. *Death Wish*, however, denies the character's sickness under the alibi that he is merely reacting against a sick society. In its skewed and reckless ideology, the film phrases the hero's reversion not as pathology but as a moral imperative. "If we're not pioneers, what are we?" the character asks, urging audiences to make the connection between this contemporary Eastern and the Westerns in which Charles Bronson himself starred as the hero. Using violence against violence ("What do you call people who, when faced with a condition of fear, just run and hide?" he asks), this urban vigilante is a rugged, lone operator who, like a Western hero cleansing the wilderness, hunts down latter-day savages.

Charles Bronson as an architect-turned-vigilante in *Death Wish* (1974) is surrounded in the reactionary city-as-nightmare thriller.

A politician mechanically intones that, "Murder is no answer to crime," but the film cannot conceal its underlying belief that it is.

Because the police see this urban swashbuckler as a deterrent to crime, they don't want to arrest him; they just want to "scare him off." In the compromised ending, the vigilante is sent out of town as the chief of police informs the media that he is still "out there." At the airport in Chicago, the new city to which he has been banished, he sees thugs roughing up a young woman and mimes shooting them with his hand. Then he breaks into a sly smile. He may have been expelled from his home city, but the architect-turned-stalker is unregenerate and determined to endure. Despite nominal disavowals, the film ends up endorsing a character made mad by a noir invasion; and in avoiding closure, it clearly creates a narrative space for a sequel in which the vigilante can continue to make war on undesirables.

Cynically playing up to middle-class white phobias about the city as an unsafe place, the film transforms New York into a landmine waiting to explode. Lurking in parks and alleys and subway trains, and storming the apartments of respectable middle-class white citizens, muggers, thieves, and stalkers seem to be omnipresent. (One of the film's transparent masquerades of playing fair is its ethnically diverse hoodlums. At first the bad guys are white guys, including the unmistakably Jewish Jeff Goldblum. Gradually, and mostly in the margins, people of color appear as muggers preying on law-abiding white citizens. To mark the filmmakers' awareness that blacks too are the victims of rampant urban crime, on a television interview, a black woman says she takes a hatpin to muggers.) Sunk in Stygian darkness or illuminated by a sickly orange light, the film's graffiti-coated city is a cauldron of crime. Out-of-towners refer to New York as "that toilet," "a war zone." "If only we had the brains to live in the country," the architect's son-in-law laments. Contaminated New York is contrasted with Honolulu, where the hero and his family vacation just before noir hits them, and with Tucson, "a beautiful place, they can breathe out there." Unlike the imaginary, studio-made cities of much of classic noir, in which a quasi-expressionist mise-en-scène reflects the protagonist's state of mind, here it is the city that's more disturbed than the character. The city is the active agent, the catalyst that inflames the character's violence.

Steeped in noir, New York is also the catalyst to crime in Martin Scorsese's *Taxi Driver* (1976), written by genre aficionado and historian Paul Schrader. But unlike the "hero" in *Death Wish*, who resorts to violence with initial reluctance and from a place of lofty social privilege only after a ghastly invasion, the taxi driver, Travis Bickle (played by Robert De Niro), has much less distance to travel to enter noir. A Vietnam vet who can't sleep and is addicted to pornography, Travis is tightly wound. His instinct for killing is deeply embedded, his semblance of normality easily exploded. Anything could set off this noir subject in the making, but it is the city itself that seems to be the linchpin.

*Death Wish* presents the city, swarming with multihued muggers, as "reality," whereas the city in *Taxi Driver* is frequently rendered from the point of view of its unbalanced protagonist. The expressionist tilt is announced at the beginning, as steam shooting up from manholes surrounds a taxi, which the circling camera inspects like an object at an exhibition. A tight closeup on Travis's staring eyes immediately follows—the shot-countershot syntax identifies Travis as our guide through an urban inferno. We're placed inside his taxi, cruising city streets that look like an X-rated pageant. Travis's New York teems with the glittering marquees of adult theaters and sex shops and with whores, pimps, and their clients. Accompanied by Travis's insinuating voiceover, in which he fulminates against "the trash" that clogs the streets, the urban vistas are bathed in underwater blues and greens accented with red neon. In the taxi driver's skewed and baffled perception, the city is a cesspool that needs to be washed clean.

Sex pushes Travis into a noir spin. For this turbulent antihero, itching to launch into crime, sex (like the city itself) is something to watch. He likes to look at women as images in pornographic tableaux, but he doesn't sleep with them; women incite but cannot fulfill his desire. Guns replace his apparently inactive phallus, as, locking himself in a basement apartment with gated windows, he hones his expertise as a crack marksman. Turning himself into a lean fighting machine, he prepares for "Armageddon." When his attempt to assassinate a presidential candidate is frustrated, his rage is transferred to the pimps who control Iris, the young prostitute he wishes to rescue from the polluted city. His orgasmic bloodbath marks his descent into a noir psychosis that has been on an inner boil for a long time.

As in *Death Wish*, the character's violence takes noir beyond the purely private space in which crime erupts in the standard classic scenario. The taxi driver's explosion, like the vigilante's, becomes a matter of public concern, as well as public misperception. The media misinterpret maniacal vengeance as the act of a latter-day savior; but unlike the fatally compromised *Death Wish*, Scorsese's film separates itself from the warped spin the media assign to the killing spree, mistaking pathology for heroism. However, like the vigilante, Travis is not caught and is certain to strike again. At the end, after he has been exalted as a hero, Bernard Herrmann's ominous score (Norman's theme from *Psycho*) signifies his madness. And his final gesture, turning his rearview mirror so that it distorts and obscures our vision, makes us see double and, as throughout the film, aligns our point of view with his.

In *Death Wish*, as police begin to lay a dragnet for the psycho vigilante, they focus their surveillance on veterans from Vietnam, Korea, and World War II—on men trained in the use of guns. *Taxi Driver* implies that Travis's experience in Vietnam contributed to his traumatic overload. The Vietnam vet, suffering from service in a discredited war and returning home in a dazed and vulnerable condition, would seem to be a rich subject for noir invasions, yet there have been far fewer returning soldiers in nouveau than in classic noir. One of the few films to connect service in Vietnam with a descent into noir is Karel Reisz's *Who'll Stop the Rain?*, based on Robert Stone's *Dogs of War*, a landmark of the literature of Vietnam. Where both *Death Wish* and *Taxi Driver* explore their protagonists' gradual immersion in noir, however, the antiheroes of Reisz's film have already made their plunge before the story opens. A soldier who has "turned" (played by Michael Moriarty) buys heroin and asks a buddy, an antisocial ex-marine (Nick Nolte) whose wartime history has made him cynical, to be his courier. Agreeing to break the law as a favor for a friend, the ex-marine is one of noir's innocent bystanders; his friend has set him up, and soon two convicts and a crooked federal agent pursue him for the stash he is carrying. Ultimately, for a decision he made on a whim, he pays with his life. How the characters became tainted—why the soldiers so easily turn to crime—remains unexplored, and the film instead settles into a prolonged chase. Placing archetypal figures drawn from noir's syllabus against promising but unexamined new thematic ground, the connection between service in a benighted war and a fall into crime, the film is a major disappointment.

While Vietnam vets have not been a fertile source for neo thrillers, since the late 1980s characters lured into a noir web have covered both genders and a wide range of classes and professions. A female therapist (*House of Games* [1987]), a screenwriter (*The Player* [1992]), dissatisfied working-class women (*Thelma and Louise* [1991]), and an unemployed middle-level executive (*Falling Down* [1993]) provide novel variations on noir's traditional border-crossing theme. These supposedly immune, law-abiding characters are inducted into crime as they become dislodged from the social contract.

Margaret, the therapist in David Mamet's tricky *House of Games* and the author of a best-seller about addictive behavior called *Driven*, seems at first almost eerily self-possessed. As enacted by Mamet's then-wife, Lindsay Crouse, a poor actress with an androgynous presence,

Margaret has the deadened eyes, flat voice, and automaton-like movements of a high 1940s somnambulist. Crouse's minimalist, almost non-acting, strikes the right note for setting up Mamet's tortuous narrative. Mike, a patient with a provocative proletarian manner (Joe Mantegna), is a compulsive gambler who persuades Margaret to accompany him to the House of Games, the gambling den he habitually frequents. In contrast to the therapist's severe white office, the den, located on skid row, is a dingy backroom bar that resembles a movie set from classic noir. As she walks down eerily lit isolated streets, the upright therapist is clearly entering the landscape of noir. Too "noir" to be real, the House of Games is, in fact, a masquerade, part of a sting set up by con artists in order to extract money from the unsuspecting therapist. When Mike

Taken to a gambling den by a seductive client (Joe Mantegna), a psychiatrist (Lindsay Crouse) enters a noir zone in *House of Games* (1987).

confesses, Margaret forgives him, but he is only setting her up for a bigger sting. All along he counts on the fact that she is attracted to him; what he hasn't figured into his scams is her own addiction to the art of the con. At the end, retaliating with a scheme of her own, she shoots him down in a liminal noir space, a no-entrance zone at an airport. In the last scene, dressed for the first time in frilly, "feminine" clothes, at lunch with a colleague, she pinches the cigarette lighter of the woman at the next table. Margaret has gone noir. Beneath her feminized, sleek, professional veneer, she's a compulsive grifter, as addicted as any of her clients and far more dangerous than Mike, who lured her onto the wild side. Mike was only a thief; Margaret's a killer.

With his trademark, hardboiled patter in which his characters address each other with repetitive, hard-hitting questions and insinuating pauses, Mamet has constructed an amoral, ironic hymn to noir. The repressed therapist, far from being punished for becoming a criminal, has been liberated by blue-collar sex and crime. In Mamet's feisty, postmodern take, who says crime doesn't pay? In his sexual politics, however, Mamet toes the traditional genre line, and *House of Games* is further insurance against Mamet becoming a patron saint of feminists. He has written a sly fable in which a proletarian homme fatale seduces and cons a career woman who proceeds to demonstrate the classic noir axiom that sexually aroused women are indeed deadlier than the male.

In *The Player*, another seemingly secure professional enters and, against all odds, subdues circumstances dipped in noir. When a desperate Hollywood producer (Griffin Mill, played by Tim Robbins), trying to stay afloat in shark-infested currents, begins to receive poison-pen postcards, he recognizes that he is being sucked into a story with a potentially noir fallout. His immediate thought is to track his mystery correspondent among authors of scripts he has rejected, and when he finds the person he thinks is the culprit, a writer who taunts him about being replaced by a new and younger player, the executive kills him. True to the noir-like plot that has claimed him, however, he kills the wrong man. The postcards continue. He becomes a murder suspect, grilled by the police and stalked by a detective. The noose tightens, and in old-fashioned noir he'd be a goner. But in Robert Altman's hip adaptation of the novel by Michael Tolkin, the lapsed executive is given a reprieve. In a police lineup, an eyewitness picks someone else. "You're free as a bird," he is told.

Happy endings for victims of the kind of mischance that befalls the movie executive are rare, and then only if the character manages to maintain immunity from the noir undercurrents. But the executive capitulates thoroughly to noir, and survives. At the end, his nemesis, who knows all, calls him directly, pitching the story of the movie we have just seen. The executive assures him he will buy it if the writer can

In the wicked black comedy *The Player* (l992), with Tim Robbins as a corrupt producer determined to maintain his place in the Hollywood sun, the movie industry itself, awash in crime both on and off the screen, is the impetus to noir.

guarantee a happy ending, which, of course, he can "if the price is right." Feeling safe at last, the player retreats to his Bel Air mansion and his beautiful, pregnant wife.

Like its vindicated protagonist, *The Player* is pleased with the way it rewrites a scenario that would seem to be heading for a crash landing. Altman's reflexive movie, in which the film industry itself is the source of noir, takes its place in a long line of acrid, self-congratulatory insider exposés of Hollywood corruption. But even so, its "happy" ending may be more truly noir than the restoration scenarios mandated by the Production Code. In this dark view of the Hollywood way of the world, the last man standing, the most manipulative, deceitful, vicious player, a studio executive willing to kill to retain his place in the California sun, is the big "winner," the man who ends up with everything. Unlike the usual middle-class victims of mischance, who collapse when they commit a crime, the executive seems immune to feelings of guilt or remorse. In this Hollywood house of games, the top player gets away with murder.

Life follows art in this film about filmmaking. As he lives like a criminal, fearful of being exposed, the producer makes a noir thriller called *The Lonely Room*, in which an innocent woman is sentenced to the gas chamber. When the film is screened for executives one year after the producer has himself been liberated from his crime, it has acquired a happy ending in which the heroine (played by Julia Roberts) is rescued at the last minute by a brawny hero (Bruce Willis). "What took you so long?" she asks breathlessly. "Traffic was bad," he says as he carries her off in his arms out of the gas chamber. At the screening, *The Player*'s one decent character asks the producer, incredulously, where "the true, unhappy ending" is. Smugly, the producer announces that the original ending tested badly in Canoga Park, and now, instead of an authentic but not commercial noir, the studio has a story with a fairy-tale ending written by the producer himself that promises to be a box-office smash.

Unlike beleaguered protagonists in classic noir, the professionals in *House of Games* and *The Player* end in queasy triumphs. Revved up by mischance, they defy doom. The characters in *Falling Down* and *Thelma and Louise* are not so lucky. The two films conform to a genre prototype (unlikely characters resort to crime) while bypassing traditional iconography. Photographed mostly in daylight and on location, neither film constructs a visual vocabulary of entrapment. Nonetheless, for their protagonists the great outdoors, sun-drenched Los Angeles in *Falling Down* and the desert vistas in *Thelma and Louise*, proves as inhospitable as the studio-built streets and interiors oozing menace in 1940s noir. Both films seem to have more than suspense on their agendas—the former is noir phrased as a white male backlash melodrama, the latter as a quasi-feminist tract. Both these ideologically symptomatic works about final journeys overstate their cases, and they are so flecked with contradictions that they veer off into incoherence.

Advertised as "the adventures of an ordinary man at war with the everyday world," *Falling Down* traces the descent into madness of a man, Bill Foster (Michael Douglas), at the end of his rope. Fired from his job at a defense plant and separated from his wife, who has taken out a restraining order against him, he is an angry white man who wanders through a city populated mostly by ethnic others. He walks away from a traffic jam and detours through marginal city districts, all the while claiming he is going home. In classic noir, the city typically was represented as spare and often empty; the Los Angeles of Bill Foster's odyssey is densely populated and, spread across the Panavision wide screen in packed compositions with contrasting directions of movement, resembles a photorealist city painting by Richard Estes. Splattered with graffiti, murals, spray paint, and a mélange of advertising signs, the film's Los Angeles is rendered as an outpost of the Third World, a gleaming, visually overloaded, infested landscape sweltering under merciless sun on the hottest day of the year.

The antihero's first encounter is with a harsh Korean grocer who charges too much for a Coke. "You're the thief, not me," Bill snaps, as he steals a baseball bat after accusing the proprietor of lacking "the grace" to learn "our language." He next collides with a sinister Hispanic gang from which he takes guns. Other ideologically loaded encounters include a neo-Nazi white supremacist (whom Bill knifes after the man claims him as a secret sharer) and racist country club members walled off from the boiling city in their own enclave. At the end, just before he is shot and killed, Bill asks the cop who has been following him, "I'm the bad guy?"

According to this deeply compromised, irresponsibly entertaining movie, the answer is, yes and no. At one level, the film suggests that all those nasty Koreans and Hispanics Bill interacts with must have had something to do with the "falling down" of this privileged patri-

An ordinary man, Bill Foster (Michael Douglas), a white urban middle-class male dispossessed in a graffiti-strewn, Third-World Los Angeles, begins his journey toward doom in *Falling Down* (1993).

arch, the man who at the starting gate would seem to have had everything. Did he lose it, as the film covertly implies, because, in Third World Los Angeles, he is now an endangered species, a middle-class white male who in this city of economic and ethnic extremes has lost his place? The film, however, disavows this reactionary (and probably unspeakable) perception by turning the dispossessed white male into a crackpot. Asking audiences to identify with the protagonist's mounting frustration with ethnic minorities, who are presented as either mean-spirited or violent, *Falling Down* solicits and plays on middle-class white xenophobia. (With typical shiftiness, the film excludes blacks from its urban melting pot.) After having constructed its put-upon wanderer as a vehicle through whom the hordes who have taken over a formerly white city can be indicted, the film then doubles back on itself, canceling its putative message because of the unreliability of the messenger. *Falling Down*, despite its ideological bad faith, is one of the choice guilty pleasures of neo-noir. Against a powerfully rendered city as inferno, it gives a forcible spin to the traditional noir trope of a bourgeois male caught in a quagmire.

Perched on safer ideological ground, *Thelma and Louise* follows a similar narrative arc. Two friends trapped in abusive marriages and low-paying jobs take off for a weekend trip that turns out to be a last hurrah. Bill Foster is driven to crime by an array of hostile others; the villains who drive Thelma and Louise over the edge belong to a single group: men who regard women as sexual objects. After the heroines turn violently against a would-be rapist, they are launched on a career as male-busters; and in the cartoonlike world Ridley Scott's film depicts, obscenely lustful men on the prowl are everywhere ripe for the picking. Susan Sarandon is tough Thelma; Geena Davis is ditsy Louise, who is capable of regressing when she meets a bodacious male (Brad Pitt, muscles rippling, in a star-making, ten-minute appearance). Because the performers are so likable, audiences are enlisted as allies on the two women's dragon-slaying odyssey.

Confronted by predatory males, Thelma and Louise begin to act like natural-born killers. Gunning their way through the rugged western landscape, they become trigger-happy outlaws protected by the rationale that they are abused women striking back at a contaminated patriarchy. But really they act like men in drag. *Thelma and Louise* is a male buddy road movie recast with women, in which women act like men, reacting to violence with greater violence. Phrased as liberation from male dominance and brutality, their journey is toward a noir madness that is as inflamed as Bill Foster's. Yet the film holds them up as feminist models, as women who stand up for their rights against men who only want to screw them. The film is a cryptolesbian fantasy in which the demented heroines can find no place for themselves in the world as it is. Death is preferable to the inevitable punishment by the male forces of law and order hot on their trail; and after they kiss each other, they drive their car off a cliff.

*Thelma and Louise* is too biased to acknowledge the fact that its protagonists are as much an ideological embarrassment as Bill Foster, aggrieved patriarch. Like him, they react to their sense of oppression by going ballistic. What the film exposes is that beneath their feminine masquerade the two characters have the criminal instincts of Bonnie and Clyde. Like *Falling Down*, the film paints itself into a corner from which the only solution seems to be killing off characters who have been steeped irreversibly in noir. Last-act recuperations in many classic noir and nouveau noir dramas are usually plausible only if you disregard the rest of the movie; but in *Falling Down* and *Thelma and Louise*, the characters' climactic deaths limn another kind of avoidance, in effect another retreat from noir. As they kill off their displaced protagonists with no homes to return to, the films wipe their hands of them. That there is no place for Bill Foster is expressed with relief, while the two women's erasure is tinged with disappointment: if only the real world could accommodate gutsy women who fight back against the male beast, even if they do become killers. By presenting them as caricatures, both films obscure the genuine sociological issues that drive their protagonists into noir. As cartoon versions of real-world grievances, the films ultimately cower behind any movie's final excuse: that they *are* only movies after all, produced as entertainment rather than sermons.

Borrowing from film noir, from the male buddy movie, and from the road movie, *Thelma and Louise* is a hoax the filmmakers got away with. If gays or blacks—or women—were portrayed with the same gross stereotyping as men are here, the film would have aroused widespread protest. Instead, it was embraced critically and commercially, and Callie Khouri's nasty screenplay won an Oscar. Some feminists who like the picture excuse it as pure fantasy, a comedy of bad manners, in effect, which offers harmless vicarious release for a shared female resentment against male rapists, a line of reasoning that is as specious as the film's. Tucked beneath its approbation of women who get back at disgusting men by turning to violence is a deeper and more generalized resentment of male sexuality.

Like all enduring genre patterns, that of the bourgeois (noncriminal) who tumbles into crime through mischance or a sudden misdeed has undergone shifts in tone. A grim, ironic humor has always informed noir stories of upright characters upended; but in the neo era, varying strains of more overt comedy have been injected. In the brilliant part-noir *Crimes and Misdemeanors* (1989), Woody Allen bisects his usual ensemble comedy of neurotic Manhattan professionals with a chilling noir story (told without a comic tremor) of a distinguished eye doctor who hires a hit man to kill a nagging mistress. To preserve his privileged social position, this man raised in a pious Jewish family decides to commit a blasphemous crime and then, in a second self-betrayal, learns after a while to make peace with it by regarding it, in a sense, as a narrative that happened to someone else. The film's double-stranded story, revealed in its title, strictly segregates noir from Allen's customary social comedy—there isn't a single comic vibration in the remarkably intense performances of Martin Landau, as the errant patriarch, and Anjelica Huston, as his insistent mistress. Yet the film's two halves are linked through characters and thematic motifs that cut across the generic divide.

Noir and comedy are more intimately conflated in the work of the movie-smart Coen brothers. In *Fargo* (1996), for example, they rinse a standard noir setup with mordant black comedy. The premise—a desperate husband hires two lowlifes to kidnap his wife in order to extract an eighty-thousand-dollar ransom from his wealthy father-in-law— would have been played entirely straight in an earlier phase of the genre. Of course the plan goes haywire: the husband is a schlemiel; his criminal employees, one a babbler, the other encased in a stony silence, are buffoons. The one that runs off at the mouth is trigger-happy: he shoots a cop who stops them because they don't have license plates; then he kills the wife's father and a hapless parking attendant. The husband, whose harebrained scheme tosses him into noir quicksand, is a failed capitalist, a car salesman with a history of misfired scams, and a born loser. He's a clown who rapidly loses control of his plan, as of every other aspect of his life, watching helplessly as his wife and father-in-law are killed and as he himself becomes ensnared by a cunning female sheriff.

Knowing noir, as they know all the classical Hollywood genres, the Coens tease black comedy and social satire out of it, while periodically, in bizarre comic contexts, violence erupts. The silent hit man kills his partner and then stuffs him headfirst into a woodchipper, his legs poking surrealistically into the air. A cockeyed optimist, wide-eyed but hardly stupid, the pregnant sheriff, Marge (Frances McDormand, in an Academy Award-winning performance, a rare honor for noir), is a delightful change from traditional dead-faced law-enforcement figures. After she has solved the case, Marge gets the last word. "Why did you do this? For just a little bit of money?" she asks the surviving kidnapper. "And here it is such a nice day today."

*Fargo* also departs from stencils in its sound and image. The hardboiled rhythms of city noir are replaced by the nasal twang of the

*Fargo* (1996), a film blanc with a know-it-all female detective (Frances McDormand), changes some genre conventions.

upper Midwest; in an idiom sprinkled with homily and platitude, the local characters address each other with a rote politeness that has a sinister underside. The filmmakers set their tale of simpletons in a blindingly white snow-covered landscape—the striking opening image is of a car emerging gradually from the sheer whiteness of snow. Reversing noir's customary shadow world, the Coens have produced a film blanc.

*Fargo's* reflexive comedy derives from the filmmakers' awareness of noir conventions; in an adjacent strain of semicomic stories of mischance, it is the characters who are self-aware. In *Kalifornia* (1993), *True Romance* (1993), and *River of Grass* (1994), the protagonists regard their entrée in crime scenes with an acute knowledge of genre. For these characters bred on movies, crime is an exciting playing field.

The hero in *Kalifornia*, Brian (David Duchovny), is writing a book on serial killers. As research, he travels across the country with his photographer-girlfriend, who shoots the places where famous murders occurred. On their journey, this middle-class couple hooks up with Early and "his woman" (Brad Pitt and Juliette Lewis). Early is a serial killer who taunts Brian about how he can write a book on a subject he knows nothing about. Brian indeed is stuck in his head. In voiceovers distributed throughout the film, he approaches noir terrain from a strictly academic perspective; his perceptions ("serial killers live their whole lives in that place, somewhere between dreams and reality") indicate that, if he ever does write his book, it won't be any good. Brian, a bourgeois egghead hooked on serial killers as the dark other—"Early lived in the moment, and I don't know if I was fascinated or frightened," he observes, spelling out his position on noir—doesn't earn his stripes until, "progressing" from thinking to doing he shoots the killer. Endorsing Brian's violence, the film is anti-intellectual and classist.

Like the scrutinizing protagonist issuing his position papers, the film's visual design is also self-conscious. The circling, craning, hyperactive camera swoons as it inspects such familiar genre sites as campy, neon-lit motel signs, an isolated gas station, and a dark pool hall. *Kalifornia's* sheer visual luster—its celebration of the poetry of vernacular architecture and of abandoned places—like its ratiocinating hero, contains the seeds of genre demolition.

The protagonist of *True Romance* is a regular postmodern kid, who works at a comics store, goes obsessively to the movies, lionizes Elvis, and drives a retro pink Cadillac. Like his creator, Quentin Tarantino, who wrote the screenplay, he is a pure product of the MTV generation, saturated in pop culture allusions. Living in a twilight realm in which the real world merges with and is often overtaken by his fantasies, he's ripe for a trip into pop noir. It begins as he sits watching Sonny Chiba in *The Street Fighter* at the Vista, his favorite theater, an old-fashioned single-screen neighborhood house. A seductive young woman, a call girl hired by his boss as a birthday present, sits down next to him; and before he knows it, just like in the movies, he's embarked on a crime spree.

After he blows away her pimp and the pimp's associates, he mistakenly takes a suitcase full of cocaine. And just like the fugitives in noir, the newly hatched criminals take to the road, traveling from cold, ice-blue Detroit in midwinter to Los Angeles, neo's land of milk and honey and gunplay, pursued by drug dealers who want to recover their suitcase. The chase climaxes at the Ambassador Hotel, a relic of old Hollywood, where there is an explosive three-way shootout among cops, a drug-snorting movie producer and his minions, and the drug people from Detroit. The showdown, one for the records in intensity and velocity, is played out against an old crime movie being projected on a

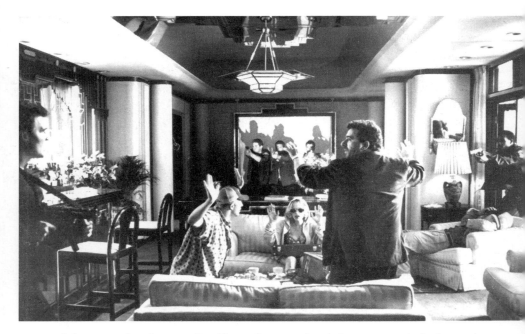

A three-way showdown—police, film producers, and mobsters—surrounds the innocent heroine (Patricia Arquette) in *True Romance* (1993), a postmodern adolescent's fever dream of a noir adventure.

large television screen. Staged with excess, the violence becomes comic—inferno and farce blended into an echt postmodern confection.

In a few places, the hip mixture of comedy and violence curdles, as in a sustained, gruesome scene in which a heavy from Detroit brutalizes the heroine. But for the most part, Tarantino has written a pulp-fiction male adolescent fantasy in which the "dreamer" is cast as the hero of a comic-book noir. The character outwits and blows away pimps and drug lords and escapes with his new, pregnant wife from a world of bad grown-ups to an idyllic island. Because it is presented as a daydream, the film can't quite be held to the same standard of morality or logic as straight "adult" noir. The character's odyssey unfolds in a kind of never-never land, and in a world in which everything is an artifact, a nice kid can use guns with impunity. In love with action movies and pop culture and intensely aware of his status in a pop fiction, the hero remains unscathed by his brush with noir. (That this is "only a movie" is underlined by the film's allusions to *Badlands*, Terrence Malick's landmark 1973 crime drama, from which it lifts music by Carl Orff and an intermittent, naive voiceover spoken by a heroine drenched in the sentiments of Harlequin Romance novels.)

In a little-seen independent, *River of Grass*, another movie with its roots in the seminal *Badlands*, a bored housewife longs for noir adventure. When she thinks she and her new beau have shot and killed a cop, she hopes they will become nationally renowned fugitives. Her boyfriend finds out that they didn't kill the cop, after all, but fears that telling her will break her fantasy of a life on the run in noirish motels. When he attempts to rob a convenience store (isn't that what killers on the run in movies like this do?), another robber intercepts him. Scaling down his ambition, he robs a Laundromat but exits only with a pile of clothes. She shoots him and then tosses him out of the car after he announces that he will get a job so they can build a life together. Imitating a criminal way of life she has seen in the movies, the rumpled, heavyset heroine has transformed herself into the character she thinks she wants to be, a notorious outlaw.

Unlike for protagonists in traditional thrillers, for this movie-made criminal, noir is solution rather than damnation, the route not the detour. Noir is adventure, a reprieve from the dead-end lives of her mother and daughter imprisoned in tract houses that border a flat landscape, Florida's river of grass. At the end, she drives away from the river of grass, heading toward Miami, where presumably she can play out her noir masquerade at full throttle.

"Mother of God, is this the end of Rico?" the gangster asks at the conclusion of *Little Caesar*. Is a film like *River of Grass*, with all its clever inversions, its ironic quotations and sense of play, its terms and tone so pointedly estranged from their origins in 1940s thrillers, a portent of the end of noir?

A natural born killer: Henry (Michael Rooker) in private, "split" in two, in *Henry: Portrait of a Serial Killer* (1989).

# Chapter 8

# Born to Be Bad

In the purest strain of noir, the set of narrative patterns I have called melodramas of mischance, crime overtakes a bourgeois setting or, solicited by one or more of the seven deadly sins, a bourgeois character eases into crime. The crucial point here is that the stories start from an opposition between lawful citizens and criminals. From the beginnings of noir, another story ensemble has focused on professional criminals, on characters who pursue a criminal way of life *before* the film begins. Noir about hard-core criminals has a different emphasis than the classic gangster saga, in which the gangster's rise from obscurity to dominance occupies most of the narrative, with his inevitable downfall reserved for a quick finale. Virtually by definition, noir fixates on downfall rather than rise. The gangster movie is customarily phrased as biographical drama (*The Public Enemy*; *Bugsy*) or as epic (*The Godfather*), neither format appropriate to noir. "Always already" criminals in noir tend to be a shabbier lot than the Depression-era lifers; and more often than not, they work on their own or link up in loosely formed cadres that have little in common with the strictly regulated hierarchies depicted in the traditional gangster opus.

Bank robbers, fugitive outlaw couples, hit men, and psychos comprise a core pantheon of noir criminal types in the neo period. The two former groups are crossovers from classic noir; the two latter, with less of a classic-era pedigree, have emerged as distinct artifacts of more recent noir. As with other paradigms in the long and lengthening nouveau period, the born-to-be-bad collection has been submitted to a wide range of idioms, from straightforward retellings from the classic era to reflexive postmodern spirals.

The failed heist, which demonstrated the truism about the lack of honor among thieves, was a classic noir staple. Three genre highlights—*Criss Cross* (1949), *The Asphalt Jungle* (1950), and *The Killing* (1956)—are about exactly the kind of doomed robbery that encapsulates a noir viewpoint. The appeal of these stories is basic. Audiences enjoy being in on the planning of a subversive act, experience vicariously the aggression that the criminals act out, then feel vindicated by the inevitable failure, the flurry of double and triple crosses cued by greed that ensure the downfall of the conspirators. As a narrative envelope, however, the heist is as confining as the rise-and-fall pattern of the old-fashioned gangster biographies. There is only so much give to the field. When Quentin Tarantino reinvented the heist film in his 1992 *Reservoir Dogs*, there had been only a handful in the intervening years since the last major entry, Robert Wise's formidable *Odds Against Tomorrow* in 1959.

Whether *Odds Against Tomorrow* is the last classic noir (though released a year after *Touch of Evil*) or the first stirring of neo-noir, it is a definitive heist film that, Janus-like, contains both traditional and new motifs. Planning a bank holdup, a cop (Ed Begley), who went wrong long before the action begins, writes his doom the moment he chooses his partners, an embittered white racist veteran (Robert Ryan) and a black musician (Harry Belafonte), who is a gambler in debt to gangsters. At first, sensing disaster, both characters resist the crooked cop's offer, but feeling pinched by failure and humiliated by the fact that their wives have had to work to compensate for their lack, they join up. In the robbery the cop devises, the musician plays a deliveryman from a local restaurant who gains entrance into the bank by bringing coffee and sandwiches to clerks toting up end-of-the-week deposits. But as the ex-cop should have realized, the vet's racism ensures the scheme's failure: because the vet refuses to allow the black man to have car keys, the robbery is foiled at a do-or-die point dependent on split-second timing. After he is wounded, the cop shoots himself so his partners won't be detained trying to rescue him. But his redemptive self-sacrifice is futile. The two survivors begin to pursue each other. Blinded by their rage, they ignore a sign that reads STOP DEAD END, running up twin gas tanks, at the tops of which they shoot each other. Following the conflagration, the police cannot distinguish the black from the white corpse. Is the apocalyptic climax to *Odds Against Tomorrow* classic noir's true epitaph?

The racism theme adds sociological stitching to a traditional heist thriller while also anticipating the way blackness is used in a distinct neo-noir cycle of the 1980s and early 1990s. Primarily, however, the film is notable as a final flourish to the original cycle. This is strongly moralistic noir before the addition of color, wide-screen composition, MTV editing, and a host of postmodern twists and renovations. Except for Harry Belafonte, the performers, including Ed Begley, Robert Ryan, Shelley Winters, and above all Gloria Grahame, a genre icon in her noir swan song in a small, decorative role (the steamy neighbor with whom the vet has a fling), carry strong association with the classic cycle. In shimmering black-and-white images, complemented by a moody jazz score, the film creates a world that insistently entraps the characters. Low-angle ceiling shots, canted angles, deep-focus shots in which characters are separated from each other within the same frame, mirror shots, a tunnel-like corridor in the cop's apartment house, a dizzying, high-angle diagonal shot as the robbers climb stairs to the top of each gas tank achieve an expressionist intensity. In a film with no wasted moments, each gesture is impregnated with noir. On an early morning walk, the bigot sees a children's game in which a black boy is encircled by his playmates, an image that resonates with the racial divide that is to lead to his death. Stippled with noir set pieces staged as if for the last time, this supremely confident film is so complete a rendition of its story type that the type all but disappeared in the 1960s. In the 1970s, in such films as *The Getaway* (1972), *Charley Varrick* (1973), and *The Outfit* (1974), the robbery narrative resurfaced in a new guise.

Gilding a heist movie with social consciousness and clearly aware of its place in a noir tradition, *Odds Against Tomorrow* works in a mythmaking terrain. It is virtuoso art-house noir. *Charley Varrick* and *The Outfit*, in notable contrast, have nothing to prove. Hoisted in a sense by remaining true to their unimportance, and stripping the bank-robber mold of higher meanings, the films are tough, lean, low-rent pulp. In both visual and moral matters, they are distinctly postclassic plein-air thrillers shot primarily in bright colors and offering only a few clues that the filmmakers are aware that they are working in noir. The casual morality of both movies, remote from the crime-and-punishment couplet that underwrites *Odds Against Tomorrow*, is of a piece with the unforced visual signature. As in *The Getaway*, the criminals are not only not punished, they are for the most part likable and even "virtuous."

Disguise rules *Charley Varrick*. In the opening heist, which thrusts us without preparation into the protagonist's world of crime, Charley (Walter Matthau) is made up as an old man with thick glasses, gray hair, a leg in a cast, and a prominent facial birthmark. Driven by his sweet-seeming wife, he is in full masquerade as a benign grandfather come to the bank to make a deposit. After he discovers that the bank he has robbed is a drop-off place for Mafia money, he dons another disguise and goes into hiding, where he pretends to be a crop duster and lives in a trailer park in a safe, ordinary town. He plays the part of a calm elderly gentleman who talks to kids and to a dotty British neighbor, skillfully concealing his criminal identity just as the film itself, with its bright rural setting, covers over most of the traces of its noir genealogy. Under cover, Charley cleverly outfoxes the Mafia hit man who comes to reclaim the mob's money. Like the original getaway couple, at the end Charley is off to Mexico and safety, money in hand, successfully refuting the crime-movie axiom that no one can steal from the mob and live.

Taking its cues from its decorous protagonist, Don Siegel's film tells a crime story with little violence and no profanity. It divests noir of much of its signature style as it also subverts the genre's moral conservatism. Charley Varrick is a decent guy just trying to earn a living. The really bad guys are the unseen mob, whose villainy is suggested by their sinister messenger (played by the hulking Joe Don Baker). In ranking its criminals, the film performs a moral sleight of hand as shifty as Charley's protectively bland façade.

In *The Outfit*, David again confronts Goliath as a low-level bank robber goes up against an omnivorous syndicate. Released from prison, a thief (Robert Duvall) becomes a marked man because, by mischance, he and his partners (like Charley Varrick) hit a mob-controlled bank. The crook as Everyman, the small-time thief and his cohorts demonstrate remarkable resourcefulness in confronting the mob. They succeed many times in penetrating the barricaded precincts of the outfit, while in between assaults on the big guns, they keep in shape by performing routine holdups. Like Charley Varrick again, the ex-con here is one cool criminal, methodical and levelheaded.

Disturbingly, the protagonists of both *Charley Varrick* and *The Outfit* occupy the narrative position assigned to heroes. They're crafty individualists squaring off against engulfing corporate giants, who recall the populist figures in Depression-era fables like *Mr. Smith Goes to Washington* and *Mr. Deeds Goes to Town*. When they escape from the syndicate dragnets with their lives and their money, audiences have been set up to sigh in relief. The small-time criminals represent "the people" rising up to slay the dragons of monolithic capitalist empires, and the fact that both sides of these battles are on the wrong side of the law is a technicality the film and, presumably, the audience conveniently forget.

In a representative later crime story like *Thief* (1981), a career robber occupies a tighter spot than the mobile, ultimately victorious felons in *Charley Varrick* and *The Outfit*. Like Charley, Frank, the thief (James Caan), conceals his criminal identity. He works in a used car lot by day, and by night he's a master safecracker who's been bought by the mob. "I own you," the head mobster sneers. The thief yearns for a regular straight life with his wife and child, but when he realizes that he is indeed an indentured servant to the mob, he becomes violent. He dynamites the Green Mill, the tavern where the mob congregates, as well as the used car lot where he works; and when he enters the mobster's house, he guns down everyone in sight. Badly wounded, he walks away from the carnage into the awaiting darkness. The climactic high-angle shot underlines his undetermined fate: Is he too shot up to live, too bruised by his past to be able to go clean?

Unlike the criminal heroes of *Charley Varrick* and *The Outfit*, the safecracker is both physically and emotionally crippled by his unlawful ways. Nonetheless, as showily directed by Michael Mann, the film is morally more problematic than the straightforward 1970s thrillers. The virtuoso opening presents the thief on the job. The film's language — quick editing, roving, athletic camera movements, a pounding rock score by Tangerine Dream that pumps up the tension, a blue alley with fire escapes that looks like a dream of the neo-noir city—in effect, enshrines the thief's job as a work of art. And despite its superficial obeisance to the fact that the protagonist suffers because of his crimes, the film sends a not-so-subliminal message that being a criminal is really a cool occupation, a trade for a real man. James Caan's thief is a tough guy, and the macho violence with which he erases his mob masters, like his safe-cracking, is rendered with a visual flair that bespeaks admiration. Years before Joe Eszterhas, Michael Mann's slick movie takes us deep into the shallow heart of designer noir.

With *Reservoir Dogs*, the prince of neo-pulp revived the heist film. Quentin Tarantino's material is conventional—a heist gone bad, the robbers by the end killed either by each other or by the law—yet as writer and director, he created a truly nouveau noir, vivid, profane, consistently surprising. The punch-counterpunch of the two opening scenes showcases the auteur's audacity, the postmodern spin with which he revises and invigorates a standard genre formula. In the pretitles opening scene, set in a diner, a handheld camera circles a group of men — the reservoir dogs—as they heatedly deconstruct the interior meanings of Madonna's "Like a Virgin." They propose alternate readings before moving on to the next topic, the etiquette of tipping, offering pro and con positions. Tarantino's bottom feeders attack unexpected subject matter in a rhythmic gutter idiom, pulp poetry written by a

Separation marks the distrust that festers among the thieves in *Reservoir Dogs* (1992). Nice Guy Eddie (Chris Penn, second from left) confronts Mr. White (Harvey Keitel, right); a bound police officer is between them, as Mr. Blonde (Michael Madsen, in the rear) and Mr. Pink (Steve Buscemi) look on.

crime-movie fan. After the titles, the film cuts abruptly to a shot of startling mayhem; in the back of a getaway car, one of the robbers, critically wounded during the failed heist, howls in pain. The lewd comedy of the first scene followed by the sudden, bloody aftereffects of the failed heist points up Tarantino's seismic shifts of genre terrain. Left out is the robbery itself. And as the film's emphatic structuring absence—the thing that is never shown—it attains a quasi-mythic status.

The robbers, in stages, repair to the prearranged meeting place, a deserted warehouse where they are to wait for the boss, Joe (played, with gravitas and dignity, by classic noir icon Lawrence Tierney). Flashbacks that identify the major players cut into the waiting time. Mr. Blonde (Joe has given his employees code names), we learn, has done time; Mr. Orange is an undercover cop. The film's fractured time scheme heightens the tension: looping, backtracking, spiraling, time encloses the characters as much as the eerily deserted warehouse does. And the nervous, circling camera, which covers space with obsessive back-and-forth movements, as if it is constantly looking over its own "shoulder," reflects the dogs' mounting distrust and anxiety.

A good part of Tarantino's revisionist cunning pivots on his use of violence. While he refuses to depict the kind of violence the audience would expect to see in a heist saga—the catastrophic gunplay at the robbery site—violence erupts elsewhere. Mr. Blonde, the resident sadist, dances to rock and roll as he tortures a cop he has abducted from the crime scene. There seems no limit to Mr. Blonde's perversity, and his escalating violence seems set up to test the audience's endurance; his madness is stopped only when, from offscreen, the wounded Mr. Orange, lying in a pool of blood, shoots him. In this scene, and in the three-way shootout, a Mexican standoff, the extreme, almost operatic violence is grazed with black comedy. In the finale, Joe holds a gun on Mr. Orange, the only dog he was not 100 percent sure of, as Mr. White, Mr. Orange's self-appointed protector, holds a gun on Joe, as Eddie, Joe's obedient son, holds a gun on Mr. White. They all shoot, and they all fall, leaving Tarantino's stage strewn with as many corpses as the fifth act of a Jacobean revenge tragedy. Only Mr. Pink, seemingly the most neurotic of the pack, survives, but the police waiting outside capture him. (Despite its postmodern glaze, the film is morally conservative in a way that earlier, classically made heist dramas, like *Charley Varrick* and *The Outfit*, are not: none of the thieves lives to profit from his crime.) *Reservoir Dogs* ends, as it began, with another exclusion. The arrival of the police and their capture of the lone bandit are confined to offscreen space.

Another Tarantino twist is the absence of romantic subplots. There are no women in the netherworld his film constructs. As the thieves bait each other about and then disavow their "secret" desires, homosexuality hides in plain sight; the joking and the rote denials express the repressed wish. The bond between Mr. White and Mr. Orange is the film's "true romance." Drawn to Mr. Orange, Mr. White believes in him when others suspect him and maintains a protective attitude. He even wants to run the considerable risk of seeking medical attention for Mr. Orange. Forming a robber's pietà, Mr. White cradles his badly wounded friend; when Mr. Orange confesses his identity, Mr. White shoots him (offscreen), a gesture that in context reveals the pain of a betrayed lover.

Attempting to imitate its betters, *Things to Do in Denver When You're Dead* (1995) models itself on *Reservoir Dogs* as rigorously as Tarantino's film "spoke" with Stanley Kubrick's classic noir heist story, *The Killing*. In *Reservoir Dogs*, despite Tarantino's revisions, a heist is still a heist whereas in *Things to Do in Denver* a caper (structurally equivalent to a holdup) is attached to higher meanings. When a murder planned by a criminal mastermind and executed by a criminal team goes bad, each member of the gang is hunted by an ace hit man. Like the gang in Tarantino's movie, the criminals here are doomed, already "dead" as they hide out waiting for the hit man to find them. And in the film's misguided, "enhanced" iconography, the killer is more than a hit man: he's a cosmic force, Destiny as unstoppable evil.

The crime that goes haywire is folded within a frame story narrated by a character who holds court in a dingy green diner as he tells stories of criminals from "the old days." Set off in a frame within the frame, the caper is presented by the gruff-voiced, hero-worshiping storyteller (Jack Warden, sounding like Lawrence Tierney) as the stuff of myth. He celebrates a legendary criminal lured out of retirement for one last gig by a former colleague who wants someone killed. The crack criminal and his tempter, a figure of Mephistophelian menace confined to a wheelchair and wearing a black glove (Christopher Walken, of course, looking more grotesque than ever), like Prince Hal and Falstaff talk about the days when they were at the top of the craft. "Those were the days" is a leitmotif of the outer and inner stories; and in doubly sentimentalizing its protagonists, the film doubly underlines its corruption, as well as its fake-pulp status. A caper noir that works overtime to find existential meaning in a routine crime story and to invest its master outlaw (played by wet-eyed heartthrob Andy Garcia) with a spurious glamour, *Things to Do in Denver When You're Dead*, as its coy title alone indicates, is strictly faux Tarantino. As if ashamed of its ancestry, the film ends up being an anti-noir gored by its pretensions.

*City of Industry* (1997), in refreshing contrast, proves that an honest, unembellished heist movie remains a workable formula. Four hoods—two brothers, a driver, and a computer whiz who fouls up the circuits—meet in Palm Springs to rob a diamond store. The driver, a cowboy with a punk haircut, a raft of lowlife women, and ties to black and Asian mobs, is the wild card; to keep all the money for himself, he attempts to blow away his partners. One of them escapes, determined to kill his enemy; as the ads proclaimed, "Wanting a man dead is worth staying alive."

Story and characters are comfortingly familiar, but the film's visual design is steeped in a neo-expressionist palette that is bolder than usual for the subgenre. All the settings exude menace. Driving on Los Angeles freeways framed by an intricate geometry of interlocking bridges and overpasses becomes for the thieves a journey into noir. Eccentric vernacular motels, gloom-laden apartments with gated windows, a smoke-filled stripper bar comprise a loser's-row portrait gallery to which the film adds the City of Industry, a world of industrial smokestacks belching fire into what seems a terminally polluted environment. With their complex networks of crisscrossing beams—their geometric gridlock—the industrial settings, which evoke the paintings of Fernand Léger and Charles Sheeler, provide a new visual lexicon for noir entrapment. Odd rectangles of light repeatedly appear in scenes otherwise shrouded in inky shadows. As the hunter (Harvey Keitel) huddles in a corner of a grungy hotel room, for example, the only light is a rectangle on the sickly green wall behind him. The unrealistic light seems to emanate from the tightly wound character, about to smash a table. This modest, little-seen but critically appreciated B thriller understands that true noir rightfully demands a continuously charged visual texture.

The film's one postmodern note is struck at the end, when the hunter mysteriously disappears. For this enigmatic figure, a solitary, grim-looking professional thief, crime not only pays it even seems to soften him. He helps the wife and children of one of his slain partners to escape the City of Industry once he has exacted his revenge against the turncoat. After he has been badly wounded in the shootout, the woman drives him to a hospital; and as she runs in for help, the hunter (in offscreen space) drives off, leaving behind a stack of money. In voiceover, the woman finishes the story: she and her kids now live far from "industry," in a remote and peaceful setting near a beach. Her deliverer mails her a watch, a totem that lets her know he is still alive, somewhere out there beyond the reach of the law.

Outwitting death and narrative plausibility, the hunter has almost supernatural power. He seems to melt into thin air, unseen, beyond the gaze of the camera, his magical survival thereby fusing with the "magic" of the medium itself. Harvey Keitel's robber has little in common with the weak, purely venal thieves in the standard classic-era heist stories; except for his occupation choice, he exhibits the behavior of a strong-willed, dedicated action-movie hero. If he isn't exactly a positive character (he's too cut off, too hidden; a life of crime has indeed done him serious emotional damage), the film nonetheless confers on him a measure of approval that wouldn't have been possible under the Production Code.

In classic and nouveau noir, sympathy for the "devil" has been traditionally extended only to the outlaw couple wandering in the American wilderness on their way toward capture or death. Their love, as well as their crime, having become legend, they are romanticized in part because they are doomed figures. Fritz Lang's 1937 thriller *You Only Live Once*, with Henry Fonda as an ethereal, falsely accused criminal and Sylvia Sidney as his dedicated spouse, established the mold. *They Live by Night* continued it into the classic noir period. Nicholas Ray's 1948 debut feature film about a couple who could not find a place for themselves in Depression America may well qualify as the most sentimental and softhearted entry in classic noir. Presented as victims of a social and economic collapse and as a couple longing for a normal life, Keechie and Bowie are the most endearing outlaw couple in American movies. In *Gun Crazy* (1950) the outlaw couple is toughened up. They are psychotics locked in a folie à deux memorialized by their fetishistic obsession with guns.

The lunar-like landscape in *Badlands* (1973) mirrors the eerie detachment of Kit (Martin Sheen), a serial killer.

In the neo era, there have been two significant criminal couples on the run, in *Badlands* and *Natural Born Killers*. *Badlands* is based on the story of real-life killer Charles Starkweather and his girlfriend Caril Ann Fugate, who embarked on a notorious cross-country murder spree in the mid-1950s. The film's young killer, Kit (Martin Sheen), seems born to be bad, while the dim high-school girl he seduces (Sissy Spacek) must be coaxed into his world of sex and crime. Kit is presented as a man without a past, a sexy wanderer and social outcast who looks like James Dean and has sudden violent eruptions. "Always already" a criminal, Kit is ever ready to shoot. When the girl's father rejects him, Kit blows the man away. But Kit doesn't need provocation to kill—he's a psycho with a gun who can kill bystanders for no reason at all.

Like its opaque, solipsistic characters, who seem incapable of making moral judgments about their crimes, the film itself seems eerily detached. The story, rejecting any trace of classic noir iconography, takes place in a picturesque rural America, a land of expansive vistas washed by wind and strong, brilliant light. Passages of Carl Orff's music in climactic moments lend further distance from the crime scenario. Writer-director Terrence Malick approaches his subject with an aesthetic eye and moral neutrality that may claim priority for his film as the original postmodern neo-noir. His celebrated, luminous crime drama is pretty poison, a radiant spectacle without a coherent moral center. While clearly an external invisible "narrator" stands outside and above the film's idiotic embedded narrator, the high-school girl who (in language borrowed from Harlequin Romance novels) blames society for misunderstanding Kit, the film remains mute about the trail of violence he blazes. In an unnerving way, Malick seems as hypnotized by Kit as the high-school girl who runs off with him. Not quite satire, not quite film noir, *Badlands* is a curious, singular hybrid, a powerful meaningless movie that has had a mostly pernicious impact on later crime dramas.

The most notorious offspring of Malick's landmark is another Quentin Tarantino screenplay (his second), bought and presumably mangled by Oliver Stone. *Natural Born Killers* (1994) is about another psychopath who "rescues" his new and innocent girlfriend by killing her father and then abducting her into his violent underworld. When a reporter asks him how he became a criminal, the media-savvy Mickey pretends to ponder the question but ends up saying he doesn't know. "I guess I'm just a natural-born killer," he smirks. In effect, Mickey turns the question of his pathological violence into a joke—the same stance that, fatally, the film adopts.

Two early scenes underscore the film's intention of presenting serial killers as vaudevillian clowns. The film opens with Mickey and Mallory (Woody Harrelson and Juliette Lewis) shooting up a roadside diner, spraying the place and the customers with a hail of bullets as they accompany their gunplay with a litany of profanities. They are performers who use violence as their text, and their outburst in the diner is presented as a hootenanny, a rip-roaring show put on to delight and to shock the spectator. Beginning with a blast, the film sets up the audience to expect (and to desire?) more fireworks. A flashback, one of many temporal disruptions, recounts how Mickey, a deliveryman, shoots Mallory's trashy parents, then seizes Mallory as his trophy. Staged in cartoonlike sets and with a laugh track, the episode is a satire of a mindless television situation comedy. Coming early, the low- farce treatment of how Mickey wins and liberates "his woman" deconstructs the characters, turning them into goofs whose uncontrolled violence is simply good for a laugh. The opening salvo in the diner, followed by the "courtship" scene, reduces pathology to sight gags and media parody.

These two emblematic sequences serve notice that wild man Oliver Stone has filtered an outlaw-couple scenario into an MTV-style grinder. With its fractured editing, abrupt switches from color to black and white, dizzying dislocations of time and space, and roving, kinetic camera, the film exploits its potentially serious subject for pure spectacle. Stone's psycho vagabonds are little more than a pretext for a free-form, state-of-the-art cinematic carnival.

Thoroughly media-savvy outlaws, Mickey and Mallory know how to monitor their celebrity status. In act one, the criminal duo consciously perform for the media always hot on their trail. In jail for most of act

Mickey and Malory (Woody Harrelson and Juliette Lewis) are maniacs on the loose in *Natural Born Killers* (1994), Oliver Stone's depraved, would-be satire of the fusion between American violence and the media.

two, they are pursued by a media whiz kid, superaggressive television journalist Wayne Gale (Robert Downey, Jr.), who wants a live interview with the globally renowned killers and is right behind them when they break out of jail. After they kill the obnoxious journalist with an appalling British accent (an act the audience has been set up to cheer), the killers leave behind, on a camcorder, the interview for which Gale has been willing to die. The criminals endure, to become a fertile hippie couple driving the American desert in a brightly colored van. Living outside the law and beyond capture, they are the progenitors of a diseased counter-patriarchy, which in a seemingly endless spiral will breed more of their kind for the media to pursue and to elevate.

Taking potshots at situation comedies, nightly news programs, and docudramas like *America's Most Wanted* (here called *American Maniacs*), *Natural Born Killers* is the crime film as would-be social and cultural satire. What better way to reveal a society's indiscriminate worship of fame than by examining how criminal psychopaths are turned into celebrities? The problem is that the film is no better than what it purports to criticize. Hopelessly compromised, it is itself a part of the web it pretends to diagnose and expose; the film at once parodies, exploits, and is complicit with its ostensible subject, the cannibalistic media. Within the film, the media are driven by an almost masturbatory desire to capture—to seize and penetrate—"live" reality: Wayne Gale lusts after the immediate experience of obtaining a live interview with the killers. As the film acknowledges, however, all image production, all processes of representation are illusionary; and as if to demonstrate the sheer untrustworthiness of the image, the film's images seem to be continually collapsing on themselves. Against an ever-shifting, fluid ground, the images repeatedly unravel, dematerialize, and re-form. In its own obsession with the artificiality of the image, *Natural Born Killers* is far more truthful than in its would-be media satire. But here, as well, Oliver Stone's excess collapses his project. Dialogue and narrative coherence are gobbled up by the director's procession of swirling, multilayered, undulating images (and sounds), and the film is reduced to the level of the visual and moral clutter it is presumably ridiculing. An utterly contaminated work, the film ends up consuming itself: an outlaw-couple neo-noir as an orgy of self-cancellation.

In the French style: the nameless protagonist (Ryan O'Neal, left) blasts a pursuer (Joseph Walsh) in Walter Hill's neo-expressionist, semi-abstract thriller, *The Driver* (1978).

The fugitive couple, offered in varying moral tones from the neutrality of *Badlands* to the approval bestowed on Thelma and Louise to the blasphemy of *Natural Born Killers*, has a long noir lineage. The hit man is, for the most part, a neo-noir prototype, raised in Quentin Tarantino's *Pulp Fiction* to the status of a postmodern antihero. As with all Tarantino's innovations, however, this too has a pop-culture pedigree. The hit man as a symbol of contemporary disengagement is the focus of Melville's 1967 *Le Samouraï*, a film Tarantino has called "perfect." And while Tarantino's bemused tone doesn't resemble Melville's Gallic solemnity, the earlier film's admiration for a hit man guided by a code of honor percolates into *Pulp Fiction*. Coming between Melville's high-art European angst and Tarantino's ripe American pulp is *The Driver*, a curious and oddly affecting 1978 neo-noir by Walter Hill, which more fully absorbs a Melvillean tone as it creates a criminal antihero the audience is primed to admire.

Like Melville's samourai, the driver (played by Ryan O'Neal) is the criminal as a contemporary underground man. Without a name, a woman, a history, a regular place to live, he dangles in existential drift.

Like the hit man, he's a criminal for hire. He's an expert with a car who speaks in monosyllables and only when he absolutely must. Most of the time, he doesn't carry a gun—the car that he handles with exquisite "masculine" control is the only weapon he needs. The film's opening establishes his virtuosity. Emerging from a hole in the ground he enters an underground garage, picks open a car, drives to a prearranged spot to meet thieves who have just robbed a casino, and then leads cops on a chase through the streets of downtown Los Angeles. Deadpan and fearless, he eludes his pursuers. The detective (Bruce Dern) who is determined to nab him refers to him as "the cowboy who's never been caught."

The bulk of the film depicts the detective's efforts to entrap this stone-cold adversary. "You play against me, pal, you're going to lose," he taunts the driver, who accepts the challenge. Their contest is played out on the margins of the city in warehouses and garages with low ceilings and in cheap hotels with crumbling walls and long, empty hallways. Geometric, industrial, and semi-abstract, space in the film is as impersonal as the driver and his hunter. Ryan O'Neal's driver is a hollow man, an untouchable loner with no apparent inner life, but in a way he's a winner. Police surround him when he goes to Union Station to retrieve robbery money he left in a locker. "Looks like we both got taken," the driver comments when he discovers that the locker is empty. Shrugging, he walks out of the station, beyond the reach of the law. He and his opponent have been motivated by a sense of masculine competition rather than greed (neither one cares where the money is). They have played the game for principles rather than profit.

A daring early neo-noir film that adopts elements of European art-house crime dramas onto native ground, *The Driver* carries genre motifs to the edge of abstraction as it places its emptied-out, nameless character in a limbolike mise-en-scène—a nowhere space for a nowhere man. Both the film and the character are too remote and too glacial to have become models for later American crime movies. One of the many ambiguous achievements of *Pulp Fiction* is that it transformed professional criminals into accessible antiheroes, comic, profane, and "one of us." Of all the ways in which Tarantino's 1994 landmark provided a fresh spin to crime-movie stencils, the most influential and enduring may be its placement of two hit men as tragicomic protagonists.

Driving on a sunny morning in the City of Angels, two men, one

Quentin Tarantino's pop-culture knockout, *Pulp Fiction* (1994), introduced an insidious nouveau noir trope, the hit man as a charming antihero (John Travolta, as hired gun Vincent Vega, dancing with the boss's wife [Uma Thurman]).

black, one white, talk about Big Macs in Amsterdam and, more generally, about restaurant etiquette in foreign cities. Thrusting and parrying, they address light topics in a brisk rhythm that identifies them as hardboiled. With their slick vernacular style, they are witty and likable and, almost coincidentally, are on their way to a hit. We follow them into an apartment where disheveled occupants are gobbling hamburgers for breakfast. One of the hit men, Jules Winnfield (Samuel L. Jackson), nabs a bite of one of the burgers; then he and his partner, Vincent

Vega (John Travolta), who till then has been lurking in the background looking blank, take out big guns and begin firing away. Talking about Big Macs, shooting up an apartment full of people—it's all in a morning's work.

The long comic episode immediately following cements our complicity with Vincent Vega. Marsellus Wallace, Vega's boss, an intimidating man nobody with regard for his life would wish to offend, has asked Vega to take his wife out on a date. The couple goes to Jack Rabbit Slim's, a retro restaurant. "Ed Sullivan" greets them. As they sit in a red car, "Buddy Holly" waits on them, while in the background "Marilyn Monroe's" skirt flies up, as it did in *The Seven-Year Itch*. But (Tarantino's slyness kicking in at high gear) John Travolta is another icon on the scene; his own pop apogee occurred nearly twenty years earlier in a similar kind of place, the 1970s disco in *Saturday Night Fever*. When Travolta twenty years on, heavy and jowly but still bursting with charm, gets up to dance, the moment is packed with pop cultural significance. And as it has been primed to do, the audience can't help but transfer feelings for the actor himself, a tarnished icon making a successful comeback, doing it again and doing it splendidly after years in the professional doldrums, to his character. Who could resist Travolta in this part, in this scene, dancing again and getting it just right? It seems incidental that this time he isn't playing a kid from Brooklyn with dreams of disco glory, but a puffy middle-aged man who kills for a living.

Vincent is not only a smooth dancer, he is also something of a buffoon. He's competent wielding a gun—his face noticeably darkens whenever he shoots—but he's also careless. Using his gun to elaborate a story, he accidentally wounds a hostage he and his partner have abducted from the apartment their visit transformed into a charnel house. Absentminded Vincent tints his violence with comedy: how can the viewer dislike a hit man in the guise of such an appealing bumbler?

To ensure a positive response to his antihero, Tarantino has yet another trick. Long before the three interlocking stories that comprise *Pulp Fiction* are completed, Vincent is killed. He's caught off guard, fatally shot as he is sitting on the john reading a pulp novel when the resident of the apartment he is watching suddenly returns. The star dies, but Tarantino has reversed the chronology, placing the last act before the second act, so Vincent is magically resurrected. It's as if Hitchcock brought back Janet Leigh for the finale of *Psycho*. When we see Vincent at the end of the film, we know the fate that has already overtaken him, and as a result his appearance is suffused with poignancy. He and Winnfield eat breakfast at a 1950s Googie-style diner (a nostalgic icon for Tarantino), thereby completing the narrative circle, returning the film to the diner where in the opening scene two customers pull an impromptu stickup. Although we don't know in the opening that the two hit men happen to be in the diner at the same time, they intercept with their expertise the attempted robbery and prevent a bloodbath. Winnfield permits the amateur thieves to leave with the money, after which he and Vincent make a triumphant exit, their mastery of the scene having ensured that no one has been hurt. The hit men appear as the people's saviors. Outside the diner, glimpsed through its venetian blinds, the two men turn and in lockstep walk offscreen, enjoying a sense of victory that we know is only temporary.

While the director, in collusion with his charismatic star, makes Vega the primary sympathetic antihero, Jackson's hit man is also humanized. In the apartment where they make their hit, the character undergoes a conversion after he and Vincent have been shot and yet do not die. He interprets their survival as a "miracle," "a sign from God that [he] should mend his ways." And in the diner, vowing to leave the life, already in the throes of his born-again ecstasy, he allows the holdup goons to leave with the money because he is in "transition."

In Tarantino's pulp-fiction world, mobsters and their molls, hit men and their victims are entirely on their own. In the absence of law-enforcement figures (the only cop in the film is a homosexual sadist who may well be wearing a police uniform simply as a fetish), the hit men are "the law." Dispensing justice according to an underworld creed, they "retire" drug dealers who try to double-cross their boss and restore order to a diner invaded by petty thieves. Without regulating agents from an outside world, the hit men are the only available or possible heroes. Even so, the film concludes with a conventional moral reckoning, in which the likable guys who kill for a living are both dead, one literally, the other, following his conversion, metaphorically.

A ribald, audacious juxtaposition of violence with black comedy, populated by a gallery of disarming rogues, *Pulp Fiction* is a rich guilty pleasure, the movie equivalent of junk food. Powerful but, both in the short run and in the final analysis, pointless, it was a crime-movie bonanza that has inevitably spawned imitations. Perhaps above all its acceptance ratified the hit man as a contemporary film hero. And whether as an avatar of existential angst, as in *Little Odessa* (1994), a romantic hero, as in *Bulletproof Heart* (1995), or a comic foil, as in *2 Days in the Valley* (1996) and *Grosse Pointe Blank* (1997), the hit man has become a recurrent presence in the crime picture. Like most original work, *Pulp Fiction* is a perilous model, and the hit men of various hues in films made in its shadow pale in comparison.

The talented novice director of *Little Odessa*, James Gray, opens and closes his film with a lingering closeup on the protagonist's eyes as he stares meditatively into offscreen space. At the beginning, the character's eyes are wary; by the end, as he stares off into the night, torn apart by what has happened to him and by what he has done to others, his gaze is notably darker. Hit men are often the most aware characters in 1990s crime movies, a point the first image here underscores. This character with a complicated inner life walks up to a man sitting on a bench and shoots him in broad daylight. A pro, he performs his job without apparent qualm; indeed, a moment's hesitation might well prove fatal. But that opening shot tells us that this character with residual feelings is trapped in a profession where feelings are impermissible.

In the early 1930s gangster sagas, the criminal antihero's Achilles' heel was typically an excess of emotion, an intense love for a mother or a sister, for instance, or for a male friend. Similarly dangerous are the feelings the hit man in *Little Odessa* has for his dying mother and for a younger brother who looks up to him. When he is called to make a hit in his old neighborhood, where his family still lives, the hit man is placed in a tight spot. He knows that going home places him and his family at risk; and yet like a Western's gunslinger reluctantly accepting one last assignment, or like the retired criminal in *Kiss of Death* persuaded to take on a job he knows in his bones he shouldn't, he returns. His former girlfriend and his beloved brother die, and as his father pronounces bitterly, "You ruined our family." Where the gangster in the classic crime movies dies, the criminal here is alive to survey and to grieve over the damage he has wrought.

Although the character is punished for his sins, the film is morally troublesome in ways classic noir and the classic gangster stories were not. A noir protagonist is typically edged or pushed into crime for reasons a films accounts for, just as the 1930s gangsters turned to crime for historically verifiable causes; but the hit man in *Little Odessa* is a criminal in a vacuum. The film's setting, the contemporary Russian immigrant community of the Brighton Beach section of Brooklyn, provides little more than exotic flavoring and a noir-ready locale. Vaguely, the new Russian immigrants' neighborhood is seen as a spawning ground for criminals, the way Italian immigrant communities were in the 1930s, but basically it is thematically immaterial that the characters are a Jewish family from Russia. The protagonist chooses to become a bad man for reasons that remain outside the film's concern. And not explaining how the character was befouled elevates him to a near-mythic status, just as the film's distanced treatment of the Russian mob turns it into a menacing, mostly offscreen presence. Seen only at the rear or the sides of the wide screen, shrouded in secrecy and semidarkness, the mob is boosted to the iconographic position of the partially seen Christ in *Ben-Hur.* What it does and who it is, the power it collectively embodies, is presumably too awesome to be fully shown.

Like *Little Odessa*, *Bulletproof Heart* opens and closes on a shot of its hero, another hit man with a soul, staring contemplatively offscreen. His job is to off a woman who owes money to the mob and can't pay. Fatally ill (a fact her executioner doesn't know), she seems to embrace her fate. But when Mick (Anthony LaPaglia) becomes attracted to her, he decides to spare her life. Unaware that Mick will not fulfill the contract, his partner, who panicked on an earlier job and now wants to prove his mettle, shoots her. The woman's death restores the hero's malaise, his conviction that he is unredeemable, a man with a bulletproof heart. Reflecting its protagonist, the film moves at a heavyhearted, viscous pace. Its solemn demeanor, however, cannot conceal its spurious intention of attempting to turn a hit man into a hero whose suffering reflects the spirit of the times.

In *Le Samouraï*, Jean-Pierre Melville was able to bring off this stunt, but to date no American movie has yet succeeded and, with luck, no further neo-noir thrillers will even try. As if recognizing that the hit man as a wounded, empathetic character is a flawed, compromised, even absurd premise, a spate of hybrid films of the 1990s have carried the character into comic terrain. In *2 Days in the Valley*, a transparent *Pulp Fiction* wannabe, a wife conspires with criminals to bump off her estranged, wealthy husband. The head hit man is sinister, reptilian—everything you would expect a hit man to be; but his assistant, a schlemiel afraid of dogs, breaks the mold. The character as played by Danny Aiello is warmhearted and dim, and like the scheming wife who, scot-free, drives off with the loot, a satisfied smile on her lips, he is given a happy end. He not only escapes with some of the money, he has also acquired a mistress. Where Tarantino deftly balances comedy with violence, the crime story in *2 Days in the Valley* dips uneasily into farce, and the triumph of the "good" criminals is a shallow rejoinder to the old Production Code mandate that crime does not and must not pay.

Completely confident in its cynicism, *Grosse Pointe Blank* is *The Graduate* for generation *x*, a put-on for the post-*Pulp Fiction* brigade. In this crime story played as farce, the hit man conducts himself like a hotshot Wall Street broker. By a rival character's count, there are too many professional killers, a situation that's bad for business, and so he favors consolidation with other outfits. But the protagonist wants to remain independent. Nobody, including his well-to-do girlfriend and her Republican father, is even momentarily phased by his career choice. "A growth industry," the father says approvingly when the young man identifies his

*2 Days in the Valley* (1996), a *Pulp Fiction* wannabe, fails in its attempt to present a has-been hit man (Danny Aiello), terrified of dogs, as an appealing comic hero. Against the smog-filled backdrop of the San Fernando Valley, a ripe site for neo-noir, comic or otherwise, the incompetent hit man tries to hold an art dealer (Greg Cruttwell) and his assistant (Glenne Headly) hostage.

line as "professional killer." As it dismantles the conventions of straight crime movies, deadpan irony is the film's single note. Its title a play on *Point Blank*, the film insistently places characters and narrative—the hit man as romantic hero who wins a girl by shooting up her placid home town—in quotatation marks, telegraphing its satiric intent.

A rare moment of self-reflection for another likable hired gun, Martin Blank (John Cusack), in the insufferably wised-up *Grosse Pointe Blank* (1997).

John Cusack, who cowrote and stars, is a likable actor with a bland Everyman presence (his character is named Martin Blank for a reason). The film (radically) scales down Hannah Arendt's perception about the banality of evil. Smugly post-serious, the movie, directed by George Armitage, is a would-be genre demolition that toys with the notion that noir taken straight is no longer playable. But like Mel Brooks's *Blazing Saddles*, which sent up Western motifs, the film's noir parody punctures but cannot erase its target. *Grosse Pointe Blank* is a one-joke movie that ultimately cancels itself out, eviscerated by its infatuation with its own nonchalance. As it tries to overturn studio-era morality with its brash, up-to-the-minute sensibility — crime *does* pay, the criminal is cute and gets the girl, and besides, shooting people is really fun, no matter what fuddy-duddy moralists contend—the film sinks into a cesspool.

If on occasion the hit man has been transformed into a semblance of being "one of us," an adjacent noir archetype, the psychotic killer, who murders out of compulsion rather than for a salary, remains confined to the category of the other. And if the hit man at times has been used as an icon of modern anxieties, the psycho killer is still a phenomenon who operates far from the madding crowd. Even in a film as morally compromised as *Natural Born Killers*, the actions of the trigger-happy protagonists are intended to shock rather than to evoke from the spectator a sense of resemblance. The psycho in neo-noir pictures comes in three basic guises: as someone within the family, lurking at close range; as a serial killer; and, a special case, as a noir superstar, a character whose virtuoso manipulations are performed as a spectacle to be savored by the audience.

At close range: Stephanie (Jill Schoelen, left), her mother (Shelley Hack), and her stepfather (Terry O'Quinn), a noir psychopath, may look like a robust, all-American family, but in *The Stepfather* (1987), appearances are indeed deceiving.

A madman hiding behind cloying dedication to family values, the protagonist of *The Stepfather* (1987) is compelled to kill the families he creates. The film opens with the character, in a kind of postorgasmic calm, walking away from the house where he has just slaughtered his family. Bland and pleasant, he takes on another identity as he establishes a new family in another town. His new wife remains oblivious, but his stepdaughter suspects that his average-seeming demeanor may be only a façade. When pressures close in on him, he prepares to kill his new family before he moves on. But his stepdaughter ends his demented circuit when she shoots him. Their house exorcized of a poisoned patriarch, she and her mother walk off arm in arm.

A prime example of the fluid boundaries between horror movies and a certain kind of noir thriller, in which the horrific has a natural rather than supernatural ontology, *The Stepfather* is a suburban Jekyll and Hyde. The antisocial protagonist harbors a doppelgänger whose origins are never explained. It would be naïve, of course, to expect this or any noir thriller to account fully for the origins of psychosis, but the character here, driven by a compulsion to murder those he has made dependent on him, is presented simply as a monster whose evil leaps out of a vacuum. Lacking thematic density, the stepfather's mania is reduced to spectacle and the viewer is placed in the position of waiting for (and desiring) the inevitable eruption when the character's social mask crumbles to reveal the killer within.

The father in *At Close Range* (1986), Brad, Sr., played by Christopher Walken at his most reptilian, coaxes his two sons into a heart of darkness. He's another fatally contaminated patriarch who, along with a band of brothers, obeys a brutal, indeed psychopathic, criminal code. When one of the extended family drowns an informer, Brad, Sr., puts a finger to his mouth to demand the silence of Brad, Jr. (Sean Penn), the son who has come to live with him after a long absence. For this demented father, expertise with guns is the supreme register of masculinity; laying a gun before his sons, he says, "I gotta see if you got something between the legs." (Forcing his sons through rituals that test their manly prowess, this father has values that represent the dark side of Reagan-era hard bodies, the cult of muscle that helps account for the improbable superstar careers of Sylvester Stallone and Arnold Schwarzenegger.)

When his sons turn against him, he retaliates, shooting Tommy (Chris Penn, Sean's brother), the son who has been loyal to him all along, and hires vigilantes to kill the prodigal son, Brad, Jr., and Brad's girlfriend, Terry. After Brad (but not Terry) survives the assault, he tries to—but realizes he cannot—kill his father. He cannot *be* his father.

Rather, arriving by helicopter, he testifies against Brad, Sr., in a court. "Who is this man?" a prosecuting attorney asks him. Chokingly, after a long pause, he answers, "My father."

*At Close Range*, powerfully directed by James Foley, a true neo-noir master, rewrites the many Oedipal texts of classic noir in which errant sons rise up against repressive bourgeois father figures. Here, a son "kills" his father in an attempt to reclaim for himself a semblance of the bourgeois order his father's blasphemy has desecrated. Convicting his father in a court of law, the son attempts some kind of moral restoration. The prodigal son who slips into then out of noir, lured into crime because he wants paternal approval and before he recognizes his father's code, is a fully realized character; and Sean Penn's edgy, kinetic performance is a genre highlight. But the father, who gradually assumes the proportions of Mephistophelian evil, remains an enigma despite, or really perhaps because of, Walken's vividly sinister presence. Walken's zeal becomes vaudevillian and enhances an aura of pretense and charade, giving the impression that the film is placing evil on display.

Classic noir was traditionally about the evolution of criminals; neo-noir films are often transfixed by a criminality that's inborn long before the narrative opens. In films on the model of *At Close Range* and *The Stepfather*, the wicked characters are presented almost purely as a spectacle, to be consumed rather than dissected. As a result, the characters become the noir equivalent of the human monsters in modern horror stories, like *Halloween*. Comfortable accounting for the psychology of the sons, *At Close Range* is virtually paralyzed in confronting that of the father. In this symptomatic thriller, with its rich Rembrandt lighting, elegantly tracking camera, and stately score, evil is at once intensely visual and superficial; beyond or resistant to interpretation, it is performed in a zone that marks it as sheer theater.

Like the hit man, the doomed serial killer, though it may seem an apt character, is a rare figure in classic noir and threatens generic boundaries. Classic noir narratives, for the most part, were encoded precisely as narratives, as stories set apart from the real world, while the serial killer carries the taint of sensational real-life crimes. By definition, the serial killer works a wide territory, another possible challenge to noir narratives, typically framed within a limited sphere. *Henry: Portrait of a Serial Killer*, a notorious 1989 film, rewrites many of noir's narrative and visual codes. As it depicts the daily routine of a serial killer, the film is disturbingly encrusted with the glaze of the real—this is noir phrased as docudrama rather than as expressionist nightmare. The actors, unknowns who provide none of the safety attached to familiar star presence, perform in a minimalist natural style from which most of the traces of standard film performance are absent. The camera behaves in a cinema verité mode as well. During violent scenes, a jerky, handheld camera and no intercutting create an illusion of immediacy—the camera does not avert its gaze during Henry's two murderous explosions—while for many other scenes, a static camera stares unflinchingly at the killer. Throughout, the camera (and therefore the spectator) remains sutured to the character, tied to him without relief.

But like the title character, masquerading as a normal citizen (Henry is an exterminator, a grotesque alibi for his secret other profession), the film's documentary gloss is only a façade, a skillful fabrication that inscribes the spectator within a voyeuristic, sadistic circuit. Doesn't the viewer, who has invested the time and money to see a portrait of a serial killer, wish to be shocked, to be given privileged access to acts of violence? The opening shot incites our voyeurism as the camera slowly retreats from a closeup to a long shot of a beautiful woman revealed to be a corpse covered with artfully arranged blood. This is violence made safe and aesthetic, a policy the film continues to pursue as, at first, it displays only the aftereffects of Henry's rampages. When Henry chooses a target, a woman randomly selected in a shopping mall, and proceeds to follow her as she drives to her house, we are placed in the position of wondering if at last we are to be permitted to see Henry kill. But a man meets the woman at her house, and Henry drives away. He returns later, however; and in an unbroken long shot, we observe him, with his exterminator equipment, talking to his potential victim at her front door. We see her hesitate about whether or not to allow the stranger inside. Does her hesitation mirror the spectator's? The audience has been set up to want the woman, a figure seen only in long shots, to admit Henry and yet is guilty about the transgressive desire the film has mobilized. When Henry and his partner, Otis, randomly break into a house and kill a family, recording the deed with a camcorder, whatever latent wish the spectator might be harboring for "forbidden" images is satiated with a vengeance. The film does not turn away from the scene of carnage, nor does it use fragmented editing to conceal the "unseeable."

After having presented violence in a layered, distanced style, the film now refuses to pull any punches. The viewer, no longer protected, is confronted by an unedited image that has been carefully constructed to look like a real event. In a stroke, "safe" movie violence has been demoted from an entertainment commodity to an unnerving simulacrum of a snuff film.

Like the movie itself, the protagonist has an invisible style. Passing for normal, he moves at random through a real world as he skillfully covers his traces. He's a self-conscious modern killer who, to avoid detection, changes his m.o. from murder to murder. With his camcorder, he records his crimes; then, with his partner, he watches them over and over, as if they are entertainment he can't get his fill of. The more he watches, the more his crimes retreat into a kind of performance framework. Henry's anonymity is so skillfully maintained that he remains at large, an untraceable killer free to pursue his criminal credo that "you have to keep moving."

Setting the killer within a real-seeming world, the film avoids traditional noir signifiers. Henry is never visually enclosed except for the times he watches himself on television. As he cruises for victims or confers with his partner or conducts a courtship of Otis's unsuspecting sister, Henry occupies bright, open spaces. This serial killer is trapped by his pathology, not by mise-en-scène. The film departs from neo-noir convention in another way as well: beneath its deadpan docudrama veneer, it investigates a psychopathic personality more fully than do most contemporary thrillers. In his childhood, Henry's prostitute-mother repeatedly abused him, and now he kills women to avenge himself against his original violator. But the film acknowledges that no single cause can account for the character's madness. Henry kills to compensate for an insatiable inner emptiness, to relieve the tedium of low-class working life, to savor the challenge of disguising his traces. He kills not only because he must but also because he can.

While *Henry: Portrait of a Serial Killer* conceals its noir origins, *Seven* (1995) puts noir insignia on spectacular display. Where *Henry* sets crime in a real world, *Seven* sets it within a highly ornamented frame. Brilliantly directed by David Fincher, *Seven* is a postmodern police procedural set in a city of perpetual gloom. The film's city is never identified, and gradually it becomes apparent that, except for some exterior location shots, the city is imaginary. It's a stylized *re*-presentation of the crime-filled, studio-built, dark city of classic noir, a place of ram-shackle derelict buildings with murky brown hallways and cluttered, warrenlike rooms into which light and air never penetrate. A city of seemingly unending rain and noise, it may well be the most richly rendered symbolic space to date in the history of neo-noir. The characters live in grim, congested rooms and nobody turns on a light—flashlights seem to be the only ready source of illumination. A young police detective and his wife, new in town, live in an apartment by an elevated train track, which emits a thunderous rumble whenever a train passes by. The serial killer's apartment is filled with the detritus of a diseased mind—a forest of crosses, journals overflowing with an anal, medieval-

In *Seven* (1995), the reaction of the investigators (Brad Pitt, left, and Morgan Freeman) prepares viewers for a gruesome countershot, a tableau staged by a serial killer.

looking scrawl. Overrun with beams, bars, gates, and nets arrayed in intersecting diagonals and verticals, the film's spaces seem ready-made to contain the mutilated bodies the killer puts on display for the investigators trying to track him down.

"John Doe," the serial killer (played by Kevin Spacey, speaking in a creepy voice), is biblically inspired. He dispenses a demented brand of justice as he punishes characters he deems guilty of one of the seven deadly sins. Unlike the usual horror-movie monster he resembles, he represents a superego out of control rather than an unbridled id. Fastidious to a pathological degree, he is repelled by human excess in any form. For each of his victims, he custom designs a death he judges to be commensurate with their crimes: he kills a fat man for his gluttony, slaughters a rich couple for their greed, arranging their bodies in tableaux that comment on their sins. His elaborate murder scenes are sermons, a form of didactic theater staged for his pursuers. Signing himself "John Doe," the killer is an auteur who leaves traces, a chain of interlocking motifs he wants and expects the investigators to decode. His envy of the rookie detective (played by Brad Pitt, cited at the time by the editors of *People* as "the sexiest man alive") ensures John Doe's own death. He constructs a scenario (by killing the detective's pregnant wife) he hopes will end with the hotheaded detective, out of wrath, killing him. "If you kill him, he wins," the detective's world-weary partner (Morgan Freeman, superb), warns him, but the young man succumbs to one of the seven deadly sins and so steps into the serial killer's master plot.

At the end, after he has shot John Doe, the detective is taken away in a police car, placed behind bars in exactly the same spot John Doe had been caged earlier. The visual rhyme—noir semiology at its most overdetermined—has no more than a superficial sheen; it's another "staging" in a film that fetishizes performance. *Seven* is a neonoir sound-and-light show in which the serial killer is a kind of ingenious performance artist who fashions gruesome, skillfully lighted and arranged murder sites scanned by a seductively tracking camera for the spectator's visual pleasure. As in the photographs of Joel-Peter Witkin, which inspired the way the film displays the killer's victims, the grotesque is raised to a transgressive art form. An unexpected box-office winner, *Seven* is compelling if morally hollow.

The copycat *Copycat* (1995) is about another designer serial killer with a postmodern self-reflexive streak. Like John Doe, this killer is intensely literary, his crimes littered with citations. He reads up on the pathology of serial murderers, then models his crime scenes on those of predecessors, like Son of Sam, Ted Bundy, and Jeffrey Dahmer. Stalking a professor of criminal psychology and the author of a seminal text on serial killers, he is determined to get an "A." As in *Seven*, however,

Serial killer Daryll Lee Cullum (Harry Connick, Jr.) in *Copycat* (1995) is trapped in his dementia.

in which John Doe is a cameo part, the killer in *Copycat* is reduced to a supporting role. The film's focus is on two females, the professor and the policewoman, who ultimately nab him. Cowritten by Anna Biderman and David Madsen, the film seems determined to prove that women are better than men at work males have traditionally performed in movies like this. (The male-baiting theme is announced in the professor's opening lecture, in which she asks the white males between twenty and thirty-five to stand up, declaring that it is from this group that serial killers are most likely to emerge.) Reversing sexual roles, men in the film are charming and to be looked at, especially the female cop's beefcake partner, a dreamboat who is mostly in the way and is killed off before the showdown. Played by Holly Hunter, a tiny woman with an intolerably scratchy voice, the officer is the hero, able to handle a big gun with far more expertise than any male in view.

In *To Die For* (1995), a psycho killer hungry for fame becomes the focus of a satire on the way the media (including thrillers like *Seven* and *Copycat*) sensationalize crime. The heroine, Suzanne Stone (played with just the right droll touch by Nicole Kidman) is a heartland reverse

Lolita eager to seize her fifteen minutes of fame. She manipulates three local kids into killing her husband, a couch potato who holds her back from pursuing her goal of becoming the next Barbara Walters, and her husband's sister. Relishing the media opportunities she knows the crime will create, she wants to become famous for being famous, in effect to achieve celebrity status for being a noir type, a sweet, lethal suburban blonde.

Having constructed herself as a media-ready subject, she is expert in playing to prying cameras and microphones now that her moment has arrived. A product of the media, she has turned herself into a commodity to be devoured by them. The media, like the unseen judge to whom the witnesses in *Rashomon* report, are the unseen countershot, the repressed reverse angle the film slyly posits as the ultimate source of knowledge and control in a media-obsessed world. Suzanne Stone is a product of images and is herself taken in by an image: the hit man who has come to off her poses as a television producer with a lucrative deal, bait that this child of the media cannot resist.

The tones differ, but in *Primal Fear* (1996) and *The Usual Suspects* (1995), a psycho killer, like the would-be heroine in *To Die For*, is presented as a cunning, entertaining trickster—a demented noir superstar. In *To Die For*, the heroine is exposed from the beginning; *Primal Fear* and *The Usual Suspects* reveal the leading characters' charades only at the end, in a strategy that compels viewers to reread the films. Like their manipulative role-playing protagonists, both thrillers engage in trompe l'oeil tactics intended to mislead and to baffle.

In *Primal Fear*, a young man accused of killing the archbishop of Chicago, captured with blood on his hands as he runs from the scene of the crime, claims to have two personalities, one of which is subject to violent episodes during which he experiences total blackouts. He persuades a powerful defense attorney (Richard Gere), who then claims innocence for his client on the grounds that it was his second self, a doppelgänger he cannot control, who killed the archbishop. After the smug hotshot lawyer wins the case, the killer admits that he has been acting all along, faking insanity in order to secure his freedom. In a holding cell, both characters are filmed behind bars, an image that underlines the lawyer's complicity in a miscarriage of justice—a potent noir theme in a post-O. J. Simpson America, where real life has, to many, seemed to offer vivid proof that indeed sometimes people can and do get away with murder. Gere's lawyer, however, is less upset about justice than the fact that he was fooled; and Edward Norton's performance as a schizophrenic invaded by an evil other has been so convincing that many viewers may also have been tricked. In *Primal Fear*, then, performance itself is the narrative crux; and along with the other characters, the spectator is placed in the position throughout the film of evaluating the authenticity of the accused. Is he only pretending, or is he for real? Emphasizing performance, the film minimizes the larger theme of how the criminal's virtuoso masquerade has confounded justice.

In the lineup, in *The Usual Suspects* (1995), who is Keyser Soze? (Left to right: Hockney [Kevin Pollak], McManus [Stephen Baldwin], Fenster [Benicio Del Toro], Keaton [Gabriel Byrne], and Verbal [Kevin Spacey]).

The thematic stakes aren't as high in *The Usual Suspects*. But the psycho trickster, the bewitchingly named Keyser Soze (Kevin Spacey in an Academy Award-winning performance), is already a genre landmark. Spacey initially appears in the guise of a weak-willed character, Verbal Kint (the first name is a tip-off), who walks with a pronounced limp and speaks in a voice dripping with apology and subservience. Keyser as Verbal narrates to a district attorney a story that has already happened about the way a legendary underworld character named Keyser Soze orchestrated a revenge plot by rounding up an ace group of criminals—the usual suspects. Impelled to a life of crime after he witnessed the slaughter of his family, Keyser embraces vengeance as a way of life. As the only survivor of a master plot that appears to have gone fatally amiss, Verbal pretends merely to have followed the orders of his infamous employer. Within the story he reconstructs for the district attorney (and for us), Verbal presents Keyser as a demonic figure, an outlaw with virtually supernatural resources, who not only eludes capture but who cannot even be positively identified. Characters within Verbal's narrative tremble at the mention of his name. Viewers are primed to regard this Nietzschean mastermind as they would the monster in a horror movie, eager to get a glimpse of him but also titillated by the way the film delays his entrance.

After he finishes his story, Verbal limps meekly out of the district attorney's office. But once out of his interrogator's sight, like Jekyll transforming himself into Hyde, Verbal straightens up, begins to walk briskly, and replaces his obsequious expression with the fierce look of a hardened criminal. And at the same time that Verbal is revealed to be Keyser, the district attorney has an epiphany in which he realizes "Verbal" isn't Verbal. He leaps out of his office to capture the man who has fooled him, but he's a beat too late. Keyser has driven off into the protection of the city, becoming another noir psycho on the loose. The killer's escape is presented as the victory of cunning over gullibility, and in the cynical 1990s, the film asks the audience to applaud the character's infernal ingenuity as a storyteller, as well as retroactively to enjoy its own misperceptions. (Even the most astute "reader" is unlikely, without prior knowledge, to have identified from the start Verbal as Keyser.)

To a degree, the film's "performance" matches Verbal's. The film itself, along with its embedded narrator, plays a teasing game with the viewer as it blocks access to the truth, withholds information, and encourages detours and misreadings. Using genre conventions like voiceover, labyrinthine plotting, spatial and temporal ruptures in new and devious ways, *The Usual Suspects* is something of a commentary on noir resources, a cunning, masterful meta-noir. The film's very cleverness, however, confines it to a narrow thematic zone. In the richest vein of classic and neo-noir, criminality vibrates with cultural, psychological, and thematic resonance. Limiting characters and narrative to a celebration of skillful performance, *The Usual Suspects* ends up being about nothing other than its own admirable, if finally hollow, ingenuity. Crime here really has, and is of, no consequence; what counts is story construction, how the filmmakers built their clever noir puzzle. To date Keyser Soze is the ultimate embodiment of a neo-noir tendency to turn a certain kind of criminal into a strutting amoral antihero, outplaying authority figures who uphold what the films imply is a repressive bourgeois culture. But to extract serious or even shallow social comment from the film is beside the point, for *The Usual Suspects*, shrewdly written (by Christopher McQuarrie) and directed (by Bryan Singer), refers only to its own mechanisms, takes seriously only its own craftiness.

Striding through mean streets: Richard Roundtree, in *Shaft* (1971), one of Hollywood's first black action-movie stars.

# Chapter 9

# Black Noir

In the early to mid-1970s, a short-lived crime-movie cycle filtered character types and plots from gangster stories and classic noir into black settings. Called "blaxploitation," the films featured black characters that, the first time around, had been either pushed to the margins or eliminated. In borrowed clothing, as it were, black actors were inserted into white crime dramas. Cheaply and quickly made (the pictures were among the first B offerings of the post-studio era), the blaxploitation program movies added a thin layer of race consciousness onto stereotyped narratives. The films did not engage in any probing way the realities of being black in America. Rather, these by-the-numbers action thrillers were addressed primarily to an audience of young, urban, black males who presumably enjoyed seeing what the dominant culture had not permitted them to see before, black males (and females) as muscular superheroes and supercrooks embroiled in activities that, for the moment, seemed "empowering."

At the time, neither the filmmakers (some, but by no means all, of whom were black) nor the target audience seemed to consider the films' ideological repressions. These, after all, were movies in which blacks on either side of the law were fully implicated in urban crime, deeply (unavoidably?) inscribed within a criminal circuit. Beneath their superficially liberating flourish, the films, which abetted white fears of blacks as an inevitably criminal underclass, were reactionary mechanisms for helping to maintain the social status quo. Borrowing the con-

ventions of canonic crime films, the blaxploitationers perpetuated seg-
regation between white and black cultures, as the historical race movies, made to be screened in blacks-only theaters, had done in earlier
decades. These shabbily made pictures earmarked for ghetto audiences
only reinforced a racial divide, recalling the separate-but-not-equal
philosophy that had always underwritten Jim Crow laws.

*Shaft* (1971), an "original" screenplay, and *Cool Breeze* (1972), a remake of *The Asphalt Jungle* (1950), are symptomatic. Crudely made, with
flat acting, a lethargic pace, and no distinctive visual insignia, the films
add nothing of value (beyond their significance as a social trace) to the
noir canon. They are prime examples of "dumbed-down" noir. John
Shaft (Richard Roundtree) is a detective with a downtown office who
has to travel uptown to Harlem. The Harlem gangster who hires Shaft
to locate his daughter, kidnapped by Italian thugs whose territory he
has invaded, tells him, "You're a black spade detective with one foot in
whitey's craw." Since the mob kingpin can't go to the police for help,
he seeks out Shaft who, like most noir detectives, occupies a liminal
zone, the threshold between the law and the underworld. As a black
detective, Shaft's position is even more tenuous, but the film is only
fleetingly concerned with its hero's race.

"I got a couple of problems," Shaft announces early on. "I was
born black and I was born poor." The film then proceeds to ignore the
statement's implications. For the most part, racial issues are reduced
to ribald jousts. "You're not so black," a white cop ribs Shaft, who responds by saying, "You're not so white." After Shaft has thrown a man
out of his office window, the white cop asks, "Come on, Shaft, what is it
with this black shit? Tell me the name of the game so I know the rules."
When Shaft visits black revolutionaries—who have a poster of Malcolm
X on their wall—one of the "soldiers," a former friend, accuses the
detective of thinking "like a white man." "And you don't think at all,"
Shaft rejoins. Gearing up for a showdown with the Italian gang, Shaft
says, "We're gonna need some more brothers, with guns this time."

Too lame to be subversive, the film treats the politics of race casually, as a sauce that doesn't in any significant way alter or enhance the
narrative conflicts. Within the parameters of the film's narrow, action-
movie formula, race is intrusive and all but irrelevant; hence, the
Malcolm X soldiers who rescue the mobster's daughter are divested of
political or ideological edge. Ben, Shaft's former friend, drops his radi-

cal stance to join "the brothers" in their assault on the hotel where the Italian mobsters are holding the kidnap victim. And in the film's most telling use of race, Ben, the would-be revolutionary, masquerades as a waiter, a role in which the Mafia goons reflexively accept him: he's black, after all.

The ostensible purpose of this retro exercise is to confer on a black actor the kind of hypermasculine persona previously reserved for white actors: at the end, it's Shaft who calls the white cop to inform him the case is closed. Like the white actors who had played detectives in classic noir, Shaft ably negotiates between the law and the underworld, as well as between whites and blacks on both sides of the law. And like the historic private eye, he is also a ladies' man, able to satisfy his white and black mistresses. As the lyrics of the title song announce (with representative finesse), Shaft is "the black private dick that's a sex machine on the chicks." "You're really great in the sack but you're shitty afterwards," his white girlfriend says, abetting racial stereotypes about black sexual supremacy. An ego ideal for young black males, Shaft became a code word for a black superhero, but the buzz that circulated around the character is hard to gauge from Richard Roundtree's blank presence. Without edge or flash or humor, Roundtree is a curiously flaccid action hero, decidedly dull rather than dashing, tired as opposed to torrid.

An original screenplay, *Shaft* has at least a sprinkling of local color. Adhering to the outlines of a prior screenplay, *Cool Breeze* is stranded in a spatial and temporal limbo from which the characters seem estranged. The actors, who seem merely to be "blacking" up to essay roles created as white characters, appear to be performing a charade. Like the contemporary all-black stage production of *Hello, Dolly!*, the film is no more than a stunt. It does not creatively rethink or truly *adapt* material conceived for a different time and place—the film does not consider the way race might have had an impact on the characters' fates. The story closely follows *The Asphalt Jungle*. Only two of the conspirators escape from a failed heist, and the protagonist still dreams of a quiet life in the country far from the asphalt jungle. Ripped out of their original context, characters and story are suspended in a blandly rendered, always sunny Los Angeles that reflects the filmmakers' self-destructive decision to avoid the look of noir. The film's iconographic charge is so indistinct that it's impossible to tell if the appallingly bad taste of the rooms in which the rich black characters live is a form of social comment or a sign of the film's minuscule budget.

Blaxploitation films on the *Shaft* model are pallid imitations. Extracting downmarket action and comedy from black crime, these ephemeral entertainment commodities are also socially irresponsible. Twenty years later, in the height of a neo-noir resurgence, a group of crime dramas with black characters have a markedly different tone and purpose. Adapting noir tropes in narrative structure and characterization, the new films are driven by a sober didactic intent. In these noir noirs, being poor and black in contemporary America is equivalent to the role of destiny in classic noir. These urban crime films set in ghetto communities suggest that to be a young, black male is virtually to be marked by and for noir. The films repeatedly argue that blackness in white America predestines a life of violence and crime. Significantly, it is primarily black filmmakers speaking primarily to black audiences who have made these crime dramas that equate blackness with noir. Like the cycle of black films in the 1970s, this one too is segregationist—white characters exist only on the margins, or are eliminated—as indeed is this chapter, which relegates black noir to the distinct subgenre that I think it is.

Like *Shaft* in 1971, *Boyz N the Hood* in 1991 sets the terms for a new crime-movie movement. Where *Shaft* models itself on the private-eye drama of classic noir, the latter film follows the narrative pattern designed around a protagonist's descent into crime. The film's opening title card, "One out of 21 black males will be killed—at the hands of another black male," wraps the protagonist, a young black male, within a deterministic vise. The statistic immediately establishes a realistic social context that was never part of the blaxploitation ethic, while at the same time it underlines the hero's vulnerability.

Establishing a pattern other black noir films will imitate, *Boyz N the Hood* begins with scenes set in the protagonist's childhood. Surrounded by violence and its aftershocks, Tre (beautifully played by Cuba Gooding, Jr.) seems targeted for noir. He walks with a group of kids down a block filled with gunshot-blasted posters of Reagan. After he gets into a fight at school, his mother, feeling unequal to raising a son on her own in a world boiling with violence, takes him to live with her estranged husband. In his father's house too crime and its consequences are inescapable facts of life. One night, after Tre's father shoots a (black) burglar, it takes a while for police to arrive; and when they do, a white cop is remote and ineffectual, and a black cop is a virulent racist, claiming he joined the force "to lessen the number of niggers in the world."

On the surface, the South Central Los Angeles neighborhood Tre moves to is clean and orderly, sunshine is plentiful and palm trees add a touch of tropical glamour. But the remnants of, and the potential for, crime are omnipresent. On a walk with new friends, Tre discovers a corpse in the grass and encounters a group of older kids itching for battle. Throughout, invisible but nonetheless penetrating, a constant reminder of a power structure that infiltrates black lives, helicopters buzz overhead, shining lights down onto the 'hood. Offscreen, sirens and gunshots pierce the air, encasing Tre in a world rumbling with danger.

*Boyz N the Hood* is told in the form of a bildungsroman that chronicles Tre's inscription into black masculinity. To assume his manhood, he must first shed his virginity, a rite of passage in which his father eagerly encourages him. But in his culture, violence and crime are also markers of manliness, and from these his father tries to restrain him. When Tre returns home from the army, the 'hood is more unstable, more easily ignited than ever. Cruising in cars along Crenshaw Boulevard, gangs from different 'hoods start a dispute that inaugurates a seemingly unstoppable cycle of violent retaliations. After his best friend, Rick, is killed, Tre is caught up in the maelstrom, feeling compelled to avenge that death with further violence. "It has nothing to do with you," his father warns as Tre stalks off gun in hand to confront his enemies. In the film's climactic moment, Tre gets out of the car in which he and his buddies are hunting their friend's slayers and returns home. In withdrawing, he breaks the chain that has clung to him from birth.

Clinging to his girlfriend (Nia Long), Tre (Cuba Gooding, Jr.) breaks down, and thereby releases himself from the chain of violence that grips his friends, in *Boyz N the Hood* (1991).

In ancient Greek drama, a cycle of revenge was broken only by the institution of Law, a court with the power to judge and to adjudicate and to which the disputants must yield. In the ghetto depicted in *Boyz N the Hood*, shattered by internecine strife, the legal system of the dominant culture is noticeably absent, and salvation seems possible only from within the community. "Increase the peace," an end title urges the audience, underlining the fact that Tre's brush with noir has been fashioned as a kind of sermon. The film dramatizes the consequences of violence in order to persuade the audience to abjure it. A postscript informs us that Tre and his girlfriend go on to college, leaving the 'hood to begin the process of transforming their lives, and that Rick's brother, Doughboy, feeling compelled to answer violence, is dead within two weeks. As Doughboy walks off to avenge his brother (and to confront his noir destiny), his image slowly dissolves.

The postscript treats the characters as if they are actual figures, and indeed the film throughout has constructed a world that, except for night scenes with flickering neon, avoids the usually stylized sheen of noir. Much of the story takes place in sunny open spaces; in this "real" world, crime doesn't need the shelter of night, and Rick is gunned down in broad daylight. *Boyz* is not a retro project awash in nostalgia, or a reflexive piece focused on resurrecting noir; rather, it uses a noir narrative paradigm as the crucible for social comment and a call for change. And unlike many crime movies from the classic and neo eras, it does not fetishize crime under the alibi of indicting the people who commit it. When Rick is shot, it is a horrifying moment, the shock compounded by the fact that the character, with a pregnant wife, was about to leave the 'hood to attend college on a football scholarship. And Doughboy's revenge leads only to his own death. But it would be naive to reduce the film's attitude toward violence as one of unwavering moral disapproval. In the world the film vividly portrays, violence is both inevitable and, if only momentarily, cathartic.

Significantly, as the opening title promises, the violence is contained within black communities. The only whites visible are a well-meaning teacher and a respectful, if flaccid, police officer; otherwise, whites remain outside the frame, an almost tangible structuring absence. Black anger against the dominant culture is focused in the character of Tre's father, named Furious, who attempts to include his son within his own field of resentments. Don't join the army, he counsels

Tre: that is the white man's game. Furious bristles with a sense of the dispossession he feels in white America. Laurence Fishburne plays the character as wounded and incomplete, a man in recovery from a deeply troubled past. Furious is a thwarted character who can't confront his failure with his wife and who remains without a woman; but nonetheless, he accepts his paternal role. And despite his anger, he raises a son who survives the ghetto, in itself a triumph. For the most part, the film avoids direct indictment of white oppression and completely bypasses black violence against whites to focus on the black rage that has turned inward or is expressed against other blacks. Seeming to absolve whites of the crimes black characters inflict on each other, the film was fervently embraced by the white critical establishment; its talented young director, John Singleton, was nominated for an Academy Award, and the film to date remains the most lauded of the noir noir cycle.

Diagonals, neon, stairs, rain, and shadows provide a high-noir mise-en-scène for a confrontation between an undercover cop (Laurence Fishburne, left) and a shifty lawyer (Jeff Goldblum), in *Deep Cover* (1992).

Bill Dukes's powerful thriller *Deep Cover* (1992) adheres more closely to a genre pattern than *Boyz N the Hood*. While Singleton's film is a coming-of-age drama—a rare noir format, to be sure—*Deep Cover* follows the more traditional curve of an underworld thriller, albeit one with an essential difference. Unlike the 1970s action movies, here blackness carries a potent ideological charge and drives the narrative. Intoned in a rhyming rap prose, a black version of classical hardboiled, the opening voiceover of the protagonist plunges us directly to the heart of noir. The narrator, John Hull (Laurence Fishburne), speaks in a dazed monotone, the voice of trauma, and in a sense the story that follows is an explanation of why the character sounds the way he does. He begins by recalling the defining moment of his childhood, when he witnessed his father, a drug addict, shot during an attempted holdup. Over and over the memory of the incident springs up from out of the past to haunt the hero. And despite the fact that he has tried to erase his heritage by "doing the right thing"—he doesn't drink or do drugs, and he has become a cop—he cannot repress the image of his father's death. When Hull is given an undercover assignment, to infiltrate a drug gang by passing himself off as a dealer new to town, before he is talked into it he doesn't want the job because he's afraid he might "revert" to being a criminal like his father. (The film's poster proclaimed, "There's a thin line between catching a criminal and becoming one.")

Relocating from Ohio to Los Angeles, Hull adopts a new persona. He lives in a seedy rooming house and goes into deep cover as he takes on the demeanor of a hardened dealer. He wears an earring; he's unshaven; and he speaks in the argot of the street. On the job, to prove to the gang that he is one of them, he is forced to kill another black man, who is a real criminal. The fateful encounter is set in a bathroom lined with mirrors in which the reflections of the two characters are hard to tell apart; the protagonist realizes, "It could have been me." Initially he's shocked by his ability to kill, but gradually he gets accustomed to underworld violence. As he feared, going undercover hurls him into his father's world. In noir noir, paternity is destiny, and recurrent flashbacks to the moment in which he saw his father killed underscore the classic noir theme of the past invading the present. As Hull makes his way up in the underworld, moving from the ghetto to an ornately decorated house in the hills, he remains a morally divided character, torn apart by the success of his charade.

Ultimately the film is as compromised and ambivalent as its protagonist. Every white character in the film is corrupt. The cop who sends the black officer into the underground is a weasel taking orders from malevolent power brokers. The drug dealers, who bring death to black people, are a group of lethal Hispanics in league with a slimy Jewish lawyer. To fight these oppressors, the undercover cop becomes a crusading hero who stands up against the drug cartel, then in court exposes the connections between the top drug lord and the highest levels of the American government, reaching up to and including the president. At the end, he keeps a good part of the eleven million dollars he walked off with from a heroic showdown with the drug lords. "What would you do?" he asks the audience in voiceover. Hull wants to do good things with the money; he has adopted the son of a Hispanic neighbor who died of a drug overdose. But after his prolonged masquerade, his use of violence, and his loss of self, his recuperation cannot be complete. In deep cover, he has begun—he has had to begin—to think like a criminal. He has been corrupted by the very world he has always tried to elude, and he knows it. At the same time, the film places him as a superhero in the *Shaft* mold: he exposes a white man's power structure engaged in its own deep cover. As the film demonstrates, violence is unavoidable in deep cover (which begins to seem a general metaphor for being a black male in America). Noir noirs suggest that crime is the black man's ineluctable destiny, equivalent to the dark fate that bedevils the antiheroes of classic noir.

As opposed to *Boyz N the Hood*, with its realistic background, *Deep Cover* is glazed with the embellishments of high-noir styling. The film envisions Los Angeles as the noir city of the 1990s, an urban wasteland as the demented Travis Bickle of *Taxi Driver* might see it. Bathed in watery blues and sharp reds, the city is depicted as a place trembling with incipient violence. Either it is packed—a dense crowd of pushers and hookers milling tensely in front of a porn shop; or it is deserted—its abandoned streets dipped in icy tones of blue and black. In recurrent montage sequences, staccato editing and different focal lengths enhance the aura of the city as a cauldron about to erupt.

If at the end of *Boyz N the Hood* Tre is able to escape from the net cast by the 'hood, Anthony (Larenz Tate), the protagonist of the Hughes brothers' far less optimistic *Dead Presidents* (1995) is locked within a system from which there is no way out. The ghetto he was born into dooms him to defeat. *Dead Presidents* is a coming-of-age story (a useful format for didactic noir noirs) that presents its protagonist at three different stages. In act one, set in the 1950s, he haunts the mean streets of a

The barefaced, empty buildings and a police squad car close in on a thief (Freddy Rodriguez) running from a failed heist, in *Dead Presidents* (l995). As in other black noir dramas, the city streets provide no exit for characters who seem predestined to crime.

black ghetto, hanging out in bars and poolrooms, as the camera glides through settings where trouble brews, waiting to ignite. An orange light alters and burnishes the real world with a neo-noir glow as Albert and Allen Hughes gild the despair of ghetto life with a touch of the poet. The youngster is attached to a father surrogate, a drug dealer, who becomes violent when a client refuses to pay him. At first the boy is shocked by the violence, but then he accepts it as a part of his inheritance, the way things are. In act two, Anthony and his buddies are in Vietnam, where they are trapped in another mise-en-scène of violence, this one created by an (absent) white patriarchy. Setting up a "rhyme" with the prologue, act two ends as the hero confronts another act of sudden, devastating violence when his buddy steps on a landmine and is blown up and dies in his arms. In act three, like soldiers in classic noir returning home to grapple with powerful feelings of displacement, he's a magnet for noir misfortune. Joining forces with a militant black woman who spouts insidious racist rhetoric, he robs a government office that burns old money ("dead presidents" is street slang for money). His partner is killed, and Anthony lands behind bars, his head doubled over in an image of terminal defeat. A victim of his environment, betrayed by his own people, as well as by the racist outsiders who control the worlds outside and inside the walls of the ghetto, he's a noir loser caught in a deterministic web.

Presenting young black males as perennial victims is not, of course, an empowering image, and indeed, the film's message is bleak, truly noir. While many classic and neo-noir stories pivot on a dark fate that is merely capricious, attacking characters for no apparent reason, noir noirs provide an explicit social framework for catastrophe. In *Dead Presidents*, noir springs from a confluence of tangible causes—the racism, poverty, and class bias that infect ghetto dwellers along with the brutalities inflicted by service in a discredited war. In act one, the character lives in a world festering with black characters who resent each other; in act three, the militant, incendiary black-power movement has added another potentially poisonous ingredient to the protagonist's environment. The Hughes brothers launch a black culture self-critique; their rambling, episodic, powerful film paraphrases classic noir themes within a specifically black perspective on which white viewers, finally, can only be eavesdroppers.

Ernest R. Dickerson's *Juice* (1992), a heist film with a strong sociological overlay, is also told from deep inside black experience. As it observes the aimless daily routine of four friends, the film's opening has the semidocumentary texture of postwar location noirs, such as *The Naked City* and *Call Northside 777*. (For most white viewers, it's likely that the opening presents an unfamiliar other world, a kind of shadow America.) The group of kids attracts and enjoys trouble. To whites they "play" black, as when they say "boo!" to a stiff white man carrying a suitcase who is so startled that he bumps into a pole. Watching *White Heat* on television, they cheer the maniacal gangster, played by James Cagney, who immolates himself on the top of a gas tank in the film's apocalyptic finale. "That motherfucker took his destiny in his own hands," one of the boys says approvingly. "If you gotta go out, that's the way to go." Bishop (Tupac Shakur), the boy destined for the greatest trouble, agrees: "You gotta go out in a blaze or you're already dead." Q (Omar Epps), the one salvageable kid in the group, wants to be a disc jockey and cautions his friends about defining themselves only within a circuit of crime and violence. But he can't talk them out of pulling a stickup. When he hesitates after they tell him they want to use him as an alibi, the ringleader, Bishop, taunts him: "This nigger's scared."

After the crew commits its first crime, the film sheds a documentary texture and its color palette changes. Noir signifiers proliferate. Shadows and diagonals dominate the mise-en-scène; sun and a sense of the natural world are banished from an urban jungle of streets washed by an infernal blue light. A vividly staged scene in a crack house, with drugged people dancing to rap in smoke-filled dens of Stygian darkness, intermittently lit by flashing strobe lights, evokes Dante's circle of hell.

As in most noir, the heist inevitably turns violent, and Q watches with growing helplessness as Bishop tumbles into a murderous rampage. "I *am* crazy," Bishop asserts with cackling bravado, recalling the gangster in *White Heat*, "and I don't give a fuck." Forced to stand up to Bishop, even if that means using a gun, Q must enter a noir zone to protect himself and others against it. Like countless American movie heroes before him, Q must "do the right thing" by demonstrating his masculine prowess; here, he proves himself with his fists rather than a gun. After he knocks Bishop over the edge of a building, one of the onlookers gives Q the ultimate endorsement in a coming-of-age ritual: "Now you have the juice." Q shakes his head, a lost, sad look in his eye, as the image freezes. The last shot is of the four young friends walking in the sun—before noir overtook their lives.

Deep in the black ghetto, stained by the crime that surrounds him (as the crazed Bishop exclaims, "We're three niggers in a police station. If you want us to be guilty, we'll be guilty."), Q has nowhere to turn except inside. He can't go to the police; no reliable black fathers are on hand to guide him; nor can he count on his friends, themselves in flight from the law. Like the sheriff in *High Noon*, he has no choice but to face his enemy on his own. Like other noir noirs, and for that matter like many classic noirs, *Juice* dramatizes a crisis in masculinity. Q represents macho under fire; and though he passes his test, he recognizes that "juice" purchased from violence has paralyzed the boys in the 'hood. In this morality tale addressed to urban black males, the fact that Q has overcome evil with his fists rather than a gun softens the price he has had to pay to claim his manhood. Where Q is carefully positioned as an ego ideal for the putative black male spectator, his antagonist, the demonic Bishop, is an enigma. Like many other villains in 1990s noir, Bishop "performs" evil in a hyperbolic style. His pathology is so extreme that it threatens to leap into another genre. He's the angry black male as a horror-film bogeyman; and if white filmmakers had conceived the character, the film might well have aroused charges of racism.

Like classic noir stories about straying bourgeois characters, black noir films in which blacks are impelled to crime through the double vise of heredity and environment are cautionary fables. Films that follow the pattern set by *Boyz N the Hood* depict violence as sometimes unavoidable but as always carrying the possibility of self-destruction. The protagonists of *Boyz* and *Juice* rise above the double strike, as Shaft baldly states it, of being poor and black; the "victory" of the undercover officer in *Deep Cover* is decidedly ambivalent, while the leading figure in *Dead Presidents* is drawn irreversibly into a noir undertow. The outcomes vary, but as with the gangster sagas of the 1930s, stories of young black males "elected" from birth into a life of crime have a limited narrative curve. The cycle seems destined to have a short but productive span.

Carl Franklin, a black director with a keen interest in noir, has taken a different approach. Like the blaxploitation filmmakers of the 1970s, Franklin appropriates other noir subgenres: the noir road movie is his inspiration for *One False Move* (1991); the classic private-eye search for a missing woman is the model for *Devil in a Blue Dress* (1995). Placing black characters in a narrative space traditionally asssociated with whites, Franklin interrogates genre conventions in a more thoughtful way than the 1970s programmers did.

The central character of *One False Move* is a light-skinned black woman, whose color seems to destine her to crime. Lured to Hollywood from a small town in Texas, Lila (Cynda Williams), who renames herself Fantasia, falls in with homicidal drug dealers (one white, one black), but unlike the now-traditional noir noir, which would focus on her descent into crime, the film instead confines her fall to its backstory. Lila/Fantasia is already a fallen woman as the story opens; now, with her partners, she is on the run after a violent encounter in which her trigger-happy colleagues have committed murder. The flight to Fantasia's hometown, Star City, Arkansas, where she wants to be reunited with the little boy she left behind and where her vicious white partner, Ray, is going to hide out with his uncle, is doomed from the beginning. Having overheard Fantasia (at a drug house under surveillance) say that she is going home, the police are on their trail.

To underscore a connection, the film crosscuts repeatedly between Fantasia on the run from Los Angeles, growing increasingly desperate, and Dale (Bill Paxton), the hometown sheriff who hopes that the net he is laying for the fugitives will ensure a longed-for promotion to the Los Angeles police force. Indeed (and improbably), Dale is revealed at the end to be the father of the boy Lila left behind with her mother when she went to Hollywood. In the showdown, playing out the heroic role he had fantasized, Dale shoots Fantasia's partners and Ray shoots Lila. After his ordeal, wounded, Dale asks his little boy to come sit down by him, for the first time acknowledging his paternity. The film fades out on the newly acquainted father and son.

Both characters model themselves on behavior steeped in film noir. Dale aspires to be like the tough cops he's seen in crime movies, while Lila/Fantasia yearns to be a Hollywood femme fatale. Dale, a white male, realizes his movie-derived dreams, while her color dooms Lila's. "Since I kinda look white you can fuck me; since I kinda look black you can dump me, what the hell," she tells Dale in a speech that resonates with her sense of defeat. The black female as a victim, the white male as an active agent undermine the miscegenation theme and the film's ecumenical distribution of villainy between white and black characters, and *One False Move* conforms to ancient stereotypes. The color coding gives the film's hoary sentimentality and retro melodramatic plotting a specious modernity (and earned it the kind of critical approbation it certainly does not merit); but at its core, it is another tribute to a white male who finally grows up.

The hero of Franklin's sixth film, *Devil in a Blue Dress*, based on a novel by Walter Mosley, is a novice private eye in postwar Los Angeles. Like many noir period pieces, the film is suffused with the kind of golden lighting that signifies time remembered, and its skillful evocation of a time that was in the history of black life in Los Angeles has a standard imaginary-museum aura. Unlike the protagonists of black noir films in contemporary settings, Easy Hawkins (Denzel Washington) is not predestined to crime; rather, he is summoned to noir in the same way as any detective. A vet, who has just moved from Texas, Easy scans the paper for job listings when destiny intrudes: a white man, a Mr. Albright, offers him one hundred dollars to find a white woman named Daphne Monet. Although Easy is not a detective, the job he is offered, a search for a missing woman who is an enigma, an empty tablet that needs to be filled, is the same as the ones undertaken by Sam Spade and Philip Marlowe. And as in the work of Hammett and Chandler, deception is on the march, almost all of it this time superintended by villainous whites. (The primary deception is that the missing woman is part black.)

Placing black characters in roles traditionally played by white actors, the film rewrites some genre conventions. Like Lila in *One False Move*, Daphne is a guiltless femme fatale marked for noir by her color: a white politician threatens to expose her; her white boyfriend will not marry her; white hit men tie her up and strap her to a chair. (As Daphne, Jennifer Beals, a white actress, has a sultry voice but none of the mystery the role requires.) The part-black female is vanquished, as in *One False Move*, while the male protagonist, this time black, emerges victorious from the noir labyrinth. Not only is he sexually potent, which

Re-creating Los Angeles's Central Avenue in the 1940s, the heart of the city's black community, for *Devil in a Blue Dress* (1995). Unlike many classic noir cities, which were products of set designers' imaginations, here a present-day Los Angeles location has been transformed into an imaginary place, a museum of a time that was.

seems a job requirement for all detectives in noir, but unlike his white predecessors he remains morally unstained. He's tough when he needs to be, and he has the deductive reasoning skills his work demands, but really he isn't hardboiled at all. As Denzel Washington plays him, Easy is a decent fellow, wary, resigned, and ironic; and the character is rewarded in ways that blacks in noir rarely are. Retiring from noir, Easy is happy to tend his own garden in his own house set on a street of similarly well-tended houses in a world of neighborly neighbors, where kids ride on bikes with mothers nearby, a world of palm trees and golden, presmog California sun. This Edenic image, suffused with a sense of well-being all but unprecedented in noir, "corrects" the standard representation of black life in crime movies made by black, as well as white, filmmakers.

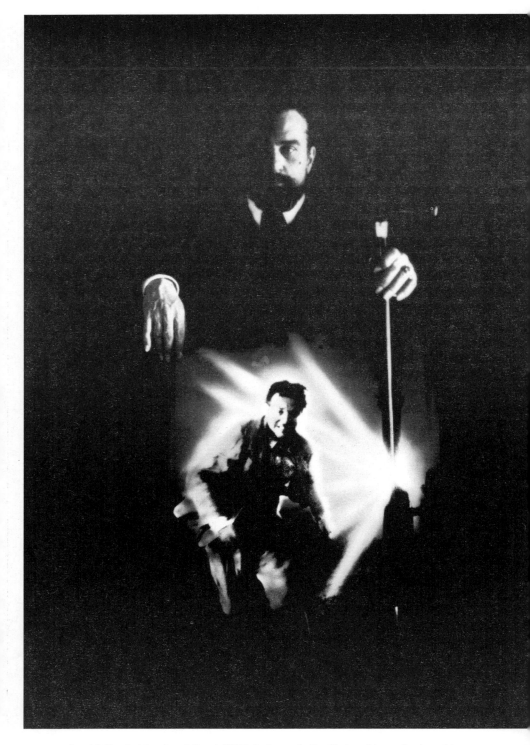

A publicity shot for *Angel Heart* (1987) that reveals the film's mixture of noir and horror-film motifs. Louis Cyphre (i. e., Lucifer [Robert De Niro] holds an image of Harry Angel (Mickey Rourke), the man whose soul he owns.

# Chapter 10

# Beyond Noir: The Roads to Ruin

Noir-like lighting, mise-en-scène, characters, and themes appeared long before they coalesced into a 1940s style retroactively named film noir and have continued to circulate long after classic noir's official expiration date. Indeed, hovering over debates about noir's entitlement to genre status has been the marked ease with which elements of noir style can be transported across a variety of more stable traditional genres. In pictures made before and after the classic era, the insignia of hard-core noir migrated to films nobody would categorize as noir. Like all kinds of movies in the postmodern age, noir has lost the "purity" it might have claimed in the studio era and, with typical contemporary fluidity, has filtered into and, in turn, been invaded by other genres.

Fragments of noir have always appeared in the horror film. Set in dark houses that look like breeding grounds for crime and inhabited by neurotic characters trapped by poisoned psyches, a tainted heredity, or a merciless destiny, classic horror tales, like *Frankenstein*, *Dracula*, and *The Old Dark House*, brim with anticipations of noir. In his script for *From Dusk Till Dawn* (1996), Quentin Tarantino literally reenacts noir's historical intimacy with the horrific. Directed by Robert Rodriguez, a south-of-the-border John Woo whose specialty is succulent violence, Tarantino's story midway negotiates an abrupt switch as, in logic-defying, postmodern fashion, he splices a noir thriller with a vampire tale. Because in a sense he is offering a two-for-one, Tarantino hasn't filled in either narrative: in act one, he provides merely the shell of a neo-noir picture about bank robbers on the run; in act two, he offers only the outer husk of a vampire movie in which lust turns literally monstrous.

In *From Dusk Till Dawn* (1996), a conventional noir narrative of two fugitives on the run flips into a vampire tale set in a surreal outpost in the Mexican desert. One of the fugitives (George Clooney) and a minister's daughter (Juliette Lewis) are the sole survivors of the generic transmutation.

In a parched southwestern landscape, the kind of hot world that's become standard neo terrain, two brothers fleeing after a bank holdup streak through a procession of dumpy motels and diners with picturesque neon signs. One brother (George Clooney) is levelheaded; the other (played by Tarantino) is a hopped-up sex fiend whose lack of restraint—offscreen he kills their first hostage, a timid female bank teller—endangers their survival chances. The second hostages are a lapsed minister (Harvey Keitel) traveling in a van with his daughter (Juliette Lewis, the trailer-trash princess of nouveau noir) and son, an Asian (a bow, however obscure, to pulp political correctness?). This hapless threesome is abducted by the robbers simply because, in classic noir fashion, they are in the wrong place at the wrong time. The brothers take their hostages across the border into Mexico, where they are to meet contacts. (Why they need hostages once they enter Mexico, always a lawless, free zone in noir, is one of the lacunae Tarantino, counting on viewers who know noir and therefore can either fill in the gap for themselves or else accept implausibility as one of the rules of the game, makes no attempt to redress.)

Once they arrive at a remote biker bar in the Mexican wilderness, where the meeting is to take place, the film shifts gears. The languid pans standard for neo-noir are replaced by staccato editing, which is a cue for upcoming action; the tensions of a developing thriller are suddenly succeeded by ribald humor. Named the Titty Twister, the theatrically oversized bar looks like a movie set in contrast to the film's realistic first act. Outside the bar, a shill (Cheech Marin) performs a shrill, lewd riff about the lures of naked women; his adolescent verbal wet dream spells immediate trouble for the film's commitment to the noir story it has begun to tell. Like the shill, the bar itself is sleaze on parade. Onstage a stripper with a thick yellow snake draped about her neck turns suddenly into a vampire, as the film, as if performing a rite of sympathetic magic, changes into a rowdy exhibit of state-of-the-art f/x. Yet, as with the noir episode, the vampire narrative adds up to, in effect, no more than a museum of genre artifacts. In authentic vampire films, of course, the monsters and their prey embody psychological, social, and sexual overtones, while here the highly contagious vampirism that overtakes almost everyone seems little more than an excuse for spectacular scenes of transformation and violence. Vampirism marks a clever shift in the film's designation of good and evil characters, for in the face of the swarthy nest of viperous bikers and their oversexed women who carry the disease, the noir outlaws are suddenly the nice guys. But ultimately a prolonged, orgasmic shootout between good guys and bad becomes the film's only concern, the guilty pleasure of watching characters blowing each other away its sole raison d'être.

The stripper's initial change, however, consciously or not, is a comment on the deadliness of a monstrous female sexuality as conjured by the males who wrote and directed this fantasy. But the economy of change at the heart of vampire lore here conforms to no coherent sexual or moral pattern. Vampirism infects all the characters—a good son, as well as a bad brother; lustful Mexicans; a minister—and the only survivors are the reasonable outlaw and the minister's daughter. To interpret vampirism as part of a universal id poised to emerge (like the vampire film that springs from the undergrowth of a routine neo-noir) is to impose a meaning that exceeds the more prosaic and primary concern of providing a good creep show. Fueled and to some extent protected by its knowing aura, *From Dusk Till Dawn* is an intergenre caprice, a pulp carnival.

Tarantino's mix-and-match jest is a blatant rather than isolated instance of the kind of border crossing, the often playful recycling that has become postmodern common currency. Without the irony or self-consciousness, noir intersected with horror in the classic period as well, in Val Lewton's celebrated B horror cycle at RKO, for instance, which visually was often indistinguishable from the nonhorror suspense films made at the same time. In *Curse of the Cat People* (1944), the heroine, a potential cat woman, takes a nighttime walk on a street of minatory shadows lined with bushes that seem to whisper ill intentions—the richly premonitory mise-en-scène could be a setup either for noir entrapment or for a supernatural eruption. Typically, the film's equation between female sexuality and the demonic resembles noir's construction of the femme fatale. In a number of Hitchcock's films, with *Psycho* the prime example, noir merges with horror, a connection literally manifested in the film's architectural contrast between a spooky Gothic mansion, traditional site of horrific deeds, and the seedy Bates Motel, an archetypal setting for noir over which the mansion hovers.

Early in the neo period, Brian De Palma, a Hitchcock "mime," mixed elements of noir and horror in a string of thrillers, including *Obsession* (1976), *Dressed to Kill* (1980), and *Body Double* (1984). *Obsession*, about a man bedeviled by a painting that reminds him of his dead wife, is the director's hollow tribute to *Vertigo*. A capitalist patriarch who neglected his wife and daughter, the distracted protagonist certainly has the makings of a noir psychopath, while the portrait has the steely gleam of a horrific icon and is photographed in a way that promises a plunge into a supernatural zone. But the film remains generically unsettled. Its clear avoidance of a noir visual signature—the story is set in New

Orleans in 1959 and in Florence, Italy, in 1975, both photographed as places of misty romance—underlines its split and diffused identity.

With duality as an insistent through-line, *Dressed to Kill* has a cleaner division between noir and horror. A sexually dissatisfied wife who momentarily strays—she has sex with a stranger she met in a museum—is slashed to death by a stalker. The housewife looks like a prostitute; a prostitute who is the only eyewitness of the slaying looks wholesome; and the killer, like Norman Bates, is a classic split personality, the wife's therapist, who is a transsexual in the making. When his patient arouses him, his emerging female self is angered and, in drag, slays her. In female masquerade, the therapist is indeed dressed to kill. As in noir, sex is lethal. The restless wife exudes an erotic aroma that is dangerous for her, as well as for the men she incites. The nearly transsexual therapist literally acts out the male fears of female sexuality that course through the canon; in his/her perverted mind, yielding to the pull of sex is to risk emasculation. Locked in an irresoluble contradiction, he is fearful of being castrated by women at the same time that he wants literally to be castrated so that his inner woman can emerge. As Bobbi, his female self, he kills with a razor, his phallic thrusts miming penetration as death. In this Gothic noir, sex is a potentially deadly game from which only the sexually adjusted prostitute, in control of her own and her clients' sexual energy, escapes unscathed. Arguing for the necessity of repression, the film, like most noir thrillers, is deeply conservative. (Although the picture was attacked at the time as virulently misogynistic, a woman is the most sensible character; it was transsexuals who ought to have been offended.)

The killer is filmed like the monster in a horror movie, his identity concealed until the finale. A blurry shadow presence, he is seen only in partial views. Like the bogeyman in contemporary slasher films on the model of *The Texas Chainsaw Massacre*, the therapist is a naturalized monster whose atavistic reversion is confined to human rather than supernatural scale. For all its frisson and a brilliantly staged sequence in a museum (lifted from *Vertigo*), this synthetic hybrid deconstructs in comparison to *Psycho*, its illustrious intertext.

Three hybrids, *Angel Heart* (1987), *Dead Again* (1991), and *Lost Highway* (1997), blend noir with horror in more original, if not finally more successful, ways than De Palma's Hitchcock tributes, which end up in a kind of generic twilight zone. *Angel Heart* begins as a standard private-eye quest narrative in which the protagonist is summoned to Harlem to find a missing singer. The characters' ripe and pulpy names—the detective is Harold Angel; the mysterious client is Louis Cyphre; the singer is Johnny Favorite—cue alert spectators to the story's upcoming generic bends. Set in New York in 1955, the film has the visual texture of noir nostalgia (an early scene takes place in a diner that recalls the one in the opening of *The Killers*). And the fact that Johnny Favorite has had his face reconstructed introduces the classic noir themes of masquerade and multiple identity. A bravura high-angle shot of Angel on a long staircase as he ascends to meet Cyphre epitomizes the intensely noir-conscious mise-en-scène. But gradually other, non-noir images and tones seep in. Two black nuns dressed in yellow sitting outside a long room filled with empty chairs, a fortune-teller filmed in eerie blue light, voodoo rituals, a recurring shot of an empty elevator interject supernatural emanations into the noir story. Are these images Angel's hallucinations? Flash-forwards? Who is "speaking" them, and in what time frame? Like the audience, the investigator becomes more and more confused. "Who the fuck are you, Cyphre?" Angel asks his employer (played by Robert De Niro with a sly, smirking quality, as if he is sharing a secret with the audience that the audience hasn't been let in on yet).

The ambiguous shifts between fantasy and reality, standard for a supernatural horror story but not for noir, are setups for the climactic revelation that Johnny Favorite sold his soul to the devil, Louis Cyphre, a.k.a. Lucifer. The only way for Johnny to escape fate was to exchange his heart. In a far-fetched narrative turn, Angel is revealed to be the young soldier Johnny selected as his victim, and now, twelve years after this chance encounter, the detective—harboring Johnny—has been summoned to settle his contract with the devil. *Angel Heart* thus recasts noir motifs (the claims of the past, a double identity, a battle with an implacable destiny, an investigator on the trail of a killer who turns out to be himself) as a tale of supernatural terror. The film's two visual codes, noir bisected by horror, reflect the protagonist's split subjectivity. "I know who I am," a horrified Angel cries out as, in the final freeze-frame, he is trapped behind an elevator cage on his descent into hell.

*Angel Heart* is a clever stunt, good for only one outing, in which noir is swept up into horror. In *Dead Again*, horror also masquerades under a noir cover. Paranoia ("it's like someone is following me and I can't see what it is . . . I can't see behind me, someone wants to kill me"), amnesia, characters haunted by traumatic events from the past—these noir standbys erupt when another niftily named private eye, Mike Church (Kenneth Branagh), conducts an investigation of a 1949 murder. Even more than in *Angel Heart*, the supernatural twist—characters from the past inhabit characters in the present to avenge a murder for which the wrong man was executed—is a deus ex machina, an alibi that asks for an unreasonably steep suspension of disbelief. Visually, such as in the sequences of staccato editing in which fragments from the murder scene in the past collide against the murder scene that is the climax of the present-tense action, as well as narratively, the far-fetched supernatural "explanation," the film engages in sleight-of-hand practices. *Dead Again* betrays the two genres it haphazardly crossbreeds.

The termination point for noir-become-horror may have been reached with David Lynch's sleek, beautifully shot *Lost Highway*. In act one, Fred, the unlucky protagonist with a perfect noir profession—saxophone player in a smoky jazz club—is charged with killing his slinky, unfaithful wife, and in no time finds himself on death row protesting his innocence to deaf ears. In act two, Pete, a character with another solid noir profession—car mechanic—is seduced by the mistress of a gangster, Mr. Eddie, who comes to his garage. (Patricia Arquette, raven-haired as the wife, blonde as the moll, plays both women.) Desperate to escape from her insanely jealous lover, the woman enlists Pete in a murder plan.

These routine noir stories of mischance, seduction, and entrapment are connected by an event that takes the film out of noir: in prison Fred disappears, mysteriously replaced by Pete. The transformation is presented as a purely uncanny spectacle the audience is expected to accept on faith, without narrative justification. In a single blow, the film dismantles noir's historical dependence on internal logic and consistency. And "permitting" itself this excursion into a supernatural action that propels, makes possible the rest of the story, *Lost Highway* narrows rather than expands noir's parameters. The film thus tips noir characterizations and themes into horror: the two femmes fatales are in league with a devil figure, a mystery man in white makeup who stage-manages the progress of both protagonists toward their awaiting doom. As in *Angel Heart*, space and time are made to "perform" elaborate charades; with a battery of flash-forwards and repetitions, the narrative circles around itself to return at the end to its point of departure, as Pete is changed back into Fred. The significance of recurrent, fragmented images, like the uncoded shot of a desert shack consumed by fire, is not revealed until the finale. In this Möbius-strip universe of dissolving and doubled identities, time and space are unreliable. Despite velvety shadows, an eerie, meticulous sound design, and the director's characteristically skillful estrangement of the familiar—Fred's walk through his ordinary house is turned into a sinister ritual—the film is merely decorative. At attempt at "cosmic" noir, *Lost Highway* is finally a self-enclosed puzzle, unsatisfactory as noir or horror, which recalls its rhymed opening and closing shots of an endless highway to nowhere.

Elements of noir have migrated less frequently into science fiction, a more defensive, resistant genre than horror. Jean-Luc Godard's 1965 attempt in *Alphaville* to unite the two genres, was a famous and perhaps symptomatic failure. From The Lands Without, Lemmy Caution, wearing the topcoat and fedora of a traditional noir private eye, is a secret agent come to Alphaville to liquidate a scientist who has made himself a dictator. A world run by computers, in which "nearly every day words disappear because they are forbidden," Alphaville is a technological dystopia whose fearful, brainwashed citizens are "replacements." Godard's future metropolis is in fact Paris circa 1964, a place of glass-and-steel high-rises, of blinking lights and cacophonous sounds, of sudden violence. The film's mise-en-scène underlines the point that the present, imaged as a place already machine dominated, contains the seeds of a horrifically depersonalizing futuristic wasteland. (Uncharacteristically, Godard offers a sentimental Hollywood ending: Lemmy rescues the mad scientist's daughter, who learns to say "I love you" as she leaves the dying city.)

Visually undernourished as noir and as science fiction, the film suggests the lack of affinity between the two genres. Noir's focus is private, domestic, psychological, while science fiction is often about the fate of the world. The automatons of Alphaville are beyond the reach of noir, immune to its network of anxieties. In science fiction, threat usually comes from the world out there, a universe distorted by scientific and technological knowledge; in noir at its best, threat comes from within.

The most celebrated marriage of noir with science fiction is Ridley Scott's *Blade Runner* ([1982] the subject of a recent book by Paul M. Sammon called *Future Noir*). In the original version, a voiceover commentary spoken by the hero, Deckard (played by Harrison Ford with an almost pitch-perfect simulation of a high 1940s deadpan monotone) coats the story with a noir patina; the omission of the voiceover in the director's cut is a significant loss. In his tone, wardrobe, and narrative function, Deckard, with or without a voiceover, recalls a 1940s detective. With rippling jazz on the sound track, he moves through smoky, noir-like environments that are retro and futuristic at the same time. His assignment, finding and terminating replicants, is distinctly science fiction rather than noir, but like a traditional private eye, he is on the prowl in a big city that itself becomes a central presence in the film. With its thrusting skyscrapers arranged in rhythmic conjugations and an array of aerial transportation, the film's imaginary cityscape recalls the one in *Metropolis* of 1926, which was inspired by director Fritz Lang's impressions of the New York skyline of the mid-1920s. The futuristic dystopia of *Blade Runner* is a city of perpetual night; fog and rain are the only weather options; the streets are thronged with people, neon, advertising, while overhead is a giant image of an Asian woman presiding as a kind of post-postmodern deity. At once glittering and decadent, bewitching and minatory, the film's city is a great foul place, a locus of noir entrapment. And like the city at night constructed by classic noir, this new dark metropolis, part *Batman*, part noir, has become the template for how cities of the future have continued to be depicted in science-fiction spectacles. The megalopolis in *Blade Runner*, like the original noir city of the 1940s, even accounting for its purely imaginary status as the projection of a city that has not yet been built, looks artificial, a city clearly produced by the cinematic imagination. Like the characters Deckard tracks (and perhaps Deckard himself), the city is a replicant, a simulacrum in a world inhabited by simulacra and therefore an exemplary postmodern mise-en-scène.

Stripping away the science-fiction accoutrements—the difficulty in distinguishing a human from a technologically perfected copy—the film rests on the quest paradigm familiar from classic and nouveau noir. Deckard recalls the hunter in *Point Blank*: both characters seek prey they must eliminate, Walker for revenge, Deckard to maintain a kind of species and ontological purity, a world kept safe for the truly and

Dressed like a film noir private eye, Deckard (Harrison Ford), the hero of *Blade Runner* (1982), tracks his quarry in a futuristic dystopia in which humans and replicants appear to be interchangeable.

exclusively human. Although in his director's cut Scott chose to eliminate the noir voiceover, he enhanced the story's connection to noir in other ways. Implying that Deckard himself is a replicant, the director's cut becomes a story, like *D.O.A.* and *The Big Clock*, steeped in pitch black irony about a character whose search ensures his own destruction. Like the characters in the most unrelenting noirs, Deckard is doomed from the start, a noir subject without a prayer. In the original version, not only is the hero less implicated with those he is charged with terminating, he escapes from the teeming, infested city to a place beyond the horizon with a pretty replicant he hopes to save. In the darker director's cut, for humans and replicants alike, there is no other place to escape to. The choking dark city has no exits.

*Strange Days* (1995) is an apocalyptic noir set in end-of-the-twentieth-century Los Angeles. (In *Blade Runner* and in *Strange Days*, centered on Broadway in downtown Los Angeles, the landmark Bradbury Building is recognizable beneath the postmodern, futuristic ornamentation). Again, future noir takes place in a nighttime city of congested streets bathed in ice-blue lighting and ablaze with agitated neon signs. The site of hyperbolic chaos, random violence, and sex for sale (Nero, the protagonist of *Strange Days* [played by Ralph Fiennes], hangs out in a stripper bar in which women on platforms perform impersonal rituals of simulated sexual stimulation), this future noir is positively Brueghelesque. Like many noir protagonists who used to be but no longer are something or someone and are thrust into a threshold space to become potential noir victims, Nero used to be a cop. Now, in this imaginary dystopia, he pursues a gruesome postmodern profession selling other people's experiences, which can be attached like earphones. Virtual reality, in the form of the merging of two "subjectivities," has come to fruition in this not-so-brave new world; and, with a vengeance, "you are there." Calling himself the magic man, the Santa Claus of the subconscious, he sells a technology that sutures spectator to image with a nasty completeness. Mocking the contemporary desire to possess, to interact with the image, his technology allows the customer to enter another consciousness while retaining a separate identity. But ultimate merger is ultimate alienation.

The narrative that emerges from the alluring noir mise-en-scène is disappointingly formulaic. Two rabidly racist white cops stop and kill a prominent black rapper. A buffed black heroine, "Mace" (Angela

The image of the protagonist (Ralph Fiennes) hovers over the "Mother of All Parties" on the eve of the new millennium, in *Strange Days* (1995). The news from the future is not good.

Bassett), who disdains the hero's career choice, is allowed a final showdown with the rogue cops, although she needs white institutional authority to bolster and ratify her revenge. After the racist cops have been killed, Nero at last recognizes that Mace loves him, and their embrace is supposed to represent recuperation for the fallen world the film vividly constructs. (But a story appealing to white guilt was seriously mistimed in the wake of the scandalous O. J. Simpson verdict, and was a notable commercial failure.) The conventional happy ending is another way in which the narrative betrays the commanding mise-en-scène. Neo-noir's self-destructive penchant for display and for seducing the eye is only increased in its marriage with science fiction, a genre traditionally dedicated to ravishing, as well as fooling, the spectator's gaze.

Like horror and especially science fiction, comedy is also potentially fatal to hard-core noir. Depending on the amount and kind, comic touches can contaminate or weaken noir to the point of parody. From at least the mid-1980s, comedy has nipped at noir's borders. Jonathan Demme's symptomatic 1986 crime comedy, *Something Wild*, mixes the genres in ways that suggested noir's vulnerability to tonal takeover. The film treats a standard noir narrative of a bourgeois male (Jeff Daniels) tempted and derailed by a femme fatale (Melanie Griffith) as a delirious mixed breed of laughs, romance, and violence. With cracks in his bourgeois armor, the protagonist is a straitlaced businessman separated from his wife. His temptress is a kook who lures him into a world of hot sex and petty theft on the order of leaving restaurants without paying. A free spirit and an inventive performer, she passes him off as her husband. The character is a femme fatale rewritten as liberating rather than dangerous; she's the carefree heroine of a latter-day screwball comedy, fun as opposed to castrating. Her escapades never quite ripen into full-fledged crime, just as the straying man never completely descends into a noir maze. Unlike the conservative classic noir tales of errant patriarchs, this postmodern variation seems to be in favor of detour: there *is* a way out, the film suggests, and it's something wild.

There's a catch in the route to the hero's liberation, however. He must commit a crime; and true to the codes of the American action picture rather than to those of film noir, he proves his masculinity through a violent act. Once he encounters his new girlfriend's ex-husband, the explosive ex-convict he is to kill in self-defense, the film's tone darkens. Being able to kill is linked with freeing his libido; both lead him to a truer manliness than he had when he was sheltered by the straight and narrow. He's rewarded by driving off with the woman who changed him. The psycho ex-husband and the violence he elicits from the hero are echoes of the "old" noir. Similarly, the places where the new lovers have their trysts, such as the Apache Motel with a postcard-perfect neon sign, are calculatedly retro touches, traces of the past from which the couple launches at the end into a world beyond noir.

*Something Wild*, which took its noir basis seriously if lightly, remained this side of parody or spoof. But it inaugurated the process of ripping at the fabric of noir, which has led to demolition derbies like *Grosse Pointe Blank*, where nothing noir is sacred. Too many parodies, with their facile deconstruction, can spell the death of any genre. A parody is ideally a stunt good for one outing; let *Dead Men Don't Wear Plaid* (1982 ), an affectionate tribute to classic noir, be a unique project. Hired by a woman wearing the requisite veil to investigate the death of her father, a cheese scientist, the detective (played by Steve Martin in black hair) encounters, in glorious black and white, "real" characters from the classic canon. On his search he interacts with fragments of Kirk Douglas in *I Walk Alone*, Ava Gardner and Burt Lancaster in *The Killers*, Veronica Lake in *The Glass Key*, Alan Ladd in *This Gun for Hire*, Bette Davis in *Deception*, Lana Turner in *The Postman Always Rings Twice*, and Humphrey Bogart in *The Big Sleep*, among others. Although the frame story is preposterous, a parody of the narrative mazes of Raymond Chandler's quest stories, the film evinces a genuine affection for the real thing, classic noir and its icons. The merging of then and now is technically seamless, as if marking the desire of the latter-day filmmakers to "mate" with the historical films from which they quote, while realizing that the films can be revisited only through citation, as frames within the frame.

Noir endures, but, inevitably, not in the same way as forty and fifty years ago. Like any genre that survives, it has had to adapt; and as a set of narrative patterns, a repertoire of images, a nucleus of character types, it has proven remarkably elastic. Against the odds, and after several premature obituaries, noir is a mainstay of commercial narrative filmmaking. Are any neo-noir movies as good as the best of the classic canon? Probably not. But over its forty-years-and-counting history, many worthy films have successfully remodeled noir to reflect, and to appeal to, contemporary perspectives. And visually, existentially, philosophically, noir has infiltrated the cultural landscape to become a widely circulated pop-culture emblem.

539-50

# Bibliography

Borde, Raymond, and Etienne Chaumeton. *Panorama du film noir américain*. Paris: Les Éditions de Minuit, 1955.

Bordwell, David, Janet Staiger, and Kristin Thompson. *The Classical Hollywood Cinema: Film Style and Mode of Production to 1960*. New York: Columbia University, 1985.

Brode, Douglas. *Money, Women, and Guns: Crime Movies from "Bonnie and Clyde" to the Present*. New York: Citadel Press, 1995.

Cameron, Ian, ed. *The Book of Film Noir*. New York: Continuum, 1993.

Christopher, Nicholas. *Somewhere in the Night: Film Noir and the American City*. New York: Free Press, 1997.

Clarens, Carlos. *Crime Movies*. New York: Da Capo Press, 1997.

Copjec, Joan, ed. *Shades of Noir*. London: Verso, 1993.

Deming, Barbara. *Running Away from Myself: A Dream Portrait of America Drawn from the Films of the Forties*. New York: Grossman Publishers, 1969.

Dijkstra, Bram. *Evil Sisters: The Threat of Female Sexuality and the Cult of Manhood*. New York: Alfred A. Knopf, 1996.

Doane, Mary Ann. *Femmes Fatales: Feminism, Film Theory, Psychoanalysis*. New York: Routledge, 1991.

Dowdy, Andrew. *The Films of the Fifties: The American State of Mind*. New York: Morrow, 1973.

Durgnat, Raymond. "Paint It Black: The Family Tree of the Film Noir." In *Film Noir Reader*, ed. Alain Silver and James Ursini. New York: Limelight Editions, 1996. Pp. 37-51.

Foucault, Michel. *The History of Sexuality*. Trans. Robert Hurley. New York: Random House, 1980.

Garnier, Philippe. *Goodis: La Vie en noir et blanc*. Paris: Éditions du Seuil, 1984.

Gomery, Douglas. *The Hollywood Studio System*. New York: St. Martin's, 1986.

Hamilton, William L. "Style Noir," *New York Times*, September 14, 1997.

Haut, Woody. *Pulp Culture: Hardboiled Fiction and the Cold War*. London: Serpent's Tail, 1995.

Higham, Charles, and Joel Greenberg. *Hollywood in the Forties*. Cranbury, New Jersey: A. S. Barnes and Company, 1968.

Hirsch, Foster. *The Dark Side of the Screen: Film Noir*. San Diego: A. S. Barnes and Company, 1981.

Jameson, Fredric. *Signatures of the Visible*. New York: Routledge, 1992.

Kaplan, E Ann. *Women in Film Noir*. London: British Film Institute, 1978.

Karimi, A. M. *Toward a Definition of the American Film Noir (1941-1949)*. New York: Arno Press, 1976.

Krutnik, Frank. *In a Lonely Street: Film Noir, Genre, Masculinity*. London: Routledge, 1991.

Madden, David, ed. *Tough Guy Writers of the Thirties*. Carbondale: Southern Illinois University Press, 1968.

McArthur, Colin. *Underworld U.S.A*. New York: Viking Press, 1972.

Muller, Eddie. *Dark City: The Lost World of Film Noir*. New York: St. Martin Griffin, 1998.

Mulvey, Laura. "Visual Pleasure and Narrative Cinema," *Screen* 16 (fall 1975): 6-18.

Naremore, James. *The Magic World of Orson Welles*. New York: Oxford University Press, 1978.

Norris, Joel. *Serial Killers*. New York: Doubleday, 1988.

O'Brien, Geoffrey. *Hardboiled America: Lurid Paperbacks and the Masters of Noir*, 2nd ed. New York: Da Capo Press, 1997.

Ottoson, Robert. *A Reference Guide to the American Film Noir: 1940-1958*. Metuchen, New Jersey: Scarecrow Press, 1981.

Palmer, R. Barton. *Hollywood's Dark Cinema. The American Film Noir*. New York: Twayne Publishers, 1994.

Polito, Robert, ed. *Crime Novels: American Noir of the 1930s & 40s*. New York: The Library of America, 1997.

—————. *Savage Art. A Biography of Jim Thompson*. New York: Alfred A. Knopf, 1995.

Porfirio, Robert G. *The Dark Age of American Film: A Study of the American Film Noir*. Ph. D. Dissertation, Yale University, 1979.

Roth, Marty. *Foul and Fair Play: Reading Genre in Classic Detective Fiction*. Athens: The University of Georgia Press, 1995.

Sammon, Paul M. *Future Noir. The Making of Blade Runner*. New York: HarperCollins, 1996.

Schrader, Paul. "Notes on *Film Noir*." In *Film Noir Reader*, ed. Alain Silver and James Ursini. New York: Limelight Editions, 1996. Pp. 53-63.

Shadoian, Jack. *Dreams and Deadends: The American Gangster/Crime Film*. Cambridge: MIT, 1977.

Silver, Alain, and James Ursini, eds. *Film Noir Reader*. New York: Limelight Editions, 1996.

Silver, Alain, and Elizabeth Ward, eds. *Film Noir: An Encyclopedic Reference to the American Style*, 3rd ed. New York: The Overlook Press, 1993.

Telotte, J. P. *Voices in the Dark: The Narrative Patterns of Film Noir*. Urbana: University of Illinois Press, 1989.

Thompson, Peggy, and Saeko Usukawa. *Hardboiled. Great Lines from Classic Noir Films*. San Francisco: Chronicle Books, 1995.

Thomson, David. *Suspects*. New York: Alfred A. Knopf, 1985.

Tuska, Jon. *Dark Cinema: American Film Noir in Cultural Perspective*. Westport: Greenwood Press, 1984.

Wood, Michael. *America in the Movies*. New York: Basic Books, 1975.

# Filmography

*After Dark, My Sweet* (Avenue, 1990). Produced by Robert Redlin and Ric Kidney. Directed by James Foley. Script by Robert Redlin and James Foley, based on the novel by Jim Thompson. Director of Photography, Mark Plummer. Production Designer, David Brisbin. Music, Maurice Jarre. Editor, Howard Smith. Starring Jason Patric (Collie), Rachel Ward (Fay), Rocky Giordani (Bert), Bruce Dern (Uncle Bud), Tom Wagner (Counterman), George Dickerson (Doc Goldman). 114 minutes.

*Against All Odds* (Columbia, 1984). Produced by Jerry Bick, Taylor Hackford, and William S. Gilmore. Directed by Taylor Hackford. Script by Eric Hughes, based on the novel *Build My Gallows High* by Daniel Mainwaring [uncredited]. Director of Photography, Donald E. Thorin. Production Designer, Richard James Lawrence; Gene Rudolph, consultant. Music, Michel Colombier and Larry Carlton. Editors, Fredric Steinkamp and William Steinkamp. Starring Rachel Ward (Jessie Wyler), Jeff Bridges (Terry Brogan), James Woods (Jake Wise), Alex Karras (Hank Sully), Jane Greer (Mrs. Wyler), Richard Widmark (Ben Caxton), Dorian Harewood (Tommy), Swoosie Kurtz (Edie). 125 minutes.

*Alphaville: Une étrange aventure de Lemmy Caution* (Chaumiane, 1965). Produced by André Michelin. Directed and written by Jean-Luc Godard. Director of Photography, Raoul Coutard. Music, Paul Misraki. Editor, Agnès Guillemot. Starring Eddie Constantine (Lemmy Caution), Anna Karina (Natacha Von Braun), Akim Tamiroff (Henri Dickson), Howard Vernon (Professor Leonard Nosferatu/Von Braun), László Szabó (Chief Engineer), Michael Delahaye (Von Braun's Assistant), Jean-André

Fieschi (Professor Heckell), Jean-Louis Comolli (Professor Jeckell). 98 minutes.

*The American Friend* [*Der Amerikanische Freund*] (Road Movie Filmproduktion, 1977). Directed and written by Wim Wenders, based on the novel *Ripley's Game* by Patricia Highsmith. Director of Photography, Robby Müller. Art Directors, Heidi Lüdi and Tony Lüdi. Music, Jürgen Knieper. Editor, Peter Przygodda. Starring Dennis Hopper (Tom Ripley), Bruno Ganz (Jonathan Zimmermann), Lisa Kreuzer (Marianne Zimmermann), Gérard Blain (Raoul Minot), Nicholas Ray (Derwatt), Samuel Fuller (The American Mobster), Peter Lilienthal (Marcangelo), Daniel Schmid (Ingraham), Jean Eustache (Friendly Man), Rudolf Schündler (Gantner). 127 minutes.

*Angel Heart* (TriStar, 1987). Produced by Alan Marshall and Elliott Kastner. Directed and written by Alan Parker, based on the novel *Falling Angel* by William Hjortsberg. Director of Photography, Michael Seresin. Production Designer, Brian Morris. Music, Trevor Jones. Editor, Gerry Hambling. Starring Mickey Rourke (Harry Angel), Robert De Niro (Louis Cyphre), Lisa Bonet (Epiphany Proudfoot), Charlotte Rampling (Margaret Krusemark), Stocker Fontelieu (Ethan Krusemark), Brownie McGhee (Toots Sweet), Michael Higgins (Dr. Fowler), Elizabeth Whitcraft (Connie), Eliott Keener (Sterne). 112 minutes.

*Asphalt Jungle* (MGM, 1950). Produced by Arthur Hornblow, Jr. Directed by John Huston. Script by Ben Maddow and John Huston, based on the novel by W. R. Burnett. Director of Photography, Harold Rosson. Art Directors, Cedric Gibbons and Randall Duell. Music, Miklós Rózsa. Editor, George Boemler. Starring Sterling Hayden (Dix Handley), Louis Calhern (Alonzo D. Emmerich), Jean Hagen (Doll Conovan), James Whitmore (Gus Ninissi), Sam Jaffe (Doc Erwin Riedenschneider), John McIntire (Police Commissioner Hardy), Marc Lawrence (Cobby), Barry Kelley (Lt. Ditrich), Anthony Caruso (Louis Ciavelli), Teresa Celli (Maria Ciavelli). 112 minutes.

*At Close Range* (Hemdale/Orion, 1986). Produced by Elliott Lewitt and Don Guest. Directed by James Foley. Script by Nicholas Kazan, based on a story by Kazan and Elliott Lewitt. Director of Photography,

Juan Ruiz Anchía. Production Designer, Peter Jamison. Music, Patrick Leonard. Editor, Howard Smith. Starring Sean Penn (Brad Whitewood, Jr.), Christopher Walken (Brad, Sr.), Chris Penn (Tommy), Mary Stuart Masterson (Terry), Millie Perkins (Julie), Eileen Ryan (Grandma), Tracey Walter (Patch). 115 minutes.

*Badlands* (Warner Bros., 1973). Produced, directed, and written by Terrence Malick. Photography, Brian Probyn, Tak Fujimoto, and Stevan Larner. Art Director, Jack Fisk. Music, George Tipton. Editor, Robert Estrin. Starring Martin Sheen (Kit), Sissy Spacek (Holly), Warren Oates (Holly's Father), Ramon Bieri (Cato), Alan Vint (Deputy), Gary Littlejohn (Sheriff), John Carter (Rich Man). 94 minutes.

*Band of Outsiders* [*Bande à part*] (Anouchka/Orsay, 1964). Directed and written by Jean-Luc Godard, based on the novel *Fool's Gold* by Dolores Hitchens. Director of Photography, Raoul Coutard. Music, Michel Legrand. Editors, Agnès Guillemot and Françoise Collin. Starring Anna Karina (Odile), Claude Brasseur (Arthur), Sami Frey (Franz), Louisa Colpeyn (Madame Victoria), Danièle Girard (English Teacher), Ernest Menzer (Arthur's Uncle), Chantal Darget (Arthur's Aunt), Michèle Seghers (Pupil), Claude Makovski (Pupil), Georges Staquet (Legionnaire). 95 minutes.

*Basic Instinct* (Carolco/TriStar, 1992). Produced by Alan Marshall. Directed by Paul Verhoeven. Script by Joe Eszterhas. Director of Photography, Jan de Bont. Production Designer, Terence Marsh. Music, Jerry Goldsmith. Editor, Frank J. Urioste. Starring Michael Douglas (Nick Curran), Sharon Stone (Catherine Tramell), George Dzundza (Gus Moran), Jeanne Tripplehorn (Dr. Beth Garner), Leilani Sarelle (Roxy), Dorothy Malone (Hazel Dobkins). 123 minutes.

*La Bête humaine* (Paris Film, 1938). Produced by Robert Hakim and Raymond Hakim. Directed and written by Jean Renoir, based on the novel by Émile Zola. Director of Photography, Curt Courant. Production Designer, Eugène Lourié. Music, Joseph Kosma. Editors, Marguerite Renoir and Suzanne de Troeye. Starring Jean Gabin (Jacques Lantier), Simone Simon (Severine), Fernand Ledoux (Roubaud,

Severine's Husband), Julien Carette (Pecqueux), Blanchette Brunoy (Flore), Jean Renoir (Cabuche, the Poacher), Gérard Landry (Dauvergne's Son), Jenny Hélia (Philomene), Colette Régis (Victoire), Jacques Berlioz (Grandmorin). 105 minutes.

*Betrayed* (MGM-UA, 1988). Produced by Irwin Winkler. Directed by Constantin Costa-Gavras. Script by Joe Eszterhas. Director of Photography, Patrick Blossier. Production Designer, Patrizia von Brandenstein. Music, Bill Conti. Editor, Joëlle Van Effenterre. Starring Debra Winger (Katie Phillips/Cathy Weaver), Tom Berenger (Gary Simmons), John Heard (Michael Carnes), Betsy Blair (Gladys Simmons), John Mahoney (Shorty), Ted Levine (Wes), Jeffrey DeMunn (Flynn). 123 minutes.

*The Big Clock* (Paramount, 1948). Produced by Richard Mailbaum. Directed by John Farrow. Script by Jonathan Latimer, based on the novel by Kenneth Fearing. Director of Photography, John F. Seitz. Production Designers, Hans Dreier, Albert Nozaki, and Roland Anderson. Music, Victor Young. Editor, Gene Ruggiero. Starring Ray Milland (George Stroud), Charles Laughton (Earl Janoth), Maureen O'Sullivan (Georgette Stroud), George Macready (Steve Hagen), Rita Johnson (Pauline York), Elsa Lanchester (Louise Patterson), Harold Vermilyea (Don Klausmeyer), Dan Tobin (Ray Cordette), Harry Morgan (Bill Womack), Richard Webb (Nat Sperling). 95 minutes.

*Black Widow* (20th Century-Fox, 1987). Produced by Harold Schneider. Directed by Bob Rafelson. Script by Ronald Bass. Director of Photography, Conrad L. Hall. Production Designer, Gene Callahan. Music, Michael Small. Editor, John Bloom. Starring Debra Winger (Alexandra), Theresa Russell (Catherine), Sami Frey (Paul), Dennis Hopper (Ben), Nicol Williamson (William), Terry O'Quinn (Bruce), James Hong (Shin), Diane Ladd (Etta). 103 minutes.

*Blade Runner* (Warner Bros., 1982). Produced by Michael Deeley. Directed by Ridley Scott. Script by Hampton Fancher and David Peoples, based on the novel *Do Androids Dream of Electric Sheep?* by Philip K. Dick. Director of Photography, Jordan Cronenweth. Production Designer, Lawrence G. Paull. Music, Vangelis. Editor, Terry Rawlings. Starring Harrison Ford (Rick Deckard), Rutger Hauer (Roy Batty), Sean Young (Rachael), Edward James Olmos (Gaff), M. Emmet Walsh (Bryant), Daryl Hannah (Pris), William Sanderson (J. F. Sebastian), Brion James (Leon), Joe Turkel (Tyrell), Joanna Cassidy (Zhora). 114 minutes.

*Blood Simple* (River Road, 1984). Produced by Ethan Coen. Directed by Joel Coen. Script by Ethan Coen and Joel Coen. Director of Photography, Barry Sonnenfeld. Production Designer, Jane Musky. Music, Carter Burwell. Editor, Roderick Jaynes (Joel Coen). Starring John Getz (Ray), Frances McDormand (Abby), Dan Hedaya (Julian Marty), M. Emmet Walsh (Private Detective), Samm-Art Williams (Meurice). 96 minutes..

*Blue Velvet* (DEG, 1986). Produced by Fred Caruso. Directed and written by David Lynch. Director of Photography, Frederick Elmes. Production Designer, Patricia Norris. Music, Angelo Badalamenti. Editor, Duwayne Dunham. Starring Kyle MacLachlan (Jeffrey Beaumont), Isabella Rossellini (Dorothy Valens), Dennis Hopper (Frank Booth), Laura Dern (Sandy Williams), George Dickerson (Detective Williams), Hope Lange (Mrs. Williams), Dean Stockwell (Ben), Priscilla Pointer (Mrs. Beaumont), Frances Bay (Aunt Barbara), Jack Harvey (Mr. Beaumont). 120 minutes.

*Bob le flambeur* [*Bob the Gambler*] (Studios Jenner/OGC/La Cyme-Play Art, 1955). Produced and directed by Jean-Pierre Melville. Script by Auguste Le Breton and Jean-Pierre Melville. Director of Photography, Henri Decaë. Art Directors, Claude Bouxin and Jean-Pierre Melville. Music, Eddie Barclay and Jean Boyer. Editor, Monique Bonnot. Starring Isabelle Corey (Anne), Daniel Cauchy (Paolo), Roger Duchesne (Bob Montagné), Guy Decomble (Inspector), André Garet (Roger), Gérard Buhr (Marc), Claude Cerval (Jean), Colette Fleury (Jean's Wife), Simone Paris (Yvonne), Howard Vernon (McKimmie). 98 minutes.

*Body Heat* (Ladd/Warner Bros., 1981). Produced by Fred T. Gallo. Directed and written by Lawrence Kasdan. Director of Photography, Richard H. Kline. Production Designer, Bill Kenney. Music, John Barry. Editor, Carol Littleton. Starring William Hurt (Ned Racine), Kathleen

Turner (Matty Walker), Richard Crenna (Edmund Walker), Ted Danson (Peter Lowenstein), J. A. Preston (Oscar Grace), Mickey Rourke (Teddy Lewis). 113 minutes.

*Le Boucher* [*The Butcher*] (La Boétie/Euro International, 1969). Produced by André Génovès. Directed and written by Claude Chabrol. Director of Photography, Jean Rabier. Production Designer, Guy Littaye. Music, Pierre Jansen. Editor, Jacques Gaillard. Starring Stéphane Audran (Helene), Jean Yanne (Popaul), Antonio Passalia (Angelo), Mario Beccaria (Leon Hamel), Pasquale Ferone (Père Cahrpy), Roger Rudel (Police Inspector Grumbach), William Guérault (Charles). 93 minutes.

*Bound* (Dino De Laurentiis/Gramercy/Spelling, 1996). Produced by Andrew Lazar and Stuart Boros. Directed and written by Larry Wachowski and Andy Wachowski. Director of Photography, Bill Pope. Production Designer, Eve Cauley. Music, Don Davis. Editor, Zach Staenberg. Starring Jennifer Tilly (Violet), Gina Gershon (Corky), Joe Pantoliano (Caesar), John P. Ryan (Mickey Malnato), Christopher Meloni (Johnnie Marconi), Richard C. Sarafian (Gino Marzzone), Barry Kivel (Shelly), Mary Mara (Bartender), Peter Spellos (Lou), Susie Bright (Jesse). 107 minutes.

*Boyz N the Hood* (Columbia, 1991). Produced by Steve Nicolaides. Directed and written by John Singleton. Director of Photography, Charles Mills. Art Director, Bruce Bellamy. Music, Stanley Clarke. Editor, Bruce Cannon. Starring Laurence Fishburne (Furious Styles), Ice Cube (Doughboy Baker), Cuba Gooding, Jr. (Tre Styles), Nia Long (Brandi), Morris Chestnut (Ricky Baker), Tyra Ferrell (Mrs. Baker), Angela Bassett (Reva Styles), Meta King (Brandi's Mom), Whitman Mayo (The Old Man), Hudhail Al-Amir (S.A.T. Man). 107 minutes.

*Breakdown* (Paramount/Dino De Laurentiis/Spelling, 1997). Produced by Dino De Laurentiis and Martha De Laurentiis. Directed by Jonathan Mostow. Script by Jonathan Mostow and Sam Montgomery, based on a story by Jonathan Mostow. Director of Photography, Douglas Milsome. Production Designer, Victoria Paul. Music, Basil Poledouris. Editors, Derek Brechin and Kevin Stitt. Starring Kurt Russell (Jeff Taylor), J. T. Walsh (Red Barr), Kathleen Quinlan (Amy Taylor),

M. C. Gainey (Earl), Jack Noseworthy (Billy), Ritch Brinkley (Al), Rex Linn (Sheriff Boyd), Moira Harris (Arleen), Kim Robillard (Deputy Len Carver), Thomas Kopache (Calhoun). 100 minutes.

*Breathless* [*À bout de souffle*] (Georges de Beauregard/Société Nouvelle de Cinéma, 1959). Produced by Georges de Beauregard. Directed and written by Jean-Luc Godard, based on a treatment by François Truffaut. Director of Photography, Raoul Coutard. Art Director, Claude Chabrol. Music, Martial Solal. Editors, Cécile Decugis and Lila Herman. Starring Jean-Paul Belmondo (Michel Poiccard), Jean Seberg (Patricia Franchini), Daniel Boulanger (Police Inspector), Jean-Pierre Melville (Parvulesco), Liliane Robin (Minouche), Henri-Jacques Huet (Antonio Berrutti), Van Doude (The Journalist), Claude Mansard (Claudius Mansard), Michel Fabre (Plainclothes Policeman), Jean-Luc Godard (An Informer). 90 minutes.

*Breathless* (Orion, 1983). Produced by Martin Erlichman. Directed and written by Jim McBride, based on the 1959 film *À bout de souffle*, written by Jean-Luc Godard, from a story by François Truffaut. Director of Photography, Richard H. Kline. Production Designer, Richard Sylbert. Music, Jack Nitzsche. Editor, Robert Estrin. Starring Richard Gere (Jesse), Valérie Kaprisky (Monica), Art Metrano (Birnbaum), John P. Ryan (Lt. Parmental). 100 minutes.

*The Bride Wore Black* [*La Mariée était en noir*] (Films du Carrosse/Productions Artistes/Dino De Laurentiis, 1967). Produced by Marcel Berbert. Directed by François Truffaut. Script by François Truffaut and Jean-Louis Richard, based on the novel by William Irish. Director of Photography, Raoul Coutard. Production Designer, Pierre Guffroy. Music, Bernard Herrmann. Editor, Claudine Bouché. Starring Jeanne Moreau (Julie), Michel Bouquet (Coral), Jean-Claude Brialy (Corey), Charles Denner (Fergus), Claude Rich (Bliss), Daniel Boulanger (Delvaux), Michel Lonsdale (Rene), Alexandra Stewart (Mlle. Becker). 105 minutes.

*Bulletproof Heart* (Keystone/Republic, 1995). Produced by Robert Vince and William Vince. Directed by Mark Malone. Script by Gordon Melbourne, based on a story by Mark Malone. Director of Photography, Tobias A. Schliessler. Production Designer, Lynne Stopkewich. Music, Graeme Coleman. Editor, Robin Russell. Starring Anthony LaPaglia (Mick), Mimi Rogers (Fiona), Matt Craven (Archie), Peter Boyle (George), Monika Schnarre (Laura), Joseph Maher (Dr. Alstricht), Mark Acheson (Hellbig), Phillip Hayes (F.B.I. Agent), Christopher Mark Pinhey (Partygoer #1), Claudio De Victor (Partygoer #2). 96 minutes.

*Cape Fear* (Melville-Talbot/Universal, 1962). Produced by Sy Bartlett. Directed by J. Lee Thompson. Script by James R. Webb, based on the novel *The Executioners* by John D. MacDonald. Director of Photography, Sam Leavitt. Art Directors, Alexander Golitzen and Robert F. Boyle. Music, Bernard Herrmann. Editor, George Tomasini. Starring Gregory Peck (Sam Bowden), Robert Mitchum (Max Cady), Polly Bergen (Peggy Bowden), Lori Martin (Nancy Bowden), Martin Balsam (Mark Dutton), Jack Kruschen (Dave Grafton), Telly Savalas (Charles Sievers), Barrie Chase (Diane Taylor), Paul Comi (Garner), Edward Platt (Judge). 105 minutes.

*Cape Fear* (Amblin/Cappa/Tribeca/Universal, 1991). Produced by Barbara De Fina. Directed by Martin Scorsese. Script by Wesley Strick, based on the screenplay by James R. Webb and the novel *The Executioners* by John D. MacDonald. Director of Photography, Freddie Francis. Production Designer, Henry Bumstead. Music, Elmer Bernstein and Bernard Herrmann. Editor, Thelma Schoonmaker. Starring Robert De Niro (Max Cady), Nick Nolte (Sam Bowden), Jessica Lange (Leigh Bowden), Juliette Lewis (Danielle Bowden), Joe Don Baker (Claude Kersek), Robert Mitchum (Lt. Elgart), Gregory Peck (Lee Heller). 130 minutes.

*Charley Varrick* (Universal, 1973). Produced and directed by Don Siegel. Script by Dean Riesner and Howard Rodman, based on the novel *The Looters* by John Reese. Director of Photography, Michael C. Butler. Art Director, Fernando Carrere. Music, Lalo Schifrin. Editor, Frank Morriss. Starring Walter Matthau (Charley Varrick), Joe Don Baker (Molly), Felicia Farr (Sybil Fort), Andrew Robinson (Harman Sullivan), John Vernon (Maynard Boyle), Sheree North (Jewell Everett), Norman Fell (Mr. Garfinkle), Benson Fong (Honest John), Woodrow Parfrey (Howard Young), William Schallert (Sheriff Bill Horton). 111 minutes.

*La Chienne* (Braunberger-Richebé, 1931). Produced by Roger Richebé. Directed and written by Jean Renoir, based on the novel by Georges de le Fouchardière. Director of Photography, Theodor Sparkuhl. Production Designer, Gabriel Scognamillo. Editor, Marguerite Renoir. Starring Michel Simon (Maurice), Janie Marèze (Lucienne), Georges Flament (Dede), Jean Gehret (Dugodet). 85 minutes.

*China Moon* (Orion/Tiger, 1994). Produced by Barrie M. Osborne. Directed by John Bailey. Script by Roy Carlson. Director of Photography, Willy Kurant. Production Designer, Conrad E. Angone. Music, George Fenton. Editors, Carol Littleton and Jill Savitt. Starring Ed Harris (Kyle Bodine), Madeleine Stowe (Rachel Munro), Benicio Del Toro (Lamar Dickey), Charles Dance (Rupert Munro), Patricia Healy (Adele), Tim Powell (Fraker), Robb Edward Morris (Pinola), Theresa Bean (Felicity Turner), Pruitt Taylor Vince (Daryl Jeeters). 99 minutes.

*Chinatown* (Paramount, 1974). Produced by Robert Evans. Directed by Roman Polanski. Script by Robert Towne. Director of Photography, John A. Alonzo. Production Designer, Richard Sylbert. Music, Jerry Goldsmith. Editor, Sam O'Steen. Starring Jack Nicholson (J. J. Gittes), Faye Dunaway (Evelyn Mulwray), John Huston (Noah Cross), Perry Lopez (Escobar), John Hillerman (Yelburton), Darrell Zwerling (Hollis Mulwray), Diane Ladd (Ida Sessions), Roy Jenson (Mulvihill), Roman Polanski (Man with Knife), Richard Bakalyan (Loach). 131 minutes.

*City of Industry* (Largo, 1997). Produced by Evzen Kolar and Ken Solarz. Directed by John Irvin. Script by Ken Solarz. Director of Photography, Thomas Burstyn. Production Designer, Michael Novotny. Music, Stephen Endelman. Editor, Mark Conte. Starring Harvey Keitel (Roy Egan), Stephen Dorff (Skip Kovich), Timothy Hutton (Lee Egan), Famke Janssen (Rachel Montana), Wade Dominguez (Jorge Montana), Michael Jai White (Odell Williams), Lucy Alexis Liu (Cathi Rose), Reno Wilson (Keshaun Brown), Dana Barron (Gena), Tamara Clatterbuck (Sunny). 97 minutes.

*Clean Slate* [*Coup de torchon*] (La Tour/Little Bear/A2, 1981). Produced by Adolphe Viezzi and Henri Lassa. Directed by Bertrand

Tavernier. Script by Bertrand Tavernier and Jean Aurenche, based on the novel *Pop. 1280* by Jim Thompson. Director of Photography, Pierre-William Glenn. Production Designer, Alexandre Trauner. Music, Philippe Sarde. Editor, Armand Psenny. Starring Philippe Noiret (Lucien Cordier), Isabelle Huppert (Rose), Jean-Pierre Marielle (Le Peron/His Brother), Stéphane Audran (Hughette Cordier), Eddy Mitchell (Nono), Guy Marchand (Chavasson), Irène Skobline (Anne), Michel Beaune (Vanderbrouck), Jean Champion (Priest), Victor Garrivier (Mercaillou). 128 minutes.

*The Conversation* (Paramount, 1974). Produced, directed, and written by Francis Ford Coppola. Director of Photography, Bill Butler. Production Designer, Dean Tavoularis. Music, David Shire. Editors, Walter Murch and Richard Chew. Starring Gene Hackman (Harry Caul), John Cazale (Stan), Allen Garfield (Bernie Moran), Frederic Forrest (Mark), Cindy Williams (Ann), Teri Garr (Amy), Harrison Ford (Martin Stett), Michael Higgins (Paul). 113 minutes.

*Cool Breeze* (MGM, 1972). Produced by Gene Corman. Directed and written by Barry Pollack, based on the novel *The Asphalt Jungle* by W. R. Burnett. Director of Photography, Andrew Davis. Art Director, Jack Fisk. Music, Solomon Burke. Editor, Morton Tubor. Starring Thalmus Rasulala (Jones), Judy Pace (Obalese), Jim Watkins (Travis), Raymond St. Jacques (Bill), Lincoln Kilpatrick (Lt. Knowles). 102 minutes.

*Copycat* (Warner Bros./Regency, 1995). Produced by Arnon Milchan and Mark Tarlov. Directed by John Amiel. Script by Ann Biderman and David Madsen. Director of Photography, László Kovács. Production Designer, Jim Clay. Music, Christopher Young. Editors, Alan Heim and Jim Clark. Starring Sigourney Weaver (Helen Hudson), Holly Hunter (Mary Jane Monahan), Dermot Mulroney (Ruben Goetz), William McNamara (Peter Foley), Harry Connick, Jr. (Daryll Lee Cullum), J. E. Freeman (Lt. Quinn), Will Patton (Nicoletti), John Rothman (Andy), Shannon O'Hurley (Susan Schiffer), Bob Greene (Pachulski), Tony Haney (Kerby), Danny Kovacs (Kostas). 123 minutes.

*Crimes and Misdemeanors* (Orion, 1989). Produced by Robert

Greenhut. Directed and written by Woody Allen. Director of Photography, Sven Nykvist. Production Designer, Santo Loquasto. Editor, Susan E. Morse. Starring Martin Landau (Judah Rosenthal), Woody Allen (Clifford Stern), Alan Alda (Lester), Mia Farrow (Halley Reed), Anjelica Huston (Dolores Paley), Jerry Orbach (Jack Rosenthal), Sam Waterston (Ben), Joanna Gleason (Wendy Stern), Claire Bloom (Miriam Rosenthal), Caroline Aaron (Barbara). 107 minutes.

*Criss Cross* (Universal, 1949). Produced by Michael Kraike. Directed by Robert Siodmak. Script by Daniel Fuchs, based on the novel by Don Tracy. Director of Photography, Franz Planer. Art Directors, Bernard Herzbrun and Boris Levin. Music, Miklós Rózsa. Editor, Ted J. Kent. Starring Burt Lancaster (Steve Thompson), Yvonne De Carlo (Anna), Dan Duryea (Slim), Stephen McNally (Ramirez), Richard Long (Slade Thompson), Esy Morales (Orchestra Leader), Tom Pedi (Vincent), Percy Helton (Frank), Alan Napier (Finchley), Griff Barnett (Pop). 87 minutes.

*Cruising* (United Artists/Lorimar, 1980). Produced by Jerry Weintraub. Directed and written by William Friedkin, based on the novel by Gerald Walker. Director of Photography, James A. Contner. Production Designer, Bruce Weintraub. Music, Jack Nitzsche. Editor, Bud Smith. Starring Al Pacino (Steve Burns), Paul Sorvino (Capt. Edelson), Karen Allen (Nancy), Richard Cox (Stuart Richards), Don Scardino (Ted Bailey), Joe Spinell (Patrolman DiSimone), Jay Acovone (Skip Lee), Randy Jurgensen (Detective Lefransky), Allan Miller (Chief of Detectives), Barton Heyman (Dr. Rifkin). 106 minutes.

*Daybreak* [*Le Jour se lève*] (Sigma, 1939). Directed by Marcel Carné. Script by Jacques Prévert, based on a story by Jacques Viot. Director of Photography, Curt Courant. Art Director, Alexandre Trauner. Music, Maurice Jaubert. Editor, René Le Hénaff. Starring Jean Gabin (François), Jules Berry (M. Valentin), Jacqueline Laurent (Françoise), Arletty (Clara), René Génin (Concierge), Mady Berry (Concierge's Wife), Bernard Blier (Gaston), Marcel Pérès (Paulo), Jacques Baumer (The Inspector), René Bergeron (Café Proprietor). 89 minutes.

*Dead Again* (Paramount/Mirage, 1991). Produced by Lindsay Doran, Charles H. Maguire, and Dennis Feldman. Directed by Kenneth Branagh. Script by Scott Frank. Director of Photography, Matthew F. Leonetti. Production Designer, Tim Harvey. Music, Patrick Doyle. Editor, Peter E. Berger. Starring Kenneth Branagh (Mike Church/Roman Strauss), Emma Thompson (Grace Sharp/ Margaret Strauss), Andy Garcia (Gray Baker), Derek Jacobi (Franklyn Madison), Robin Williams (Dr. Carlisle), Hanna Schygulla (Inga). 111 minutes.

*Dead Men Don't Wear Plaid* (Universal, 1982). Produced by David V. Picker and William E. McEuen. Directed by Carl Reiner. Script by George Gipe, Carl Reiner, and Steve Martin. Director of Photography, Michael Chapman. Production Designer, John DeCuir. Music, Miklós Rózsa. Editor, Bud Molin. Starring Steve Martin (Rigby Reardon), Rachel Ward (Juliet Forrest), Carl Reiner (Field Marshall Von Kluck), Reni Santoni (Carlos Rodriguez), George Gaynes (Dr. Forrest), Frank McCarthy (Waiter), Adrian Ricard (Mildred). 89 minutes.

*Dead Presidents* (Buena Vista/Hollywood/Caravan/Underworld, 1995). Produced and directed by Albert Hughes and Allen Hughes. Script by Michael Henry Brown, from a story by Allen Hughes, Albert Hughes, and Michael Henry Brown. Director of Photography, Lisa Rinzler. Production Designer, David Brisbin. Music, Danny Elfman. Editor, Dan Lebental. Starring Larenz Tate (Anthony), Keith David (Kirby), Chris Tucker (Skip), Freddy Rodríguez (Jose), Rose Jackson (Juanita), N'Bushe Wright (Delilah), Bokeem Woodbine (Cleon). 119 minutes.

*Death Wish* (De Laurentiis/Paramount, 1974). Produced by Hal Landers, Bobby Roberts, and Michael Winner. Directed by Michael Winner. Script by Wendell Mayes, based on the novel by Brian Garfield. Director of Photography, Arthur J. Ornitz. Production Designer, Robert Gundlach. Music, Herbie Hancock. Editor, Bernard Gribble. Starring Charles Bronson (Paul Kersey), Hope Lange (Joanna Kersey), Vincent Gardenia (Frank Ochoa), Steven Keats (Jack Toby), William Redfield (Sam Kreutzer), Stuart Margolin (Aimes Jainchill). 93 minutes.

*Deep Cover* (New Line, 1992). Produced by Pierre David and Henry Bean. Directed by Bill Duke. Script by Michael Tolkin and Henry Bean.

Director of Photography, Bojan Bazelli. Production Designer, Pam Warner. Music, Michel Colombier. Editor, John Carter. Starring Laurence Fishburne (John Hull), Jeff Goldblum (David Jason), Victoria Dillard (Betty), Clarence Williams III (Taft). 112 minutes.

*Desperate Hours* (Dino De Laurentiis/MGM, 1990). Produced by Dino De Laurentiis and Michael Cimino. Directed by Michael Cimino. Script by Lawrence Konner, Mark Rosenthal, and Joseph Hayes, based on the novel by Joseph Hayes. Director of Photography, Douglas Milsome. Production Designer, Victoria Paul. Music, David Mansfield. Editors, Peter Hunt and Christopher Rouse. Starring Mickey Rourke (Michael Bosworth), Anthony Hopkins (Tim Cornell), Lindsay Crouse (Chandler), Kelly Lynch (Nancy Breyers), Elias Koteas (Wally Bosworth), David Morse (Albert). 105 minutes.

*The Desperate Hours* (Paramount, 1955). Produced and directed by William Wyler. Script by Joseph Hayes, based on his novel and play. Director of Photography, Lee Garmes. Art Directors, Hal Pereira and Joseph MacMillan Johnson. Music, Gail Kubik. Editor, Robert Swink. Starring Humphrey Bogart (Glenn), Fredric March (Dan Hilliard), Arthur Kennedy (Jesse Bard), Martha Scott (Eleanor Hilliard), Dewey Martin (Hal), Gig Young (Chuck), Mary Murphy (Cindy), Richard Eyer (Ralphie), Robert Middleton (Kobish), Alan Reed (Detective). 112 minutes.

*Devil in a Blue Dress* (TriStar/Clinica Estetico/Mundy Lane, 1995). Produced by Jesse Beaton and Gary Goetzman. Directed and written by Carl Franklin, based on the novel by Walter Mosley. Director of Photography, Tak Fujimoto. Production Designer, Gary Frutkoff. Music, Elmer Bernstein. Editor, Carole Kravetz. Starring Denzel Washington (Easy Rawlins), Tom Sizemore (DeWitt Albright), Jennifer Beals (Daphne Monet), Don Cheadle (Mouse), Maury Chaykin (Matthew Terell), Terry Kinney (Todd Carter), Mel Winkler (Joppy), Albert Hall (Odell), Lisa Nicole Carson (Coretta James), Jernard Burks (Dupree Brouchard). 102 minutes.

*Diabolique* (Morgan Creek/Marvin Worth/Warner Bros., 1996). Produced by Marvin Worth and James G. Robinson. Directed by Jeremiah

S. Chechik. Script by Don Roos, based on the 1955 film *Les Diaboliques* [uncredited] written by Henri-Georges Clouzot, Jérôme Geronimi, Frédéric Grendel, and René Masson, and the novel *Celle qui n'était plus* by Pierre Boileau and Thomas Narcejac. Director of Photography, Peter James. Production Designer, Leslie Dilley. Music, Randy Edelman. Editor, Carol Littleton. Starring Sharon Stone (Nicole), Isabelle Adjani (Mia), Chazz Palminteri (Guy), Kathy Bates (Shirley), Spalding Gray (Simon Veach), Allen Garfield (Leo Katzman), Adam Hann-Byrd (Erik). 108 minutes.

*Les Diaboliques* (Filmsonor, 1955). Produced and directed by Henri-Georges Clouzot. Script by Henri-Georges Clouzot, Jérôme Géronimi, Frédéric Grendel, and René Masson, based on the novel *Celle qui n'était plus* by Pierre Boileau and Thomas Narcejac. Director of Photography, Armand Thirard. Art Director, Léon Barsacq. Music, Georges Van Parys. Editor, Madeleine Gug. Starring Simone Signoret (Nicole Horner), Véra Clouzot (Christina Delasalle), Paul Meurisse (Michel Delasalle), Charles Vanel (Inspector Fichet), Jean Brouchard (Plantiveau), Noël Roquevert (Herboux), Pierre Larquey (Drain), Michel Serrault (Raymond), Yves-Marc Maurin (Moinet). 107 minutes.

*Dirty Harry* (Warner Bros., 1971). Produced and directed by Don Siegel. Script by Harry Julian Fink, Rita M. Fink, John Milius [uncredited], and Dean Riesner, based on an unpublished story by Rita M. Fink and Harry Julian Fink. Director of Photography, Bruce Surtees. Art Director, Dale Hennesy. Music, Lalo Schifrin. Editor, Carl Pingitore. Starring Clint Eastwood (Harry Callahan), Reni Santoni (Chico), Harry Guardino (Bressler), Andrew Robinson (Scorpio), John Mitchum (DeGeorgio), John Larch (Chief), John Vernon Mayor), Mae Mercer (Mrs. Russell), Lyn Edgington (Norma), Ruth Kobart (Bus Driver). 102 minutes.

*Disclosure* (Warner Bros./Baltimore/Constant C, 1994). Produced by Barry Levinson and Michael Crichton. Directed by Barry Levinson. Script by Paul Attanasio, based on the novel by Michael Crichton. Director of Photography, Tony Pierce-Roberts. Production Designer, Neil Spisak. Music, Ennio Morricone. Editor, Stu Linder. Starring Michael Douglas (Tom Sanders), Demi Moore (Meredith Johnson), Donald

Sutherland (Bob Garvin), Roma Maffia (Catherine Alvarez), Caroline Goodall (Susan Hendler), Dennis Miller (Mark Lewyn), Dylan Baker (Philip Blackburn), Nicholas Sadler (Don Cherry), Allan Rich (Ben Heller), Rosemary Forsyth (Stephanie Kaplan). 127 minutes.

*D.O.A.* (United Artists, 1950). Produced by Leo C. Popkin. Directed by Rudolph Maté. Script by Russell Rouse and Clarence Greene. Director of Photography, Ernest Laszlo. Art Director, Duncan Cramer. Music, Dimitri Tiomkin. Editor, Arthur H. Nadel. Starring Edmond O'Brien (Frank Bigelow), Pamela Britton (Paula Gibson), Luther Adler (Majak), Beverly Campbell (Miss Foster), Lynne Baggett (Mrs. Philips), William Ching (Halliday), Henry Hart (Stanley Philips), Neville Brand (Chester), Laurette Luez (Marla Rakubian). 83 minutes.

*D.O.A.* (Silver Screen/Touchstone, 1988). Produced by Ian Sander and Laura Ziskin. Directed by Rocky Morton and Annabel Jankel. Script by Charles Edward Pogue. Director of Photography, Yuri Neyman. Production Designer, Richard Amend. Music, Chaz Jankel. Editor, Michael R. Miller. Starring Dennis Quaid (Dexter Cornell), Meg Ryan (Sydney Fuller), Charlotte Rampling (Mrs. Fitzwaring), Daniel Stern (Hal Petersham), Christopher Neame (Bernard). 96 minutes.

*Double Indemnity* (Paramount, 1944). Produced by Joseph Sistrom. Directed by Billy Wilder. Script by Raymond Chandler and Billy Wilder, based on the novel by James M. Cain. Director of Photography, John F. Seitz. Art Directors, Hal Pereira and Hans Dreier. Music, Miklós Rózsa. Editor, Doane Harrison. Starring Fred MacMurray (Walter Neff), Barbara Stanwyck (Phyllis Dietrichson), Edward G. Robinson (Barton Keyes), Porter Hall (Mr. Jackson), Jean Heather (Lola Dietrichson), Tom Powers (Mr. Dietrichson), Byron Barr (Nino Zachette), Richard Gaines (Mr. Norton), Fortunio Bonanova (Sam Gorlopis), John Philliber (Joe Pete). 106 minutes.

*Dressed to Kill* (Cinema 77/Warwick/Filmways, 1980). Produced by George Litto. Directed and written by Brian De Palma. Director of Photography, Ralf D. Bode. Production Designer, Gary Weist. Music, Pino Donaggio. Editor, Jerry Greenberg. Starring Michael Caine (Dr. Robert Elliott), Angie Dickinson (Kate Miller), Nancy Allen (Liz Blake), Keith

Gordon (Peter Miller), Dennis Franz (Detective Marino), David Marguilies (Dr. Levy), Ken Baker (Warren Lockman), Brandon Maggart (Cleveland Sam), Susanna Clemm (Betty Luce), Fred Weber (Mike Miller). 105 minutes.

*The Driver* (20th Century-Fox/EMI, 1978). Produced by Lawrence Gordon. Directed and written by Walter Hill. Director of Photography, Philip Lathrop. Production Designer, Harry Horner. Music, Michael Small. Editors, Tina Hirsch and Robert K. Lambert. Starring Ryan O'Neal (The Driver), Bruce Dern (The Detective), Isabelle Adjani (The Player), Ronee Blakely (The Connection), Matt Clark (Red Plainclothesman), Felice Orlandi (Gold Plainclothesman), Joseph Walsh (Glasses), Rudy Ramos (Teeth). 91 minutes.

*The Drowning Pool* (Warner Bros., 1975). Produced by Lawrence Turman and David Foster. Directed by Stuart Rosenberg. Script by Tracy Keenan Wynn, Lorenzo Semple, Jr., and Walter Hill, based on the novel by Ross Macdonald. Director of Photography, Gordon Willis. Production Designer, Paul Sylbert. Music, Michael Small. Editor, John C. Howard. Starring Paul Newman (Harper), Joanne Woodward (Iris Devereaux), Tony Franciosa (Detective Broussard), Murray Hamilton (Kilbourne), Gail Strickland (Mavis Kilbourne), Melanie Griffith (Schuyler Devereaux). 108 minutes.

*Elevator to the Gallows* [*Ascenseur pour l'échafaud*] (Nouvelles Éditions, 1957). Produced by Jean Thuillier. Directed by Louis Malle. Script by Roger Nimier and Louis Malle, based on the novel by Noël Calef. Director of Photography, Henri Decaë. Production Designers, Rino Mondellini and Jean Mandaroux. Music, Miles Davis. Editor, Léonide Azar. Starring Jeanne Moreau (Florence Carala), Maurice Ronet (Julien Tavernier), Georges Poujouly (Louis), Yori Bertin (Veronique), Jean Wall (Simon Carala), Elga Andersen (Frau Bencker), Iván Petrovich (Horst Bencker), Lino Ventura (Inspector Cherier), Charles Denner (Inspector Cherier's Assistant), Félix Marten (Subervie), Jean-Claude Brialy (Chess Player at Motel). 87 minutes.

*Experiment in Terror* (Columbia/Geoffrey-Kate, 1962). Produced and directed by Blake Edwards. Script by Gordon Gordon and Mildred Gordon, based on their novel. Director of Photography, Philip Lathrop. Art Director, Robert Peterson. Music, Henry Mancini. Editor, Patrick McCormack. Starring Glenn Ford (John Ripley), Lee Remick (Kelly Sherwood), Stefanie Powers (Toby Sherwood), Roy Poole (Brad), Ned Glass (Popcorn), Ross Martin (Red Lynch), Anita Loo (Lisa), Patricia Huston (Nancy), Gilbert Green (Special Agent), Clifton James (Capt. Moreno), William Bryant (Chuck). 123 minutes.

*Face/Off* (Paramount/WCG, 1997). Produced by David Permut, Barrie M. Osborne, Terence Chang, and Christopher Godsick. Directed by John Woo. Script by Mike Werb and Michael Colleary. Director of Photography, Oliver Wood. Production Designer, Neil Spisak. Music, John Powell. Editors, Steven Kemper and Christian Wagner. Starring John Travolta (Sean Archer), Nicolas Cage (Castor Troy), Joan Allen (Eve Archer), Alessandro Nivola (Pollux Troy), Gina Gershon (Sasha Hassler), Dominique Swain (Jamie Archer), Nick Cassavetes (Dietrich Hassler), Harve Presnell (Victor Lazarro), Colm Feore (Dr. Malcolm Walsh), John Carroll Lynch (Prison Guard Walton). 130 minutes.

*Falling Down* (Warner Bros., 1993). Produced by Arnold Kopelson, Timothy Harris, and Herschel Weingrod. Directed by Joel Schumacher. Script by Ebbe Roe Smith. Director of Photography, Andrzej Bartkowiak. Production Designer, Barbara Ling. Music, James Newton Howard. Editor, Paul Hirsch. Starring Michael Douglas (Foster/ D-Fens), Robert Duvall (Detective Prendergast), Barbara Hershey (Beth), Rachel Ticotin (Sandra), Tuesday Weld (Mrs. Prendergast), Frederic Forrest (Surplus Store Owner), Lois Smith (D-Fens's Mother), Joey Hope Singer (Adele), Ebbe Roe Smith (Man on Freeway), Michael Paul Chan (Mr. Lee). 115 minutes.

*Farewell, My Lovely* (EK/ITC,1975). Produced by George Pappas and Jerry Bruckheimer. Directed by Dick Richards. Script by David Zelag Goodman, based on the novel by Raymond Chandler. Director of Photography, John A. Alonzo. Production Designer, Dean Tavoularis. Music, David Shire. Editors,Walter Thompson and Joel Cox. Starring Robert Mitchum (Philip Marlowe), Charlotte Rampling (Helen Grayle), John Ireland (Lt. Nulty), Sylvia Miles (Mrs. Florian), Jack O'Halloran (Moose Malloy), Anthony Zerbe (Laird Burnette), Harry Dean Stanton

(Billy Rolfe), Jim Thompson (Judge Grayle), John O'Leary (Lindsay Marriott), Kate Murtagh (Frances Amthor). 97 minutes.

*Fargo* (PolyGram/Gramercy/Working Title, 1996). Produced by Ethan Coen. Directed by Joel Coen. Script by Ethan Coen and Joel Coen. Director of Photography, Roger Deakins. Production Designer, Rick Heinrichs. Music, Carter Burwell. Editor, Roderick Jaynes (Joel Coen). Starring Frances McDormand (Marge Gunderson), William H. Macy (Jerry Lundegaard), Steve Buscemi (Carl Showalter), Peter Stormare (Gaear Grimsrud), Harve Presnell (Wade Gustafson), John Carroll Lynch (Norm Gunderson), Kristin Rudrud (Jean Lundegaard), Tony Denman (Scotty Lundegaard), Steve Park (Mike Yanagita), Steven Reevis (Shep Proudfoot). 98 minutes.

*Fatal Attraction* (Paramount, 1987). Produced by Stanley R. Jaffe and Sherry Lansing. Directed by Adrian Lyne. Script by James Dearden. Director of Photography, Howard Atherton. Production Designer, Mel Bourne. Music, Maurice Jarre. Editors, Michael Kahn and Peter E. Berger. Starring Michael Douglas (Dan Gallagher), Glenn Close (Alex Forrest), Anne Archer (Beth), Ellen Hamilton Latzen (Ellen), Stuart Pankin (Jimmy), Ellen Foley (Hildy), Fred Gwynne (Arthur). 119 minutes.

*La Femme Nikita* (Cecchi Gori Group/Tiger/Gaumont, 1990). Produced, directed, and written by Luc Besson. Director of Photography, Thierry Arbogast. Production Designer, Dan Weil. Music, Eric Serra. Editor, Olivier Mauffroy. Starring Anne Parillaud (Nikita). Jean-Hugues Anglade (Marco), Tchéky Karyo (Bob), Jeanne Moreau
(Amande), Jean Reno (Nikita's Partner), Jean Bouise (Cabinet Chief), Philippe Du Janerand (Ambassador), Roland Blanche (Police Investigator), Philippe Leroy-Beaulieu (Commander Grossman), Marc Duret (Rico). 115 minutes.

*52 Pick-Up* (Cannon, 1986). Produced by Menahem Golan and Yoram Globus. Directed by John Frankenheimer. Script by Elmore Leonard and John Steppling, based on the novel by Elmore Leonard. Director of Photography, Jost Vacano. Production Designer, Philip Harrison. Music, Gary Chang. Editor, Robert F. Shugrue. Starring Roy

Scheider (Harry Mitchell), Ann-Margret (Barbara Mitchell), Vanity (Doreen), John Glover (Raimy), Robert Trebor (Leo), Kelly Preston (Cini), Clarence Williams III (Bobby Shy). 114 minutes.

*Final Analysis* (Warner Bros., 1992). Produced by Charles Roven, Paul Junger Witt, and Tony Thomas. Directed by Phil Joanou. Script by Wesley Strick, based on a story by Strick and Robert Berger. Director of Photography, Jordan Cronenweth. Production Designer, Dean Tavoularis. Music, George Fenton. Editor, Thom Noble. Starring Richard Gere (Isaac Barr), Kim Basinger (Heather Evans), Uma Thurman (Diana Baylor), Eric Roberts (Jimmy Evans), Keith David (Detective Huggins), Paul Guilfoyle (Mike O'Brien). 124 minutes.

*Frantic* (Warner Bros., 1988). Produced by Thom Mount and Tim Hampton. Directed by Roman Polanski. Script by Roman Polanski and Gérard Brach. Director of Photography, Witold Sobocinski. Production Designer, Pierre Guffroy. Music, Ennio Morricone. Editor, Sam O'Steen. Starring Harrison Ford (Richard Walker), Emmanuelle Seigner (Michelle), Betty Buckley (Sondra Walker), John Mahoney (Williams), Jimmie Ray Weeks (Shaap), Yorgo Voyagis (Kidnapper). 120 minutes.

*Frisk* (Strand, 1995). Produced by Marcus Hu. Directed by Todd Verow. Script by Jim Dwyer, George LaVoo, and Todd Verow, based on the novel by Dennis Cooper. Director of Photography, Greg Watkins. Production Designer, Jennifer Graber. Music, Lee Ranaldo. Editor, Todd Verow. Starring Michael Gunther (Dennis), Jaie Laplante (Julian), Craig Chester (Henry), Raoul O'Connell (Kevin), Michael Stock (Uhrs), Parker Posey (Ferguson), James Lyons (Gypsy Pete), Alyssa Wendt (Susan), Alexis Arquette (Punk), Eric Sapp (Samson), Bonnie Dickenson (Jennifer). 83 minutes.

*From Dusk Till Dawn* (A Band Apart/Los Hooligans/Miramax/Dimension, 1996). Produced by Gianni Nunnari and Meir Teper. Directed by Robert Rodriguez. Script by Quentin Tarantino, from a story by Robert Kurtzman. Director of Photography, Guillermo Navarro. Production Designer, Cecilia Montiel. Music, Graeme Revell. Editor, Robert Rodriguez. Starring George Clooney (Seth Gecko), Quentin Tarantino (Richard Gecko), Harvey Keitel (Jacob Fuller), Juliette Lewis (Kate

Fuller), Ernest Liu (Scott Fuller), Cheech Marin (Border Guard/Chet Pussy/Carlos), Fred Williamson (Frost), Salma Hayek (Santanico Pandemonium), Marc Lawrence (Old Timer), Michael Parks (Texas Ranger Earl McGraw). 108 minutes.

*The Game* (Propaganda/PolyGram, 1997). Produced by Steve Golin and Cean Chaffin. Directed by David Fincher. Script by John D. Brancato and Michael Ferris. Director of Photography, Harris Savides. Production Designer, Jeffrey Beecroft. Music, Howard Shore. Editor, Jim Haygood. Starring Michael Douglas (Nicholas Van Orton), Sean Penn (Conrad Van Orton), Deborah Kara Unger (Christine), James Rebhorn (Jim Feingold), Peter Donat (Samuel Sutherland), Carroll Baker (Ilsa), Anna Katarina (Elizabeth), Armin Mueller-Stahl (Ansen Baer), Charles Martinet (Nicholas's Father). 128 minutes.

*The Getaway* (Solar/First Artists, 1972). Produced by David Foster and Mitchell Brower. Directed by Sam Peckinpah. Script by Walter Hill, based on the novel by Jim Thompson. Director of Photography, Lucien Ballard. Art Directors, Angelo Graham and Ted Haworth. Music, Quincy Jones. Editor, Robert L. Wolfe. Starring Steve McQueen (Doc McCoy), Ali MacGraw (Carol McCoy), Ben Johnson (Jack Benyon), Sally Struthers (Fran Clinton), Al Lettieri (Rudy Butler), Slim Pickens (Cowboy), Richard Bright (Thief), Jack Dodson (Harold Clinton), Dub Taylor (Laughlin), Bo Hopkins (Frank Jackson). 122 minutes.

*The Getaway* (Largo/JVC/Turman Foster/John Alan Simon, 1994). Produced by David Foster, Lawrence Turman, and John Alan Simon. Directed by Roger Donaldson. Script by Walter Hill and Amy Holden Jones, based on the novel by Jim Thompson. Director of Photography, Peter Menzies, Jr. Production Designer, Joseph C. Nemec III. Music, Mark Isham. Editor, Conrad Buff. Starring Alec Baldwin (Doc McCoy), Kim Basinger (Carol McCoy), Michael Madsen (Rudy Travis), James Woods (Jack Benyon), David Morse (Jim), Jennifer Tilly (Fran), James Stephens (Harold), Richard Farnsworth (Slim). 115 minutes.

*The Grifters* (Cineplex Odeon, 1990). Produced by Martin Scorsese, Robert A. Harris, James Painten, and Peggy Rajski. Directed by Stephen Frears. Script by Donald E. Westlake, from the novel by Jim Thompson. Director of Photography, Oliver Stapleton. Production Designer, Dennis Glassner. Music, Elmer Bernstein. Editor, Mick Audsley. Starring Anjelica Huston (Lilly Dillon), John Cusack (Roy Dillon), Annett Bening (Myra Langtry), Jan Munroe (Guy at Bar), Pat Hingle (Bobo), Richard Holden (Cop). 119 minutes.

*Grosse Pointe Blank* (Hollywood/New Crime/Caravan, 1997). Produced by Susan Arnold, Donna Arkoff Roth, and Roger Birnbaum. Directed by George Armitage. Script by Tom Jankiewicz, D. V. DeVincentis, Steve Pink, and John Cusack. Director of Photography, Jamie Anderson. Production Designer, Stephen Altman. Music, Joe Strummer. Editor, Brian Berdan. Starring John Cusack (Martin Q. Blank), Minnie Driver (Debi Newberry), Dan Aykroyd (Grocer), Alan Arkin (Dr. Oatman), Joan Cusack (Marcella), Jeremy Piven (Paul Spericki), Hank Azaria (Lardner), Barbara Harris (Mary Blank), K. Todd Freeman (McCullers), Mitchell Ryan (Mr. Newberry). 107 minutes.

*Gun Crazy* [a.k.a. *Deadly Is the Female*] (United Artists, 1950). Produced by Frank King and Maurice King. Directed by Joseph H. Lewis. Script by MacKinlay Kantor and Millard Kaufman, from the *Saturday Evening Post* story "Gun Crazy" by MacKinlay Kantor. Director of Photography, Russell Harlan. Production Designer, Gordon Wiles. Music, Victor Young. Editor, Harry W. Gerstad. Starring Peggy Cummins (Annie Laurie Starr), John Dall (Bart Tare), Berry Kroeger (Packett), Morris Carnovsky (Judge Willoughby), Anabel Shaw (Ruby Tare), Harry Lewis (Clyde Boston), Nedrick Young (Dave Allister), Trevor Bardette (Sheriff Boston), Mickey Little (Bart Tare, 7), Russ Tamblyn (Bart Tare, 14), Paul Frison (Clyde Boston, 14), Dave Bair (Dave Allister, 14). 87 minutes.

*Hammett* (Orion/Warner/Zoetrope, 1983). Produced by Fred Roos, Ronald Colby, and Don Guest. Directed by Wim Wenders. Script by Ross Thomas, Dennis O'Flaherty, and Thomas Pope, based on the novel by Joe Gores. Photography, Philip Lathrop and Joseph Biroc. Production Designers, Eugene Lee and Dean Tavoularis. Music, John Barry. Editors, Barry Malkin, Marc Laub, Robert Q. Lovett, and Randy Roberts. Starring Frederic Forrest (Hammett), Peter Boyle (Jimmy Ryan), Marilu Henner (Kit Conger), Roy Kinnear (Hagedorn), Lydia Lei (Crystal Ling). 97 minutes.

*Harper* (Warner Bros., 1966). Produced by Elliott Kastner and Jerry Gershwin. Directed by Jack Smight. Script by William Goldman, based on the novel *The Moving Target* by Ross Macdonald. Director of Photography, Conrad L. Hall. Art Director, Alfred Sweeney. Music, Johnny Mandel. Editor, Stefan Arnsten. Starring Paul Newman (Harper), Lauren Bacall (Mrs. Sampson), Julie Harris (Betty Fraley), Arthur Hill (Albert Graves), Janet Leigh (Susan Harper), Pamela Tiffin (Miranda Sampson), Robert Wagner (Alan Traggert), Robert Webber (Dwight Troy), Shelley Winters (Fay Estabrook), Harold Gould (Sheriff Spanner), Strother Martin (Claude). 121 minutes.

*Heat* (Warner Bros./Forward Pass/New Regency, 1995). Produced by Art Linson and Michael Mann. Directed and written by Michael Mann. Director of Photography, Dante Spinotti. Production Designer, Neil Spisak. Music, Elliot Goldenthal. Editors, Dov Hoenig, Pasquale Buba, William Goldenberg, and Tom Rolf. Starring Al Pacino (Vincent Hanna), Robert De Niro (Neil McCauley), Val Kilmer (Chris Shiherlis), Jon Voight (Nate), Tom Sizemore (Michael Cheritto), Diane Venora (Justine), Amy Brenneman (Eady), Ashley Judd (Charlene), Mykelti Williamson (Drucker), Wes Studi (Casals). 160 minutes.

*Henry: Portrait of a Serial Killer* (Maljack, 1989). Produced by Lisa Dedmond, Steven A. Jones, and John McNaughton. Directed by John McNaughton. Script by Richard Fire and John McNaughton. Director of Photography, Charlie Lieberman. Art Director, Rick Paul. Music, Steven A. Jones and Robert McNaughton. Editor, Elena Maganini. Starring Michael Rooker (Henry), Tom Towles (Otis), Tracy Arnold (Becky), Ray Atherton (Fence), David Katz (Henry's Boss), Eric Young (Parole Officer), Mary Demas (Hooker #1/Dead Prostitute/ Dead Woman), Kristin Finger (Hooker #2), Anne Bartoletti (Waitress), Erzsebet Sziky (Hitchhiker). 83 minutes.

*The Hot Spot* (Film Now/Orion, 1990). Produced by Paul Lewis. Directed by Dennis Hopper. Script by Nona Tyson and Charles Williams, based on the novel *Hell Hath No Fury* by Charles Williams. Director of Photography, Ueli Steiger. Production Designer, Cary White. Music, Jack Nitzsche. Editor, Wende Phifer Mate. Starring Don Johnson (Harry Madox), Virginia Madsen (Dolly Harshaw), Jennifer Connelly

(Gloria Harper), Charles Martin Smith (Lon Golick), William Sadler (Frank Sutton), Jerry Hardin (George Harshaw). 128 minutes.

*House of Games* (Filmhaus/Orion, 1987). Produced by Michael Hausman. Directed and written by David Mamet, based on a story by David Mamet and Jonathan Katz. Director of Photography, Juan Ruiz Anchía. Production Designer, Michael Merritt. Music, Alaric Jans. Editor, Trudy Ship. Starring Lindsay Crouse (Dr. Margaret Ford), Joe Mantegna (Mike), Mike Nussbaum (Joey), Ricky Jay (George), Lilia Skala (Dr. Littauer), J. T. Walsh (Businessman/Con Artist), Willo Hausman (Girl with Book). 101 minutes.

*Human Desire* (Columbia, 1954). Produced by Lewis J. Rachmil. Directed by Fritz Lang. Script by Alfred Hayes, based on the novel *La Bête humaine* by Émile Zola. Director of Photography, Burnett Guffey. Art Director, Robert Peterson. Music, Daniele Amfitheatrof. Editor, Aaron Stell. Starring Gloria Grahame (Vicki Buckley), Glenn Ford (Jeff Warren), Broderick Crawford (Carl Buckley), Edgar Buchanan (Alec Simmons), Kathleen Case (Ellen Simmons), Peggy Maley (Jean), Diana DeLaire (Vera Simmons), Grandon Rhodes (John Owens), Dan Seymour (Bartender). 90 minutes.

*Internal Affairs* (Paramount, 1990). Produced by Frank Mancuso, Jr. Directed by Mike Figgis. Script by Henry Bean. Director of Photography, John A. Alonzo. Production Designer, Waldemar Kalinowski. Music, Mike Figgis, Anthony Marinelli, and Brian Banks. Editor, Robert Estrin. Starring Richard Gere (Dennis Peck), Andy Garcia (Raymond Avila), Nancy Travis (Kathleen Avila), Laurie Metcalf (Amy Wallace), Richard Bradford (Grieb), William Baldwin (Van Stretch). 115 minutes.

*I, the Jury* (American Cinema/20th Century-Fox, 1982). Produced by Robert H. Solo. Directed by Richard T. Heffron. Script by Larry Cohen, based on the novel by Mickey Spillane. Director of Photography, Andrew Laszlo. Production Designer, Robert Gundlach. Music, Bill Conti. Editor, Garth Craven. Starring Armand Assante (Mike Hammer), Barbara Carrera (Dr. Charlotte Benett), Alan King (Charles Kalecki), Laurene Landon (Velda), Geoffrey Lewis (Joe Butler), Paul Sorvino (Detective Pat Chambers), Judson Scott (Kendricks). 109 minutes.

*Jackie Brown* (A Band Apart/Miramax, 1997). Produced by Lawrence Bender. Directed and written by Quentin Tarantino, based on the novel *Rum Punch* by Elmore Leonard. Director of Photography, Guillermo Navarro. Production Designer, David Wasco. Editor, Sally Menke. Starring Pam Grier (Jackie Brown), Samuel L. Jackson (Ordell Robbie), Robert Forster (Max Cherry), Bridget Fonda (Melanie), Michael Keaton (Ray Nicolette), Michael Bowen (Mark Dargus), Robert De Niro (Louis Gara), Chris Tucker (Beaumont Livingston), Hattie Winston (Simone), Lisa Gay Hamilton (Sheronda). 154 minutes.

*Jagged Edge* (Columbia/EMI, 1985). Produced by Martin Ransohoff. Directed by Richard Marquand. Script by Joe Eszterhas. Director of Photography, Matthew F. Leonetti. Production Designer, Gene Callahan. Music, John Barry. Editors, Sean Barton and Conrad Buff. Starring Glenn Close (Teddy Barnes), Jeff Bridges (Jack Forrester), Peter Coyote (Krasny), Robert Loggia (Sam Ransom), Leigh Taylor-Young (Virginia), John Dehner (Judge Carrigan). 108 minutes.

*Jeopardy* (MGM, 1953). Produced by Sol Baer Fielding. Directed by John Sturges. Script by Mel Dinelli. Director of Photography, Victor Milner. Art Directors, William Ferrari and Cedric Gibbons. Music, Dimitri Tiomkin. Editor, Newell P. Kimlin. Starring Barbara Stanwyck (Helen), Barry Sullivan (Doug), Ralph Meeker (Lawson). 69 minutes.

*Juice* (Paramount/Island World, 1992). Produced by David Heyman, Neal H. Moritz, and Peter Frankfurt. Directed by Ernest R. Dickerson. Script by Ernest R. Dickerson and Gerard Brown. Director of Photography, Larry Banks. Production Designers, Lester W. Cohen and Brent Owens. Editors, Sam Pollard and Brunilda Torres. Starring Omar Epps (Q), Tupac Shakur (Bishop), Jermaine Hopkins (Steel), Khalil Kain (Raheem), Cindy Herron (Yolanda), Vincent Laresca (Radames), George O. Gore (Brian), Grace Garland (Q's Mother), Queen Latifah (Ruffhouse M.C.). 91 minutes.

*Kalifornia* (Rank/Propaganda/PolyGram/Viacom, 1993). Produced by Steve Golin. Directed by Dominic Sena. Script by Tim Metcalfe, based on a story by Stephen Levy and Tim Metcalfe. Director of Photography, Bojan Bazelli. Production Designer, Michael White. Music, Carter Burwell. Editor, Martin Hunter. Starring Brad Pitt (Early Grayce),

Juliette Lewis (Adele), David Duchovny (Brian Kessler), Michelle Forbes (Carrie Laughlin), Sierra Pecheur (Mrs. Musgrave), Gregory Mars Martin (Walter Livesy). 118 minutes.

*The Killer* [*Die xue shuang xiong*] (Film Workshop/Golden Princess/Magnum, 1989). Produced by Tsui Hark. Directed and written by John Woo. Director of Photography, Wong Wing-Hang. Art Director, Luk Man-Wah. Music, Lowell Lowe. Editor, Fan Kung-Ming. Starring Chow Yun-Fat (Jeffrey Chow), Sally Yeh (Jennie), Danny Lee (Detective "Eagle" Lee), Kenneth Tsang (Sgt. Randy Chung), Chu Kong (Sydney Fung), Lam Chung (Willie Tsang), Shing Fui-On (Johnny Weng), Ye Rongzu (Tony Weng), Yi Fan Wei (Frankie Feng), Wong Kwong Leung (Wong Tong). 110 minutes.

*The Killer Inside Me* (Devi/Warner Bros., 1976). Produced by Michael W. Leighton. Directed by Burt Kennedy. Script by Edward Andrew Mann and Robert Chamblee, based on the novel by Jim Thompson. Director of Photography, William A. Fraker. Music, Tim McIntire and John Rubinstein. Editors, Danford B. Greene and Aaron Stell. Starring Stacy Keach (Lou Ford), Susan Tyrrell (Joyce Lakeland), Tisha Sterling (Amy Stanton), Keenan Wynn (Chester Conway), Charles McGraw (Howard Hendricks), John Dehner (Bob Maples). 99 minutes.

*The Killers* (Universal, 1946). Produced by Mark Hellinger. Directed by Robert Siodmak. Script by Anthony Veiller and John Huston, based on the story by Ernest Hemingway. Director of Photography, Elwood Bredell. Art Directors, Jack Otterson and Martin Obzina. Music, Miklós Rózsa. Editor, Arthur Hilton. Starring Burt Lancaster (Swede), Ava Gardner (Kitty Collins), Edmond O'Brien (Jim Reardon), Albert Dekker (Big Jim Colfax), Sam Levene (Lt. Lubinsky), Virginia Christine (Lilly Lubinsky), John Miljan (Jake), Vince Barnett (Charleston), Charles D. Brown (Packy Robinson), Donald MacBride (Kenyon). 102 minutes.

*The Killers* (Revue, 1964). Produced and directed by Don Siegel. Script by Gene L. Coon, based on the story by Ernest Hemingway. Director of Photography, Richard L. Rawlings. Art Directors, Frank Arrigo, George Chan and George O'Connell. Music, John Williams. Editor, Richard Belding. Starring Lee Marvin (Charlie), Angie Dickinson (Sheila

Farr), John Cassavetes (Johnny North), Ronald Reagan (Browning), Clu Gulager (Lee), Claude Akins (Earl Sylvester), Norman Fell (Mickey), Virginia Christine (Miss Watson), Don Haggerty (Mail Truck Driver), Robert Phillips (George). 93 minutes.

*The Killing* (Harris-Kubrick/United Artists, 1956). Produced by James B. Harris. Directed by Stanley Kubrick. Script by Stanley Kubrick and Jim Thompson, based on the novel *Clean Break* by Lionel White. Director of Photography, Lucien Ballard. Art Director, Ruth Sobotka Kubrick. Music, Gerald Fried. Editor, Betty Steinberg. Starring Sterling Hayden (Johnny Clay), Coleen Gray (Fay), Vince Edwards (Val Cannon), Jay C. Flippen (Marvin Unger), Marie Windsor (Sherry Peatty), Ted de Corsia (Randy Kennan), Elisha Cook, Jr. (George Peatty), Joe Sawyer (Mike O'Reilly), Timothy Carey (Nikki Arane), Jay Adler (Leo). 83 minutes.

*A Kiss Before Dying* (United Artists/Crown, 1956). Produced by Robert L. Jacks. Directed by Gerd Oswald. Script by Lawrence Roman, based on the novel by Ira Levin. Director of Photography, Lucien Ballard. Art Director, Addison Hehr. Music, Lionel Newman. Editor, George A. Gittens. Starring Robert Wagner (Bud Corliss), Jeffrey Hunter (Gordon Grant), Virginia Leith (Ellen Kingship), Joanne Woodward (Dorothy Kingship), Mary Astor (Mrs. Corliss), George Macready (Leo Kingship), Robert Quarry (Dwight Powell), Howard Petrie (Chesser), Bill Walker (Butler), Molly McCart (Annabelle), Marlene Felton (Medical Student). 94 minutes.

*A Kiss Before Dying* (Universal/Initial, 1991). Produced by Robert Lawrence. Directed and written by James Dearden, based on the novel by Ira Levin. Director of Photography, Mike Southon. Production Designer, Jim Clay. Music, Howard Shore. Editor, Michael Bradsell. Starring Matt Dillon (Jonathan Corliss), Sean Young (Ellen/Dorothy Carlsson), Max Von Sydow (Thor Carlsson), James Russo (Dan Corelli), Diane Ladd (Mrs. Corliss). 95 minutes.

*Kiss of Death* (20th Century-Fox, 1947). Produced by Fred Kohlmar. Directed by Henry Hathaway. Script by Ben Hecht and Charles Lederer, based on a story by Eleazar Lipsky. Director of Photography, Norbert

Brodine. Art Directors, Lyle R. Wheeler and Leland Fuller. Music, David Buttolph. Editor, J. Watson Webb, Jr. Starring Victor Mature (Nick Bianco), Brian Donlevy (D'Angelo), Coleen Gray (Nettie), Richard Widmark (Tommy Udo), Karl Malden (Sgt. William Cullen), Taylor Holmes (Earl Howser), Howard Smith (Warden), Anthony Ross (Williams), Mildred Dunnock (Ma Rizzo). 98 minutes.

*Kiss of Death* (20th Century-Fox, 1995). Produced by Barbet Schroeder and Susan Hoffman. Directed by Barbet Schroeder. Script by Richard Price, based on the 1947 film *Kiss of Death*, written by Ben Hecht and Charles Lederer, from a story by Eleazar Lipsky. Director of Photography, Luciano Tovoli. Production Designer, Mel Bourne. Music, Trevor Jones. Editor, Lee Percy. Starring David Caruso (Jimmy Kilmartin), Samuel L. Jackson (Calvin), Nicolas Cage (Little Junior), Helen Hunt (Bev), Kathryn Erbe (Rosie), Stanley Tucci (Frank Zioli), Michael Rapaport (Ronnie), Ving Rhames (Omar), Philip Baker Hall (Big Junior), Anthony Heald (Jack Gold). 101 minutes.

*Klute* (Warner Bros., 1971). Produced and directed by Alan J. Pakula. Script by Andy Lewis and Dave Lewis. Director of Photography, Gordon Willis. Art Director, George Jenkins. Music, Michael Small. Editor, Carl Lerner. Starring Jane Fonda (Bree Daniel), Donald Sutherland (John Klute), Charles Cioffi (Peter Cable), Dorothy Tristan (Arlyn Page), Nathan George (Trask), Roy Scheider (Frank), Rita Gam (Trina), Vivian Nathan (Psychiatrist). 114 minutes.

*L.A. Confidential* (Warner Bros./Regency, 1997). Produced by Arnon Milchan, Curtis Hanson, and Michael G. Nathanson. Directed by Curtis Hanson. Script by Brian Helgeland and Curtis Hanson, based on the novel by James Ellroy. Director of Photography, Dante Spinotti. Production Designer, Jeannine C. Oppewall. Music, Jerry Goldsmith. Editor, Peter Honess. Starring Kevin Spacey (Jack Vincennes), Russell Crowe (Bud White), Kim Basinger (Lynn Bracken), Guy Pearce (Ed Exley), James Cromwell (Dudley Smith), David Strathairn (Pierce Patchett), Ron Rifkin (D.A. Ellis Loew), Danny De Vito (Sid Hudgeons). 138 minutes.

*The Last Seduction* (Incorporated Television/Oakwood/DBA Kroy, 1994). Produced by Jonathan Shestak. Directed by John Dahl. Script by Steve Barancik. Director of Photography, Jeff Jur. Production Designer, Linda Pearl. Music, Joseph Vitarelli. Editor, Eric L. Beason. Starring Linda Fiorentino (Bridget Gregory), Peter Berg (Mike Swayle), J. T. Walsh (Frank Griffith), Bill Pullman (Clay Gregory), Bill Nunn (Harlan), Brien Varady (Chris), Donna Wilson (Stacy). 110 minutes.

*Little Odessa* (New Line/Live/Fine Line, 1994). Produced by Paul Webster. Directed and written by James Gray. Director of Photography, Tom Richmond. Production Designer, Kevin Thompson. Music, Dana Sano. Editor, Dorian Harris. Starring Tim Roth (Joshua), Edward Furlong (Reuben), Moira Kelly (Alla), Vanessa Regrave (Irina), Maximilian Schell (Arkady), Paul Guilfoyle (Boris). 98 minutes.

*The Long Goodbye* (Lion's Gate/EK/United Artists, 1973). Produced by Jerry Bick Directed by Robert Altman. Script by Leigh Brackett, based on the novel by Raymond Chandler. Director of Photography, Vilmos Zsigmond. Music, John Williams. Editor, Lou Lombardo. Starring Elliott Gould (Philip Marlowe), Nina Van Pallandt (Eileen Wade), Sterling Hayden (Roger Wade), Mark Rydel (Marty Augustine), Henry Gibson (Dr. Verringer), David Arkin (Harry), Jim Bouton (Terry Lennox), Warren Berlinger (Morgan), Jo Ann Brody (Jo Ann Eggenweiler), Jack Knight (Hood). 112 minutes.

*Lost Highway* (Asymmetrical/October Films/CiBy 2000, 1997). Produced by Deepak Nayar, Tom Sternberg, and Mary Sweeney. Directed by David Lynch. Script by David Lynch and Barry Gifford. Director of Photography, Peter Deming. Production Designer, Patricia Norris. Music, Angelo Badalamenti and Barry Adamson. Editor, Mary Sweeney. Starring Bill Pullman (Fred Madison), Patricia Arquette (Renee Madison/Alice Wakefield), Balthazar Getty (Pete Dayton), Robert Blake (Mystery Man), Natasha Gregson Wagner (Sheila), Robert Loggia (Mr. Eddy/Dick Laurent), Gary Busey (Bill Dayton), Richard Pryor (Arnie), Jack Nance (Phil), John Roselius (Al), Lou Eppolito (Ed). 135 minutes.

*The Maltese Falcon* (Warner Bros./First National, 1941). Produced by Henry Blanke. Directed and written by John Huston, based on the novel by Dashiell Hammett. Director of Photography, Arthur Edeson. Art Director, Robert Haas. Music, Adolph Deutsch. Editor, Thomas

Richards. Starring Humphrey Bogart (Sam Spade), Mary Astor (Brigid O'Shaughnessy), Gladys George (Iva Archer), Peter Lorre (Joel Cairo), Barton MacLane (Detective Lt. Dundy), Lee Patrick (Effie Perine), Sydney Greenstreet (Kasper Gutman), Ward Bond (Detective Tom Polhaus), Jerome Cowan (Miles Archer), Elisha Cook, Jr. (Wilmer Cook). 100 minutes.

*The Manchurian Candidate* (United Artists/MC, 1962). Produced by George Axelrod and John Frankenheimer. Directed by John Frankenheimer. Script by George Axelrod, based on the novel by Richard Condon. Director of Photography, Lionel Lindon. Production Designer, Richard Sylbert. Music, David Amram. Editor, Ferris Webster. Starring Frank Sinatra (Bennett Marco), Laurence Harvey (Raymond Shaw), Janet Leigh (Rosie), Angela Lansbury (Raymond's Mother), Henry Silva (Chunjin), James Gregory (Senator John Iselin), Leslie Parrish (Jocie Jordon), John McGiver (Senator Thomas Jordon), Khigh Dhiegh (Yen Lo), James Edwards (Cpl. Melvin). 126 minutes.

*Manhunter* (De Laurentiis, 1986). Produced by Richard A. Roth. Directed and written by Michael Mann, based on the novel *Red Dragon* by Thomas Harris. Director of Photography, Dante Spinotti. Production Designer, Mel Bourne. Music, The Reds and Michel Rubini. Editor, Dov Hoenig. Starring William L. Petersen (Will Graham), Kim Greist (Molly), Joan Allen (Reba), Brian Cox (Dr. Lecter), Dennis Farina (Crawford), Tom Noonan (Francis Dollarhyde). 118 minutes.

*Marlowe* (MGM/Katzka-Berne/Cherokee, 1969). Produced by Gabriel Katzka and Sidney Beckerman. Directed by Paul Bogart. Script by Stirling Silliphant, based on the novel *The Little Sister* by Raymond Chandler. Director of Photography, William H. Daniels. Art Directors, George W. Davis and Addison Hehr. Music, Peter Matz. Editor, Gene Ruggiero. Starring James Garner (Philip Marlowe), Gayle Hunnicutt (Mavis Wald), Carroll O'Connor (Lt. Christy French), Rita Moreno (Dolores Gonzales), Sharon Farrell (Orfamay Quest), H. M. Wynant (Sonny Steelgrave), Jackie Coogan (Grant W. Hicks), Kenneth Tobey (Sgt. Fred Beifus), Nate Esformes (Paleface), Bruce Lee (Winslow Wong), Christopher Cary (Chuck), Paul Stevens (Dr. Lagardie). 95 minutes.

*Masquerade* (MGM-UA, 1988). Produced by Michael I. Levy. Directed by Bob Swaim. Script by Dick Wolf. Director of Photography, David Watkin. Production Designer, John Kasarda. Music, John Barry. Editor, Scott Conrad. Starring Rob Lowe (Tim Whalen), Meg Tilly (Olivia Lawrence), Doug Savant (Mike McGill), Kim Cattrall (Brooke Morrison), John Glover (Tony Gateworth), Dana Delany (Anne Briscoe). 91 minutes.

*The Mississippi Mermaid* [*La Sirène du Mississippi*] (Films du Carrosse/ Productions Artistes/Delphos, 1969). Produced by Marcel Berbert. Directed and written by François Truffaut, based on the novel *Waltz into Darkness* by Cornell Woolrich. Director of Photography, Denys Clerval. Art Director, Claude Pignot. Music, Antoine Duhamel. Editor, Agnès Guillemot. Starring Jean-Paul Belmondo (Louis), Catherine Deneuve (Julie/ Marion), Michel Bouquet (Comolli), Nelly Borgeaud (Berthe Roussel), Marcel Berbert (Jardine), Martine Ferrière (Landlady), Roland Thénot (Richard). 123 minutes.

*The Moon in the Gutter* [*La Lune dans le caniveau*] (Palace/Gaumont/ TF1/SFP Cinéma/Opera Film, 1983). Produced by Lise Fayolle. Directed and written by Jean-Jacques Beineix, based on the novel by David Goodis. Director of Photography, Philippe Rousselot. Art Director, Hilton McConnico. Music, Gabriel Yared. Editors, Alessandro dell'Orco, Monique Prim, and Yves Deschamps. Starring Gérard Depardieu (Gerard), Nastassja Kinski (Loretta), Victoria Abril (Bella), Bertice Reading (Lola), Gabriel Monnet (Tom), Dominique Pinon (Frank), Miléna Vukotic (Frieda). 137 minutes.

*The Morning After* (20th Century-Fox/Lorimar, 1986). Produced by Bruce Gilbert. Directed by Sidney Lumet. Script by James Hicks and Jay Presson Allen [uncredited]. Director of Photography, Andrzej Bartkowiak. Production Designer, Albert Brenner. Music, Paul Chihara. Editor, Joel Goodman. Starring Jane Fonda (Alex Sternbergen), Jeff Bridges (Turner Kendall), Raul Julia (Joaquin Manero), Diane Salinger (Isabel), Richard Foronjy (Sgt. Greenbaum). 103 minutes.

*Mrs. Winterbourne* (TriStar/A&M/Sony, 1996). Produced by Dale Pollock, Ross Canter, and Oren Koules. Directed by Richard Benjamin.

Script by Phoef Sutton and Lisa-Marie Radano, based on the novel *I Married a Dead Man* by Cornell Woolrich. Director of Photography, Alex Nepomniaschy. Production Designer, Evelyn Sakash. Music, Patrick Doyle. Editors, Jacqueline Cambas and William Fletcher. Starring Shirley MacLaine (Grace Winterbourne), Ricki Lake (Connie Doyle), Brendan Fraser (Bill/Hugh Winterbourne), Miguel Sandoval (Paco), Loren Dean (Steve DeCunzo), Peter Gerety (Father Brian), Jane Krakowski (Christine), Debra Monk (Lt. Ambrose), Kate Hennig (Sophie), Susan Haskell (Patricia Winterbourne). 106 minutes.

*Mulholland Falls* (MGM/Largo/PolyGram/Zanuck, 1996). Produced by Richard D. Zanuck and Lili Fini Zanuck. Directed by Lee Tamahori. Script by Pete Dexter, based on a story by Pete Dexter and Floyd Mutrux. Director of Photography, Haskell Wexler. Production Designer, Richard Sylbert. Music, Dave Grusin. Editor, Sally Menke. Starring Nick Nolte (Max Hoover), Melanie Griffith (Katherine), Chazz Palminteri (Coolidge), Chris Penn (Relyea), Michael Madsen (Eddie Hall), Treat Williams (Fitzgerald), Jennifer Connelly (Allison Pond), Andrew McCarthy (Jimmy Fields), John Malkovich (Timms). 107 minutes.

*Murder, My Sweet* (RKO, 1944). Produced by Adrian Scott. Directed by Edward Dmytryk. Script by John Paxton, based on the novel *Farewell, My Lovely* by Raymond Chandler. Director of Photography, Harry J. Wild. Art Directors, Albert S. D'Agostino and Carroll Clark. Music, Roy Webb. Editor, Joseph Noriega. Starring Dick Powell (Philip Marlowe), Claire Trevor (Velma/Mrs. Grayle), Anne Shirley (Ann), Otto Kruger (Amthor), Mike Mazurki (Moose Malloy), Miles Mander (Mr. Grayle), Douglas Walton (Marriott), Don Douglas (Lt. Randall), Ralf Harolde (Dr. Sonderborg), Esther Howard (Mrs. Florian). 95 minutes.

*The Naked Kiss* (Allied Artists, 1964). Produced, directed and written by Samuel Fuller. Director of Photography, Stanley Cortez. Art Director, Eugène Lourié. Music, Paul Dunlap. Editor, Jerome Thoms. Starring Constance Towers (Kelly), Anthony Eisley (Griff), Michael Dante (Grant), Virginia Grey (Candy), Patsy Kelly (Mac), Karen Conrad (Dusty), Betty Robinson (Bunny), Gerald Michenaud (Kip), George Spell (Tim). 90 minutes.

*Narrow Margin* (Carolco/TriStar, 1990). Produced by Jonathan A. Zimbert and Jerry Offsay. Directed by Peter Hyams. Script by Peter Hyams, based on the 1952 film *The Narrow Margin*, written by Earl Felton. Director of Photography, Peter Hyams. Production Designer, Joel Schiller. Music, Bruce Broughton. Editor, James Mitchell. Starring Gene Hackman (Caulfield), Anne Archer (Hunnicut), James B. Sikking (Nelson), J. T. Walsh (Michael Tarlow), M. Emmet Walsh (Sgt. Dominick Benti), Susan Hogan (Kathryn Weller). 97 minutes.

*The Narrow Margin* (RKO, 1952). Produced by Stanley Rubin. Directed by Richard Fleischer. Script by Earl Felton, based on a story by Martin Goldsmith and Jack Leonard. Director of Photography, George E. Diskant. Art Directors, Albert S. D'Agostino and Jack Okey. Editor, Robert Swink. Starring Charles McGraw (Walter Brown), Marie Windsor (Mrs. Neall), Jacqueline White (Ann Sinclair), Gordon Gebert (Tommy Sinclair), Queenie Leonard (Mrs. Troll), David Clarke (Kemp), Peter Virgo (Densel), Don Beddoe (Gus Forbes), Paul Maxey (Jennings), Harry Harvey (Train Conductor). 71 minutes.

*Natural Born Killers* (New Regency/Ixtlan/J.D., 1994). Produced by Jane Hamsher, Don Murphy, and Clayton Townsend. Directed by Oliver Stone. Script by David Veloz, Richard Rutowski, and Oliver Stone, based on a story and script by Quentin Tarantino. Director of Photography, Robert Richardson. Production Designer, Victor Kempster. Music, Trent Reznor. Editors, Hank Corwin and Brian Berdan. Starring Woody Harrelson (Mickey Knox), Juliette Lewis (Mallory Knox), Robert Downey, Jr. (Wayne Gale), Tommy Lee Jones (Dwight McClusky), Tom Sizemore (Jack Scagnetti), Rodney Dangerfield (Mallory's Dad), Russell Means (Old Indian), Edie McClurg (Mallory's Mom), Balthazar Getty (Gas Station Attendant), Joe Grifasi (Duncan Homolka). 120 minutes.

*The Net* (Columbia, 1995). Produced by Irwin Winkler and Rob Cowan. Directed by Irwin Winkler. Script by John D. Brancato and Michael Ferris. Director of Photography, Jack N. Green. Production Designer, Dennis Washington. Music, Mark Isham. Editor, Richard Halsey. Starring Sandra Bullock (Angela Bennett), Jeremy Northam (Jack Devlin), Dennis Miller (Dr. Alan Champion), Diane Baker (Mrs. Bennett), Wendy Gazelle (Impostor), Ken Howard (Bergstrom), Roy

McKinnon (Dale). 114 minutes.

*Nick of Time* (Paramount, 1995). Produced and directed by John Badham. Script by Patrick Sheane Duncan. Director of Photography, Roy H. Wagner. Production Designer, Philip Harrison. Music, Arthur B. Rubinstein. Editor, Frank Morriss. Starring Johnny Depp (Gene Watson), Christopher Walken (Mr. Smith), Charles S. Dutton (Huey), Peter Strauss (Brendan Grant), Roma Maffia (Ms. Jones), Gloria Reuben (Krista Brooks), Marsha Mason (Gov. Eleanor Grant), Courtney Chase (Lynn Watson), Bill Smitrovich (Officer Trust), G. D. Spradlin (Mystery Man). 89 minutes.

*Night and the City* (20th Century-Fox, 1950). Produced by Samuel G. Engel. Directed by Jules Dassin. Script by Jo Eisinger, based on the novel by Gerald Kersh. Director of Photography, Mutz Greenbaum. Art Director, C. P. Norman. Music, Franz Waxman. Editors, Nick De Maggio and Sydney Stone. Starring Richard Widmark (Harry Fabian), Gene Tierney (Mary Bristol), Googie Withers (Helen Nosseross), Hugh Marlowe (Adam Dunn), Francis L. Sullivan (Phil Nosseross), Herbert Lom (Kristo), Stanislaus Zbyszko (Gregorius), Mike Mazurki (Strangler), Charles Farrell (Beer), Ada Reeve (Molly). 95 minutes.

*Night and the City* (20th Century-Fox/Penta, 1992). Produced by Jane Rosenthal and Irwin Winkler. Directed by Irwin Winkler. Script by Richard Price, based on the novel by Gerald Kersh. Director of Photography, Tak Fujimoto. Production Designer, Peter Larkin. Music, James Newton Howard. Editor, David Brenner. Starring Robert De Niro (Harry Fabian), Jessica Lange (Helen Nasseros), Cliff Gorman (Phil Nasseros), Jack Warden (Al Grossman), Alan King (Boom Boom Grossman). 105 minutes.

*Night Moves* (Warner Bros., 1975). Produced by Robert M. Sherman. Directed by Arthur Penn. Script by Alan Sharp. Director of Photography, Bruce Surtees. Production Designer, George Jenkins. Music, Michael Small. Editor, Dede Allen. Starring Gene Hackman (Harry Moseby), Susan Clark (Ellen Moseby), Edward Binns (Ziegler), Harris Yulin (Marty Heller), Kenneth Mars (Nick), Janet Ward (Arlene Iverson), James Woods (Quentin), Anthony Costello (Marv Ellman), John Crawford (Tom Iverson), Melanie Griffith (Delly Grastner). 100 minutes.

*No Way Out* (Neufeld/Ziskin/Garland, 1987). Produced by Laura Ziskin and Robert Garland. Directed by Roger Donaldson. Script by Robert Garland, based on the novel *The Big Clock* by Kenneth Fearing. Director of Photography, John Alcott. Production Designer, Dennis Washington. Music, Maurice Jarre. Editor, Neil Travis. Starring Kevin Costner (Tom Farrell), Gene Hackman (David Brice), Sean Young (Susan Atwell), Will Patton (Scott Pritchard), Howard Duff (Sen. Willy Duvall), George Dzundza (Dr. Sam Hesselman), Jason Bernard (Maj. Donovan), Iman (Nina Beka), Fred Dalton Thompson (Marshall), Leon Russom (Kevin O'Brien). 114 minutes.

*Obsession* (Columbia/Yellow Bird, 1976). Produced by George Litto and Harry N. Blum. Directed by Brian De Palma. Script by Paul Schrader, based on a story by Paul Schrader and Brian De Palma. Director of Photography, Vilmos Zsigmond. Art Director, Jack Senter. Music, Bernard Herrmann. Editor, Paul Hirsch. Starring Cliff Robertson (Michael Courtland), Geneviève Bujold (Elizabeth Courtland/Sandra Portinari), John Lithgow (Robert LaSalle), Sylvia "Kuumba" Williams (Judy), Wanda Blackman (Amy Courtland), J. Patrick McNamara (Kidnapper #3), Stocker Fontelieu (Dr. Ellman). 98 minutes.

*Odds Against Tomorrow* (United Artists/HarBel, 1959). Produced and directed by Robert Wise. Script by Abraham Polonsky and Nelson Gidding, based on the novel by William P. McGivern. Director of Photography, Joseph C. Brun. Art Director, Leo Kerz. Music, John Lewis. Editor, Dede Allen. Starring Harry Belafonte (Johnny Ingram), Robert Ryan (Earl Slater), Shelley Winters (Lorry), Ed Begley (Dave Burke), Gloria Grahame (Helen), Will Kuluva (Bacco), Richard Bright (Coco), Lew Gallo (Moriarity), Fred J. Scollay (Cannoy), Carmen De Lavallade (Kittie). 95 minutes.

*One False Move* (I.R.S. Media, 1991). Produced by Jesse Beaton and Ben Myron. Directed by Carl Franklin. Script by Billy Bob Thornton and Tom Epperson. Director of Photography, James L. Carter. Production Designer, Gary T. New. Music, Peter Haycock and Derek Holt. Editor, Carole Kravetz. Starring Cynda Williams (Fantasia/Lila), Bill Paxton (Dale "Hurricane" Dixon), Billy Bob Thornton (Ray Malcolm), Jim Metzler (Dud Cole), Michael Beach (Pluto), Earl Billings (McFeely),

Natalie Canerday (Cherylann). 105 minutes.

*Out of the Past* (RKO, 1947). Produced by Warren Duff. Directed by Jacques Tourneur. Script by Daniel Mainwaring, based on his novel *Build My Gallows High*. Director of Photography, Nicholas Musuraca. Art Directors, Albert S. D'Agostino and Jack Okey. Music, Roy Webb. Editor, Samuel E. Beetley. Starring Robert Mitchum (Jeff Bailey), Jane Greer (Kathie Moffett), Kirk Douglas (Whit Sterling), Rhonda Fleming (Meta Carson), Richard Webb (Jim), Steve Brodie (Fisher), Virginia Huston (Ann), Paul Valentine (Joe), Dickie Moore (The Kid), Ken Niles (Eels). 97 minutes.

*The Outfit* (MGM, 1974). Produced by Carter De Haven. Directed and written by John Flynn, based on the novel by Richard Stark. Director of Photography, Bruce Surtees. Art Director, Tambi Larsen. Music, Jerry Fielding. Editor, Ralph E. Winters. Starring Robert Duvall (Earl Macklin), Joe Don Baker (Cody), Karen Black (Bett Jarrow), Timothy Carey (Jake Menner), Robert Ryan (Mailer), Marie Windsor (Madge), Jane Greer (Alma), Henry Jones (Doctor), Emile Meyer (Amos), Roy Roberts (Bob). 103 minutes.

*The Parallax View* (Paramount, 1974). Produced and directed by Alan J. Pakula. Script by David Giler and Lorenzo Semple, Jr., based on the novel by Loren Singer. Director of Photography, Gordon Willis. Production Designer, George Jenkins. Music, Michael Small. Editor, John W. Wheeler. Starring Warren Beatty (Joseph Frady), Hume Cronyn (Editor Edgar Rintels), William Daniels (Austin Tucker), Paula Prentiss (Lee Carter), Kelly Thordsen (Sheriff L. D.), Earl Hindman (Deputy Red), Chuck Waters (Busboy-Assassin), Bill Joyce (Sen. Carroll), Bettie Johnson (Mrs. Carroll), Bill McKinney (Art, an Assassin). 102 minutes.

*Pickpocket* (Lux, 1959). Produced by Agnès Delahaie. Directed and written by Robert Bresson, based on the novel *Crime and Punishment* by Fyodor Dostoevsky. Director of Photography, Léonce-Henri Burel. Production Designer, Pierre Charbonnier. Music, Jean-Baptiste Lully. Editor, Raymond Lamy. Starring Martin LaSalle (Michel), Marika Green (Jeanne), Jean Pélégri (Police Inspector), Dolly Scal (Michel's Mother),

Pierre Leymarie (Jacques), Kassagi (Master Pickpocket), Pierre Etaix (Accomplice), César Gattegno (Detective). 75 minutes.

*Pierrot le fou* (Rome-Paris/De Laurentiis Cinématografica, 1965). Produced by Georges de Beauregard. Directed and written by Jean-Luc Godard, based on the novel *Obsession* by Lionel White. Director of Photography, Raoul Coutard. Art Director, Pierre Guffroy. Music, Antoine Duhamel. Editor, Françoise Collin. Starring Jean-Paul Belmondo (Ferdinand/"Pierrot"), Anna Karina (Marianne), Dirk Sanders (Marianne's Brother), Raymond Devos (Man on the Pier), Graziella Galvani (Ferdinand's Wife), Roger Dutoit (Gangster), Hans Meyer (Gangster), Jimmy Karoubi (Dwarf), Christa Nell (Madame Staquet), Pascal Aubier (Brother #2), Samuel Fuller (Himself), László Szabó (Political Exile), Jean-Pierre Léaud (Young Man in Cinema). 110 minutes.

*The Player* (Avenue/Guild/Spelling, 1992). Produced by David Brown, Michael Tolkin, and Nick Wechsler. Directed by Robert Altman. Script by Michael Tolkin, based on his novel. Director of Photography, Jean Lépine. Production Designer, Stephen Altman. Music, Thomas Newman. Editors, Maysie Hoy and Geraldine Peroni. Starring Tim Robbins (Griffin Mill), Greta Scacchi (June Gudmundsdottir), Fred Ward (Walter Stuckel), Whoopie Goldberg (Detective Avery), Peter Gallagher (Larry Levy), Brion James (Joel Levison), Cynthia Stevenson (Bonnie Sherow), Vincent D'Onofrio (David Kahane), Dean Stockwell (Andy Civella), Richard E. Grant (Tom Oakley). 123 minutes.

*Point Blank* (MGM/Judd Bernard and Irwin Winkler, 1967). Produced by Judd Bernard and Robert Chartoff. Directed by John Boorman. Script by Alexander Jacobs, David Newhouse, and Rafe Newhouse, based on the novel *The Hunter* by Richard Stark. Director of Photography, Philip H. Lathrop. Art Directors, George W. Davis and Albert Brenner. Music, Johnny Mandel. Editor, Henry Berman. Starring Lee Marvin (Walker), Angie Dickinson (Chris), John Vernon (Mal Reese), Keenan Wynn (Fairfax/"Yost"), Carrol O'Connor (Brewster), Lloyd Bochner (Frederick Carter), Michael Strong(Stegman), Sharon Acker (Lynne), James B. Sikking (The Shooter). 92 minutes.

*Point of No Return* (Warner Bros., 1993). Produced by Art Linson.

Directed by John Badham. Script by Robert Getchell and Alexandra Seros, based on the 1990 film *La Femme Nikita*, written by Luc Besson. Director of Photography, Michael W. Watkins. Production Designer, Philip Harrison. Music, Hans Zimmer. Editor, Frank Morriss. Starring Bridget Fonda (Maggie), Gabriel Byrne (Bob), Dermot Mulroney (J. P.), Miguel Ferrer (Kaufman), Anne Bancroft (Amanda), Olivia d'Abo (Angela), Richard Romanus (Fahd Bahktiar), Harvey Keitel (Victor the Cleaner), Lorraine Toussaint (Beth), Geoffrey Lewis (Drugstore Owner), Mic Rogers (Cop). 108 minutes.

*Port of Shadows* [*Le Quai des brumes*] (Ciné-Alliance, 1938). Produced by Gregor Rabinovitch. Directed by Marcel Carné. Script by Jacques Prévert, based on the novel *Le Quai des brumes* by Pierre MacOrlan. Director of Photography, Eugen Schüfftan. Production Designer, Alexandre Trauner. Music, Maurice Jaubert. Editor, René Le Henaff. Starring Jean Gabin (Jean), Michele Morgan (Nelly), Michel Simon (Zabel), Pierre Brasseur (Lucien), Robert Le Vigan (Michel Krauss), Jenny Burnay (Lucien's Friend), Marcel Pérès (Chauffeur), Réne Génin (Doctor), Edouard Delmont (Panama), Raymond Aimos (Quart-Vittel). 91 minutes.

*The Postman Always Rings Twice* (MGM, 1946). Produced by Carey Wilson. Directed by Tay Garnett. Script by Harry Ruskin and Niven Busch, based on the novel by James M. Cain. Director of Photography, Sidney Wagner. Art Directors, Cedric Gibbons and Randall Duell. Music, George Bassman. Editor, George White. Starring Lana Turner (Cora Smith), John Garfield (Frank Chambers), Cecil Kellaway (Nick Smith), Hume Cronyn (Arthur Keats), Leon Ames (Kyle Sackett), Audrey Totter (Madge Gorland), Alan Reed (Ezra Liam Kennedy), Jeff York (Blair), Charles Williams (Doctor), Cameron Grant (Willie). 113 minutes.

*The Postman Always Rings Twice* (Paramount/Lorimar, 1981). Produced by Bob Rafelson and Charles Mulvehill. Directed by Bob Rafelson. Script by David Mamet, based on the novel by James M. Cain. Director of Photography, Sven Nykvist. Production Designer, George Jenkins. Music, Michael Small. Editor, Graeme Clifford. Starring Jack Nicholson (Frank Chambers), Jessica Lange (Cora Papadakis), John Colicos (Nick Papadakis), Michael Lerner (Katz), John P. Ryan (Kennedy), Anjelica Huston (Madge), Christopher Lloyd (Salesman). 125 minutes.

*Primal Fear* (Paramount/Rysher, 1996). Produced by Gary Lucchesi. Directed by Gregory Hoblit. Script by Steve Shagan and Ann Biderman, based on the novel by William Diehl. Director of Photography, Michael Chapman. Production Designer, Jeannine C. Oppewall. Music, James Newton Howard. Editor, David Rosenbloom. Starring Richard Gere (Martin Vale), Edward Norton (Aaron/Roy), Laura Linney (Janet Venable), John Mahoney (John Shaughnessy), Alfre Woodard (Judge Miriam Shoat), Frances McDormand (Dr. Molly Arrington), André Braugher (Tommy Goodman), Maura Tierney (Naomi Chance). 131 minutes.

*The Professional* [*Léon*] (Gaumont/Films du Dauphin, 1994). Produced, directed, and written by Luc Besson. Director of Photography, Thierry Arbogast. Production Designer, Dan Weil. Music, Eric Serra. Editor, Sylvie Landra. Starring Jean Reno (Léon), Natalie Portman (Mathilda), Gary Oldman (Stansfield), Danny Aiello (Tony), Peter Appel (Malky); Willie One Blood, Don Creech, Keith A. Glascoe, Randolph Scott, Jernard Burks, and Matt De Matt (Stansfield's Men); Ellen Greene (Mathilda's Mother), Michael Badalucco (Mathilda's Father), Elizabeth Regen (Mathilda's Sister). 110 minutes.

*Psycho* (Paramount, 1960). Produced and directed by Alfred Hitchcock. Script by Joseph Stefano, based on the novel by Robert Bloch. Director of Photography, John L. Russell. Production Designers, Joseph Hurley and Robert Clatworthy. Music, Bernard Herrmann. Editor, George Tomasini. Starring Anthony Perkins (Norman Bates), Janet Leigh (Marion Crane), Vera Miles (Lila Crane), John Gavin (Sam Loomis), Martin Balsam (Milton Arbogast), John McIntire (Sheriff Chambers), Lurene Tuttle (Mrs. Chambers), Simon Oakland (Dr. Richmond), Frank Albertson (Tom Cassidy), Patricia Hitchcock (Caroline). 109 minutes.

*Pulp Fiction* (A Band Apart/Jersey/Miramax, 1994). Produced by Lawrence Bender. Directed and written by Quentin Tarantino, based on stories by Quentin Tarantino and Roger Avary. Director of Photography, Andrzej Sekula. Production Designer, David Wasco. Editor, Sally Menke. Starring John Travolta (Vincent Vega), Samuel L. Jackson (Jules Winnfield), Uma Thurman (Mia Wallace), Harvey Keitel (Winston, a.k.a.

The Wolf), Tim Roth (Pumpkin), Amanda Plummer (Honey Bunny), Bruce Willis (Butch), Maria de Medeiros (Fabienne), Ving Rhames (Marsellus Wallace), Eric Stoltz (Lance), Rosanna Arquette (Jody). 149 minutes.

*Purple Noon* [*Plein Soleil*] (Paris/Panitalia/Titanus, 1960). Produced by Robert Hakim and Raymond Hakim. Directed by René Clément. Script by René Clément and Paul Gégauff, based on the novel *The Talented Mr. Ripley* by Patricia Highsmith. Director of Photography, Henri Decaë. Art Director, Paul Bertrand. Music, Nino Rota. Editor, Françoise Javet. Starring Alain Delon (Tom Ripley), Marie Laforêt (Marge), Maurice Ronet (Philippe Greenleaf), Bill Kearns (Freddy Miles), Erno Crisa (Inspector Riccordi), Frank Latimore (O'Brien), Ave Ninchi (Gianna), Viviane Chantel (Belgian Tourist). 115 minutes.

*Red Rock West* (Polygram/Propaganda, 1992). Produced by Sigurjon Sighvatsson and Steve Golin. Directed by John Dahl. Script by John Dahl and Rick Dahl. Director of Photography, Marc Reshovsky. Production Designer, Robert Pearson. Music, William Olvis. Editor, Scott Chestnut. Starring Nicholas Cage (Michael), Lara Flynn Boyle (Suzanne), Dennis Hopper (Lyle), J. T. Walsh (Wayne), Craig Reay (Jim), Vance Johnson (Mr. Johnson), Robert Apel (Howard), Bobby Joe McFadden (Old Man), Dale Gibson (Kurt). 98 minutes.

*Reservoir Dogs* (Dog Eat Dog/Live/Miramax, 1992). Produced by Lawrence Bender. Directed and written by Quentin Tarantino. Director of Photography, Andrzej Sekula. Production Designer, David Wasco. Music Supervisor, Karyn Rachtman. Editor, Sally Menke. Starring Harvey Keitel (Mr. White), Tim Roth (Mr. Orange/Freddy), Michael Madsen (Mr. Blonde), Chris Penn (Nice Guy Eddie), Steve Buscemi (Mr. Pink), Lawrence Tierney (Joe Cabot), Eddie Bunker (Mr. Blue), Quentin Tarantino (Mr. Brown). 99 minutes.

*Romeo Is Bleeding* (Rank/PolyGram/Working Title, 1993). Produced by Hilary Henkin. Directed by Peter Medak. Script by Hilary Henkin. Director of Photography, Dariusz Wolski. Production Designer, Stuart Wurtzel. Music, Mark Isham. Editor, Walter Murch. Starring Gary Oldman (Jack), Lena Olin (Mona), Annabella Sciorra (Natalie), Juliette

Lewis (Sheri), Roy Scheider (Don Falcone), Dennis Farina (Nick). 108 minutes.

*Le Samouraï* (Filmel/CICC/Fida Cinématografica, 1967). Produced by Eugène Lépicier and Raymond Borderie. Directed and written by Jean-Pierre Melville, based on the novel *The Ronin* by Joan McLeod. Director of Photography, Henri Decaë. Production Designer, François de Lamothe. Music, François de Roubaix. Editors, Monique Bonnot and Y. Maurette. Starring Alain Delon (Jef Costello), François Périer (Superintendent), Nathalie Delon (Jane Lagrange), Cathy Rosier (The Piano Player), Michel Boisrond (Wiener), Robert Favart (Bartender), Jean-Pierre Posier (Olivier Ray), Roger Fradet (Inspector #1), Carlo Nell (Inspector #2), Robert Rondo (Inspector #3). 95 minutes.

*Scarlet Street* (Universal, 1945). Produced and directed by Fritz Lang. Script by Dudley Nichols, based on the novel and play *La Chienne* by Georges de la Fouchardière. Director of Photography, Milton Krasner. Art Director, Alexander Golitzen. Music, H. J. Salter. Editor, Arthur Hilton. Starring Edward G. Robinson (Christopher Cross), Joan Bennett (Kitty March), Dan Duryea (Johnny Prince), Margaret Lindsay (Millie), Rosalind Ivan (Adele Cross), Jess Barker (Janeway), Arthur Loft (Dellarowe), Samuel S. Hinds (Charles Pringle), Vladimir Sokoloff (Pop Lejon), Charles Kemper (Patcheye). 103 minutes.

*Sea of Love* (Bregman/Universal, 1989). Produced by Martin Bregman and Louis A. Stroller. Directed by Harold Becker. Script by Richard Price. Director of Photography, Ronnie Taylor. Production Designer, John Jay Moore. Music, Trevor Jones. Editor, David Bretherton. Starring Al Pacino (Frank Keller), Ellen Barkin (Helen), John Goodman (Sherman), Michael Rooker (Terry), William Hickey (Frank, Sr.), Richard Jenkins (Gruber), Paul Calderon (Serafino). 113 minutes.

*Serpico* (Paramount, 1973). Produced by Martin Bregman. Directed by Sidney Lumet. Script by Waldo Salt and Norman Wexler, based on the book by Peter Maas. Director of Photography, Arthur J. Ornitz. Production Designer, Charles Bailey. Music, Mikis Theodorakis. Editors, Dede Allen and Richard Marks. Starring Al Pacino (Frank Serpico),

John Randolph (Chief Green), Jack Kehoe (Tom Keough), Biff McGuire (Capt. McClain), Barbara Eda-Young (Laurie), Cornelia Sharpe (Leslie), Tony Roberts (Bob Blair). 129 minutes.

*Seven* (New Line, 1995). Produced by Arnold Kopelson and Phyllis Carlyle. Directed by David Fincher. Script by Andrew Kevin Walker. Director of Photography, Darius Khondji. Production Designer, Arthur Max. Music, Howard Shore. Editor, Richard Francis Bruce. Starring Brad Pitt (Detective David Mills), Morgan Freeman (Lt. William Somerset), Gwyneth Paltrow (Tracy), Richard Roundtree (Talbot), John C. McGinley (California), Kevin Spacey (John Doe), John Cassini (Officer Davis), Peter Crombie (Dr. O'Neill), Reg E. Cathey (Dr. Santiago), Richard Portnow (Dr. Beardsley). 107 minutes.

*Shaft* (MGM, 1971). Produced by Joel Freeman. Directed by Gordon Parks. Script by Ernest Tidyman and John D. F. Black, based on the novel by Ernest Tidyman. Director of Photography, Urs Furrer. Art Director, Emanuel Gerard. Music, Isaac Hayes. Editor, Hugh A. Robertson. Starring Richard Roundtree (John Shaft), Moses Gunn (Bumpy Jonas), Victor Arnold (Charlie), Charles Cioffi (Lt. Vic Androzzi), Christopher St. John (Ben), Gwenn Mitchell (Ellie), Lawrence Pressman (Tom). 98 minutes.

*Shattered* (MGM, 1991). Produced by Wolfgang Petersen, John Davis, and David Korda. Directed and written by Wolfgang Petersen, based on the novel *The Plastic Nightmare* by Richard Neely. Director of Photography, László Kovács. Production Designer, Gregg Fonseca. Music, Alan Silvestri. Editors, Hannes Nikel and Glenn Farr. Starring Tom Berenger (Don Merrick), Bob Hoskins (Gus Klein), Greta Scacchi (Judith Merrick), Joanne Whalley-Kilmer (Jenny Scott), Corbin Bernsen (Jeb Scott). 97 minutes.

*Shock Corridor* (Allied Artists, 1963). Produced, directed, and written by Samuel Fuller. Director of Photography, Stanley Cortez; color sequences by Samuel Fuller. Art Director, Eugène Lourié. Music, Paul Dunlap. Editor, Jerome Thoms. Starring Peter Breck (Johnny Barrett), Constance Towers (Cathy), Gene Evans (Boden), James Best (Stuart), Hari Rhodes (Trent), Larry Tucker (Pagliacci), William Zuckert (Swanee),

Philip Ahn (Dr. Fong), Neyle Morrow (Psycho), John Matthews (Dr. Cristo). 101 minutes.

*Shoot the Piano Player* [*Tirez sur le pianiste*] (Pléïade, 1960). Produced by Pierre Braunberger. Directed by François Truffaut. Script by François Truffaut and Marcel Moussy, based on the novel *Down There* by David Goodis. Director of Photography, Raoul Coutard. Art Director, Jacques Mély. Music, Georges Delerue. Editors, Cécile Decugis and Claudine Bouché. Starring Charles Aznavour (Charlie/Edouard), Marie Dubois (Lena), Nicole Berger (Theresa), Michèle Mercier (Clarisse), Albert Rémy (Chico Saroyan), Jean-Jacques Aslanian (Richard Saroyan), Richard Kanayan (Fido Saroyan), Claude Mansard (Momo), Daniel Boulanger (Ernest), Serge Davri (Plyne). 80 minutes.

*Someone to Watch Over Me* (Columbia, 1987). Produced by Thierry de Ganay and Harold Schneider. Directed by Ridley Scott. Script by Howard Franklin. Director of Photography, Steven Poster. Production Designer, James D. Bissell. Music, Michael Kamen. Editor, Claire Simpson. Starring Tom Berenger (Mike Keegan), Mimi Rogers (Claire Gregory), Lorraine Bracco (Ellie Keegan), Jerry Orbach (Lt. Garber), John Rubinstein (Neil Steinhart), Andreas Katsulas (Joey Venza). 106 minutes.

*Something Wild* (Religiosa Primitiva, 1986). Produced by Jonathan Demme and Kenneth Utt. Directed by Jonathan Demme. Script by E. Max Frye. Director of Photography, Tak Fujimoto. Production Designer, Norma Moriceau. Music, John Cale and Laurie Anderson. Editor, Craig McKay. Starring Jeff Daniels (Charles Driggs), Melanie Griffith (Audrey Hankel), Ray Liotta (Ray Sinclair), Margaret Colin (Irene), Tracey Walter (The Country Squire), Dana Preu ("Peaches"), Jack Gilpin (Larry Dillman), Su Tissue (Peggy Dillman), Kristin Olsen (Tracy), John Sayles (Motorcycle Cop). 113 minutes.

*Spoorloos* [*The Vanishing*] (Golden Egg/Argos/MGS/Ingrid, 1988). Produced by Anne Lordon and George Sluizer. Directed and written by George Sluizer, based on the novel *The Golden Egg* by Tim Krabbé. Director of Photography, Toni Kuhn. Art Directors, Santiago Isidro Pin and Cor Spijk. Music, Hennie Vrienten. Editors, George Sluizer and Lin Friedman. Starring Gene Bervoets (Rex Hofman), Johanna ter Steege (Saskia Wagter), Bernard-Pierre Donnadieu (Raymond Lemorne), Gwen Eckhaus (Lieneke), Bernadette Le Saché (Simone Lemorne), Tania Latarjet (Denise), Lucille Glenn (Gabrielle), Roger Souza (Manager), Caroline Appéré (Cashier), Pierre Forget (Farmer Laurent). 107 minutes.

*The Stepfather* (ITC, 1987). Produced by Jay Benson. Directed by Joseph Ruben. Script by Donald E. Westlake, based on a story by Carolyn Lefcourt, Brian Garfield, and Donald E. Westlake. Director of Photography, John Lindley. Production Designer, James William Newport. Music, Patrick Moraz. Editor, George Bowers. Starring Terry O'Quinn (The Stepfather), Jill Schoelen (Stephanie Maine), Shelley Hack (Susan Blake), Charles Lanyer (Dr. Bondurant), Stephen Shellen (Jim Ogilvie), Stephen E. Miller (Al Brennan), Robyn Stevan (Karen), Jeff Schultz (Paul Baker), Lindsay Bourne (Art Teacher), Anna Hagan (Mrs. Leitner). 90 minutes.

*Still of the Night* (MGM-UA, 1982). Produced by Arlene Donovan. Directed by Robert Benton. Script by Robert Benton, based on a story by Robert Benton and David Newman. Director of Photography, Nestor Almendros. Production Designer, Mel Bourne. Music, John Gibson. Editors, Jerry Greenberg and Bill Pankow. Starring Roy Scheider (Dr. Sam Rice), Meryl Streep (Brooke Reynolds), Jessica Tandy (Grace Rice), Sara Botsford (Gail Phillips), Josef Sommer (George Bynum), Joe Grifasi (Joseph Vitucci). 91 minutes.

*Strange Days* (First Light/Lightstorm, 1995). Produced by James Cameron and Steven-Charles Jaffe. Directed by Kathryn Bigelow. Script by James Cameron and Jay Cocks, based on a story by James Cameron. Director of Photography, Matthew F. Leonetti. Production Designer, Lilly Kilvert. Music, Graeme Revell. Editor, Howard Smith. Starring Ralph Fiennes (Lenny Nero), Angela Bassett (Lornette "Mace" Mason), Juliette Lewis (Faith Justin), Tom Sizemore (Max Peltier), Michael Wincott (Philo Gant), Vincent D'Onofrio (Burton Steckler), Glenn Plummer (Jeriko One), Brigitte Bako (Iris), Richard Edson (Tick), William Fichtner (Dwayne Engelman). 145 minutes.

*Taxi Driver* (Columbia/Bill-Phillips, 1976). Produced by Michael Phillips and Julia Phillips. Directed by Martin Scorsese. Script by Paul Schrader. Director of Photography, Michael Chapman. Art Director, Charles Rosen. Music, Bernard Herrmann. Editors, Marcia Lucas and Tom Rolf. Starring Robert De Niro (Travis Bickle), Cybill Shepherd (Betsy), Jodie Foster (Iris Steensman), Peter Boyle (Wizard), Harvey Keitel (Sport), Albert Brooks (Tom), Leonard Harris (Charles Palantine), Martin Scorsese (Passenger), Diahnne Abbott (Concession Girl), Frank Adu (Angry Black Man). 112 minutes.

*Thelma and Louise* (MGM/Pathé/Percy Main, 1991). Produced by Ridley Scott, Mimi Polk, Callie Khouri, and Dean O'Brien. Directed by Ridley Scott. Script by Callie Khouri. Director of Photography, Adrian Biddle. Production Designer, Norris Spencer. Music, Hans Zimmer. Editor, Thom Noble. Starring Susan Sarandon (Louise), Geena Davis (Thelma), Harvey Keitel (Hal), Michael Madsen (Jimmy), Christopher McDonald (Darryl), Brad Pitt (J. D.). 128 minutes.

*They Live by Night* (RKO, 1948). Produced by John Houseman. Directed by Nicholas Ray. Script by Charles Schnee and Nicholas Ray, based on the novel *Thieves Like Us* by Edward Anderson. Director of Photography, George E. Diskant. Art Directors, Albert S. D'Agostino and Al Herman. Music, Woody Guthrie and Leigh Harline. Editor, Sherman Todd. Starring Cathy O'Donnell (Keechie), Farley Granger (Bowie), Howard Da Silva (Chickamaw), Jay C. Flippen (T-Dub), Helen Craig (Mattie), Will Wright (Mobley), Marie Bryant (Singer), Ian Wolfe (Hawkins), William Phipps (Young Farmer), Harry Harvey (Hagenheimer). 95 minutes.

*Thief* (United Artists, 1981). Produced by Jerry Bruckheimer and Ronnie Caan. Directed and written by Michael Mann, based on the novel *The Home Invaders* by Frank Hohimer. Director of Photography, Donald E. Thorin. Production Designer, Mel Bourne. Music, Tangerine Dream. Editor, Dov Hoenig. Starring James Caan (Frank), Tuesday Weld (Jessie), Robert Prosky (Leo), Tom Signorelli (Attaglia), Dennis Farina (Carl), James Belushi (Barry), Willie Nelson (Okla). 122 minutes.

*Thieves Like Us* (United Artists, 1974). Produced by Jerry Bick and

George Litto. Directed by Robert Altman. Script by Calder Willingham, Joan Tewksbury, and Robert Altman, based on the novel by Edward Anderson. Director of Photography, Jean Boffety. Editor, Lou Lombardo. Starring Keith Carradine (Bowie), Shelley Duvall (Keechie), John Schuck (Chicamaw), Bert Remsen (T-Dub), Louise Fletcher (Mattie), Ann Latham (Lula), Tom Skerritt (Dee). 123 minutes.

*Things to Do in Denver When You're Dead* (Miramax/Woods/Buena Vista, 1995). Produced by Cary Woods. Directed by Gary Fleder. Script by Scott Rosenberg. Director of Photography, Elliot Davis. Production Designer, Nelson Coates. Music, Michael Convertino. Editors, Éva Gardos and Richard Marks. Starring Andy Garcia (Jimmy the Saint), Christopher Walken (Man with the Plan), Gabrielle Anwar (Dagney), William Forsythe (Franchise), Treat Williams (Critical Bill), Christopher Lloyd (Pieces), Bill Nunn (Easy Wind), Jack Warden (Joe Heff), Steve Buscemi (Mister Shhh), Fairuza Balk (Lucinda). 115 minutes.

*This World, Then the Fireworks* (First Independent/Largo, 1997). Produced by Chris Hanley, Brad Wyman, and Larry Gross. Directed by Michael Oblowitz. Script by Larry Gross. Director of Photography, Tom Priestley, Jr. Production Designer, Maia Javan. Music, Pete Rugolo. Editor, Emma Hickox. Starring Billy Zane (Marty Lakewood), Gina Gershon (Carol Lakewood), Sheryl Lee (Lois Archer), Rue McClanahan (Mom Lakewood), Seymour Cassel (Harris), Will Patton (Lt. Morgan), Richard Edson (Joe), William Hootkins (Jake Krutz). 100 minutes.

*To Die For* (Columbia, 1995). Produced by Laura Ziskin. Directed by Gus Van Sant. Script by Buck Henry, based on the novel by Joyce Maynard. Director of Photography, Alan Edwards. Production Designer, Missy Stewart. Music, Danny Elfman. Editor, Curtiss Clayton. Starring Nicole Kidman (Suzanne Stone), Matt Dillon (Larry Maretto), Joaquin Phoenix (Jimmy Emmett), Casey Affleck (Russell Hines), Illeana Douglas (Janice Maretto), Alison Folland (Lydia Mertz), Dan Hedaya (Joe Maretto), Wayne Knight (Ed Grant), Kurtwood Smith (Earl Stone), Holland Taylor (Carol Stone). 100 minutes.

*Touch of Evil* (Universal, 1958). Produced by Albert Zugsmith. Directed and written by Orson Welles, based on the novel *Badge of Evil* by

Whit Masterson. Director of Photography, Russell Metty. Art Directors, Alexander Golitzen and Robert Clatworthy. Music, Henry Mancini. Editors, Virgil Vogel and Aaron Stell. Starring Charlton Heston (Ramon Miguel "Mike" Vargas), Janet Leigh (Susan Vargas), Orson Welles (Hank Quinlan), Joseph Calleia (Pete Menzies), Akim Tamiroff ("Uncle Joe" Grandi), Valentin De Vargas ("Pancho"), Ray Collins (District Attorney Adair), Dennis Weaver (Motel Clerk), Joanna Moore (Marcia Linnekar), Mort Mills (Schwartz). 95 minutes (1958, theatrical release); 108 minutes (1976, with restored footage).

*True Romance* (August/Morgan Creek, 1993). Produced by Bill Unger, Gary Barber, Samuel Hadida, and Steve Perry. Directed by Tony Scott. Script by Quentin Tarantino. Director of Photography, Jeffrey L. Kimball. Production Designer, Benjamín Fernández. Music, Hans Zimmer. Editors, Michael Tronick and Christian Wagner. Starring Christian Slater (Clarence Worley), Patricia Arquette (Alabama), Dennis Hopper (Clifford Worley), Val Kilmer (Elvis), Gary Oldman (Drexl Spivey), Brad Pitt (Floyd), Christopher Walken (Vincenzo Coccotti), Michael Rapaport (Dick Ritchie), Bronson Pinchot (Elliot Blitzer), Samuel L. Jackson (Big Don). 119 minutes.

*2 Days in the Valley* (Rysher/Redemption/MGM, 1996). Produced by Jeff Wald and Herb Nanas. Directed and written by John Herzfeld. Director of Photography, Oliver Wood. Production Designer, Catherine Hardwicke. Music, Anthony Marinelli. Editors, Jim Miller and Wayne Wahrman. Starring Danny Aiello (Dosmo Pizzo), James Spader (Lee Woods), Greg Cruttwell (Allan Hopper), Jeff Daniels (Alvin Strayer), Teri Hatcher (Becky Foxx), Charlize Theron (Helga Svelgen), Glenne Headly (Susan Parish), Peter Horton (Roy Foxx), Marsha Mason (Audrey Hopper), Paul Mazursky (Teddy Peppers). 105 minutes.

*The Underneath* (Gramercy/Populist, 1995). Produced by John Hardy. Directed by Steven Soderbergh. Script by Sam Lowry and Daniel Fuchs, based on the novel *Criss Cross* by Don Tracy. Director of Photography, Elliot Davis. Art Director, John Frick. Starring Peter Gallagher (Michael Chambers), Alison Elliott (Rachel), William Fichtner (Tommy Dundee), Adam Trese (David), Joe Don Baker (Clay), Paul Dooley (Ed), Elisabeth Shue (Susan). 99 minutes.

*Union City* (Kinesis, 1980). Produced by Graham Belin. Mark Reichert, based on the story "The Corpse Next Door" by Cornell Woolrich. Director of Photography, Edward Lachman. Production Designer, George Stavrinos. Music, Chris Stein. Editors, Lana Tokel, Eric Albertson, and J. Michaels. Starring Dennis Lipscomb (Harlan), Debbie Harry (Lillian), Irina Maleeva (Contessa), Everett McGill (Larry Longacre), Pat Benatar (Jeanette), Sam McMurray (Young Vagrant). 87 minutes.

*The Usual Suspects* (Rosco/Blue Parrott/Bad Hat Harry/PolyGram/ Spelling, 1995). Produced by Bryan Singer and Michael McDonnell. Directed by Bryan Singer. Script by Christopher McQuarrie. Director of Photography, Newton Thomas Sigel. Production Designer, Howard Cummings. Music and editing, John Ottman. Starring Kevin Spacey (Verbal), Chazz Palminteri (Agent Dave Kujan), Gabriel Byrne (Dean Keaton), Stephen Baldwin (McManus), Benicio Del Toro (Fenster), Kevin Pollak (Hockney), Pete Postlethwaite (Kobayashi), Suzy Amis (Edie), Giancarlo Esposito (Jack Baer), Dan Hedaya (Sgt. Rabin). 96 minutes.

*U-Turn* (Clyde Is Hungry/Illusion/Phoenix, 1997). Produced by Dan Halsted and Clayton Townsend. Directed by Oliver Stone. Script by John Ridley, based on his novel *Stray Dogs*. Director of Photography, Robert Richardson. Production Designer, Victor Kempster. Music, Ennio Morricone. Editors, Hank Corwin and Thomas J. Nordberg. Starring Sean Penn (Bobby Cooper), Billy Bob Thornton (Darrell), Powers Boothe (Sheriff), Jennifer Lopez (Grace McKenna), Nick Nolte (Jake McKenna), Julie Hagerty (Flo), Joaquin Phoenix (Toby N. Tucker), Jon Voight (Blind Man), Claire Danes (Jenny), Laurie Metcalf (Bus Station Clerk), Liv Tyler (Girl in Bus Station). 125 minutes.

*The Vanishing* (20th Century-Fox, 1993). Produced by Larry Brezner and Paul Schiff. Directed by George Sluizer. Script by Todd Graff and George Sluizer, based on the 1988 film *Spoorloos* and the novel *The Golden Egg* by Tim Krabbé. Director of Photography, Peter Suschitzky. Production Designer, Jeannine C. Oppewall. Music, Jerry Goldsmith. Editor, Bruce Green. Starring Jeff Bridges (Barney), Kiefer Sutherland (Jeff), Nancy Travis (Rita), Sandra Bullock (Diane), Park Overall (Lynn), Maggie Linderman (Denise), Lisa Eichhorn (Helene), George Hearn (Arthur Bernard), Lynn Hamilton (Miss Carmichael), Garrett Bennett

(Cop at Gas Station), George Catalano (Highway Cop), Frank Girardeau (Cop at Apartment). 110 minutes.

*Vertigo* (Paramount, 1958). Produced and directed by Alfred Hitchcock. Script by Alec Coppel and Samuel Taylor, based on the novel *D'Entre les morts* by Pierre Boileau and Thomas Narcejac. Director of Photography, Robert Burks. Art Directors, Hal Pereira and Henry Bumstead. Music, Bernard Herrmann. Editor, George Tomasini. Starring James Stewart (John "Scottie" Ferguson), Kim Novak (Madeleine/Judy), Barbara Bel Geddes (Midge), Tom Helmore (Gavin Elster), Henry Jones (Coroner), Raymond Bailey (Doctor), Ellen Corby (Hotel Manager), Konstantin Shayne (Pop Leibel), Lee Patrick (Older Mistaken Identity), Paul Bryar (Capt. Hansen). 128 minutes.

*Vivre sa vie* [*Her Life to Live/It's Her Life*] (Pléiade, 1962). Produced by Pierre Braunberger. Directed and written by Jean-Luc Godard, inspired by the study *Où en est la prostitution?* by Marcel Sacotte. Director of Photography, Raoul Coutard. Music, Michel Legrand. Editors, Agnès Guillemot and Lila Lakshmanan. Starring Anna Karina (Nana Kleinfrankenheim), Sady Rebbot (Raoul), André-S. Labarthe (Paul), Guylaine Schlumberger (Yvette), Brice Parain (The Philosopher), Peter Kassovitz [voice dubbed by Jean-Luc Godard] (Young Man), Dimitri Dineff (Dimitri), Monique Messine (Elizabeth), Gérard Hoffman (Man Who Buys Nana), Gilles Quéant (Client), Paul Pavel (The Photographer), Jean Ferrat (Man at Jukebox), László Szabó (Wounded Man), Henri Attal (Arthur), Jean-Paul Savignac (Young Soldier in Bar), Mario Botti (The Italian). 85 minutes.

*Weekend* [*Le Week-end*] (Comacico/Films Copernic/LIRA/Ascot Cineraid, 1967). Directed and written by Jean-Luc Godard. Director of Photography, Raoul Coutard. Music, Antoine Duhamel. Editor, Agnès Guillemot. Starring Mireille Darc (Corinne), Jean Yanne (Roland), Jean-Pierre Kalfon (Leader of the F.L.S.O.), Valérie Lagrange (His Moll), Jean-Pierre Léaud (Saint-Just/ Man in Phone Booth), Yves Beneyton (Member of the F.L.S.O.), Paul Gégauff (Pianist), Daniel Pommereulle (Joseph Balsamo), Blandine Jeanson (Emily Bronte/Girl in Farmyard), Virginie Vignon (Marie-Madeleine). 95 minutes.

*While You Were Sleeping* (SST/Caravan/Hollywood, 1995). Produced by Joe Roth and Roger Birnbaum. Directed by Jon Turteltaub. Script by Daniel G. Sullivan and Fredric Lebow. Production Designer, Garreth Stover. Music, Randy Edelman. Editor, Bruce Green. Starring Sandra Bullock (Lucy Moderatz), Bill Pullman (Jack), Peter Gallagher (Peter), Peter Boyle (Ox), Jack Warden (Saul), Glynis Johns (Elsie), Michael Rispoli (Joe, Jr.), Jason Bernard (Jerry), Micole Mercurio (Midge), Ally Walker (Ashley Bacon). 100 minutes.

*Who'll Stop the Rain?* (United Artists, 1978). Produced by Herb Jaffe and Gabriel Katzka. Directed by Karel Reisz. Script by Judith Rascoe and Robert Stone, based on the novel *Dog Soldiers* by Robert Stone. Director of Photography, Richard H. Kline. Music, Laurence Rosenthal. Editor, John Bloom. Starring Nick Nolte (Ray), Tuesday Weld (Marge), Michael Moriarty (John), Anthony Zerbe (Antheil), Richard Masur (Danskin), Ray Sharkey (Smitty), Gail Strickland (Chairman). 125 minutes.

*The Woman in the Window* (Christie/International/RKO, 1945). Produced by Nunnally Johnson. Directed by Fritz Lang. Script by Nunnally Johnson, based on the novel *Once Off Guard* by J. H. Wallis. Director of Photography, Milton Krasner. Art Director, Duncan Cramer. Music, Arthur Lange and Hugo Friedhofer. Editors, Thomas Pratt, Marjorie Johnson, and Gene Fowler, Jr. Starring Edward G. Robinson (Professor Richard Wanley), Joan Bennett (Alice Reed), Raymond Massey (Frank Lalor), Edmund Breon (Dr. Michael Barkstane), Dan Duryea (Heidt/Doorman), Thomas E. Jackson (Inspector Jackson), Arthur Loft (Claude Mazard/Frank Howard), Dorothy Peterson (Mrs. Wanley), Frank Dawson (Collins, the Steward), Carol Cameron (Elsie Wanley). 99 minutes.

**—Compiled by Ian Cook**

# Illustrations

# INDEX